WITHDRAWN
No longer the property of the
Boston Public Library.
Sale of this material benefits the Library.

D1253685

Loving Literature

Loving Literature

A Cultural History

DEIDRE SHAUNA LYNCH

The University of Chicago Press

CHICAGO AND LONDON

DEIDRE SHAUNA LYNCH is the Chancellor Jackman Professor
of English at the University of Toronto.

The University of Chicago Press, Chicago 60637
The University of Chicago Press, Ltd., London
© 2015 by The University of Chicago
All rights reserved. Published 2015.
Printed in the United States of America

24 23 22 21 20 19 18 17 16 15   1 2 3 4 5

ISBN-13: 978-0-226-18370-1 (cloth)
ISBN-13: 978-0-226-18384-8 (e-book)
DOI: 10.7208/chicago/9780226183848.001.0001

The University of Chicago Press gratefully acknowledges the generous support of
the Chancellor Jackman Professorship at the University of Toronto toward
the publication of this book.

Library of Congress Cataloging-in-Publication Data
Lynch, Deidre, author.
Loving literature : a cultural history / Deidre Shauna Lynch.
pages cm
Includes bibliographical references and index.
ISBN 978-0-226-18370-1 (cloth : alk. paper) — ISBN 978-0-226-18384-8
(e-book) 1. English literature—Appreciation. 2. English literature—History
and criticism. I. Title.
PR129.U5L96 2015
820.9—dc23
2014015454

♾ This paper meets the requirements of ANSI/NISO Z39.48–1992
(Permanence of Paper).

Contents

Illustrations

Introduction

Although since the era of Thomas Kuhn the natural sciences have inspired attempts to historicize their basic epistemological assumptions, research protocols, and social practices, we continue to await, Lorraine Daston has recently lamented, comparable self-reflection from and on behalf of humanists: accounts of "what they do" and "how they know what they know."[1] In *Loving Literature* I aim to help English studies contribute to the project that Daston calls for. More precisely, I aim to suggest why self-reflection on our ways of knowing will not suffice when we seek to assess English professors' characteristic mode of practicing humanist study: I aim to honor, instead, the central role that affective labor—our ways of feeling, then, as well as knowing—has been assigned within English studies, and I aim to consider how through our cooperation with that assignment we have come to inhabit a profession that is paradoxically beholden to statements of personal connection. *Loving Literature* turns to literary studies' eighteenth- and nineteenth-century prehistory—to early definitions of literariness, to histories of criticism, canonicity, literary history, and "heritage," and, above all, to the emergence during this period of new etiquettes of literary appreciation—so as to examine how it has come to be that those of us for whom English is a line of *work* are also called upon to *love* literature and to ensure that others do so too.

Following Max Weber, William Clark states that the "modern bureaucratic distinction allowing the formation of a public-professional, expert self, and its insulation from the interests and hobbies of the amateur, private self, lies in the distinction between office and home."[2] The freewheeling

ways of many salaried, professional practitioners of English studies, however, confound that dichotomy and the norms it upholds. Those who are
employed at all (a population that diminished over the years in which I
wrote this book, as humanities departments downsized and their labor force
became increasingly casualized) must make their peace with the fact that
viewed from the outside their work does not look like work. For those professing English, it is all in a day's work to reread the novel one has read for
pleasure and convert it into material for a class or an article. Many of us
regularly engage in bringing our work home or, worse, bringing our home
to work—as when we make last year's bedtime reading the object of analysis
for this year's seminar and thereby rearrange social space so that the bedroom abuts on the classroom. Without exactly intending this state of affairs,
we seem to have more personal time in our working day than others do,
though the downside to such exemption from the time discipline that would
have us clocking in and clocking out is that the parameters that ought to
delimit the workload and working hours within our industry tend to be
treated as though they might be expanded almost infinitely.[3]

Taking a long view, auto-ethnographers of our discipline have often delineated the history of English studies over the last century and a half as
the story of how each new call for the professionalization that might better secure the English professor's claim to expertise has been followed, in
another swing of the pendulum, by a new round of amateur envy. Carol
Atherton engages along these lines the equivocal procedures of the late
nineteenth-century campaigners who established English literature as an
academic specialty within the English universities. Even as those campaigners insisted that, distinguished as their subject was by disinterested, ratio-
nalized methods of inquiry, it was as "susceptible of serious, methodical,
and profitable treatment as history itself," they could not, Atherton notes, re-
linquish their investments in this subject's moral benefits. Aspiring to have
things two ways, they presented English both as a knowledge practice and
as an instrument of pastoral care and character building. Given this dualistic
setup, it is understandable that our pursuits of rigor or campaigns for a new
professionalism have often been shadowed by expressions of nostalgia for
a past ostensibly readier to acknowledge that the project of really understanding literature necessarily eludes the grasp of expert cultures—readier
to acknowledge that literature involves readers' hearts as well as minds, and
their sensibility as well as training.[4]

Two fictions that influenced the late twentieth-century public's perceptions of schooling in English exemplify this tendency to identify literary

studies with the love of the subject and to identify that love with amateurs not yet subjected to the affective deformation that supposedly comes with formal education. The Victorianist protagonists of A. S. Byatt's 1990 novel *Possession*, one of them still seeking employment as a university teacher, the other having successfully secured her professional position, begin to fall in love when they discover that for all their methodological and socioeconomic differences they had alike decided to "work" in their professional lives as researchers on "what could survive our education," on the few poems that "stayed alive." People who "work" on poetry must resign themselves to a position of moral compromise, Byatt intimates via this passage of dialogue, because their very work as professional researchers and educators puts that poetry at risk.[5] In the 1989 Peter Weir film *Dead Poets Society*, the lesson plan that the newly hired English teacher John Keating prepares for his first day of class at Weldon Academy seems designed to avert that risk: it requires Keating, played by Robin Williams, to lead his bemused students *out of* their classroom and out of his workplace, while he recites Robert Herrick and Walt Whitman and urges the class to take up arms against "armies of academics . . . measuring poetry."[6] (This free spirit, needless to say, will soon be stifled by an institution that cannot countenance such independence of mind.) "The very atmosphere of the class-room, with its paraphernalia of study, is one in which the wings of poesy cannot readily beat," stated the Newbolt Report on *The Teaching of English in England*, the 1921 document of the campaign that eventually succeeded in installing imaginative literature—rather than English composition exclusively—at the center of Britain's national education system. It is as though Mr. Keating misread the Newbolt Committee and took a wistful aside as the core of their message.[7]

Still, an equally plausible way to describe the boundary confusion that shapes the practice of literary study would be to invert the dynamic that Mr. Keating's extramural English class and his embrace of his outsider status illustrate. We might say, instead, that the English professor's affective life is *supposed to* slop over onto her job; it's all in a day's work when it does. I don't believe that the equation between professionalization and the suppression of feeling that A. S. Byatt and Peter Weir intimate suffices as a description of how we experience our working lives. My experience does not suggest to me that the personal is *repressed* when departments of English go about their ostensibly clinical official business. For our classes—even the graduate seminars—regularly come to be invested, as Lauren Berlant has noted, with "anxieties and needs for mirroring one normally associates with the institutions of privacy and domestic intimacy," and those intimacy expectations prompt all concerned, at significant cost in an era of soaring student-teacher ratios, to think of teaching and learning as processes that must, by definition, involve personal contact. A recent *New York Times Book Review* essay by Dean Bakopoulos confirms Berlant's account as it wags a finger at the professorate who have centered the curriculum on theory and historical contexts and who have thereby marginalized their *real* subject, reading as a "process of seduction."[8] Eve Sedgwick once quipped that the scene of liberal arts education represents an "erogenous zone" for the academy: a statement that registers how the literary profession especially defines itself around (a properly administered) pleasure and (a properly disciplined) sensitivity and how this line of work mandates as much as represses a "personal touch." In characterizing our vocation in this puckish way, Sedgwick captured the embarrassment that such oddly public practices of intimacy and this oddly intimate profession can occasion.[9]

How did literary pedagogy and criticism end up located in so eccentric a relationship to post-Enlightenment culture's conventional and gendered schema for segregating "personal life" from the public sphere, feeling from knowing, and recreation from labor? Approaching that question from diverse angles, the chapters composing this book engage with a variety of the cultural forms in which English literature was transmitted during the eighteenth and nineteenth centuries, in which literature's distinctiveness from other kinds of discourse was demarcated, and which people used to ponder their relationship with it: treatises on taste, belletristic appreciations, lives and editions "of the poets," early literary histories, projects of bibliography and bibliophilia, commonplace books, albums of friendship, accounts of keep-fit regimens of rereading, and travelogues mapping authors' "homes and haunts," among other things. These chapters span a period in British cultural history that extends from the mid-eighteenth to the mid-nineteenth century. The records of reading that center my first and second chapters thus originate from decades that saw the debut in provincial dissenting academies and in the Scottish universities of new lectures on "rhetoric and belles-lettres"; those decades also saw important changes in the marketplace of print, as the copyright decisions underwriting new accounts of vernacular literature as a national property facilitated the appearance in that marketplace of multivolume, canon-making sets of "the British poets." By the time I wind up my story in chapter 6 of this book my subjects are contemporary with the mid-nineteenth-century founding at the British universities of dedicated chairs in the subject henceforth known as "English literature" (and renaming of chairs formerly dedicated to rhetoric and belles lettres):

the former development was engendered in part by new government policies that required candidates for the civil service to be evaluated and ranked
through a system of formal examinations, including those testing their
knowledge of literary history. Collectively these chapters aim to outline
how since its late eighteenth-century/early nineteenth-century reinvention,
also the inaugural moment of its disciplinization, "English literature" has
always been something more than an object of study, even for the architects of that disciplinization. It has also been implicated in its audiences' libidinal dramas and in their understandings of their families and their erotic
histories—hence English studies' eccentric relation to the norms of publicness and impersonality that seem to govern other knowledge-producing
occupations. To ponder this implication, *Loving Literature* navigates among
poetics, the history of aesthetics, and book history, on the one hand, and the
histories of psychology, sexuality, and the family, on the other. It surveys the
redefinitions of literary experience—and of the interior spaces of the mind
and home—that had to occur in order for the *love* of literature to become
part of English studies' normal science.

The account a single book can provide of how that state of affairs came to
be will necessarily be circumscribed. This history of the literary affections
cannot directly address, though I hope it illuminates, the later nineteenth-
century developments and debates that helped lay the ground for the love
troubles still vexing English in the university setting. There are, for example,
the materials set out in Ian Hunter's *Culture and Government*, which describe
how English pedagogy, by virtue of its absorption of romantic norms of
individual correction through self-expression, emerged in the late Victorian
schoolroom as the privileged embodiment of liberal technologies of moral
supervision: Hunter's materials might be seen as forming a prequel of
sorts to Berlant's and Sedgwick's discussions of the role of the personal
touch in pedagogic practice.[10] It is worth briefly mentioning, in addition,
the intriguing fact that in the late nineteenth century some commentators
who resisted English's absorption by the universities pointed to the success
of the National Home Reading Union, founded in 1889, as proof that the
Arnoldian and Ruskinian project of installing a literary sensibility in the
largest possible constituency was already under way without the academy's
help (a fact about the discipline's prehistory that indexes the longevity of
the ongoing rivalry between the classroom and book club, between, for example, E N G 3 2 3 H 1 F, Jane Austen and Her Contemporaries, and the Toronto

chapter of the Jane Austen Society of North America, and makes one wonder how much the aura exercised by the home might color our institutional practices even now).[11] Also noteworthy is the parting of the ways that occurred at this same time between historians and professors of literature (the same people frequently held both offices earlier in the century), when the former group began to define itself in relationship to an "objectivity question" and to norms of value-free scientific investigation—norms that, even in the heyday of philology, never seemed as compelling for literary studies.[12]

As I have indicated, however, this book engages an earlier moment, before *English* named an educational program, and before the school system could claim anything like the sway that would later belong to it as the primary institution overseeing the transmission of the literary heritage and regulating the population's access to the cultural capital with which that literary heritage was freighted. During the century I examine, the project of canon formation was a more diversely sanctioned enterprise; the literary subjectivity assembled through encounters with that recommended reading flourished in multiple cultural locales.[13] Accordingly, I treat schooling only incidentally here (the secret poetry clubs frequented by some eighteenth-century Oxford undergraduates engage me in chapter 2; in chapter 4 I investigate the role of rereading in both our classroom practices and nineteenth-century definitions of canonicity). My emphasis falls instead on how the rearrangements of the discursive field that produce a new idea of literature for the later eighteenth and early nineteenth centuries also represent a watershed in the history of the emotions and intimate life. To an extent that previous work on the historicity of literature fails to acknowledge, the foundational texts of criticism, aesthetic theory, and literary history and biography that were generated during these decades were inflected by the imperatives of a long era of sensibility.[14] Though I often make a point here of looking beyond the public (masculine) face of the emergent discipline of English studies, one doesn't need to stray much beyond the canonical texts by figures like Samuel Johnson, Thomas Warton, or Samuel Taylor Coleridge to discover traces of how that new idea of literature was intimately experienced. Those texts not only document the historicity of concepts of the literary, they also show (not least by revealing some of the architects of literary criticism and literary study to have been closet men of feeling) that this history cannot be understood apart from the history of emotional practice.

I thus return to those texts in part to explore how British culture came to accede to an arrangement, now almost too familiar to be visible, that had literature become available to readers first and foremost as private, passional persons rather than as members of a rational, civic-minded public. (Perhaps too sweepingly, Simon During dates to the 1760s "a fissure between literature and civility.")[15] But because the relationality of the reader to her reading matter is one of my principal fields of investigation, my subject also ends up being the species of sociably minded animism that readers indulge when they designedly make a home with romantic poetry or keep company with their favorite authors—whenever they conceive of literature as something more than an object that might instruct or move them or prompt their admiration. The practices of personification that underwrite an alternative account of literature's ontology, an account of literature as an object soliciting its audiences' involvement and affection and fidelity, are a recurrent topic in this book.[16] Sometimes I explore too resistances to this arrangement. As we shall see, certain founding figures of modern literary criticism give signs of having had an intensely vexed, love-hate relationship to literary love.

An important body of scholarship emerged in the 1980s and 1990s to remind English studies of the historical mutability of the meanings of its keyword "literature." It is now part of our disciplinary common sense that eighteenth- and nineteenth-century Anglo-American culture reinvented "literature" as a new sort of object of study, appreciation, marketing, and pedagogy. Of course, the rearrangement of the field of writing that this process entailed was not a punctual event, and it is tricky to track accordingly.[17] When James Boswell stated in 1791 that the "love of literature" did not fail Samuel Johnson on his deathbed, he used "literature" in older senses of the term that either designated a particular aptitude, literacy, or provided a synonym for erudition or learning in general. Boswell was indicating that the dying Johnson continued to *read* and to *study*. However, Boswell's cultivation of the role of fan and insistence on revering his favorite author, even during the latter's lifetime, as a quasi-imaginary being (a ghost or fictional character, who had, Boswell asserted, "grown up in my fancy into a kind of mysterious veneration") speak volumes about the new uses to which "literature" was already being harnessed.[18] The anonymously published *Extracts from the Diary of a Lover of Literature* (1810), in which one Thomas Green went public with his feelings about his reading matter, illuminates those uses as well. The *Extracts* do this only in part by recording *what* the eponymous Lover reads: although *Paradise Lost* and *Joseph Andrews* form part of his "miscellaneous course of reading," these are ranged alongside political writings (Edmund Burke's and the Abbé Barruel's discussions of the origin of the French Revolution) that to twenty-first-century audiences might seem deficient in the imagination we require of instances of literariness. Equally significant is the Lover's evident conviction that his affective responses to his reading are worthy of remark, that it matters, for instance, that to the "fascinating influence" of the *Arabian Nights' Entertainment* he finds himself "quite ductile," that "Towered Cities please us then" is for him the most pleasing line in Milton's "L'Allegro" (he compares it the "animating" effects of a change from minor to major keys in "some entrancing Symphony"), or that he feels mournful when he contemplates his inability to recapture the hallucinatory intensity of his first youthful reading of *Robinson Crusoe*.[19] Such observations suggest how the emergence during the long era of sensibility of a new understanding of literature was necessarily accompanied by the emergence of the form of subjecthood that During has called "literary subjectivity"—a kind of work on the self that proceeds through the psychological intensities that reading creates and that begins with a "recognition of oneself as a distinct type who takes literature seriously."[20]

The *Extracts* also brings to view other criteria for marking off literature's boundaries that will be mobilized in the new literary era. The fact that the Lover tends to write about old books rather than the newly published is notable, given a definition of literature as writing that "signifies the cultural heritage versus writing deemed merely topical."[21] (This definition also hints, of course, at how in the nineteenth century especially "English" would operate in the wider culture as an apparatus for the transmission of national feeling.) And another defining trait of the literary discernible here seems worth flagging for my argumentative purposes. In the *Extracts* the Lover's reading and commenting on books are presented as ends in themselves. And, indeed, texts that were works of "literature" (texts either written or recast and reappraised in those terms) required their readers to eschew in these special cases the practices of text indexing and epitomizing, of gutting for content, and "digesting," that before the eighteenth century had so often defined all kinds of reading. With those works a different relation was required. In the newer account, what literature isn't, is something to be used. We don't treat literature as a thing but as a person: lovers of literature construct the aesthetic relation as though it put them in the presence of other people and with the understanding that the ethical relations so conjured must not be instrumentalized. The case *may* well be different with the writing designated as the belles lettres—to use the French rubric that nineteenth-century English studies ended up rejecting. Belles lettres may solicit admiration, as a requisite homage to the beauty that is enshrined in their very name (an egregiously French name at that). But literature, something to be taken personally by definition, demands love.[22]

Literature so defined emerges, as Trevor Ross's 1998 history of canonicity outlined, when an earlier "rhetorical culture" in which texts had served as instruments of social power, and old texts had been valued only as a backdrop to ongoing cultural production, began to give way to a cultural arrangement centered on "appreciation": on the close, historically sensitive but tasteful reading of "classics," or on a devoted engagement with contemporary writers of genius who (*as* geniuses, a breed apart) occupied an aesthetic realm positioned at a distance from worldly conflicts.[23] Registering the fallout from a broader realignment of the older divisions of knowledge, this new category of writing, a narrowed canon of especially valuable, exclusively imaginative works, would in addition come to exclude texts addressed primarily to the understanding—the science, philosophy, history, and politics that counted as "literature" so long as that rubric designated erudition in general. The later eighteenth century's investment in a notion of the literary as, instead, that idiom which the passions made their own is apparent in the praise that in 1791 the philosopher Thomas Reid bestowed on the lectures on rhetoric George Jardine was then delivering to his students at the University of Glasgow: "No subjects are likely to be more interesting to young minds, at a time when their taste and feelings are beginning to open." Reid also intimates here that English really is a young person's subject.[24] "How frosty is the feeling associated with [the] names [of Archimedes and Galileo] . . . by comparison with that which . . . many a young innocent girl . . . cherishes in her heart for the name and person of Shakspeare," Thomas De Quincey put it in 1839 in a statement about canon love that doubles as an exercise in mapping the disciplines: "How different, how peculiar, is the interest which attends the great poets who have made themselves necessary to the human heart."[25]

Previous historicist scholarship has adopted various approaches to assess the cultural work it took to naturalize this modern, narrowed, and aestheticized sense of "literature." Sometimes this scholarship has produced, for instance, an account of the domestic politics of the vernacular canon: an account of how booksellers', editors', and anthologists' new canon of English serviced the needs of a rising middle class eager to exploit a new apparatus for the distribution of social distinction and cultural capital.[26] At other times, it has focused on demonstrating how instrumental the institution of English was both for the work of British national unification and for the extension of the domain of standard English under the auspices of colonialism.[27] Still other scholars have told the story, often expressing regret for the wrong turns that were taken, of how a belletristic, aestheticized concept of high culture organized around the classics of bygone times came in the eighteenth century to occlude the rhetorical orientation of a socially responsive and practical pedagogy. Listen closely enough to some of these scholars and one can hear an undertone of regret for how the shift toward new, aestheticized notions of literature's autonomy entailed the sacrifice of literature's public significance: nostalgia for an older configuration of literature that was spared "the burden of 'literariness,' " and—maybe this is audible only to the ears of a female scholar—nostalgia for a manliness that was lost at the same time that version of literature was.[28] The template for this work has generally been sociological, predisposing it to emphasize how struggles over contending definitions of literature either cooperate with or contest projects of social stratification (or of "distinction" as per Pierre Bourdieu) and/or dominant myths of national community.[29]

That orientation to the agon of cultural production helps explain why studies of the late eighteenth-/early nineteenth-century reinvention of literature have tended to overlook how that reinvention also created a new object for people's affections—one that altered the practices and protocols of those affections in its turn. In the romantic period, Jonah Siegel observes, "more writers become the objects of a fantastic admiration . . . than in all previous centuries combined." But, he continues, that ramping up of esteem need not be attributed to a "dramatic increase in . . . quality" in writing, but rather to "a notable increase in the need to admire."[30] Notwithstanding the emergence of this new affective economy, the scholars on whom I build here generally distribute their attention in a manner that suggests that although literature is an abstraction that had to be invented (much as the canon, as John Guillory proposes, is also an abstraction, defined by its perpetual evasion of materialization in any finite list of texts), this is not so with literary appreciation.[31] In their studies, literature is a cultural construction, but its appreciation comes naturally. And these studies have had even less to say about something that will be a recurrent topic here: the circumstances under which in the period's records of reading, the language of approbation or admiration is found insufficient and recourse is had to the stickier, subjectivity-saturated language of involvement and affection.

This failure to explore readers' wish for relationship registers, among other things, humanities disciplines' long-held investment in the notion that there may be a special epistemic virtue in practicing criticism from a position of alienation. The methodological challenges that inevitably accompany any effort to construct a history of reading—the history of an activity that leaves few traces—have been a factor as well. Those scruples come with costs, however. The reluctance to engage the affective attachments that have connected readers to the institutions of English has inhibited us from bringing our histories of aesthetics between 1750 and 1850 into dialogue with accounts of this century as a pivotal epoch in the history of emotion, intimacy, and sexuality. Yet the attachments that have connected Anglo-American readers to the institutions of English are crucial to the history of private life, because the aesthetic sphere is a site for the dramas of individuals' identity formation, and also because encountered, for example, in the form of "the Family Shakespeare" or "the Sir Walter Scott birthday book," the canon has mediated the relationships that define home. The changing paradigms that readers had for codifying the pleasures of texts are crucial resources for understanding the eighteenth-century practice of sensibility—that remapping of the human heart that served to personalize the passions, which earlier had been thought of as impersonal forces moving the individual from the outside.[32] They are also crucial resources for understanding nineteenth-century concepts of domesticity and how they brought loving feeling into a new and potentially tricky relationship with habit and routine.

This is not to gainsay that those discourses on sentiment and home themselves could be vehicles for the nationalist, geopolitical projects that histories of literariness have often been readier to reference. When in one of his elephantine marginal notes, written in 1808 on the flyleaf of a folio edition of Milton, Coleridge records his high esteem for Milton's poetry, he is unable to refrain from taking an interest as well in other people's—indeed a whole other nation's—abnormal emotional responses. Coleridge's encomium, which I've had to abridge severely, declares that Milton's

> poetry belongs to the whole world [and] .. is alike the property of the churchman and the dissenter, the Protestant and the Catholic, . . . and of every country on earth except the kingdom of Dahomey in Africa, for the PRESENT at least; and of France (as long as it shall be inhabited by Frenchmen) FOREVER! A mine of lead could sooner take wing and mount aloft at the call of the sun . . . than the witty, discontinuous intellect, and sensual sum-total of a Frenchman could soar up to religion, or to Milton and Shakespeare. It is impossible.

Coleridge derides a nation that doesn't get either intellection or devotion right (other commentators, we will see, also cite the French nation's deficient commitment to home life). His note reminds us that lovers of literature often hate in literature's name.[33] The consequence is that the scholar who seeks to assemble a historical phenomenology of literariness does not have to choose between eros and agon. Indeed, she often can't.

Of course, particular texts had been lauded for moving the passions since Longinus's day at least. But in the emergent literary era that this book explores individuals needed to *learn* to develop and to legitimate their own private, individuated relationships with that abstraction, the canon, the "literature" that had, in the wake of copyright decisions of the late eighteenth century, come to constitute Britons' public domain. They also needed to learn the strategies enabling them to think of their intensely felt transactions with their reading matter as something other than enthrallment to empty fictions or empty rhetoric and to think of literature, instead, as the locus of ethical transactions whose essence was human contact. The "pervasive association of reading in the West with the private social spaces and meanings of the erotic," Daniel Boyarin observes in *The Ethnography of Reading*, is both historically generated and culturally precarious; it continues to require much cultural effort to sustain it.[34] In its engagement with the love of literature, *Loving Literature* is also guided, accordingly, by the presupposition that the many accounts we have of the professionalization of literary study and criticism are incomplete without a consideration of literature's *personalization* and the practices and institutions of reading by which it was supported. We produce a partial picture only when we narrate the prehistory of English departments as though it were simply the story of the separation of a specialist caste of interpreters from a general reading public and the divvying up of meaning and feeling, knowledge and pleasure, between the two.[35] For a start, that narrative leaves us unable to assess the entanglements of the institutional and the intimate within the informal, everyday practice of English studies, within that psycho-pedagogy of everyday life that defines the discipline's real effectivity just as much as our publications in literary criticism do.

That narrative, I have been noting, also leaves feeling and pleasure without a history. It exempts love from scrutiny, so that its historical dimensions escape discussion and so that we forget that its meanings are negotiable and contestable and have varying effects in the world. Rather than bracketing questions about intimacy, gratitude, and emotional commitment, I have written in the belief that these phenomena themselves demand historical investigation. Borrowing from queer theory and putting historical pressure on the voluntarism that links aesthetic preference and sexual preference alike has provided me with one way to do that investigating.[36] There can be something irksomely normalizing about the way people inside and outside academe mobilize the concepts of love and aesthetic pleasure and invigilate others for signs of the passion that they present both as ethical obligation and as index of psychological normality. Boyarin reminds us of this at a witty moment in the essay I just cited. He admits his estrangement from the community of feeling that is invoked in accounts of how "we" all know how "to get lost in a book" and says that naturalizing accounts of the privatized, eroticized reading of fiction that make that reading practice seem a "given of being human"—a bit like sex, in short—sometimes fill him with a "feeling of inadequacy": "Perhaps that feeling should lead me to seek a reading therapist, who would presumably provide me with a surrogate book."[37] But it is also worth underscoring that this book's account of how English literature came to represent a home away from home for hundreds of thousands of readers does not portray that domestication as inevitably conservative in its effects. Domestication in my book is something more than a straightforward process of homogenization and assimilation. The logics of affect reconstructed in *Loving Literature* are often perverse, aligning individuals and their desires in unexpected ways, or casting love as something that can collapse time and connect the living and dead.

Like other scholars who have investigated the historical constitution of literature and literariness, I have been driven in part by my worries over the future of English studies—though I take comfort from the knowledge that in prefacing *The Rise of English Literary History* René Wellek likewise declared that his history's aim was to "show by what ways the present . . . *impasse* of literary studies has been reached."[38] (This was in 1941. The discipline's crises also constitute its long-standing business as usual.) The scholars in the 1980s and 1990s who continued Wellek's investigations into English studies' prehistory did so against the backdrop of the canon wars, deeming it useful to place in a deeper historical context recent conflicts over the proper nature of our discipline's object. But in some respects these scholars, in their reluctance to address English as an object of the affections, ended up writing at cross-purposes with those critical attacks, originating both inside and outside academe, on the new disciplinary constellations of the late twentieth century, and to this day those who did that attacking adhere tenaciously to the premise that the field's turn to cultural studies or theory spelled the end of love in our classrooms. Media coverage of university English studies thus continues to proceed as though it were a given that the state of English professors' hearts should be a matter for public concern. "There is something about love that does not sit well with the literary academy," Zadie Smith writes ruefully at the start of a much-quoted essay published in the

Guardian.[39] *New Yorker* film critic David Denby's *Great Books*, a chronicle of the year the middle-aged Denby spent working his way through Columbia University's freshman curriculum, is more aggressive in the criticism it hurls in the academy's direction: Denby repeatedly puts on hold the encomiums his title implies and turns to denouncing the joylessness of the academic left—"dry-souled clerics" "who do not love literature."[40] I've already suggested that what actually goes on in departments of English has little to do with caricatures like Denby's. It is just as plausible to think of the academy as helping to glamorize literary passion by making it a thing of stolen moments that are embezzled from the institution, the impromptu gush of feeling, say, that breaks through the impersonal lecture. Before English studies commits wholly to what Daniel Cottom has called an "erotic rearmament campaign" in a bid to regain its lost public legitimacy, it might be better to stop and think a bit longer about what an emotional commitment to literature *is*.[41] This book aims to provide that thinking space.

That aim informs the strategy I have pursued to organize this account of the literary affections. It represents, in part, a riposte to how, within recent discussions of the fortunes of English studies, the phrase "the love of literature" gets used as though its meaning were transparent and as if the structure of feeling that it designated were wholly healthy and happy. It is as though those on the side of the love of literature had forgotten what literary texts themselves say about love's edginess and complexities. By focusing my book on those complexities I mean to emphasize, by contrast, that this love too can be a matter of misrecognition, overvaluation, self-congratulation, aggressivity, transference, fetishism, and/or jealousy, that it too brings with it (sometimes unreasonable) intimacy expectations, and that, in these relations too we rather enjoy taking the presence of the other for granted. The better to isolate such dimensions of the literary affections, the better to divest the love of literature of that aura of self-evidence, I decided not to organize this book as a series of studies of individual authors or for that matter of individual readers. I also rejected early on the notion that I might proceed by engaging the various genres through which ideas of literature have been mediated, promoted, and regulated (the literary anecdote, the lecture, the essay in appreciation, and so forth).[42] I have opted instead to investigate the peculiarity of the emotional practices ushered in with the new definitions of the literary canon—and highlighted accordingly the psychic challenges would-be lovers had to surmount once, for instance, the canon came to be deemed as common cultural property, or when canonical writers came to be seen as ageless figures who would always, perennially, be with their readers.

I catalogue varieties of love and sometimes varieties of perversity. The chapters that follow are divided into four parts, devoted, respectively, to grateful love, to possessive love, to love that is a habitual, everyday affair, and, finally, to loving and losing (that elegiac love that has an investment in the loss of its object). I'll conclude this introduction by outlining those parts.

Part 1, "Choosing an Author as You Choose a Friend," first fleshes out some of the claims about the personalizing of literature I've made in this introduction and then turns to a series of disputes in the late eighteenth-century periodical press that pitted Anna Seward against James Boswell and involved the character and critical authority of the recently deceased Samuel Johnson. There I use Seward's quarrel with Johnson and his acolyte to illuminate in a preliminary fashion the changing ways in which the problem of love has resurfaced in English. I examine Seward's complaint that Johnson was a critic who, lamentably, reasoned rather than felt and who, deficient in prepossessions, had no *favorite* authors; I turn as well to the *Lives of the Poets* and Boswell's *Life*, so as to reconstruct Johnson's own love-hate relationship to literary love and his uneasiness, in particular, with the demand that one should feel gratitude to the English authors.

David Hume wrote in 1740 that "'tis remarkable, that goods, which are common to all mankind, and have become familiar to us by custom, give us little satisfaction; tho' perhaps of a more excellent kind, than those on which, for their singularity, we set a much higher value."[43] The account in part 2 that I give of "Possessive Love" examines the fantasy of being left alone with the canon and having that public domain, "common to all," to oneself. Part 2 begins by investigating the possessiveness informing the literary histories produced by eighteenth-century men of letters—and the way an investment in historical specificity (in Richard Hurd's words, an investment in cultural conditions that "never did subsist but once and are never likely to subsist again") supplied the precondition for an investment in esoterica.[44] Literary history was (then as now) understood as an exercise in public service, giving British reading audiences access to their cultural birthright, but when period commentators referred, sourly, to the "nest of British . . . antiquities" that Thomas Warton, the author of the first narrative history of English poetry, had assembled around himself in his Oxford cubbyhole, they were also registering how the Gothic revival implemented by his history and its source studies had carved out a space for romance and a space for opposition to the sober, adult responsibilities of modern public life.[45] The attention that in his critical writings Warton lavishes on the singular and recondite, the energy that he expends on locating the materials that will bit by bit fill in the big picture, help to reclaim the literary past for the public of the present day. At the same time, such attention also has the potential to render that past the object of a more suspect, solipsistic form of engagement. It can remake literary study as an arena for private gratification and secret enjoyment. The second half of part 2 takes a second look at the antiquarian books with which Warton lined his nest and, considering the rare book as cult object, goes on to reconstruct that early nineteenth-century episode in the history of British bookselling that contemporaries dubbed "the bibliomania." It also considers anthologists and essayists like Charles Lamb, Leigh Hunt, and Thomas De Quincey, members of the first generation to confront a ready-made canon, born readers of the libraries of the English poets that had been compiled in the eighteenth century as already-recommended reading. These early nineteenth-century figures fostered a love of English literature as a cultural service, but, as Julie Carlson has observed, they also found being subjected to other people's conceptions of the poets an infringement on their individuality and interiority.[46] In the bibliomania, however, they found cues as to how they might make an impersonal canon into property of the most personal and private kind.

Part 3, "English Literature for Everyday Use," takes a different tack to examine what is involved in rendering "English literature" *home ground*, emphasizing not the esoteric but the regular, routinized, and habitual. The authority that literary discourse achieves after the late eighteenth century is in some ways a function of the way that the new category of "the modern classic" seems to promise, as a kind of preventative medicine, to keep its readers steady: literature is an object with which, in effect, one might *go steady*, and to demonstrate that, this section of the book examines the alliances forged between literature and new late eighteenth- and early nineteenth-century discourses on psychology, health, and domestic timetables. After discussing the new, quasi-medical accounts of the pleasures of poetic meter produced by associationist psychology at the turn of the century, I move to outlining how, later in the nineteenth century, novels (Jane Austen's especially) would absorb some of poetry's therapeutic functions. The novel, defined by its privileged relation to duration, has the advantage among literary forms when it comes to presenting itself as a committed reader's companion for the long haul—a guise in which literature occasions a love that is so uncalculated, so habitual, that it runs on automatic pilot, with no effort of the will required.

Part 4, "Dead Poets Societies," explores the elegiac aspects of the love of literature as it considers literary studies' investment, since the romantic period, in dark tales of loss that enable us to indulge in the passions of mourning. In both chapters in part 4, I aim to show that current laments over the death of literature (Denby compares the great books he loves to species that "[hover] near extinction") have been nested within a romantic-period idiom.[47] In the first, I discuss how the period's female-authored gothic romances make reading itself look like haunting, portraying texts as legacies and readers as mourners. Set in ancient mansions that echo to the sound of remote generations, adorned with chapter epigraphs that quote Shakespeare, Milton, and the graveyard poets, the gothic novel shares enough traits with the new historical anthologies with which it is contemporary to rank as one of romantic culture's chief institutions of canon love. In the second chapter, I discuss literary biographies and reminiscences (Boswell's of Johnson, De Quincey's of Wordsworth), along with Victorian editions of the romantic poets that ornamented the poems with photographic illustrations. This chapter follows its predecessors in excavating a rhetoric that links the "belief" in authors to a belief in ghosts and that ascribes to the literary canon something like the enigmatic authority that a gothic heroine's dead parents have, the authority of those who preexist us. In the wake of the efforts of the eighteenth-century and nineteenth-century canon makers explored in the earlier chapters of *Loving Literature*, literature came to represent a cultural space of posthumousness. This transformation installed the barrier of death between dead poets and living readers (and sometimes, as in De Quincey's *Lake Reminiscences*, between living poets, already leading their posthumous existence, and their living readers), but that barrier, I contend as I conclude, proved paradoxically essential to the personalization that transmutes admiration into love.

PART I

Choosing an Author as You Choose a Friend

CHAPTER ONE

Making It Personal

It is not enough to admire. Admiration is a cold feeling.

HUGH BLAIR, lecturing to his students at the University of Edinburgh
ca. 1760–62

Machiavelli, whom Milton admired, reasoned that a prince who was feared
would survive longer than one who was loved. Literature does not work that
way.

GARY TAYLOR, "Milton and Shakespeare: Battle of the Bards,"
Time Magazine, May 15, 2008

Thanks to mediation, we are surrounded with communication situations that
are fundamentally interpretive rather than dialogic. Only the Lonelyhearts
of the world expect a personal reply from the movie, phonograph record, or
radio program. Or to be more precise, we are all Lonelyhearts inasmuch as we
"interact" with books, pets, infants, or distant correspondents.

JOHN DURHAM PETERS, *Speaking into the Air: A History of the Idea of
Communication* (2001)

"THE PROPERTIES . . . OF FLESH AND BLOOD"

In the early twentieth century, the original designers of the home telephone
took pains to give it an anthropomorphic appearance, meaning thereby to
ease the transition to prosthetized speech. The candlestick phone's bodily
presence—the rounded contours, which accommodated beholders' efforts
to see in it a resemblance to the human form, the positioning of the trans-
mitter, which obliged those placing or taking calls to engage the instrument
"face" to "face"—helped to reassure the new technology's users, who still
hesitated to equate electronic sounds transmitted across wires with real human voices. "One is not alone or speaking to oneself; the instrument, 'like'
a human figure, stands before one's eyes, responding to one's gestures, listening with its own ear."[1] The twenty-first century has had reason to repeat
those lessons in personalization, coping with the various computational
creatures that have been designed to interact with humans sociably and
elicit humans' attachments. Robotic pets such as Tamagotchi, for instance,
present themselves as objects with whom we might relate and might even

exchange tendernesses. Nowadays, accordingly, computer scientists' discussions of "aliveness" involve more than assessments of robotic intelligence and competence. They also involve experiences of robot connection and of ethical commitments to robot well-being.

Sherry Turkle comments that now that we have begun to share our emotional lives with these "non-biological" "relational artefacts," it is high time that humans pondered seriously just what "loving" has come to mean.[2] I believe such sharing and pondering have gone on longer than Turkle acknowledges. For in the eighteenth century, a comparable kind of anthropomorphizing numbered among the several transformations that led to the emergence onto the cultural stage of literature in the modern sense of the term. This century witnessed various projects intended to affirm the humanity that was lodged in the artifacts of the book market and thus to close some of the gaps between the living world and the paper world. "Literature" owed much to new stories about authors, about the figure of the literary genius particularly, and to hermeneutic procedures that attached writing to a self-expressive, original, outsize personality—as opposed, say, to casting it as an imitation of the best models, or a reiteration of favorite stories, or a citation from a Book of Nature conceptualized as an intertext of multiple correspondences and connections. Literary biography helped produce among print's eighteenth-century consumers the sense of a passionate human presence, a supererogatory something lying behind certain books that made them something more than repositories of disembodied words. Taken as a group, biographies (especially collective biographies such as Samuel Johnson's *Lives of the English Poets*, whose reception history focuses this chapter's second half) worked to establish that in their private lives too the authors were a breed apart—a proposition that served to buttress the claims of literature in that new, narrowed sense of the term. And by the early nineteenth century, the biographical writers' and biographical readers' determination to individuate authors and personalize writing had helped bring about a consequential transition. The old literary "lists"—the most apt rubric for the hybrids of authorial dictionaries and catalogues of worthies that had appeared on the scene in the seventeenth century—gave way to something more demanding and deserving of emotional investment, a literary canon.[3]

Trying out a thought experiment in which the history of the love of literature figures as part of this larger history of nonbiological relational artifacts, I am not, of course, contending that before literature assumed its modern meaning in the eighteenth century, readers of poetry and narrative had no regard for authors.[4] The seventeenth-century catalogues I just mentioned are evidence to the contrary. Nor do I mean to suggest that we will get a handle on the love of literature simply by determining the number of authors the category comprehends and then tallying up the amount of affection that readers expend in their love for each of them. A more complicated calculus is at issue in this affective economy. Since the eighteenth century, the love of literature has been shaped, in addition, by newly nationalized concepts of the cultural heritage, new concepts of home and home life, adaptations of the old liturgical calendar, and modern concepts of historical distance, the historical period, and of nostalgia—as my subsequent chapters will indicate. But throughout this book I am presupposing a close relation between, on the one hand, the rearrangements and reclassifications of discourse that produced literature as a distinct category and, on the other hand, an emerging consensus that the transactions that would count as literary would involve heart-to-heart relations. They would involve, as well, what was most individual in the reader's individuality.

Our bookish activities need not always be a forum for interpersonal relations. Michel Foucault reminded us of this fact in an essay that has been seminal for many self-reflexive investigations of the discipline of English. Whereas, following the seventeenth century, the authority of scientific discourse would increasingly be a function of that discourse's facelessness and detachment from particular biographical entities, the reverse happened with "literary discourse," which, Foucault proposed, "was acceptable only if it carried an author's name." In those texts we now call literary, individuals take possession of language and make it express their selves. In another essay on authorship, Leah Marcus thinks analogously about how strangely cacophonous early modern books can look to modern eyes, thanks to their first users' habit of converting books' margins and blank pages to discrepant purposes and of binding together unrelated, multiply-authored materials between the covers of a single volume. She comments that in the Renaissance "the bound printed book" was conceptualized less as a "surrogate body of the author" and more "as a storage unit"—like, she proposes, a portfolio file or a computer disk. Of course, there was also, in the Renaissance, a countervailing tendency to understand the book as a surrogate self of its author, as Marcus concedes. This "hybridization between the human organism and technology" (a term Marcus uses when discussing John Milton's understanding of authorial presence) gained ground with time.[5] In 1759 a contributor to the *Critical Review* declared accordingly that "we are desirous of attaching esteem to the person of an ingenious writer; we love to compare the lineaments of his mind with the features of his face."[6]

This chapter investigates certain eighteenth-century readers' accounts of the benefits *and* obligations that followed when, as Samuel Taylor Coleridge later put it, "poems . . . assume the properties of flesh and blood."[7] Throughout I emphasize the resistances that made the emergence of an account of literary reading as a *personal* matter an uneven process. The traces that those resistances have left in the writings of the eighteenth-century architects of English deserve a higher profile when we historicize our disciplinary object. Their neglect has sustained, and been sustained by, an understanding of reading as a straightforward process of acculturation and of readers as passive receptacles: I contend, however, that just that understanding needs to be contested if we are to see how the literary affections have a history. Following an overview that builds on and redirects some recent analyses of the eighteenth-century making of the English canon so as to foreground this issue, the first half of this chapter investigates descriptions of literature as a gift that genius bestows on posterity and corresponding descriptions of the love of literature as a grateful love. With the mobilization of the author function, literary reading became subject to new expectations of affective obligation and dilemmas of affective entanglement. Accordingly, talk of what it meant to love literature was necessarily in dialogue, as I will show, with the period's discussions of freedom and constraint and equality and hierarchy: discussions in which gratitude was a burden to be carried, as well as an emotional state engendered spontaneously.

In its second half, this chapter turns to Johnson's *Lives* and Boswell's *Life of Johnson* and highlights in these texts Johnson's expressions of discomfiture over the very arrangements for biographical reading that he himself had advanced, suggesting that he also mistrusted these arrangements as an occasion for emotional profligacy. Johnson can sometimes look to be convinced that any amount of love for an object that cannot reciprocate one's affections is already a case of loving too much. I tack between his uneasiness with the way that readerly transactions with poetry were being pressured by the imperatives of a new age of sensibility and the sometimes explicitly anti-Johnsonian modeling of the role of the lover of literature undertaken by Anna Seward, who disagreed with Johnson about how a subject ought to conduct herself in relationship to aesthetic objects.

I want, however, to begin at some distance from these case studies in how "aesthetics" lines up with "ethos" and "philia" in the era of the man and woman of feeling, and so I begin a little earlier in the eighteenth century. Let us start by marking some eighteenth-century instances in which the proposition that aesthetic experience was a scene of personal congress gets belied just where we might expect it to be credited.

USING, ADMIRING, LOVING

It can be disorienting, for instance, to look at printed collections of poetry from the early eighteenth century—the ancestors of the multivolume anthology of English verse for which in 1777–81 Johnson produced his *Lives of the English Poets* as prefaces. These earlier collections are not really about authorial achievement at all. Falling short in the anthropomorphizing department, they thwart our wish to see in them the sources of more modern habits of literary appreciation. Take, for instance, from 1738, *The British Muse, or a Collection of Thoughts Moral, Natural, and Sublime of Our English Poets*. The editor of this compilation of sixteenth- and seventeenth-century verse, Thomas Hayward, arranged for his books' contents to be arrayed "according to the Order of Time in which [our English poets] wrote." That format, of course, remains fundamental to the discipline's presentation of "literature": it is partly in becoming an object with a past that literature comes into visibility in the discursive field. At the same time, the announced motive for Hayward's choice of organizational scheme, which is "to shew the gradual Improvements of our Poetry and Language," evokes an unfamiliar account of how that past unfolded as a story.[8] The determination that chronology should reveal "Improvement," and so poetry's perfectibility, might seem to us wrongheaded. (For later antiquarians smitten with medieval romances, among many others, it would instead be axiomatic that literature by its nature could not conform to the linear shape of a progressive history, and that instead genius flourished most in the earliest stages of society.) Even odder is the framework to which this chronological presentation is subordinated in *The British Muse*. The three volumes are in fact arranged alphabetically, and the letters of the alphabet are the finding aids that one uses to discover not authors' names but poetical topics. Thus volume 1 commences with *Abbeys*. Under that heading Hayward arrays, moving forward through time, excerpts of Shakespeare's drama and verse by Samuel Daniel and others. Next comes *Absence*: a sequence that makes it seem, evocatively, as if the anthologist were rehearsing the history of the Reformation and of the passing of the faith of his fathers, a loss that had also been referenced in the first passage found under the *Abbeys* heading, from a source identified as "Shakespeare's Cromwell" (i.e., *Henry VIII*, that favorite of eighteenth-century playgoers). Under *Absence*, one finds verse by (in chronological order) Edmund Spenser, Michael Drayton, John Donne (represented by "A Valediction: Forbidding Mourning," though, disconcertingly, not in its entirety), Ben Jonson, Thomas Carew, and Sir John Suckling. The first volume, having taken us from *A* through *F* in the alphabet, ends with the heading

Friend. Though it features the same authors, this eighteenth-century proto-anthology reads less like the textbooks professors of English assign in survey classes and more like an overgrown index.

A later example of this phenomenon, *The Beauties of Poetry Display'd*, from 1757, documents the contemporary scene, rather than documenting poetry's past and paying homage "to neglected and expiring merit" as Hayward had twenty years earlier.[9] However, it shares the format of its predecessor, likewise embracing the impersonality of alphabetical order in a way that seems to make poetical images and sentiments float free of the people who are poets. The definition of language as a self-expressive medium that will inform later accounts of literary genius, the presupposition that literary texts might be read biographically for hints of the history of feelings that they vouchsafe to a sensitive reader: these are accommodated badly by this book. Having opened *The Beauties of Poetry Display'd*, the reader begins with the heading *Abandoned*, illustrated by a long extract from Alexander Pope's *Sappho to Phaon* and also an extract from a poem of Mrs. [Aphra] Behn's. Then one moves to *Age, golden, iron, etc.* and encounters a specimen of "Wharton's Virgil" (the edition prepared by Joseph Warton); thence to *Animaculus*—represented by James Thomson's *The Seasons*—and to *Astonishment—Hamlet* and *Julius Caesar*; and finally to *Autumn*—a poem by "Mrs." [Mary] Leapor. Next up is the letter *B.*

These poetry collections register an unfamiliar understanding of English poetry as existing to be used, rather than existing to be read and appreciated.[10] In his overview of "All of the Collections of This Kind That Were Ever Published" that he contributed as a preface to the third volume of *The British Muse*, William Oldys mentions Edward Bysshe's *The Art of English Poetry* (first published in 1703 and by the 1730s in its eighth edition):[11] the latter is a book in which the "Collection of the most Natural, Agreable, and Sublime Thoughts . . . . that are to be found in the best English poets" ends up placed cheek by jowl with "A Dictionary of Rhymes." That reference to Bysshe thus confirms how from a certain angle these collections resemble how-to manuals. They also resemble ready-made commonplace books, their digests of the poetic tradition easing the work load for the would-be collector of commonplaces. For the books not only preselect poetic flowers and nuggets of meaningfulness. They also set out in advance the headings that a reader should use in tabulating these.[12] Such motives had for some time shaped the editorial practice of the booksellers and compilers who mediated between poets and publics. In, for instance, *The New Academy of Complements, Erected for Ladies, Gentlewomen, Courtiers, Gentlemen, Scholars, Soldiers, Citizens, Countrymen, and*

All Persons, of What Degree Soever, of Both Sexes; Stored with Variety of Courtly and Civil Complements . . . With an Exact Collection of the Newest and Choicest Songs à la Mode (1669), poetry is framed explicitly as an adjunct to examples of eloquence. Poetry offers itself to readers not as a love object, but rather as a source of instruction in how to speak fair (the literary tradition is annexed to elocutionary training) and thus in how to woo love objects and advance in the world. This poetry book presupposes its implementation in a domain of practice beyond reading's paper world.

Trevor Ross's magisterial account of the eighteenth-century emergence of literature, *The Making of the English Literary Canon* (1998), can help us place these books historically so as to explain the seemingly perverse relation these books have to our modern expectation that the poetic anthology should be the site of the imaginative communion joining readers to people called authors. A rhetorical culture, Ross states, as he reconstructs notions of literature before "Literature," values texts from the past only as a backdrop to ongoing cultural production, as possibly useful models for new compositions and spurs to new acts of eloquence. As an example of this arrangement, he instances Sir Philip Sidney's perfect courtier, who aimed "not onely to read others *Poesies*, but to *poetise* for others reading."[13] But in the eighteenth century that arrangement gradually gave way to one organized around the historically sensitive but tasteful *reading* of the "classics" of the past.[14] This culture values literature "as a type of moral technology that could enrich students by virtue of the labour required to . . . appreciate it" (226).

Ross lays out this before-and-after contrast pithily: "Poetry is composed and spoken," he declares, but "literature [is] read and studied" (300). As this formulation indicates, Ross is especially interested in how, given altered social conditions, the critic's task as canon maker began to be reconceived in the eighteenth century, geared to reception rather than invention. If previously the literary canon had been something that each generation of writers was expected to produce anew, in the eighteenth century, as readership expanded and as aristocratic patronage was displaced by a market in print, that literary canon began, instead, to be a precious, ever-more-fragile tradition that critics *re*produced on audiences' behalf. The critic's role had been to enforce linguistic correctness and so ensure that the polishing and improvement of the English tongue (as Thomas Hayward might put it) would proceed without interruption. Gradually, another role became conspicuous: that of granting each generation of readers the awareness that would enable them to negotiate the alterity of the treasure trove of canonical texts. Thus in the eighteenth century there is, for the first time, evidence of vernacular (rather than Latin, Greek, or Hebrew) texts being scrutinized and taught in order to bring out their meaning. Only then, by extension, is there some consensus that general readers' desire for literature is a desire to be equipped to appreciate it rather than to create literature themselves. That emergent presupposition about the general reader also helps to account for the distance separating the poetry collections I mentioned above from something like, for instance, William Hazlitt's *Select British Poets* (1824): readers of this book, the frontispiece especially promises, will be learning about a tradition, and not simply as they encounter great poems but also as they make the acquaintance of the great poets (fig. 1.1).[15]

The changes that Ross chronicles as he recounts how literature arose upon the ruins of an old rhetorical culture include, as well, a shift in the temporal orientation of the critic. The critic became the guardian of the canon of the dead. The other side of the emergence of an autonomous aesthetic sphere was a relocation into an ever more remote past of real literary value—that is, value deriving no "advantages . . . from local customs or temporary opinions," as Samuel Johnson wrote about Shakespeare's merit. Literary antiquity was no longer conceptualized as the unpolished, unimproved prelude to modernity. Instead, by 1765, when Johnson's edition of Shakespeare's plays appeared, Shakespeare's historical remoteness represented a good thing, since it ensured that he was valued for the right reasons. Shakespeare's works had outlived their century, Johnson stated, and so they "support no opinion with arguments, nor supply any faction with invectives . . . but are read without any reason than the desire of pleasure."[16] The close connection between pastness and canonicity, as Johnson implies, was not simply a function of how older works that were still talked about had prima facie passed the test of time. It was also a function of the decontextualizing wrought by historical distance and the depoliticizing effects that entailed. The reading of old works was an end in itself, without utilitarian purpose, which meant that these works' credentials as *aesthetic* objects were more easily determined. The reeducation in the reading of Milton that Joseph Addison's *Spectator* papers imparted to their audience in 1712 provides another case in point. These essays downplayed the didactic aims of *Paradise Lost*. Instead, they engaged the reader's pleasure, tracing how the poem's beauties worked to "unbend the Mind of the Reader."[17]

Within the culture of appreciation whose emergence Ross describes through examples like these, literature and its reading thus exist in a relationship of mutual definition. Literature comes to name a distinctive, exclusive category of expression that sponsors a special mode of reading—an

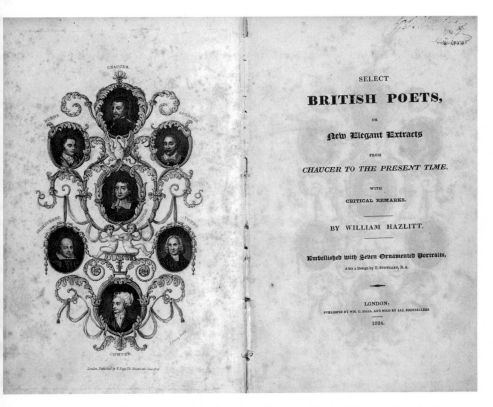

SELECT

BRITISH POETS,

OR

New Elegant Extracts

FROM

CHAUCER TO THE PRESENT TIME,

WITH

CRITICAL REMARKS.

BY WILLIAM HAZLITT.

Embellished with Seven Ornamented Portraits,

After a Design by T. STOTHARD, R.A.

LONDON:
PUBLISHED BY WM. C. HALL, AND SOLD BY ALL BOOKSELLERS.

1824.

FIGURE 1.1 Frontispiece and title page from William Hazlitt's 1824 compilation *Select British Poets, or New Elegant Extracts from Chaucer to the Present Time.* Assembling the portrait busts of Chaucer, Spenser, Shakespeare, Milton, Young, Cowper, and Burns, this frontispiece depicts the literary tradition not as a collection of poetic beauties, as in the earlier tradition of poetic miscellanies, but as a gallery of poets. Photograph: Courtesy of the John Graham Library, Trinity College, University of Toronto.

activity that will be personally enriching and yet also, at the same time, its own reward. Literature's specialness is also shored up by the premise that to read texts that have outlived their time requires a particular kind of receptivity: an exercise of the sympathetic imagination, a striving to bridge the distance between self and other and now and then. And literary reading comes to be understood, as well, as an activity requiring a certain amount of critical or pedagogical supervision. Readers would require expert assistance if they were to discover the value of the literary texts, so distant from their contemporary moment, on which they were to exercise their sensibilities.

One additional feature that Ross and others highlight in describing these new arrangements needs to be reckoned with. Throughout *The Making of the English Literary Canon*, Ross associates the shift from reading for use to reading for appreciation, which for him heralds the emergence of literature, with a "feminization" of eighteenth-century culture. He assigns considerable evidentiary weight, accordingly, to declarations like the one Johnson made to Boswell that their age was distinctive from prior eras because "we have more knowledge generally diffused; all our ladies read . . . , which is a great extension."[18] Through ladies' reading, Ross suggests, literature was precipitated out from an older culture of argument and eloquence in which acquaintance with poetry had been valued as a vehicle to social action. Early modern women had not been well positioned to pursue the goal-oriented, appropriative reading that had defined that rhetorical culture. The under-examined implication here is that women were instead born readers, as it were, of the kind of anthology that solicits and presupposes "love of genius"; when it came to reading as interpersonal connection, women were naturals. When "the eighteenth century invents the canon" and with it a new concept of the aesthetic, Douglas Lane Patey proposes in an argument congruent with Ross's, it develops in tandem an account of the poetical character that is newly female-friendly by virtue of excluding "erudition and participation in practical affairs." And the eighteenth century begins, Patey says, to describe the taste that aesthetic objects require from their audience in terms that highlight passivity—a receiving of pleasure, a yielding of the self to the emotions that a composition arouses.[19] The historian of reading William Sherman deploys a similar binary framework when introducing his account of the age of the commonplace book. Stressing modern people's distance from that epoch of "used books," when, in contrast to now, reading was a matter of busy text-indexing, epitomizing, gutting for content, and digesting, Sherman encapsulates the transition from early modern to modern thus: "We have moved from a culture in which readers take hold of texts for specific purposes to one in which texts generally take hold of readers."[20] With the institutionalization of literature, Sherman's formula implies, reading becomes a matter of passive surrender. At that point readers exit history as active agents; readers of "literature" have nothing left to do.

But adapting to literature was not something that just happened. Such formulae are too pat. Occluded by the oppositions between producer/consumer, active/passive, composition/ appreciation, and masculine/feminine that shore up these before-and-after narratives are the eighteenth century's uncertainties about how readers were to comport themselves in relationship to aesthetic objects, and just what the reader's remit would be once certain special literary books were no longer to be used, but instead to be felt with and felt for. As we shall see, one area of uncertainty involved the question of exactly what kind of gendered practice the new practice of appreciation might be: a question bracketed by the thesis of cultural feminization, however, which simplifies how gender norms inflect the protocols for literary attachments. More generally, the tidy symmetry of accounts framed in this manner seems to divert these scholars from investigating the possibility that for eighteenth-century people appreciation might not have brought closure to a story of cultural transition, but might instead have brought new challenges. It was not so easy for readers to accommodate the notion that the book was not a storage unit but a surrogate self, a hegemonic notion once it was agreed that—as Simon During puts it—literature is "writing which has 'authors' versus writing which is anonymous."[21] It took time and trouble to naturalize the changed conditions of social interactivity engendered as readers came to feel themselves (or suppose that they ought to feel themselves) in relation with those selves also.

Eighteenth-century debates about those personal relations are given short shrift in contemporary scholars' accounts of the emergence of *literary* reading. One reason may be that we have to accommodate a now standard account of what, as the so-called century of taste, the eighteenth century accomplished. This account presupposes that judgment and attachment are to be placed in opposition rather than apposition, and assumes that only the first is to be thought of as a historical achievement whose establishment involved real cultural effort. The most often-cited histories of aesthetics, as David Marshall notes, tend to read eighteenth-century discussions teleologically—as preparing the ground for Immanuel Kant's *Critique of Judgment* (1790)—and they center accordingly on the process by which the disinterestedness and detachment proper to the connoisseur became during the Enlightenment the core principles of aesthetic experience.[22] These histories pivot on the consolidation of a scheme that sees aesthetic experience occupy a separate realm that is at a neat remove from the realm of quotidian need and desire (hence the premises about the autonomization of art that underwrite Trevor Ross's history of canonicity): this understanding of aesthetic experience is applauded for how it underwrites a disinterested "respect" for the art object as an end in itself.

Within these histories, the attainment of a proper aesthetic attitude depends on the production and preservation of professional distance. But even so, as Marshall stresses, eighteenth-century discussions of aesthetic experience often tend to bring aesthetic experience "home," to "domestic settings" and "everyday life."[23] Furthermore, as Denise Gigante has observed, the seventeenth- and eighteenth-century alignment of the aesthetic with the sense of "taste" and the swerve that this alignment involves from "a classical aesthetics primarily linked to the higher senses of sight and hearing" leave aesthetic experience bound up with the body. There are implications to the gustatory metaphor that underwrites Enlightenment discussions of the man of taste, in other words, that seem to countermand those discussions' insistence on the distance that the connoisseur should preserve between himself and the object of his contemplation and evaluation. Taste also names an intimate, interiorized pleasure that, precisely in not accommodating itself easily to objective laws, plays an essential role in "generating our very sense of self."[24]

Conforming oneself to "the standard of Taste," David Hume famously asserts in a 1757 essay of that name (often read as prefiguring Kant's *Critique*), means laying aside all personal considerations: I forget "my individual being and my peculiar circumstances." Hume requires the true judge, he who seeks to establish the universal standard of taste and so to evaluate works from distant epochs and climes as they should be evaluated, to have a "strong sense . . . cleared of all prejudice." But even so, this evacuation of "prejudice" from the scene of taste does not entail a total banishment of "predilection." (Hume's term "predilection" combines, the *Oxford English Dictionary* tells us, the prefix "pre" with "dilection," a noun derived from the Latin for "to select to oneself from others, to esteem highly, hold dear, love.") If "it is plainly an error in a critic to confine his approbation to one species or style of writing," nonetheless, "it is almost impossible not to feel a predilection for that which suits our particular turn and disposition": the latter statement launches an account, reaffirming the particularities of individuals' attachments and their identities, of how certain nations and age groups have "favourite authors" and naturally so, because "we choose our favourite author as we do our friend, from a conformity of humour and disposition."[25] This idea that the man of taste will cleave to a favorite author in the same way that he also cleaves to a friend registers, in a foreseeable way, the impact of those new notions of authorship that were gradually making (as we have seen) certain sorts of anthologies obsolete—those sorts that collected "poetical sentiments" more than "poets" and represented reader's transactions with books as an occasion for an encounter with "beauties," and not as an occasion on which readers sustained the company of other people. But it is harder than many of Hume's commentators acknowledge to accommodate this idea to the account of the connoisseur as judge who must transcend his personal particularities so as to take a disinterested view of the aesthetic object. Momentarily, Hume gestures toward an alternate picture of the connoisseur as a lover, who, as such, will have and play favorites and will suspend the norms of impartiality to that end. As we shall see later, several contemporary readers of his *Lives of the Poets* would fault Samuel Johnson for falling short as a literary lover: Edmund Cartwright, for instance, would note, in terms that chime with Hume's, how in the pages of Johnson's *Lives* "whole beauties are passed over with the neutrality of a stranger and the coldness of a critic." Hume cannot part with the investments that he has by virtue of belonging to his "own age and country," but Johnson, Cartwright complains, "appears to have little more brotherly kindness [for his contemporaries] than they might have expected at Constantinople."[26]

A more fleshed-out version of this picture of connoisseur as lover, a version in which affective gratification and judgment are explicitly linked, appears in an earlier essay of Hume's, "Of the Delicacy of Taste and Passion" (1742). This essay promotes the study of "poetry, eloquence, music or painting" by proposing that, in obtaining the wherewithal to make aesthetic judgments, and in learning to mark the "differences and gradations" which separate adequacy from excellence, the connoisseur ends up a truer friend. The affections of the man who "has well digested his knowledge both of books and men" are "confined within a narrow circle"; what is more, "he carries them further than if they were more general and undistinguished."[27] He is capable of a feeling deeper and more ardent than a general esteem. In the way it confuses, rather than separates, art and life, this early essay especially suggests that Hume may have loved love more than the historians of aesthetics, preoccupied with the emergence of a properly Kantian account of aesthetic disinterestedness, do. It suggests the extent to which the history of the aesthetic overlaps with a history that sees Britons revise from the inside an inherited discourse of civic humanism, redistributing the dignity that had for their forefathers accrued to public virtues exclusively and granting it to what Hume calls here the small "delicacies" of love and friendship.

Through this brief excursus on that aspect of aesthetic discourse, I mean to have taken a step toward filling in the lacunae, noted above, in the recent scholarship engaging the eighteenth-century emergence of the category of literature. This scholarship tends to assume that we already know what literary appreciation is and that it came and comes naturally—especially to a female or feminized reading public. Such an assumption casts the particular reading practice that literature has solicited as a simple act of entextualization and acculturation, in a way that removes this practice from history.

Scholarship on taste proceeds similarly. To the extent that a predilection for a favorite author appears on the radar of historians of aesthetics, it is as the timeless compulsion that true connoisseurs will have learned to overcome in attaining the proper aesthetic disinterestedness. But the consolidation of literature was also a chapter in the history of intimate, private life, as in the history of the emotions. Neglect of those dimensions of literature's history has left us ill equipped to engage the particular turn that the formation of subjectivities began to take when eighteenth-century lovers of literature began to find wanting the tasteful language of approbation or admiration and when they took recourse instead in the stickier, subjectivity-saturated language of affection and involvement.

We are thus poorly prepared to gauge those readers' insecurities as they found themselves navigating the evaluative field that was created by statements like John Dryden's in *Of Dramatic Poesy* (1668): "If I would compare [Ben Jonson] with Shakespeare, I must acknowledge him the more correct poet, but Shakespeare the greater wit. . . . I admire him, but I love Shakespeare." Originating from that eminent source, the statement must have exerted some pressure on more humble readers, leaving them worrying whether it was an error, in that case, to admire Shakespeare and bestow more tender feelings on Jonson—wondering, more generally, how they themselves might contrive to embed an idiolect of personal affection within the sociolect of taste. In a 1797 essay, the philosopher and novelist William Godwin warned that the youth who begins reading late will never have the capacity to make authors into his intimates—he "makes a superficial acquaintance . . . but is never admitted into the familiarity of a friend"; "stiffness and formality are always visible between them." Godwin's statement provokes its reader's consternation; it suggests how tricky it might be, even a century after Dryden, to get a loving reading right. [28] In coming onto the scene as a new sort of object for people's affections, literature altered the practices and protocols of those affections in its turn. Thorny problems of ethics and etiquette thus beset readers at the dawn of the literary era, as they accommodated these new paradigms for codifying the pleasures of their texts.

The protocols that were to guide them in thinking of their bookish encounters as scenes of personal congress were not straightforward. Was it appropriate to share one's emotional life with the people in books? Should one love authors as persons? (If so, *all* authors?) Was love what the reader owed them? (Or did the reader *owe* anything?) Did the author's claims for tribute from the reader extend to this reader's heart? Or would liking, rather than loving, do, and was love supererogatory, beyond the call of duty? Where to locate the line between appreciation and fetishistic enslavement—an idolatry that valued excessively and irrationally? In 1759, the bluestocking author Elizabeth Carter, on hearing that she had an admirer in a certain Anne Pitt, professed, in a letter to an acquaintance she shared with that reader, how much she deplored the manner in which this Mrs. Pitt understood her own aesthetic predilection. Hers is one view on those questions:

> She might *admire* me if I were a vocal statue, or a walking tripod; but no such queer curiosity am I, I walk upon two feet like other folks. . . . Surely then, it is very hard that Mrs. Pitt should think of sticking me up in a cabinet, like a mere object of *vertu*, to be *admired* and perish with cold, when I am so much better entitled to be placed in some obscure snug corner by a warm fire-side. I should be quite undone if you had considered me in the same view of *admiration*, and placed me among your vases, and your Chinese dolls.[29]

In his ethical writings, Aristotle had made mutual recognition crucial to the definition of friendship: "Of the love of lifeless objects," Aristotle writes in *The Nicomachean Ethics*, "we do not use the word 'friendship' for it is not mutual love, nor is there a wishing of good to the other."[30] (Wine is Aristotle's example of such an object; Elizabeth Carter's complaint that admiration makes her into a "mere" collectible provides another.) Do we delude ourselves then, stretch the concept of friendship too far, when, like the "early reader" of Thomson and Milton in Godwin's essay, we count long-dead authors who never knew us, much less returned our feelings, as our "companions"? And yet that offer of companionship exemplifies, contrariwise, an alternative proposal about friendship set out in Aristotle's *The Eudemian Ethics* that held that the most praiseworthy friends were those who continued to love their dead, precisely because they loved without hope of a return: "They know, but are not known."[31] Though from one angle it resembles the deluded intimacy expectations of a Miss Lonelyhearts, as flagged in this chapter's third epigraph, love for the dead author might also be considered ethically exemplary. The intimacies promised to the lover of literature are irrefragably linked to an awareness of distance. The pages that follow continue to explore such affective conundrums, considering them as central dramas within the story of the personalization of literature.

LOVE, DEBT, AND LITERATURE AS LARGESSE

This section launches that exploration by zeroing in on those particular conundrums that were generated for eighteenth-century readers by representations of readerly gratitude as authors' due and of books as, correspondingly, the gifts that should be repaid with that gratitude. Such representations remain familiar to this day. A review by Christopher Ricks of Lawrence Lipking's *Samuel Johnson: The Life of an Author* (2000), for instance, congratulates Lipking for modeling the conviction "that the literature of the past should prompt not griping but gratitude." "Gratitude ... becomes us," Ricks later instructed fellow readers of Pope, Burns, Wordsworth, and Tennyson in his own *Allusions to the Poets* (2003).[32] With this seemingly commonsensical expectation about how readers should comport themselves during their aesthetic experiences, Ricks was actually asking a lot. To suggest as much, I aim in this section to trace the manner in which some eighteenth-century readers (both real and imagined) balked at such prescriptions. That resistance to an account of the love of literature as a grateful love may bespeak, I want to suggest, a resistance to the personalization of the aesthetic relation—a resistance traceable even on the part of Samuel Johnson himself, even though as a proponent of literary biography and in this guise an architect of the author love so crucial to the institution of literature, he helped prepare its ground. Ricks *ethicalizes* readers' transactions with texts. More or less overtly, the readers that I look at in this section, as a context for this chapter's concluding sections on Johnson's *Lives of the English Poets*, declared themselves discomfited by the burden of gratitude that such ethicalization creates.

In Trevor Ross's description of the eighteenth-century emergence of literature, one distinction between a modern objectivist culture and an earlier rhetorical culture is the rigid separation between authors and readers that the former presupposes. No longer are the two parties involved in literary transactions placed on an even playing field. The latter suggestion about their relative positioning seemed to inform, as we saw, the older poetry collections, such as *The New Academy of Complements*, that were oriented to readerly use. In the new arrangement, authors and readers are decisively separated by the barrier of death, old works now having the monopoly on canonicity. They are separated too by asymmetric endowments of imagination and talent.[33] "A man of Genius," stated William Duff, is "a kind of different being from the rest of his species": the statement from 1770 documents how the term "genius" had then already begun the transition that would take it from being a designation for an aptitude, a characteristic disposition ("he has a genius for"), to a designation for character type ("he was a genius"), a larger-than-life figure of preternatural powers. (That transition is another aspect of the rearrangements of the discursive field that created modern literature.) Another celebration of genius unfolds in Edward Young's *Conjectures on Original Composition* (1759), which designates "author" as a "noble title." That charged word, "noble," also indicates how, under this new arrangement, the author's cultural authority was also something obtained at the expense of the aristocratic patron. In the new arrangement, only one party, the author, is patrician, leaving in the plebeian position even the aristocrats who had traditionally been charged with the encouragement of learning.[34]

The gulf between the reader and the author that was engendered by what one might call, extending Foucault, "the genius function" made great authors into figures whom mere readers could only look up to. To Goethe's hero Wilhelm Meister in 1796, Shakespeare's plays seem the "performances of some celestial genius" who "descend[s] among men" so as to instruct them. The beneficence of the canonized authors includes that willingness to *condescend*, in the rapidly vanishing sense of the term that is written up in Johnson's *Dictionary* and that usually designated the noblesse oblige of aristocratic patrons who indulgently "sooth[ed]" their inferiors with "familiarity."[35] Such accounts of the distance between the parties whom literature involves were in friction both with the democratic impulses of the era and with the intimacy expectations that eighteenth-century readers were forming as they learned to read biographically.

One way to explore that friction, this section will suggest, is through the premise holding that the beneficence of the canonical author is made concrete in the literary texts that he (or more rarely she) gives to posterity. Late eighteenth-century readers encountered a particularly explicit form of that premise in the copyright cases of their day. Through much of the century, a publishing cartel had acted as though perpetual copyright had a basis in common law and had demanded accordingly that others (especially Scots publishers) recognize their exclusive title to texts such as *Paradise Lost* and Thomson's *The Seasons*. In the decision in *Donaldson v. Becket* in 1774 the Law Lords denied this claim to perpetual copyright: the judgment, Trevor Ross has commented, amounted to a recognition that British literature "belonged to the British people" or that at the very least the texts that had stood the test of time, and in the meantime gone out of copyright, did. The concept of a public domain that the judgment thereby ratified—the concept of an ideal space housing those special texts—would have crucial ramifications for the notions of a canon.[36] Occasionally in the debating that paved the way for the Law Lords' ratification of the concept of a public domain, classic authors were described as having *given* their works to the public. (Notably, such an account of author-reader relations sidelines an idea of the public as being poets' "patrons," a relationship implying a rather different arrangement

of power.) "In every language, the words which express the publication
of a book express it as giving it to the public," Justice Yates declared in
Millar v. Taylor, the 1769 case that was the dry run for *Donaldson v. Becket*.[37]
Shakespeare's works, said Justice Camden, "were surely given to the public
if ever author's were."[38] Reference was made, as well, to how booksellers' illiberal and mercenary attempts to perpetually engross the cultural heritage
had defeated that noble authorial intention. Authors, by contrast to booksellers, were beyond worldly need. In this view, then, authors appear as a
group distinguished by their munificence, a liberality that is also a call on
readerly gratitude.

Literary culture of the late eighteenth century was discovering what
good gifts books make. In a break with past practice, giving presents was
no longer primarily an activity connecting patrons to their dependents but
becoming instead an exchange linking the generations and so defining the
intimate sphere.[39] By the early nineteenth century, British poetry would find
a new home in a medium called the "gift book" that was destined for exactly that style of exchange. Grappling with the commercial proliferation
that was fueled in part by the new practices of giving, literary culture was
also discovering something useful in this account of authors' munificence.
Unlike the sale of a commodity, the giving of a gift tends to establish a relationship between the parties.[40]

Still, readers who had been taking lessons in love from eighteenth-
century novels would have readily recognized the potential for tension
in the affective economy so established. A recurring interest in "unequal
marriages" (Mr. Bennet's term in *Pride and Prejudice*) and "disproportioned
friendships" (as Mr. Bennet's fictional ancestor Dr. Primrose calls them in
The Vicar of Wakefield) had long put grateful love on the novel's agenda,
as the name of a central semantic problem—*Was love founded on gratitude
real love?*—as well as a problem of emotional self-management—*Could such
love last?* Could hearts "bowed down by obligation, and goodness never to
be returned" ever succeed in rising to familiarity with "the obligers"? The
heroine of Samuel Richardson's *The History of Sir Charles Grandison* (1753–
54) broods over the latter question: Harriet Byron's consciousness of all she
owes to the eponymous hero, a figure of inexhaustible beneficence, makes
it unavoidable. There is no way to be "even" with Sir Charles Grandison in
anything, Harriet marvels, and the realization both pleases her as further
evidence of the merit of her beloved and makes her uneasy. "What shall I do
with my gratitude?" she asks with bewilderment.[41]

Eighteenth-century and romantic-period discussions of the dynamics of literary appreciation sometimes disclose an equivalent to this uneasiness. The very people who claim distinction through their author love can appear a bit put out by the vocabulary of munificence that was supposed to bestow moral dignity on authorship. A curious example of that perturbation can be found in the opening of *Biographia Literaria*, Samuel Taylor Coleridge's 1816 account of his authorial tribulations and literary affections. While recounting his youthful reading, Coleridge appears, at first glance, self-protectively to be setting limits to expectations about readerly gratitude. He states that it is only the literary works of one's contemporaries that "assume the properties of flesh and blood": "recit[ing], extol[ing], contend[ing] for" those works, he concedes, is "but the payment of a debt due to one, who exists to receive it" (*Biographia*, 1:15). (While a schoolboy at Christ's Hospital, Coleridge made forty transcriptions of Bowles's sonnets, by way of presents to friends: that labor may have given him a way of paying off his debt to the poet.)[42] But, Coleridge insists, there is nothing like this degree of involvement with the "great works of past ages," which "seem to a young man things of another race, in respect to which his faculties must remain passive and submiss, even as to the stars and mountains" (1:12). In setting out this contrast, Coleridge apparently aims to convince us that the distance separating the contemporary reader from the classic works (as far away as are starry skies and mountain summits) is not a problem. On the contrary, that very distance means that readers are released from the obligations they feel as the debtors of their contemporaries. The burdens that arise in the cases in which texts "assume the properties of flesh and blood" do not arise with these works. But in that reference to "passive and submiss faculties," one may hear a contrary note that suggests that Coleridge does in fact continue to personalize his relations to those works. There is some audible balking at how this account of the literary field grants authors an unchallengeable monopoly over the category of activity. Virginia Woolf might have been aiming to provoke just these worries in an intimidating statement she made a century later: "Jane Austen we needs must adore; but she does not want it; she wants nothing, our love is a by-product, an irrelevance; with that mist or without it her moon shines."[43] In these passages from Coleridge and Woolf, the association of literary genius and heavenly bodies—stars and the moon—intimates that the gift of literature would necessarily be a gift disbursed from above. That verticality is a problem.

The contemporary essayist Margaret Visser evokes an important context for the challenges the grateful lover of literature must navigate when she reminds us of the extent to which modernity created itself through suspicion of the gift. Moderns, she notes, have been hyperaware of how equality and independence require protection from giving—especially from the kind of unilateral, de haut en bas giving, that has come into view over my last few pages. That awareness was perhaps most acute in the eighteenth century, when the terms "patronize" and "condescension" first begin to designate bad things, and when the patron-client relationships that had organized the conferral and reception of benefits came under suspicion in new ways.[44] In a *Rambler* essay from October 1750 Johnson spotlighted the problem:[45] "Benefits which cannot be repaid, and obligations which cannot be discharged, are not commonly found to increase affection; they excite gratitude indeed, and heighten veneration, but commonly take away that easy freedom and familiarity of intercourse without which, though there may be fidelity, and zeal, and admiration, there cannot be friendship. The great effect of friendship is beneficence, yet by the first act of uncommon kindness it is endangered, like plants that bear their fruit and die." Acknowledging this aspect of the context in which figures such as Coleridge developed their literary affections makes the notes of recalcitrance in his devotion easier to hear.

That gratitude is an edgier emotion for loving readers than a commentator like Christopher Ricks acknowledges is evidenced by how the annals of literary reading seem quite often to turn up variations on a fantasy of author rescue that seems structured to take care of gratitude's burdensome aspects and help readers manage the strong and disconcerting feelings that great writing arouses. This fantasy was familiar to Jane Austen herself, who knew fandom from both sides. (She outs herself as a fan in a November 3, 1813, letter, in which, gleeful over the recent publication of *Pride and Prejudice*, she begins spinning a fantasy in which she rides her success all the way to a marriage with Frances Burney's son, the teenaged Alexandre D'Arblay—a union enabling her to realize the literary fan's dream of a close, quasi-familial connection with her favorite author.)[46] Consider the conversation in a scene early in Austen's *Sense and Sensibility* (1811) which shows us the three Dashwood sisters, who have just been disinherited, imagining what they would do if someone gave them a large fortune apiece. "The day of your windfall will be a fine day for booksellers, music-sellers and print-shops," their friend Edward Ferrars declares, going on to specify the project that Marianne Dashwood particularly would pursue in these circumstances: "'I know her greatness of soul! ... Thomson, Cowper, Scott—she would buy them all over and over again; she would buy up every copy, I believe, to prevent their falling into unworthy hands. ... And the bulk of [her] fortune would be laid out in annuities on the authors or their heirs.'" Edward is perhaps being unkind in this scene. He has forgotten how Marianne's recent experience likely makes her conceive of herself as an object, not a subject, of charity. Still his conjecture about Marianne's behavior is persuasive in light of a snarky comment Marianne has made earlier about how unresponsive Edward proved when reading Cowper.[47] Through Edward's conjectures, Austen reveals herself to be a shrewd observer of her era's culture of literary appreciation. As she recognizes, a portionless girl like Marianne might well want to rescript poetry love and reimagine herself, not as the poets' beneficiary, but as a Lady Bountiful who commands the wherewithal to shower annuities on her favorite authors and their posterity. Marianne manipulates the social frameworks for literary appreciation so as to claim admiration for her individual way of admiring.

Edward's comments hint, as well, that the problem with the gift giving of the authors is that it is disbursed indiscriminately. In *Of Favours* (circa AD 60), an exhaustive treatment of gratitude, the Stoic moralist Seneca had meditated repeatedly on this kind of gift, at one point suggestively linking the gifts of the gods, such as the sunshine, the "showers and waters filling the springs, the winds that blow regularly," things "devised for the benefit of all . . . the good and bad alike," with "works of genius, [which] even if they are going to meet with unworthy readers, are edited and published."[48] Marianne does not like to think of authors' gifts as bestowed upon—or creating—a collective world, as showers, waters, and winds do. Worried by literature's general solicitations, Marianne desires a fortune (Edward says) in order to be able to bar unworthy or unintended recipients.

The wish links this character to an actual bookish teenager from the 1790s, William Henry Ireland, who supplies this section's last example of a fantasy of author rescue. Of course, Ireland usually figures in literary history in a contrary guise, as an author-imposter of ill repute. In 1794 the seventeen-year-old's claim to his Shakespeare-loving father that he (Ireland Jr.) had discovered a treasure trove of "miscellaneous papers and legal instruments under the hand and seal of William Shakspeare" set in motion a process that would see him in the next year managing briefly to pass off his own writings as literary historical finds—as an authentic *King Lear* and a previously unknown Shakespearean tragedy *Vortigern and Rowena*, both of which he had recovered from obscurity. Through his counterfeiting, Ireland obtained proof that *his* genius was equal to Shakespeare's, though the opening night at Drury Lane in April 1796, when *Vortigern* was hooted off stage, likely renewed doubt about that comparison. Less commented on than this hubristic ambition is the fact that among the earliest of Ireland's forgeries were a promissory note supposedly in the hand of the Bard and a deed of gift, made out by this same hand as a record of a debt that has provoked the debtor to try to make a return.

The author's debts encompassed, as it turns out, a huge one to a certain sixteenth-century William Henry Ireland, who had heroically saved the careless Bard from drowning in the Thames, and who, in return, as quid pro quo, had received the plays *Lear, Henry IV, Henry V,* and *Henry III* (!), all the profit from which, the Bard wrote on this deed of gift, were "wholly toe bee for sayde Ireland and atte hys deathe thenne toe hiys fyrst Sunne alsoe William Henry . . . ande soe on for everre inn hys lyne" (fig. 1.2). The deed of gift that disposes of the Bard's plays is in actuality an IOU. It conceals a history, one that Ireland has recovered, in which Shakespeare is (an) Ireland's beneficiary: he owes something to the man who has saved his life and uses the plays to cancel the debt. At the same time that it establishes the Ireland family's moral right to possess these plays, this alternate history of the Shakespeare canon facilitates a repossession and privatization of Shakespeare. The author is moved out of the public domain and into protective custody. (The story resembles in this way Edward Ferrars's vision of Marianne Dashwood as meaning to monopolize all copies of Thomson, Cowper, and Scott.) And when Ireland positions an earlier Ireland in such a way that he can do the giving and exact the gratitude, the hierarchy of munificent genius and grateful audience that usually structures the culture of literary appreciation is suspended. It is largesse and not a gift, Margaret Visser states, "to give to someone while making it plain that this person cannot give anything back, [and] that she has nothing to offer [the giver] that the giver wants."[49] That Shakespearean IOU that the sixteenth-century Ireland obtains through his valor both symptomatizes and palliates an anxiety over the prospect that the gift of literature that prompts readers' grateful love might resemble largesse: a gift disbursed from above that underlines the passivity of the recipient. The story engages head-on with readers' anxieties about the inactivity and ineffectuality of appreciation.

Psychoanalytically inflected readings of Ireland's Shakespearean counterfeiting usually emphasize how it enabled a young man who was never able to extract a full account of his parentage from his father to concoct a genealogy. Suffering from an aberrant relation to the Oedipal situation, he looked to literary history for the materials from which to invent his own inheritance and construct the prehistory of his self.[50] The drawback of this interpretation of what Ireland did when he made literature *personal* is the

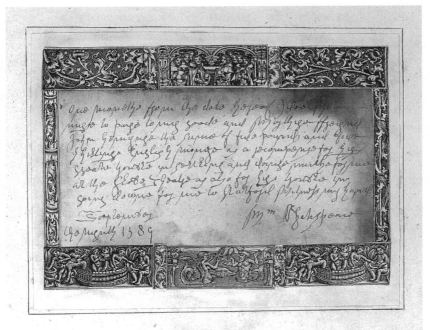

FIGURE 1.2 A "Promissory Note Purporting to Be from Shakspeare to Heminges" from the William Henry Ireland papers. Dated 1805, the papers consist of Ireland's own extra-illustrated edition of the *Miscellaneous Papers and Legal Instruments under the Hand and Seal of William Shakspeare*, first published by Ireland (and, before that, forged) in 1796. The "purported" recipient of this IOU, John Heminges was an actor and a manager of the King's Men. Ireland enjoyed thinking of the Bard as other people's debtor. Photograph: Courtesy of the Lilly Library, Indiana University, Bloomington, Indiana.

extent to which it highlights his feelings about his father at the expense of his feelings about Shakespeare. The author love that Ireland enacts gets explained away as really being about something else. But attention to the psychic drama and the feelings of ambivalence attendant on being Samuel Ireland's loving son need not occlude the psychic drama and feelings of ambivalence attendant on being Shakespeare's loving reader.

SAMUEL JOHNSON'S INGRATITUDE

Samuel Johnson made his name as the late eighteenth century's master reader. "Said he to an intimate, 'I have done tolerably well without sleep for I have been able to read like Hercules.' But he picked and culled his companions for his midnight hours; 'and chose his author as he chose his friend.' " As this passage from a biographical sketch published in the *Gentleman's Magazine* in 1784 suggests, not least by insinuating that the author, Thomas Tyers, has inside knowledge about who—or whose books—it is that Johnson cuddles up with during his midnight hours, Johnson's biographers were determined to make the silent life of their subject's reading as audible as possible.[51] In engaging this celebrity reader's "domestick privacies" the biographers took their cue, as Boswell in particular insisted in his opening to the *Life of Johnson*, from Johnson's own practice. They trod again a path that Johnson had blazed: in his *Life of Mr. Richard Savage*, his essays on the dignity of biography that he had included in the *Rambler*, and especially in the series of biographical and critical prefaces Johnson wrote between 1777 and 1781 for the conger of London booksellers who, pressured by the Law Lords' decision in *Donaldson v. Becket*, had determined to pool the copyrights to which they had once asserted their title and to assemble an elaborate, multivolume edition of *The Works of the English Poets*.

This section and the next, however, look to those prefaces, *The Lives of the Most Eminent English Poets* as they came to be known, so as to recover the complexities in Johnson's relationship to the increasingly hegemonic account of literary appreciation as a process in which readers seek to be introduced personally to authors and to become involved personally with these figures to whom they owe thanks. Canon-making projects of the kind pursued by the London booksellers who commissioned Johnson's prefaces helped consolidate an understanding of the canon as a set of authorial oeuvres rather than a set of particular poems and so helped consolidate our modern understanding of literature as writing that has authors as opposed to writing that does not. From John Bell's *Poets of Great Britain* (1777), the main competition for Johnson's *Poets*, to Charles Cooke's portable *Pocket Edition of Select British Poets* (1792), biographical prefaces were mandatory features of such sets, a format that contributed to the idea that the experience of literature was the experience of a prolonged encounter with a person. Biography assisted that personalization of literature that helps make it an object of the affections as well as an object of admiration.[52] But, as we shall see, Johnson betrayed some skepticism about this development in the very writings in which he contributed to it. In the *Rambler* essay from October 1750 praising how biography leads our thoughts into its subjects' "domestick privacies" Johnson also writes of how no other species of writing "can more certainly enchain the heart by an irresistible interest" (*Rambler*, 60: 319). Mingled with the praise is a hint of nervousness about the enforced passivity that might be the lot of the loving reader whose heart, "enchained," is no longer at his or her own disposal. Whether texts should have the power to make demands on readers and their emotions is a live question for Johnson, for all his devotion *as* a reader. It complicates his relationship to biography, and especially to the notion that the form might serve as the forum in which the public might give its thanks for the gifts of authors.[53] Johnson had mixed feelings about the enlargement of the empire of eros that occurred when literature was reinvented as an object of the affections.

This is not to deny the impress in the *Lives* of that new fixing of disciplinary boundaries and that tradeoff that the editors of *Reading the Early Modern Passions* describe in commenting on how in the early modern period "artistic work trades an expansive set of interests . . . for its status as a privileged venue of affective expression."[54] For these writings reveal a Johnson who as a reader is on the hunt for love in his books and who within his criticism is ready to make lovability one criterion of evaluation. John Dryden, for example, is in the "Life of Dryden" faulted by Johnson for not being able to portray all the forms of love and especially for seldom conceiving in his works that true love that is "correspondent kindness" (a mutuality that is presumably the antitype of the friendship scuppered by a power imbalance, by the "benefits which cannot be repaid" and "obligations which cannot be discharged" that Johnson had earlier discussed in the *Rambler* 64 [344]). Dryden's poetry is also, in another wonderful phrase, denied the power to "awaken those ideas that slumber in the heart."[55] In the "Life of Cowley" the metaphysical poets are faulted for their inhuman detachment: "they wrote rather as beholders than partakers of human nature" (1:201), Johnson says, painting them as unfeeling pen pushers who failed both in "representing" "the affections" and in "moving" them (1:200). Abraham Cowley's "The Mistress," Johnson declares, personifying the poem known by this title, "has no power of seduction: 'she plays round the head, but comes not at the heart'" (1:218).[56]

But, as we have begun to see, the understanding of textual transactions as relations in which we sustain the company of other people creates emotional obligations. Accordingly, there are counterbalancing moments in Johnson's criticism when he patently seeks relief from those obligations—passages in which he seems to be parading his commitment phobia or playing dumb. Generations of Johnson's admirers have ended up therefore having to respond to the charge that, offsetting the books' championing of poetic excellence, there is in the *Lives* an excessive investment in throwing cold water on other readers' ardors. Throughout this collective biography Johnson can appear an awfully detached participant in the literary attachments of his era. Whether they wish to or not, his audience is forced to become as self-conscious as he is about its emotional expenditures.

Reconstructing an embarrassing incident in the annals of author love, Johnson recounts how *Essay on Man*, when published anonymously, was actually condemned by some professed admirers of the poetry of Alexander Pope who afterward, when the poem's authorship was revealed, had egg on their faces. He takes a swipe at "those who like only when they like the author, and who are under the dominion of a name" (4:38) and so to discomfiting effect, reminds his readers of the affectation potentially lurking within their affections. The *Lives* exhaustively records, as well, the fallibilities and peccadilloes of the poets—Pope's myriad ways of testing the patience of his friends' domestic staff, Swift's stinginess, Milton's fussiness about the meteorological conditions in which poetic composition might proceed. The anecdotes seem selected to demonstrate that the genius who soars also comes down to earth and partakes equally with the meanest specimens of humanity of a common human nature.

Johnson at times appears almost indecently ready to see that descent accelerated. In the "Life of Phillips," for instance, he lauds how John Philips's mock-Miltonic, mock-epic "The Splendid Shilling" (1701) set out to bring Milton down a peg, "degrade" Milton's stately construction in *Paradise Lost* by applying it to low, trivial things. Phillips's project "gratifies the mind," Johnson says, "with a momentary triumph over that grandeur which hitherto held its captives in admiration" (2:69).

When he addresses Milton's works directly, Johnson's need to break free from captivity is especially apparent. For the first readers of the *Lives* it made the "Life of Milton" a byword for an "envious hatred of greatness" (1:85)—exactly the psychological trait that, as it happens, Johnson names, belittlingly, as a cause of Milton's republican political notions. This "Life" famously stages a strange dynamic of mingled admiration, identification, and hostility. Christine Rees and Roger Lonsdale have described it as the expression of Johnson's uneasiness, also apparent in his Shakespearean criticism, with the way that irrational literary pleasures threaten a reader's self-control. Johnson, they observe, can be disconcerted by the intensity of his emotional responses to literature—and by the discovery that what commands his love does not always earn his approbation. In the gendered psychodrama of his criticism, poetic beauties are dominatrices and enchantresses. They compel a reluctant attraction, followed by seduction, guilty surrender, shameful captivity, and then revulsion.[57] At the same time, even as he performs in the "Life of Milton" the role of resisting, ingrate reader, Johnson seems still to be testifying to the depth of his identification with this poet, since those performances not only repeat Milton's own, but they also follow scripts of Milton's own authoring. Johnson slots himself into the role of the rebel Satan of *Paradise Lost*, a figure who is envious of eminence and who experiences God's gift of grace as an assault on his freedom. (As we shall shortly see, the poetess Anna Seward read the "Life of Milton" as a series of clues to the envy and ingratitude that were part of Johnson's psychological makeup.) Johnson also reenacts the story of Milton's Samson Agonistes, presenting himself as a beguiled victim of poetry's Dalila-like power to seduce.

How should we take all this acting out? For a start, it seems in some measure a function of Johnson's conviction that love is taxing that the encounters with Miltonic sublimity that Addison in the *Spectator* had celebrated as part of a program of personal enrichment will instead both exalt *and* depress Milton's reader. His feelings for Milton disarm Johnson, he all but avows in the "Life," and the excitements of Miltonic poetry—of *Paradise Lost* specifically—are also therefore felt as a painful perturbation. "He only is the master who keeps the mind in pleasing captivity," Johnson wrote in the "Life of Dryden," proposing in a much-quoted passage that works of imagination were to be valued according to their power to detain the attention (2:147). Johnson's metaphor of captivity, however, also insinuates the pain—the coerciveness and challenge to self-possession—that inhabits and inhibits readerly pleasure. The version of this proposition included in the "Life of Milton" runs thus: "Such is the power of [Milton's] poetry, that his call is obeyed without resistance, the reader feels himself in captivity to a higher and nobler mind, and criticism sinks in admiration" (1:104).

The "Life of Milton" is constructed overall as a tissue of intellectual and affective reversals. One passage that begins as a hardheaded analysis of Milton's outlandish, un-English idiom, identified as the effect of the poet's study of other literatures and (so Johnson asserts) his pedantry, concludes with the critic letting down his guard. Johnson states that Milton's language is, its faults notwithstanding, "the vehicle of so much instruction and so much pleasure, that, like other lovers, we find grace in its deformity" (1:104). The reversal suggests how Milton robs Johnson of his self-control over his subject and his own reaction. His judgment is good; he actually knows better than to value that style, but, infatuated, he loves it all the same.[58] Conversely, in the most notorious passage of the "Life," Johnson denies altogether that love, infatuated or not, has had anything to do with his relationship to Milton. The passage stages the critic's abrupt resignation from the Milton fan club to which in the pages immediately preceding he has finally seemed to belong, as it recasts that relationship almost wholly in terms of compulsion and resistance: *"Paradise Lost* is one of those books which the reader admires and lays down, and forgets to take up again. None ever wished it longer than it is. Its perusal is a duty rather than a pleasure. We read Milton for instruction, retire harassed and overburdened, and look elsewhere for recreation; we desert our master and seek for companions" (1:100). Johnson added these sentences as a second thought in 1783, when his "Prefaces" were reissued as the *Lives.* They represent one last act of defiance, hurled at a public desiring (as Johnson put it to his friend Edmond Malone) "honeysuckle lives."[59]

The language used in this passage of the "Life" to capture the experience of reading Milton is significant for evoking one aspect of the sociological context in which the *Lives'* performances of affective disturbance are embedded. It indicates how Johnson positions the literary affections within a world systematically structured by inequalities of political and economic power. The mention of mastery aligns the readerly relations in which Milton's fans are enrolled and which Johnson seeks to desert with interactions defined by the bonds of *service*—relations that subject some persons to the will and the condescension of others, and in which their devotion and grateful affection are thoroughly entangled with their dependence and obedience. The Shakespearean David Schalkwyck has recently outlined just how natural it was for Renaissance English society, not yet governed by modernity's impersonal economic nexus, to make the relations between master and servant the template for all sorts of affiliations, even the most intimate. He points out how pervasively, accordingly, love and service were conjoined in this society, with the first cast as the very ground of the second. "Peculiar modes of social organization and personal intimacy made [love and service] work together and sound off each other," and so "the metaphor of being enslaved by love is . . . tied to sociological conditions of mastery and service in more than merely imaginative or literary ways."[60] Viewed against this backdrop, Johnson reveals himself as paradigmatically modern, someone estranged from older, precapitalist, paternalist traditions, who displays that estrangement by emphatically setting himself against any possible align-

ment of mastery and belovedness. (It is tempting, however, to think that
he is identifying with Milton's antihero as he performs this estrangement:
Satan explains, after all, in a passage that bespeaks Milton's own problems
with paternalism, that his rebellion against God was a way to be "quit" of
"the debt immense of endless gratitude / So burthensome still paying, still
to owe.")[61] We might also in this connection recall the desire for affective
equality that was audible in Johnson's *Rambler* essay 64, with its comments
on how unrepayable benefits and undischargeable obligations prove fatal
to friendship. When ranged alongside the other *Rambler* essays that address
the topic directly, this essay reads as an attempt to work out the complex
ethical and affective calculus of a patronage economy that identifies virtue
mainly with the beneficence of patrons and casts ingratitude (of their cli-
ents) as the worst of vices. Johnson was always sensitive to "the interlocking
of patronage with subservience," and that sensitivity makes him skeptical
about the very possibility of the free gift. Giving for him sometimes seems
an act prone to instrumentalization by the giver, prone to engender debt in
the recipient.[62]

Milton is "the least indebted of all the borrowers from Homer," Johnson
observed in an earlier passage in the "Life" (1:105). If there is a hint of exasperation in this account of the independence of an author "confident of his
own abilities and disdainful of help," it may be because Johnson is simultaneously aware that those abilities levy a tribute of gratitude on him (1:105).
Dwelling on the idea that Milton is no debtor, that he has preserved his
independence, seems to trigger in Johnson an uneasiness over the possibility that as Milton's enthralled reader and beneficiary of his gifts he is very
differently positioned. Johnson also gets testy when he notices the embarrassment Milton's earlier biographers evinced, the poet's nephew Edward
Philips particularly, when dealing with their hero's turn in early life to the
trade of school-teaching. Consumed by status anxiety, they bent over backward to make it seem that Milton "did not sell literature to all comers at an
open shop; he was a chamber-milliner [i.e., a milliner who transacts her
business from a private home], and measured his commodities only to his
friends" (1:60). ("Literature" in this passage carries, as the term often does
in Johnson's writings, the older meaning that makes it a synonym for "erudition.") These lives, in Johnson's account of them, envisioned a Milton
who succeeds in so limiting the scope of his market transactions that they
become identical with the transactions of friendship. Gifts that can create
ties of personal obligation, that demand a return that is not simply money
but also gratitude toward the giver, are nested within Milton's literary

commodities. Milton somehow gets to have it both ways. To Johnson, that seems plain unfair.

ANNA SEWARD AND "THE DISEASE OF NOT ADMIRING" IN THE AGE OF JOHNSON

Though Johnson depicted his poetry love as enthrallment, something compelled and uncomfortable, comments like the one in the "Life of Milton" about deludedly finding "grace" in the "deformity" of Milton's "Babylonish dialect" do at least ally him with "other lovers" as a group. Generally, the popular imagination has tended since the Victorian period to remember Johnson doing just that—that is, rejoicing to concur with the common reader, as he does at the conclusion of the "Life of Gray," in a famous passage that has been pivotal for Johnson's modern reputation as virtuous amateur and that has acquired a touchstone status in modern polemics against literary professionals' insensibility and/or prejudice. "In the character of his Elegy," Johnson wrote in this "Life," "I rejoice to concur with the common reader; for by the common sense of readers . . . must be finally decided all claim to poetical honours" (4:184).

This is how the popular imagination remembers Johnson—as a model of literary appreciation—but, by contrast, much of the immediate response to the *Lives of the Poets* disputed vehemently Johnson's right to characterize himself as a lover of literature. It represented Johnson instead as an austere, illiberal, heartless martinet. Considerable consensus arose around the position that the unresponsive Johnson was not built for love. That assertion informs, for example, the cartoon that James Gillray engraved after the appearance of the *Lives*, "Apollo and the Muses Inflicting Penance on Dr. Pomposo, round Parnassus," which imagines poetry taking its revenge on Johnsonian criticism (fig. 1.3). The contrast between the slender, delicate figures of Apollo and his entourage and the ungainly, overweight body on which they are inflicting a shameful corporal punishment is central to the argument of the image. With it, Gillray asserts something that even Johnson's number one fan James Boswell conceded in the *Life* when, recording his regret that a poet whom he read with fondness had left Johnson unmoved, he tells us that at the time he comforted himself "with thinking that the beauties were too delicate for [Johnson's] robust perceptions" (*Life*, 837).[63] Writing fifty years after Johnson's death, the bibliographer and antiquarian Sir Samuel Egerton Brydges (1762–1837) filled his autobiography with complaints about the *Lives*, which had apparently dashed Brydges's dreams of being a poet himself: Johnson brought a "dissecting knife" to

FIGURE 1.3 James Gillray's "Apollo and the Muses, Inflicting Penance on Doctor Pomposo, round Parnassus," a caricature print published in 1783. Equipped with a dunce's cap that is also a pyramid erected to the fame of Milton, Otway, Waller, Gray, Shenstone, and Lyttelton, Samuel Johnson does penance for the transgressions he committed in the *Lives of the Poets*. Photograph (detail): Courtesy of the Lewis Walpole Library, Yale University.

his practice of life writing, "reasoned rather than felt, and therefore had little sentiment," and aspired "to be the evil magician, at the touch of whose spear delusions fled."[64] And so forth. The reading public's injured feelings evidently took a while to heal.

The most vocal exponent of this view of Johnson as an unresponsive, untender, wet blanket of a critic was Anna Seward, woman of letters and elegiac poet—"th'Immortal MUSE of Britain" according to one contemporary admirer—famed for her *Elegy on Captain Cook* (1780) and her *Llangollen Vale* (1796).[65] In many respects, Seward used Johnson's negative example to craft her own relation to the public space of criticism. In Seward's mind, the services she might perform for literature also comprehended the services that an *Immortal* MUSE *of Britain* performed as a genteel *reader* (and exuberant reciter). And her sex, rather than an obstacle, was an asset in that endeavor. "A masculine education cannot spare from professional study, and the necessary acquisition of languages, the time and attention which I have bestowed on the compositions of my countrymen," she wrote in a letter included in the preface to her posthumous *Poetic Works*.[66] Indeed, the fact that the universities British men attended were places from which British poets were banished was an insuperable handicap for masculine taste, "since superior to the Greek, Roman and Tuscan bards, are the bards of Britain."[67] If she was excelled by many in "the power of writing verse," she was certainly not surpassed, Seward declared, when it came to "the vivid and strong sensibility of its [verse's] excellence, or . . . the ability to estimate its claims."[68] For Seward, whose pronounced sense of entitlement would make her a figure of fun for later writers (including, sadly enough, her literary executor, Sir Walter Scott), the consumption as well as the production of literature might be an activity carried out under the sign of genius.

That view came to seem increasingly eccentric as an age of authors entrenched itself. As I noted earlier in this chapter, this era's new concepts of literature seemed to involve new separations between active authors and passive readers, with the concept of genius pressed into service in new ways to mark the distance between these groups. Seward, however, was certain that enthusiasm for poetry, especially in combination with a zeal for friendship, could serve as the basis for a life led on a grander scale than that of ordinary people. She loved love accordingly—a stance that I want briefly to explore, because it casts into relief Johnson's mixed feelings about *his* favorite authors and about the partiality and prepossession that the very idea of a favorite author involves. We'll return to Johnson at this chapter's end.

Seward is a figure of increasing interest for scholars of women's romantic poetry and romantic friendships. Johnsonians and historians of criticism who engage her tend, by contrast, mainly to remember how she and Boswell did battle over Johnson and the *Lives* from 1786 to 1794, with Boswell at the high tide mark of the quarrel reminding readers that "poetesses . . . have too often been not of the most exemplary lives."[69] This war of words, carried out in successive letters published in the *Gentleman's Magazine*, was sparked by Seward in a pseudonymous letter sent to the *Gentleman's* editor that derided Johnson's recent biographers for idolizing him as a beneficent saint. Rapidly, Johnson's own balking when it came to idolizing became the central point of contention between Seward and Boswell, whose *Life of Johnson* was at the outset of hostilities still in the works. Seward declared herself vexed, as in fact many late eighteenth-century readers did, by the short shrift that Johnson's *Lives of the Poets* had given to the generation of poets who were successors to Pope; he had ignored, she felt, authors whose achievements in the lyric had, in her view, begun to repair in the domain of letters the loss of glory that the military and political failures of the 1780s had inflicted on Britain.[70] As Seward wrote in a posthumously published letter, "Servile adulation to the fame of Johnson as a critic on poetry . . . becomes no lover of literature, since, to the memory of the shining poetic lights of Great Britain, it is that species of ingratitude of which Lear so forcibly expresses his feeling, when he exclaims to his second daughter, 'O Regan! Wilt thou take her by the hand?' "[71] In his replies, Boswell played the gender card. His polemical strategy involved contrasting Johnson's straight shooting with his antagonist's feminine propensity to embroider on the facts (the pseudonymous Benvolio was soon outed as a female) and with the "little arts" "employed by a cabal of minor poets and poetesses" who were "sadly mortified that Dr. Johnson . . . assigned [them] their proper station."[72]

Historians of this pamphlet war usually deem Boswell to have been the victor. Certainly, Seward's efforts to present her warm feelings for the English poets as publicly exemplary never met with the success that Boswell's Johnson devotion continues to enjoy. Her orotund prose has done her no favors, to be sure. But the discrepancy also indexes how gender norms have inflected the protocols both of literary attachments and of criticism, and it suggests the limits of the arguments that historicize literary appreciation by pointing to a feminization of eighteenth-century culture.

Seward passed the whole of her life, from age eight on, in Lichfield, the Midlands cathedral town that was Johnson's birthplace and where her own family had long been resident. (Her father was the prebendary of Lichfield Cathedral; her maternal grandfather had been Johnson's schoolmaster.) Johnson, her elder by thirty-three years, had hightailed it for London long before her birth, but she remained in the provinces, at the heart of a community fond of gossiping about their famous native son. From this home base, Seward had been able to supply Boswell with the information about Johnson's childhood that he required as he worked through the 1780s on the *Life*. That contributory role perhaps helped prepare the way for the pamphlet war these two conducted: Boswell, a possessive lover, was zealous about having Johnson to himself, so Seward's inside knowledge likely irked as much as it gratified him. Multiple biographical links make up the Johnson-Boswell-Seward triangle, in fact, but it is important to acknowledge that the squabbling that involved the latter two had larger stakes than personal rivalry. It attests, in addition, to the lack of consensus about how in this emergent literary culture readers should comport themselves in relation to aesthetic objects. To take seriously Seward's disputes with the *Lives* thus can serve as a way to recover the period's contests about how much the authority of that master reader, the literary critic, should or should not owe to this reader's sense of personal connection with literature and thus to this reader's prepossessions and partiality.

For what is often at issue in Seward's complaints about Johnson's criticism in the *Lives* is not so much Johnson's flawed taste, nor the Tory political prejudice that made him an illiberal commentator on poets, like Milton, who had been significant for a Whig tradition of liberty—not so much Johnson's underestimation of particular authors' powers of pleasing, then—as the hardheartedness, in Seward's words, the "morbid deficiency in the judgement and the affections," that such errors expressed. In this quotation from a posthumously published letter of 1786, Seward responds to the rough handling to which "Lycidas" had been subjected in Johnson's "Life of Milton" and in particular to Johnson's announced, perverse incapacity, in her paraphrase of the "Life," to "read Lycidas without pleasure . . . [and] without frequent recurrence." Elsewhere in her comments Johnson appears as an ingrate, in relation to his friends and to the poets whose gifts he receives thanklessly, and, in another faint reminiscence of Milton's Satan, as a "gloomy spirit."[73] The language of diagnosis in such passages is worth noticing. As she makes her case against the *Lives*, Seward participates in the vigilance about normal and abnormal emotional response that was one outgrowth of the eighteenth-century cult of sensibility. Sliding between aesthetic and ethical registers, Seward's critique of his biographical criticism implies that Johnson's aberrant emotional makeup is the real issue. Seward even wrote poetry pursuing her case: her *Original Sonnets on Various Subjects* of 1799 included one sonnet, for instance, entitled "On the Posthumous Fame of Doctor Johnson," and another entitled "On Doctor Johnson's Unjust Criticisms in His Lives of the Poets." The latter is printed with a note asserting that whereas Johnson's "adorers seek to acquit him of wilful misrepresentation by alledging that he wanted ear for lyric numbers, and taste for the higher graces of poetry," this is impossible to believe when we look at the *Rambler* essays and encounter the "poetic efflorescence, metaphoric conception, and harmonious cadence" that adorn Johnson's prose.[74] Seward therefore proposes an alternative diagnosis: "We must look for the source of his injustice in the envy of his temper." The sonnet itself continues in the same vein. Drawing on anecdotes collected in Hester Piozzi's 1786 biography of Johnson, it ascribes to Johnson a "pain / which writh'd o'er *Garrick's* fortunes" and then spells out what that serpentine, Satanic-sounding writhing betrays: it "shows us clear / Whence all his spleen to Genius."[75] This need to psychologize and ethicalize Johnson's critical reactions is a striking feature of her reaction to the *Lives*. Such speculation about Johnson's inner feelings is licensed if one believes, with Seward, that the qualifications for criticism include not only powers of judgment but also capacities for gratitude and enthusiasm.

Around 1784, just when the position of the age's master reader was left vacant by Johnson's death, Seward, then forty-two, began collecting, transcribing, rewriting, and even adding footnotes to her literary correspondence. Rather than her poems, those letters, to a great extent the documents of her warm feelings for other people's poetry, represented, she had determined, the better bet for her posthumous reputation. That determination registered her conviction that the shaping of public taste should be the work of genteel amateurs in the provinces and that it should accordingly be recaptured from the professional London authors, like Johnson, who had begun to monopolize it—premises that the modern book trade and dawning of modern notions of literature had already rendered somewhat beside the point.[76] "Authorism," as Seward termed it, was in fact something to be regarded with mistrust; "authorism" went hand in hand with a "jealousy" that would impair the individual's "candour"—a term that Seward used in that special late eighteenth-century sense of responsiveness that involves kindliness and a favorable disposition.[77] Her correspondence was the forum in which she undertook to exercise that virtue of candor. An extensive network of like-minded men and women of feeling received from Seward letters that traded compliment for compliment (sometimes a shade sycophantically), weighed in on questions of prosody, promoted lyric poetry, which "has risen higher in this than in any age," and decried writings in which she saw the muse quit "the mazes of . . . pathetic description, and generous sentiment" for the "thorny paths of acrimonious satire."[78] If it had been possible in the late eighteenth century, Seward would, I feel certain, have reveled in being a member of an online community. She would have blogged and been a frequent, irksome presence in the comment threads of the blogs of others.

In the framework created by her epistolary sociability, poetry was valued, as Seward's frequent references to "our poets" indicate, as a medium for social sharing. It enhanced and was enhanced by friendship. This under-standing is especially in evidence in the letters from the 1790s in which Seward praised the literary community of a particularly distinctive kind that she encountered when visiting the picturesque Welsh Vale of Llangollen—letters whose praise was likely all the more fervent because this community was so evidently the antitype of the Literary Club depicted in the *Life of Johnson*. Llangollen Vale had come by the 1790s to figure on the itineraries of many tourists in quest of sentiment and the picturesque, who were often drawn there by their curiosity about the life that two celebrity paragons of female friendship, Lady Eleanor Butler and Sarah Ponsonby, had made to-gether in that location following their 1778 elopement from Kilkenny in Ire-land. When Seward traveled to "that retreat, which breathes all the witchery of genius, taste, and sentiment," she was fascinated by both the romantic attachment of these Ladies of Llangollen (as the pair came to be known over the five decades in which they inhabited Llangollen Vale) and by the ambitious agenda for self-cultivation to which the Ladies devoted them-selves. Literary enthusiasms matching Seward's own—studying Dante and Madame de Sevigné, making extracts to fill up commonplace books—were an important element in the Ladies' performance of virtuous rural retire-ment, a performance that by and large screened them from hostile scrutiny of their sexual improprieties. At the same time, however, the love of litera-ture was also the very forum of their queer intimacy. (Lady Eleanor's jour-nals keep track of the books—Spenser's, Sterne's, Rousseau's, "no. 97 of the Rambler written by Richardson, author of those inimitable Books, *Pamela, Clarissa, Sir Charles Grandison*"—that she has read aloud nightly to Sarah Ponsonby, "my Beloved." The desiring practices defining life at Llangollen appear to have mingled seamlessly the identities of lover and reader.)[79] Lady Eleanor's "taste for works of imagination is very awakened, and she ex-presses all she feels with an ingenious ardour, at which the cold-spirited be-ings stare," Seward wrote in a 1795 letter reporting on her visit to Llangollen and heralding a kindred spirit. The Ladies had remade one room of the cot-tage as a "Gothic library," fitted it up with an Aeolian harp and stained glass windows, and stored it with "the finest editions, superbly bound"—interior decorating, celebrated in Seward's letters and in two stanzas of her 1796 poem *Llangollen Vale*, that inscribed a sapphic scenario into a household space traditionally serving to display masculine privilege (fig. 1.4).[80]

As we saw earlier, David Hume in "Of the Delicacy of Taste and Passion" had called on readers to cultivate their taste on the grounds that literary ap-preciation would enrich real-world affinities and alliances. The emotions it

The R.ᵗ Honᵇˡᵉ Lady Eleanor Butler and Miſs Ponsonby.
"The Ladies of Llangollen."

From a Drawing by LADY LEIGHTON carefully taken from life.
Drawn on Stone by R.J.LANE A.R.A.
Printed by J. Graf.

Died Dec.ʳ 8ᵗʰ 1831. Aged 76.

Died June 2ᵈ 1829. Aged 90.

FIGURE 1.4 "The Ladies of Llangollen." Lady Eleanor Butler and Sarah Ponsonby are depicted in the "Gothic library" of their cottage orné at Plas Newydd in Wales. This late Victorian lithograph (ca. 1887) by Richard James Lane is based on a drawing "carefully taken by life" by Lady Leighton. It includes facsimiles of the Ladies' signatures. Photograph: © National Portrait Gallery, London.

excites "dispose to tranquillity; and produce," he wrote, "an agreeable melancholy, which, of all dispositions of the mind is best suited to love and friendship."[81] For Seward, the Ladies' bookish intimacies demonstrated magnificently that, as Hume had intimated, the possessor of taste and the votary of love could and should be one and the same. Their example affirmed her in her determination to counter Johnson's flinty-hearted discussions of "our poets" with her own ardor.

For later commentators, the sense of entitlement tincturing Seward's anti-Johnsonian campaigning and the confidence with which she opposed her ethos of sentiment to Johnson's authorism have been a bit embarrassing. Certainly her subject's contrarian refusal to accept the Boswellian message that she had been living in the Age of Johnson all along discomfited Margaret Ashmun, who wrote a biography of Seward at Yale in the late 1920s, with, as it happens, dean of Boswell studies Frederick Pottle looking over her shoulder. One sign of this discomfiture is that Ashmun wishfully imagined Seward into a different age altogether: "One wonders why she did not do better than she did. . . . Miss Seward ought to have lived in an age when women were not afraid to go forth from the home and use their powers in wage-earning and in social service."[82] Norma Clarke opens her *The Rise and Fall of the Woman of Letters* with an anecdote from 1808, in which the writer Robert Southey reports on an awkward close encounter with Seward's literary enthusiasm: as she did him tribute, Southey had to choke down his laughter. Clarke uses the story to signal how emphatically romanticism brought down the curtain on the era that her book charts. In this account too then, Seward is misplaced in literary historical time, and her function within Clarke's argument is to embody a figure left behind by cultural change. The woman of letters disappeared from public life at the end of the eighteenth century, as the social transactions that had defined a culture of polite letters gave way to those more rigid protocols organizing literature in the modern sense of the term. Under the new conditions, a poetry enthusiast like Seward lost her access to the authority that previously had been anchored in her sensibility and zeal for demonstrating her appreciation.[83] In an age developing new narratives of career and profession, feeling would no longer count as achievement or activity (Seward's decision that her letters would be more important than her poems for her posthumous reputation indexes, however, her mistaken belief that it would).

But as easy as it is to conclude that Seward, woefully miscalculating, ended up on the wrong side of the verdicts of literary history, it is also a tad misleading. Scholars of her dispute with Johnson's criticism might as

justifiably find Seward the more modern figure of the two, since her complaints about the *Lives* illuminate so well Johnson's discomfort with some of
the defining aspects of the age that bears his name. She and James Boswell
alike—card-carrying woman and man of feeling respectively—were much
more comfortable than Johnson was, with his mixed feelings about amorous captivity, in the commercialized climate of manufactured and manip-
ulable passions that was the late eighteenth-century culture of sensibility.
They were more at ease living in a world that had begun casting loving
feeling as that which was to be incited and required instead of repressed.
The word would not be coined for another century, but we could label these
two "fans." Seward especially locates her identity in part in the act of pitting
her aesthetic experience against that of the critic and pitting her intimacy
expectations against the critic's truth claims.

For the historian of literary appreciation such fractiousness is useful. It
reveals that during this era in which literature was becoming a love object
there was little consensus about just what readers' and critics' remit should
henceforth be. (The multiple, mutually inconsistent definitions that are supplied by the *Oxford English Dictionary*'s entry on "appreciation" might be
seen as a symptom of that dissonance: the reader who appreciates can be
engaged either in "the action of estimating qualities" or in "sympathetic recognition of excellence." We can guess which option Seward would prefer.)[84]
Thus Johnson could at once be heralded as the era's master reader and still
appear to his contemporaries to be getting reading wrong, omitting, for instance, to carry it out in the proper spirit of gratitude. Seward, who so loved
having favorite authors, was put out by what she identified as Johnson's
frigid incapacity for that prepossession and partiality to which the reader
who has favorites commits.[85] She came close to suggesting that Johnson's
insistence on conferring praise and blame justly was simply the cover for
that incapacity. For loved ones, you are supposed to make allowances; you
approach their faults with "brotherly kindness," as Edmund Cartwright put
it. Johnson, it appears, didn't do this enough to satisfy these readers.

Not long after the publication of Johnson's *Lives*, a poet who had appeared to be in the running to be Seward's new favorite author, William
Cowper, disappointed her with a comparably icy refusal of personal connection to literary genius, in a manner that made Seward lament that the
age was "polished," "cold," and "sick of the disease of NOT admiring."[86]
Seward's marginalia in her copy of Cowper's *The Task* memorialize her dis-
may over lines in which Cowper surveyed from a satiric distance the bard-
olatry occasioned by the 1769 Shakespeare Jubilee and in which, prompted

by those ceremonials of consecration and thanksgiving, he worried about man's propensity to praise man, not God. The actor and theatre manager David Garrick's deliberate analogies on that occasion between the pleasures of literary consumption and the rites of religious practice appear to have rubbed Cowper the wrong way. Cowper observed one of the most elaborate eighteenth-century exercises in giving thanks for the gifts of genius and pointed out what such panegyric had in common with the idolatrous perversion of the fetish worshipper. "O Wintry spirit!" Seward wrote in the margins of her copy of *The Task*, marking up the passage that documented Cowper's detachment from his contemporaries' literary devotions. Sixteen lines of blank verse effusion followed.[87]

CODA: ON NOT EXERTING ONESELF FOR THE MAN WHO HAS WRITTEN A GOOD BOOK

In a conversation with Boswell from March 1783 that is recorded in the *Life of Johnson*, we once again catch sight of a Johnson who refuses to follow the affective scripts of the age of sensibility. We see him reacting against literary attachments and, worse still for Boswell (given the latter's fannish instincts), forgoing them on his own behalf. In this scene, during a breakfast visit paid to Dr. Johnson, Boswell has attempted to initiate a discussion of the contemporary neglect of literary genius, with Johnson himself providing the prime example. In setting this discussion topic, Boswell might well have taken his cue from earlier Milton biographies, which often deplored the slow sales of *Paradise Lost* during Milton's lifetime (in *his* "Life of Milton," Johnson, by contrast, took pains to vindicate the public against this charge of neglect and proposed that since the "call for books was not in Milton's age what it is in the present," the sale should rather be viewed as "an uncommon example of the prevalence of genius" [1:270]). In replying to Boswell, Johnson insists, however, that gratitude and affection are supererogatory, not the genius's due. "There is no reason why any person should exert himself for a man who has written a good book: he has not written it for *any individual*. I may as well make a present to the postman who brings me a letter" (*Life*, 1200). At this moment Johnson likely recalls lines from Seneca's *Of Favours*: "A kindness accorded to just anyone wins gratitude from no one. No one at an inn or tavern sees himself as a personal guest. Nor will he think himself the guest of the host at a public banquet; where it can be said: What, after all, has he done for me?"[88]

We want to think that authors write for us, motivated by personal concern. Thwarting that wish, Johnson moves in this exchange with Boswell to undo what the biographical project of his *Lives of the English Poets* seemed to have effected: he moves to preempt the personalization requisite to the love of literature. His analogy between author and letter carrier, deliberately coarse, turns a forum that Boswell would like to dedicate to the union of hearts into a space of modern commerce. It demotes the celestial literary genius; he becomes a low-level civil servant, and, one infers from Johnson, in our transactions with him we do not need to leave a tip (Johnson's term "present" appears to designate the kind of gift given from on high, by a social superior to a dependent).

This conversation between Boswell and Johnson later caught the attention of an author who, as we saw during our eavesdropping on Austen's *Sense and Sensibility*, was a love object for romantic-period readers. In the "Introductory Epistle" to *The Fortunes of Nigel* (1822) Sir Walter Scott reiterated and reversed Johnson's terms, writing a vignette in which the Author of *Waverley* is told, by an indiscreet character of his own creating, that "common gratitude to the public" who so love him should make him less hasty in his design of those novels' plots. When the Author replies, he entreats his visitor, first, to do as Dr. Johnson had once advised and "free [his] mind from cant." Do not look for love in all the wrong places, the Author then warns: "To the public I stand pretty nearly in the relation of the postman who leaves a packet at the door of the individual," and "the bearer of the despatches is . . . as little thought on as the snow of last Christmas." "I deny," he concludes, "there is any call for gratitude, properly so called, either on one side or the other."[89]

When the author becomes a letter carrier, he does get paid (after all, it was the recipients of letters who assumed the cost of postage at this period), but that payment is merely for transporting words with which he has no personal connection to a series of destinations on an anonymous circuit of reproduction and distribution. His work involves a short-term transaction with the public, not an enduring relationship. The letter carrier is no gift giver. Conversely, no gratuity is required from us either. This author as letter carrier does not do what he does either out of or in expectation of love. In this Johnsonian account, the man who writes a good book has no need of the individual who is *me* and, correspondingly, there is no good that *I* can do him.

PART 2

Possessive Love

CHAPTER TWO

Literary History and the Man Who Loved Too Much

If the Fairy Queen be destitute of that arrangement and oeconomy which epic severity requires, yet we scarcely regret the loss of these while their place is so amply supplied, by something which more powerfully attracts us: something, which engages the affections of the heart, rather than the cold approbation of the head.

THOMAS WARTON, *Observations on the Fairy Queen of Spenser* (2nd ed.,1762)

To constitute a relish for the Black-Letter, a certain degree of literary Quixotism is highly requisite: he who is unwilling to penetrate the barren heath and the solitary desert, he who cannot encounter uneasiness, perplexity, and disquietude; he who is not actuated by an enthusiasm for his employment, is no true knight, and unfit such service.

HENRY HEADLEY, preface to *Select Beauties of Ancient English Poetry* (1787)

"ACADEMIC BOWERS"

In this chapter, my project of tracing the ups and downs in literary studies' love-hate relationship with love leads me to the mid-eighteenth-century origins of historicism in English studies. I wish to press harder than other historians of literary historicism have on the fact that Britons' turn to their new classics, the works of Chaucer, Shakespeare, Spenser, and Milton, occurred at just the moment when taste seemed disappointingly chilly when it was not validated by "the affections of the heart."

To get a feel for the ambivalence this development engendered, let's consider a phrase that was bandied about with some energy in 1755—"academic bowers." "It may gratify curiosity," Samuel Johnson stated that year as he prefaced his *Dictionary*, "to inform it that the *English Dictionary* was written with little assistance of the learned, and without any patronage of the great; not in the soft obscurities of retirement, *or under the shelter of academic bowers*, but amidst inconvenience and distraction, in sickness and in sorrow."[1] As he vindicated the scholarship that *he* undertook outside bowers' shelter, in the school of hard knocks, Johnson participated in a tradition, dating back to the *Spectator* papers, that identified the redemption of learning with its relocation from "libraries, schools, and colleges" and into a public sphere of open, rational dialogue.[2] This announcement of its author's outsider status makes Johnson's preface an early entry in the record of bad publicity that dogs literary critics inside the academy. It makes sense, then, that Johnson's sniping caught the attention of his friend Thomas Warton (1728–1790), poet, fellow of Trinity College, Oxford professor of poetry, pioneering literary historian and editor, and a figure whose bookishness will loom large in this chapter. There are signs that Warton took it personally. In an April 1755 letter to his older brother Joseph, Warton copied out the sentence I have just quoted and then identified Johnson's preface as both "noble" and, Warton mused, liable to provoke "disgust," thanks to Johnson's evident "consciousness of superiority."[3] He likely noticed that with his reference to "academic bowers" Johnson had severed Warton's home base in the university from the world of public utility and responsibility.

At the moment when he caps his lexicographic labors, Johnson in the preface retroactively equates the lexicographer's expulsion from the Arcadian-Oxbridgean bower with engagement in real work. (In 1731, Johnson's poverty had forced him to curtail his studies at Oxford, which he left before obtaining a degree.) The embowered academic, by contrast, his equation insinuates, has it easy. One thinks of pastoral retirement and naps on clover. Warton, who wrote fondly of the "elbow chairs" that after 1756 introduced new comfort levels to Oxford's Bodleian Library, and whose own chair of ample proportions is still preserved at Trinity College, might have thought of just such things himself. In December 1758 Warton contributed to Johnson's periodical essay series *The Idler* a spoof called "Journal of a Senior Fellow," ostensibly "just transmitted from Cambridge," and prefaced it with the claim that in these pages the reader of Johnson's periodical would at last encounter what Johnson's title had promised, a "genuine Idler."[4]

But the bower is a site both of pastoral play and of love—and loving, as much as working, is an activity for which those inside academe are often held to be ill suited. A. D. Nuttall titled his study of the scholar's image in the popular imagination *Dead from the Waist Down*.[5] The charge that they are emotionally stunted applies whether academics are seen as given over wholly to joyless and irrelevant pedantry or, alternately, given over wholly to self-seeking careerism. Of course, Johnson often gets identified as an ally by those making this accusation as well. Commentators who deplore the professionalization of English and, with it, the late twentieth-century advent of theory and/or cultural studies have often cast him in the role of the incorruptible outsider, an amateur who is the foil of the heartless, tenure-seeking technocrat.

The previous chapter, however, in exploring Johnson's mixed feelings about the demand that literature be loved, suggested that this casting might have made Johnson himself uneasy. Moreover, his famous esteem for the common reader notwithstanding, Johnson was also an active participant in one of the changes that helped make it appear that criticism was necessarily an expert's practice, that "English literature" was something looming above the everyday writing and reading of the contemporary moment, and something that was by contrast frozen "in the past."[6] For instance, the illustrative quotations that Johnson had collected for that 1755 *Dictionary* were, in his words, selected exclusively from "our ancient volumes."[7] The *Dictionary*'s display of the literary heritage pointedly omitted all examples originating after the Restoration.

Loving Literature engages how literature, in just this time period when it came to name an object possessed of a history distinct from the history of writing in general, came as well to name an object of the affections. Although Marjorie Garber observes wittily that "the love question" always hovers around literature, "like a pesky putto," the recent histories of literary history's eighteenth-century origins that have done so much to document Johnson's and Thomas Warton's contributions to this historicism are uniformly silent when it comes to this question.[8] Their reticence might, of course, represent a way to play it safe. As we have already seen, it can be tricky to locate the disciplinary work of English in relation to those normative mappings of experience that demarcate the institutional from the intimate and expertise from sensibility. Perhaps the elbow chairs' introduction into the Bodleian helped begin that boundary confusion. What changed when scholarship began taking place in chairs that accommodated bodies' varying forms rather than imposing the same vertical rectitude on all? Or perhaps this question should target another alteration of the furniture of the Oxford libraries. After the Bodleian's and the college libraries' unchaining in the closing decades of the eighteenth century of the last of the books that they had hitherto fettered to lecterns, scholars could loll back inside their chairs in the expectation that, rather than their attending on the books, all books, even the folio volumes, should come to them there.

Speculations like this one, about what physical spaces might do to shape a discipline's objects and to house its scholars' subjectivity, will repeatedly find their way into this chapter, since I seek here to trace the particular strategies for *inhabiting* the archive that Thomas Warton developed as he undertook his research into medieval verse romances and their readers. That research was foundational for an emergent discipline of English. Warton retrieved the record, arcing back centuries, of successive readerly dalliances with romance; his histories were valued by his contemporaries for giving the modern public access to the archetypal sources of a distinctively national genius, one whose antiquity was, in new ways, key to its shimmering charm. His other crucial contribution to the making of the English canon was, quite precisely, to *periodize* it: he and those he influenced deployed on vernacular texts critical techniques that had been previously trained mainly on Greek and Roman classics, and did so in ways that, in emphasizing the othernesses of those texts' diction, references, and verse forms, also emphasized "our elder authors"' remoteness from the modern moment of criticism. Poetry, he thus demonstrated, could be made to contribute to the project of modeling the historicity of culture: even the poetry of the Middle Ages, that period of chivalry and romance and magic when the imagination seemed particularly exuberant and untrammeled by limitations of time or space. Warton situated works of literature in specific historical contexts—historical conditions, in the piquant words of his ally Richard Hurd, that "never did subsist but once, and are never likely to subsist again."[9] I am interested in how within this historicism, that singularity Hurd references acquired a strange affective charge.

The attention that in his critical writings Warton lavishes on the particular and recondite and the energy that he expends on locating the materials that will bit by bit fill in the big picture help to reclaim the literary past for the public of the present day. At the same time, such attention also has the potential to render that past the object of a more suspect, solipsistic form of engagement. It can remake literary study as an arena for private gratification and secret enjoyment, where a scholar like Warton might fashion himself as a truant man of feeling. Thus as I study Warton and some of his allies studying—as I examine the peculiar intertwinings of pedantry and privacy, bookishness and romance that mark this mid-eighteenth-century brand of historicism—I will seek to make visible historicism's occasional collusion with possessive love. I aim by this means to reconstruct historicism's links to that personalization of literature that by Warton's day was the other side of the professionalization of criticism.

The even newer new historicism whose heyday was the 1980s and early 1990s tended to make its commitments seem a matter of discipline and rectitude. Yet attaching works of literature to their *own* time and place and taking the measure of the linguistic and cultural distance separating the time of the works' writing from the time of their reading might in fact double as a way to have those works to oneself. In what follows I approach this conjunction of historicist study and possessive love indirectly, beginning in my first two sections with the mixed feelings that Warton's bookishness occasioned for his contemporary readers. The chapter's second half engages with the fact that literary historicism first took shape as a rescue mission on behalf of romance particularly. From the start, the literary historian's intellectual labor was expended on behalf of writing that was valued precisely for sidelining the claims of the mind in favor of the claims of the heart and for promoting fancy over reason. To illuminate further the paradoxes of this situation, I conclude, in the last section, by speculating on how this historicism might have been imprinted by late eighteenth-century Oxford's local culture of poetry appreciation and the particular performances of private life that culture hosted.

"TO NARROW SPACE CONFINED": SPECIALIZATION

"Bowers" is a bookish word. It invokes a pastoral world that—as Johnson would be the first to insist—exists almost exclusively in the pages of poets. (And even in those pages, bowers are defined by their discontinuity from the real, waking world. They are sites of slumber and sleepy shade, to recall the lullaby lines that Spenser used in *The Faerie Queene* to depict the "Bower of Bliss"—spaces of truancy in which "warlike arms," "the idle instruments / Of sleeping praise," go rusty with neglect.)[10] Johnson's reference to bowers in his conclusion to the preface to the *Dictionary* is readable, in fact, as a souvenir of the lexicographer's own history of dalliances with the Elizabethan verse that Warton's histories had made pivotal to the period's reconceptualizing of the literary heritage. Understood that way, the reference backhandedly registers the importance of Warton's own scholarly labors, which merit rehearsing. In 1754 Warton published *Observations on the Fairy Queen of Spenser*—which Johnson had praised, in fact, for modeling how scholars might profitably study "our ancient authours ... by [perusing] the books which those authours had read."[11] He followed it with a revised and extended edition in 1762. Between 1774 and 1781 he published three volumes of his *The History of English Poetry*—a book that, although left unfinished at his death in 1790, is generally held to be the inaugural example of narrative literary history.[12] Warton was in 1770 an editor of Theocritus and, later, of Milton, undertaking in 1785 an edition of Milton's "smaller poems"—as, endearingly, the verse preceding *Paradise Lost* was called.[13] His

efforts toward this edition usurped work on what was to have been the projected fourth volume of the *History*—the volume reserved for a conclusion
that would have taken Warton, full circle, back to the poetry of Spenser.
Whatever appeal such symmetry might have exerted, an elderly Warton was,
as it turned out, more energized by his vexation over the rough handling to
which, unamiably, Johnson had subjected Milton's sonnets and "Lycidas" in
the *Lives of the English Poets* six years before. Warton throughout his writing life also published his own poetry: *The Pleasures of Melancholy* in 1747,
thirty years later, a collection of *Poems* that has been credited with inspir-
ing the Romantic poets' resurrection of the sonnet form, which the Augus-
tans had shunned, and then, in 1782, his currently most anthologized poem,
"Verses on Sir Joshua Reynolds's Painted Window at New-College Oxford."
George III named him poet laureate in 1785.

But another distinction that the laureate, fellow of Trinity College, Oxford,
and professor of poetry might have announced on his CV is worth mentioning. Warton was also, as David Fairer has reckoned, the reader who in the
year 1753 accounted single-handedly for *one-ninth* of the book requests at
the Bodleian Library. The statistic evidences, of course, the diligence informing the source studies that Warton undertook so as to illuminate Spenser's
and (later) Milton's knowledge of their poetic predecessors. The discussion
of Spenser's engagements with Chaucer and with the "old Romances"—
"romances of the dark ages, founded on Saracen superstitions, and filled
with giants, dwarfs, damsels, and enchanters"—began the work of illustrating centuries of composition that had hitherto been blanks to Warton's contemporaries. *The History of English Poetry* continued that work. Excavating
what his friend the Chaucerian editor Thomas Tyrwhitt called "those sepulchres of MSS, which, by courtesy are called libraries," and reading (as
few for generations had read) old ballads and writings by Malory, Lydgate,
Surrey, and other, often anonymous authors, Warton was able to reintro-
duce the nation's classic authors back to the eighteenth-century reading
public as, first and foremost, the heirs and transmitters of prior traditions.[14]
(Not incidentally, that reintroduction also made an argument for the historical continuity of Britain's national culture.) In this guise the classic authors
appeared as readers of the past *themselves*, likewise attracted by its charms.
(Warton's attraction to portraits of the artist as a young reader, and to the
particularly intimate reader relations such portraits can sponsor as they mirror the reader back to himself, will become evident later.)

In the long term Warton's example transfigured the "Gothic library" of
obsolete stuff that Alexander Pope had dismissed in *The Dunciad*—a collec-

tion, as that poem's pedants put it, in a boastful yet self-condemning phrase, of "all such Reading as was never read."[15] Increasingly, this library became required reading for all who would pretend to critical expertise, and people began, as well, to call the rooms in which they stored their books their Gothic libraries (as Eleanor Butler and Sarah Ponsonby did in their cottage in the Vale of Llangollen). Warton's testy response to Pope's quip about the "Gothic library," found in the postscript to the second edition of his *Observations on the Fairy Queen*, recalls Pope's work as a Shakespearean commentator, only to insinuate that someone capable of jeering at source study would scarcely have been qualified for that work: "If Shakespeare is worth reading he is worth explaining; and the researches used for so valuable and elegant a purpose, merit the thanks of genius and candour, not the satire of prejudice and ignorance" (2:264).

Evidently, by 1762, when Warton struck back at Pope, increasing numbers, many of them Warton's correspondents, counted on meeting with those thanks. And there was reason for their optimism. For one thing that distinguished a *"Gothic* library" from any other kind was that the materials it assembled were, in their uncouth and yet sublime ebullience, deemed *British*—and, as such, the antitheses of overrefined, Continental court culture. The year 1762 also saw Richard Hurd—afterward bishop of Worcester—publish his *Letters on Chivalry and Romance*, another effort to illustrate feudal manners at the dawn of English literary history and so recover that "lost . . . world of fine fabling" that was Spenser's inspiration in *The Faerie Queene*. Thomas Percy, another cleric who at the midcentury was casting about for the fast track to preferment, published his *Reliques of Ancient English Poetry* in 1765. This collection of (touched up) old ballads and (antiqued) new ballads continued the aesthetic rehabilitation of English literature's dark ages. Two years later, Percy's correspondent Richard Farmer, master of Emmanuel College at Cambridge, published his *An Essay on the Learning of Shakespeare*, which proposed that "nothing but an intimate acquaintance with the writers of [Shakespeare's] time, who are frequently of no other value, can point out his allusions, and ascertain his Phraseology." For Shakespeare's sake, Farmer too was willing to fall martyr to, as he announced, "all such reading as was never read."[16] And so forth. In 1818 a *Blackwood's Magazine* reviewer would summarize the change to which these individuals contributed in the following terms: "In our Augustan age we see the mind of the country tending with determined force *from* that ancient literature; and in these latter days, we have seen it returning upon the treasure of these older times, with an almost passionate admiration."[17] What was pedantry in Pope's dunces had been redefined, under the auspices of this new, Wartonian mode of his-torical imagination, as a "labour which . . . essentially contributes to the service of true taste" (*Observations*, 2:265).

Historicism—the endeavor "to place ourselves in the writer's situation and circumstances" (*Observations*, 2:87)—was presented by Warton as labor and service. His argument ran along now familiar lines. As a component of scholars' self-abnegating identification with the poets whom they study, they are to read what those poets read, and to persevere with these obscure texts however tedious or difficult they might find them. That said, the ex-orbitance of the figure that Fairer arrives at in his account of Warton's li-brary doings—one-ninth of all the requisitions!—might well suggest to us something in excess of *selfless* professionalism, an energy that is surplus to Warton's duties—and maybe something more private than public spirit. Duty and devotion are evident here, but there is a hint of the pack rat too.

I, at least, detect a sense of the voracity that Sir Walter Scott fingered in an 1804 review when he identified Warton's excessive attachment to the objects of the Gothic library as the reason for the failure of his *The History of English Poetry*. As most nineteenth-century commentators did, Scott acknowledged Warton as a prime mover in that sea change in definitions of canonicity that made English antiquity into "the moment of literary achievement against which all subsequent writing would be measured," and that had obliged the literary critic to become perforce a literary historian.[18] But Scott none-theless faulted Warton. Pondering the reason why at the present moment of 1804, "a . . . connected history of our poetry" remained an unsatisfied "desideratum" for English letters, Scott stated that such a project was a task to which "Johnson was unequal [in *Lives of the Poets*], through ignorance of our poetical antiquities" and "in which," he added, "Warton failed, perhaps, because he was too deeply enamoured of them."[19] Warton failed because he loved too much.

That the *History*, left unfinished, was not a success even in its own terms has seldom been disputed. It is not clear, though, that it could ever have lived up to the elevated expectations the later eighteenth-century public brought to it. As Warton knew, many hoped that their era's new commentar-ies on poetical antiquities would be the setting for a long-awaited reconcili-ation of the polite man of taste with the curious antiquary. Ever since the Renaissance, these two had been cast as each other's foes, a guise in which they could personify frictions inherent to the life of letters. Innovative prac-tices of philology had first set certain early modern readers worrying "that too much learning might be a dangerous thing for the classics" and that the scholarly enterprise, if pursued too energetically, might damage the aura of unassailable timelessness that had made the works of Homer and Virgil classic in the first place. Recounting how Renaissance humanism became divided against itself in this manner, Joseph Levine demonstrates the unnerving effects of the new historical descriptions of the manners of Virgil's age and of editions of Homer that used the forensic methods of the new textual scholarship or drew attention to the mutability of the Greek language. Among those unnerved were the many gentlemen in the habit of revering the classical authors as the models of imitation they would draw on in forming their style and taste.[20]

But when he set out to recover the reading that had formed the taste of "our elder English classics," Warton cast his own enterprise as proof that such enmities could now be consigned to the past. Antiquaries of a former age, he admitted, had left the romances that were so important to the nation's classic authors to "moulder, unattended," in "our libraries" because they foolishly believed it was better to "employ their industry in reviving obscure fragments of uninstructive morality or uninteresting history." But "the present age" was able to "make amends": subjects of George III were well placed to connect—as Warton declared, in a self-promoting phrase—"the curiosity of the antiquarian" to "taste and genius" (*History*, 1:209). In launching his *Reliques of Ancient English Poetry* in 1765 Thomas Percy had likewise announced a concord between the antiquary and the man of taste and genius: in the 1794 preface to the fourth edition he proudly declared the *Reliques* satisfactory both as history and as "refined entertainment," both acceptable to the "judicious antiquary" and admissible into "the most elegant libraries."[21]

Yet even in 1794 confidence on such points was probably premature, for several reasons. A culture of aristocratic hegemony, which was still not persuaded that work should or even could be a component of a gentlemanly identity, was bound to have mixed feelings about the *labor* that erudition involved. This culture continued to be ill prepared to value the antiquary's or textual critic's propensity for being "anxious about little things" as a sign of virtuous diligence. There was, in other words, no certainty about the kind of class affiliation that could be read off the practice of literary history—or about the extent to which "the labour that contributes essentially to the service of true taste" could or should begin to resemble the real work of rude mechanics. It was incontestable that Warton's good breeding entitled him to mingle in the politest social circles, but reception of his *History* was inevitably shaped by the fact that many of his contemporaries believed firmly that a "mere antiquarian" was, as Johnson put it, "a rugged being."[22] That the antiquary Thomas Hearne, sometime assistant at the Bodleian and foremost scholar of medieval culture in the generation before Warton's, had had in his youth to resort to agricultural labor was through the middle decades of the eighteenth century too juicy a fact for defenders of gentlemanly privilege to overlook. Solicitude over particulars continued to be dismissible as social ineptitude—whether that solicitude informed textual editors' compilations of variant readings or historically minded critics' accounts of the cultural and linguistic differences registered by their new schemes of periodization. Faux pas in this mode were "impertinence," and in that eighteenth-century sense of the term that combines boring irrelevance with bad-mannered insolence.

Familiar to present-day students of the discipline's history thanks to Simon Jarvis's 1995 book on the controversies surrounding the eighteenth-century editing of Shakespeare, these disputes about the class politics of literary labor intersect with another, less familiar debate: the one that Scott's reference to Warton's excessive amorousness highlights, the one that comes to the fore if we think about how the engagement with minutiae that makes study that much more laborious also supplies the ground for that state of intimacy we now call "close reading." While they balanced the claims of learning and taste—whether they pronounced their reconciliation a fait accompli, postponed it to some as yet unwritten piece of literary history, or declared it an impossibility—commentators were also rehearsing their uncertainties about the kind of *emotional practice* literary study should be. On the one hand, since denizens of the world of learning were thought to be excessively irascible in their disputes—no analogy between "men and other animals" being "stronger than this, that they get fierce from being kept in the dark"— the prospect of the antiquaries' socialization and gentrification was valued for how it might temper and moderate their expressions of partisan feeling. Antiquaries ought not to make of their pursuit "an article of faith, but to treat all the parts of it with coolness and candour, as matters of the merest indifference": John Pinkerton here in his 1784 *Essay on Medals* counsels his comrades in the antiquarian trenches to cultivate a kind of Chesterfieldian urbanity.[23] They get too emotional, he seems to suggest. Controversy should not be taken so personally. And yet, on the other hand, the footnotes that cluttered the antiquaries' compositions, and their reluctance to present their materials in the narrative form that might engage a reader's sensibilities, were construed by contemporaries as a sign that the learned were irredeemably obtuse about the claims of human interest.

Distinguished by his torpor and insensibility, the antiquary sometimes figured in late eighteenth-century discussion as a negative object lesson in what it means to be excluded from the pleasures of sympathy. Antiquarian writing's deficit in reader friendliness suggested to many a deficit in that geniality that was the proper province of the man of the world. In the later eighteenth century it was also possible to propose that what learning needed was to be taught to feel.

Had Warton learned that lesson? Had he learned it too well? These questions interested certain readers of the time intensely, but they were divided in their responses. In a 1774 letter, Horace Walpole, himself notorious both for his hoarding up of antiquarian trinketry and for the hauteur he displayed while distancing himself from grubby fact-hunting of other people's studies, anticipated Walter Scott's verdict on Warton's *History*: "I am sorry that Mr. Warton has contracted such an affection for his materials." (This lament appears in one of a succession of the bulletins Walpole sent to his friends as he responded to each new volume of Warton's *History*.) At the same time a diametrically contrasting account of the *History*'s flaws also had adherents. It is likely Warton whom William Godwin, for instance, was referencing when, in the preface to his 1804 *Life of Chaucer*, he complained, in a passage that exasperated Scott when he reviewed the *Life*, that the study of the literary past had hitherto been the preserve of "men of cold tempers."[24] (A language of temperature ran throughout later eighteenth-century belletrism: Warton in his *History* downgraded some medieval writers, like Hoccleve, for their "cold" geniuses and "frigid lines," and Isaac D'Israeli, in a 1795 book that sought to redeem the anecdote collector's attention to small things from the charge of antiquarian pettiness, disparaged the "frigid rapture" that "a [Thomas] Hearne" would feel "if he could discover the name of a Saxon king unrecorded in our annals." Samuel Johnson famously quipped that a reader's overexposure to the explanatory notes of a Shakespearean scholiast would leave his "mind . . . refrigerated by interruption.")[25] Still, whichever account of the *History*'s under-performance one opted for, it remains the case that it was the state of Warton's affections—his sensibility—that occasioned the commentator's worried scrutiny.

This makes sense once we recollect that the decade in which the *History* appeared was also the moment when Englishmen and women were vociferous in complaining that Dr. Johnson did not love poetry enough. We have already seen Anna Seward ascribing to Johnson "a morbid deficiency . . . in the affections."[26] In Augustan England, accounts of literary criticism's positioning in relation to its object had been negotiated through the metaphorics of a battle of the books, as in, for instance, the wars of the Ancients against the Moderns. But, as the previous chapter suggested, increasingly in the later eighteenth century participants in literary culture were expected to make love, not war. What was required of them was the wherewithal for prepossession, signs of the tenderheartedness that would make allowances for a favorite author or, as in Warton's case, a favorite epoch. These interrogations of Warton's affective capacities register that change, while they illuminate a lack of consensus during this formative era for English over how an individual's critical authority might or might not accommodate a sense of personal, emotional connection with literature.

Of course, that uncertainty is not only a feature of this formative moment in the literary era; it is ongoing. David Simpson has captured it in his assertion that "literary criticism as a socio-educational complex is neither wholly objectivist nor wholly personalized, but subsists by a seemingly inevitable struggle between the two."[27] Simpson's observation helps me to specify how, in my reading of Wartonian historicism, I differ from other scholars who have studied Warton's contribution to the eighteenth-century making of the English canon. Take, for instance, Jonathan Kramnick's treatment of Warton's Spenserian studies in *Making the English Canon*. The story of canon making that Kramnick recounts is grounded in the dialectical development of public-sphere publicity, on the one hand, and academic specialization, on the other. In Kramnick's scheme, Warton's role is to personify the university intellectual. Kramnick calls attention accordingly to how the title pages of Warton's literary histories, spelling out their author's institutional affiliation and university titles, explicitly declared a seat at the university to be the place for a proper discussion of poetry. As Kramnick details, an inherited division between the feudal world of the court and the commercial world of the city was updated in the *Observations*: Warton, Kramnick proposes, cast the literary past, as mediated by a community of scholarly expertise, as an antidote to that commodified literary present that was at his moment being shaped—or rather misshaped—by Grub Street, hack novels, and circulating libraries.[28]

Still, even if this announcement that literature had taken up residence at the college was unprecedented in eighteenth-century England, I think that twenty-first-century readers of *Making the English Canon* will spot familiar features in Kramnick's portrayal of the university intellectual. This is the scholar as the thief of enjoyment. Scholars' putative incapacity to appreciate aesthetic appreciation, their downplaying of encomium in favor of that explication that roots texts in specific, bygone times and places, are contrasted by Kramnick with the self-assigned task of that other professional reader, the journalist—who aspires to bring a nation of readers together by way of their shared appreciation of beauty. Hence, for instance, the role that his argument assigns to *The Observer Observ'd* (1756), William Huggins's pugnacious rejoinder to Warton's *Observations on the Fairy Queen*, which decries the impediment to that aesthetic communion that is produced when a coterie imposes its self-serving professional dialect on the practice of criticism.

In his eagerness to engage head-on the association of current literary studies with killjoy politics and pedantry, Kramnick seems to accept as a given the polarizing of enjoyment and discipline, aesthetic pleasure and the historicist critic's engagements with the detritus of the past. But this way of proceeding risks overlooking the discipline's "enjoyment of discipline," the "pleasure we take in renouncing pleasure for the stern alterities of history."[29] It risks overlooking something crucial to the history of literary historicism and of the emotional practices it incites: the particular—adamantly particularized—pleasures of laboriously recovered, recondite information. To court public perception as a thief of enjoyment is—as the medievalist Aranye O. Fradenburg explains in the essay from which I borrow that phrase—to make oneself suspicious in *two* ways.[30] Those decried for spoiling the public's enjoyment of its pleasures are equally liable to attract suspicion as figures who seem to monopolize some secret source of pleasure inaccessible to the wider world.[31]

When, in his 1733, pro-Pope and anti-Theobald poem on the editing of Shakespeare, David Mallet sneeringly declared the textual critic, the Augustan satirists' poster boy for pedantry, to be "to narrow cares in narrow space confined," he had in mind the cramped margins on the page where that critic's conjectures are printed, as well as the shabby garrets that were thought to be fitting sites for the pursuit of such minutiae.[32] Practitioners of recondite learning high-mindedly accept that narrowness—and resign themselves to disdain from the Mallets of the world—in conformity with what might be called the sacrificial conception of the historiographical project: historicism demands that the responsible philologist renounce personal presuppositions and contemporary tastes, this as the trade-off for scholarly access to history's secret truth.[33]

This does not gainsay, however, that the "narrow spaces" to which recondite learning is confined may also be experienced as pleasurably "snug," as sites of hiding and privacy. Recondite, as it happens, derives from the Latin for "to hide." It names a category profoundly involved in those transformations that the sociologist of modernity Georg Simmel delineated when he traced the interconnections between individualization and the rise of secrecy—a human achievement, he says, that produces an "enlargement of life"—"the possibility of a second world alongside the manifest world."[34] In prefacing his edition of Shakespeare, Johnson was in fact delightfully up front about that possibility in the passage in which he adverts to the narrow concerns of a textual critic's notes: "Since I have confined my imagination to the margin, it must not be considered very reprehensible if I have suffered it to play some freaks in its own domain."[35]

As he sets out the social context in which mid-eighteenth-century critics first learned to treasure the antiquity of English writing, Kramnick draws on Jürgen Habermas's discussion of the structural transformation of the public sphere. However, he brackets the parallel transformation of that new sphere of intimacy which for Habermas was the eighteenth-century public sphere's first staging ground: those innovations that, for instance, converted houses into homes, and which, more generally, detached the category of the private from its negative associations with deprivation and linked it instead to individuals' aspiration to self-fulfillment. Downplaying these developments in eighteenth-century people's ways of organizing experience preempts consideration of how the literary discipline at its inception might also have been impacted by the fallout from another salient change during this period: the personalization of literature that was the other side of reading's professionalization.[36]

BONDING WITH BOOKS

Scrutiny of the library culture of the eighteenth-century university can reveal even this public stage for knowledge work as a site incorporating sanctuaries where subjectivity could, as Johnson would put it, play in its own domain. Warton's interest in the elbow chairs that were introduced into his primary place of work, the Bodleian, has already been mentioned. He also seems, at the time he was preparing his edition of Theocritus, to have rigged up a kind of unofficial, prototypical library carrel for himself there: he received special dispensation enabling items from the Bodleian's collections to be delivered to, and to accumulate inside, a kind of study granted him in the gallery. Of course, somebody who had in one year made one-ninth of the Bodleian's book requests would have pressing reasons to arrange things so that those books could be kept together and at hand. But this customized "narrow space" might also (as with the Bodleian elbow chairs) have facilitated this reader's intimate bonding with the books.[37] Warton's contemporaries and immediate successors noted, not always approvingly, how he appeared to have negotiated a space for the personal within a scholarly enterprise otherwise oriented to the supra-personal and appeared to have negotiated ways of being private even in settings that were, like the Bodleian, dedicated to reading in company.

Another way that Warton did this was in arranging for his writing to stage not only his relationship with an idea of the literary past, but also something less abstract: his relationship to particular books—the material copies he had *handled* rather than the texts that he had *read*. Indeed, a twenty-first-century reader of Warton's *History* may be surprised at how often it refers to books in contradistinction to texts. Warton was sensitive to medium and often, in recounting poetry's history, called attention to that history's dependence on the history of media, but he also seems simply to have *liked* recalling that books, in contradistinction to texts, are *things* and, moreover, things whose stories are tied up with those of particular individuals, who acquire and lose them and place their marks on them. Hence in volume 3 Warton mentions, in a section on translations from the classics in sixteenth-century England, that "my copy [of Chapman's Homer] once belonged to Pope" (3:444) and mentions "the books of my friend the late Mr. William Collins of Chichester, now dispersed," a collection of comic stories in prose from 1570 that included, Warton thinks, a source for the frame story of Shakespeare's *Taming of the Shrew* (3:292–94). Warton's candor in this passage about the haziness of his memory got him in hot water with a rival student of literary antiquities, Joseph Ritson, whose *Observations* on the *History* I shall engage later. At this point, I want to emphasize how this reference to the dispersed library of the late Mr. William Collins, itemizing the evidence with a degree of detail surpassing the needs of Warton's argument, worked to interject into this historiography a plaintive note of autobiography. With it, Warton erects a monument to his friendship with his schoolfellow the poet Collins, who had died young, in a madhouse, in 1759. This was autobiography, however, recounted as stories of books, as well as friends, gained and lost.

In 1711, the classical philologist and textual critic Richard Bentley prefaced the work in which he aimed to establish the "true" reading of Horace with a justification of textual emendations founded on "what arises from Conjecture" rather than "the Authority of Books." Bentley's words betray an interesting disdain for the material, marketable *stuff* of study and a determination to see it abstracted away: "I wou'd not . . . have you pay a blind Veneration to dealers in Books alone, but dare you to think for yourself."[38]

Later eighteenth-century culture, we have seen, in some measure sur-
mounted that fastidiousness about hobnobbing with "dealers in Books."
Warton and associates such as Percy and Farmer—even Johnson—had instead decided that it was in *libraries* above all that the sources of the nation's
literary imagination were to be sought. "You can make a poem walking
in the fields or lying in bed," Johnson said; but elaborating a tradition—
"composing a Dictionary," for example—was a different affair, "requir[ing]
books and a desk."[39]

To consider old books, however shabby, as potentially revelatory objects
seemed advisable in the wake of Warton's proposal that texts and meanings
from the literary past were best established by reading what authors had
read themselves. But this later eighteenth-century historicism also strained
in contrary directions, in ways mandating a program of policing and self-
policing on the part of its practitioners. Hence, as suggested earlier, the frequent insistence that antiquarianism had disqualified itself as legitimate
knowledge practice, as a consequence of its excessive devotion to the tangible, obdurately particular and appealingly graspable stuff through which
it knew the past. Even as antiquarianism's empirical methods infiltrated
the more prestigious discourses that mediated the public's access to other
times, antiquarians themselves continued to be derided. The specialization
that their narrow studies seemed to portend made people anxious; so too
their collecting practices and the privatized, possessive pleasures those practices appeared to sponsor. For, tellingly, the faults ascribed to, say, a Thomas
Hearne (whose writings bear titles such as "A Dissertation concerning the
Word Sir" and "The Copy of an Inscription on the Ivory Handle of a Whip")
were not simply condemned as error—as, say, overinvestment in details or
refusal to assimilate singularities to the big picture.[40] As Susan Manning has
observed, especially perturbing were the *proprietorial* responses evoked in
the antiquary by, for instance, *this* moth-eaten ledger, *that* bit of Saxon bric-
a-brac: responses that seemed symptomatic of this figure's self-delighting
immersion in the hermetic world of his collection.

As Manning explains, the specter evoked by the antiquarian enterprise
was "the power of solipsistic pleasure to undermine social connection."[41]
Just that specter is being exorcised in that 1804 essay in which Walter Scott
faulted Warton's excessive attachment to "our poetical antiquities." Warton
had produced, Scott averred, not a *History of English Poetry* but rather "an
immense commonplace-book of *memoirs to serve for such a history.*"[42] The
complaint is that what should have been a "connected" narrative had turned
out instead to be a *collection* of bits and pieces. (In his off hours Warton did

collect, in fact—fragments of medieval stained glass.) The project had run aground, Scott in effect indicates, because, as he put it in another essay two years later, Warton was too *close* to his materials: "Whenever he has occasion to mention a tale of chivalry, in his *History of English Poetry*, it seems to operate like a spell, and he feels it impossible to proceed with the more immediate subject of his disquisition, until he has paced through the whole enchanted maze, and introduced his reader into all its labyrinths. Of the great variety of . . . digressions, with which that work abounds . . . , a large proportion arose solely from his attachment to this romantic lore."[43] And Warton was too close to his materials in a couple of senses—on the one hand, unable to abstract an argument from an unmethodical welter of detail and, on the other hand, too emotionally intimate with all those particulars.

Too close to "his" materials? In the first of the quoted passages above, Scott gestures toward the impropriety of that closeness by using the first person plural possessive pronoun—"too enamoured of *our* poetical antiquities." The poetical antiquities are *ours*, not *his*; in getting so close and in subjecting them to *his* amatory designs, Warton has stepped out of line. Of course, as we have begun to see, this way of perplexing the public order of books with his idiosyncratic predilections does not make Warton singular among contemporary scholars of the literary past. In his day, scholars' relationship to the possessive pronoun could not reliably be left to go without saying.

Consider, for example, a moment in the flurry of epistolary activity that accompanied Percy's editorial work on the *Reliques of Ancient English Poetry*. In 1762 the poet and connoisseur William Shenstone wrote to Percy to outline some options Percy seemed to have for handling the seventeenth-century manuscript, "the parcel of old ballads," that was foundational for the initial stages of that work.[44] Those "old MSS" are like "pure gold in Dust or Ingots," Shenstone declares in the letter. (I proceed slowly through his argument, whose convoluted nature Shenstone acknowledges when he wraps up the letter with the signature "Chaos / From Mr. Shenstone's Brain.") The manuscripts are bullion that his friend may "either mint himself, or dispose of in the shape he found it." But if Percy, when he publishes, ends up opting for the latter alternative—namely, leaving the language of the ballads unmodernized and "un-improved"—the "noble treasures" will never attain the status of being "every one's money." In that case, the pieces that Percy assembles in the *Reliques* will be "a prize merely for . . . virtuosoes," and Percy will have missed his opportunity to reactivate the ballads' communal power and to make the popular entertainment of other times into a modern medium of national solidarity. But that may not be so bad, Shenstone muses. For in that case "the disadvantage" under which "the purchasers" "will lie" will "not [be] incident to the present owner; who possesses his treasure in secret, and not in common with all mankind."[45] Envisioned monopolizing his treasure in secret and so forestalling its circulation, Percy in Shenstone's description is a kind of miser. When he ponders Percy's relationship to an account of literary value that would tie it to literature's standing as a shared social currency, Shenstone thinks about the resistance the miser mounts both to the proposition that, as currency, money is by definition "every one's money" and to the proposition that follows, which is (in Georg Simmel's words now, not Shenstone's), that "money is the expression and agent of the relationship that makes the satisfaction of one person always mutually dependent upon another person."[46]

In the event, Percy published the materials now known as the *Reliques* in a touched-up form and alongside ballad imitations. And thereafter, embarrassed by his project (by the fourth edition he was downplaying it as "an amusement of his youth") and no longer enchanted by the rude energies of minstrelsy's materials, he kept the actual manuscript that had been the catalyst for the *Reliques* out of public view. It was "locked away," Nick Groom comments, "like some dreadful family secret, a mad changeling" until 1867, long after Percy's death. Such inconsistencies and backtrackings were owing in part, one suspects, to Percy's uncertainty about how best to perform the class privileges that his literary successes had procured for him, the son of a grocer. Groom mentions eighteenth-century scholars' awareness that the manuscript materials that they were identifying as the antique sources of the nation's literary imagination also permitted, in their uniqueness and obscurity, a kind of "monopoly scholarship."[47]

The backdrop to the investigations into the pleasures of intimate possession that I have referenced was a situation in which national treasures were, as often as not, in private hands. Even as the new historicist approaches stressed the source studies, cross-referencing, and contextualization that only breadth of reading could supply, it continued to matter immensely who owned and who would lend what, and who could afford to own and who was obliged to borrow.

In a panning review of 1804, for instance, Walter Scott, already irritated by the sneers at cold-tempered antiquaries with which William Godwin had prefaced his *Life of Chaucer*, wrote that Godwin should also have kept to himself his regret over how his researches for the *Life* were impeded by private collectors' reluctance to "part with their treasures." According to Scott, in the suavely scathing passage that ended the review, "the Maxims concerning property, contained in [Mr. Godwin's] 'Political Justice,' were not altogether calculated to conciliate confidence."[48] (Throughout his political treatise of 1793 Godwin had intimated that society's attainment of genuine justice would have to involve a redistribution shifting property from the haves to the have-nots.) In a 1791 pamphlet Joseph Ritson set out his grievance against the eighteenth-century scholarly establishment by referencing this establishment's relationship to scarce materials: "It is a very common, but, at the same time, very unreasonable practice in commentators and others to bid their readers *see* this or that scarce book, of which it is, as they well know, frequently impossible for them to procure a sight."[49] The immediate occasion for this comment was the putatively slipshod job Edmond Malone and George Steevens had done in their 1790 edition of Shakespeare's plays, though Percy and Warton also often found themselves on the receiving end of Ritsonian lambastings.[50]

If Warton represented for scholarship the prospect that one might over-internalize the demands of a culture of sensibility and of literary appreciation and love too much, Ritson for his part became a byword for obtuseness to those demands. His ferocity was famous. The fact that Ritson was by the 1790s an associate of Godwin's and fellow political radical was not, of course, irrelevant to his reputation. Warton's firsthand experience of that ferocity came when Ritson published *Observations on the First Three Volumes of the History of English Poetry* (1782). In a devilish bit of sabotage, Ritson arranged for the paper and font used for this book to match those used for Warton's *History*, an arrangement permitting readers to bind his and Warton's volumes together: Ritson had determined to supply this record of Warton's omissions (no Anglo-Saxon poetry!) and blundered references as, he insisted disingenuously, "a very useful *Appendix*."[51] Elsewhere Ritson recorded his perturbation over the fact that "no one save Warton seems ever to have seen those three works which had an ephemeral existence in the library of the poet Collins, of which Warton gave descriptions from memory in his *History*." I suggested earlier that that offending passage might be read as a demonstration of how in Warton's hands research, otherwise oriented to collective ends, might be refashioned so as to lodge private associations. Ritson's own scholarly life made room for the claims of sentimental melancholy. He dedicated a "memorial bookcase" to the memory of John Baynes, who had bequeathed him his collection of early English romances. Even so, to him Warton's record of his privileged access to Collins's books was readable apparently either as a display of class entitlement (a gentleman's bibliography might fudge details because of his conviction that exactitude was plebeian) or as evidence that Warton had perpetrated scholarly fraud (the lost books might have been undiscoverable because they never existed).[52]

The class politics of property left other imprints on the *History*, as a Ritson might easily have discovered. "On the Introduction of Learning into England," the second of the two "dissertations" that Warton wrote to open the *History*, appears to reproduce as its manifest content the latent conditions of literary scholarship in Warton's own era. The account gets around only belatedly to the topics its title might appear to predict—for instance, the beginnings of lay education, or the increasing prevalence of vernacular translation from the classics. In fact, informed by the micro-materialism of antiquarian learning, the dissertation verges on being the literary-historical equivalent of an eighteenth-century object narrative, likewise thing-centered. Books are in the foreground in Warton's survey of learning's introduction into England and are represented less as the objects that subjects create and more as the things that make persons act in particular ways. Warton thus noted the ceremonies that monasteries staged to commemorate their acquisition of a book, their regulations about book lending, and the punishments that they inflicted on those hanging on to volumes beyond the allotted time. Pinning down the larger meaning that Warton imputed to these details is hard. On the one hand, an Anglican line on a pre-Reformation past of superstition and priestcraft informs this second dissertation's comments on how, in contrast to "the present diffusion of literature," back then a few churchmen "surpassed by the most disproportion [*sic*] degrees in point of knowledge, all other members of the community." On the other hand—and since this dissertation is in counterpoint with the previous dissertation, "Of the Origin of Romantic fiction in Europe," there *is* another hand—Warton concluded the dissertation by admitting that, however deplorable, "the gloom of ignorance and superstition" nonetheless forms a congenial habitat for "those spectres of illusive fancy, so pleasing to the imagination, . . . which form so considerable a part of the poetry of the succeeding centuries."[53] Ultimately, then, Warton admitted that *romantic fiction*'s interests were at cross-purposes with *learning*'s.

The admission captures the problem that Warton was obliged to negotiate throughout the *History* and that his juxtaposition of the two dissertations announces: the problem of balancing discrepant timelines in the aftermath of his "discovery that the nation's ecclesiastical and poetic histories seemed to have inversely coordinated epochs of consummation."[54] As many have observed, in Warton's pages, a history ordered by the conviction that the belles lettres improved with time (the conviction that literature's story, like that of the wider culture, was one of ever-increasing refinement) competed with a story of loss. Bishop Richard Hurd had anticipated his friend's articulation of those antinomies. Hurd's historicist defense of Spenser's Gothicism in his 1762 *Letters on Chivalry and Romance* had ended by consigning the aesthetic of *The Faerie Queene* to history, via some wistful lines about how during the second half of the seventeenth century reason had driven the "tales of faery . . . off the scene" and how, if we had "gotten by this revolution . . . a great deal of good sense," we had, all the same, "lost . . . a world of fine fabling" (154). At the close of his second volume of the *History*, Warton repeated Hurd's elegy for "romantic poetry" almost word for word: "The lover of true poetry will ask, what have we gained by this revolution? It may be answered, much good sense, good taste, and criticism. But in the mean time, we have . . . parted . . . with fictions that are more valuable than reality" (2:463).

These Protestant clerics' and critics' vocation was, in some sense, to chronicle the widening dissemination of words and the Word. The *History* thus keeps tally of the increasing availability of Scripture in England, and one of its turning points is the sixteenth-century moment when "every pen was employed in recommending, illustrating, and familiarising the Bible, which was now laid open to the people" (3:161). Warton's own esteem for rare books, to the extent that it was sometimes founded *on* their rarity, put him in an odd relation to the *History*'s celebration of printing presses' powers of multiplication. Warton also made things tricky for himself and his scholarly peers by equating the modern diffusion of books with the suppression of feeling—doing so at the same time that he intimated that feeling, rather than knowledge, was poetry's vital principle.

"FEEL GOTHIC": MAKING ROMANCE HISTORY

As his choice of topic for the first dissertation of *The History of English Poetry* indicated, Warton also identified poetry with "romance." He had declared as much earlier: "So magnificently marvellous are [romances'] fictions, and fablings, that they contribute, in a wonderful degree, . . . to store the fancy with those sublime and alarming images, which *true* poetry best delights to display" (*Observations*, 2:268; emphasis added). For Warton, the narrative entertainments of the Middle Ages—and not the period's legends of saints so much as its metrical tales of enchantment and mad love—represented the gold standard for what was most authentic in poetical production. The history of poetry was synonymous with the history of, in Warton's idiom, "romantic poetry."[55] Important consequences for both his *History* and the literary discipline he shaped followed from that identification of the fortunes of poetry in general with those of the romance, a genre without a future, whose associations with dispelled gloom and dissolved magic meant that it could emblematize all sorts of pleasures that are fated to be renounced. One legacy of eighteenth-century scholars' romance with bygone romances has been an understanding of literature that situates practitioners of literary studies in a nostalgic relationship to their object. I have been discussing the pleasures of possession as an aspect of historicism by reconstructing the centrality assigned to particular rare and curious books and manuscripts in that practice and the worry that this assignment provoked. In this section I want to think about possessive love as something that literature, as reconfigured by these scholars of romance, sponsors by definition—by the new definition that was established when they harnessed their historiography to a narrative of imagination lost and bowers renounced.

As other historians of eighteenth-century literary history have emphasized, periodization, that historiographical "discourse of separation," was crucial to multiple aspects of the eighteenth-century historicists' discussions of romance.[56] This section of this chapter treats the affective situation that those historicists' periodizing schemes engendered. There is a strange counterpoint between the early literary historians' resuscitation of the stuff of the Gothic library and their periodizing insistence on an unbridgeable historical distance between its then and their own now. Their historicist romance with romance, which in some respects shaped a definition of literature as that which culture outgrows, also opened up new possibilities for understanding literary appreciation as a performance of privacy, a secret enjoyment engaging one's private rather than one's public self.

One way that Warton endowed poetry's history with continuities that carried across period divisions was by imagining poetic succession as the story of how one poet after another (re)discovered the romance as a vital source for the imagination. One poet after another, rather than looking around him, at his contemporaries, instead "nourished the sublime" by looking backward, to a dim and distant past (*Observations*, 1:188). For Warton, new poetry, time and again, was the fruit of a poet's retrospective reading of the past's romances. "Our author's imagination was entirely possessed with that species of reading," he wrote in *Observations on the Fairy Queen of Spenser* (1:65). Warton's Milton edition of 1785 depicted a Milton who delighted in "choral church-music . . . Gothic cloysters, the painted windows of a venerable ca-

thedral, . . . tilts and tournaments." "One is surprised," Warton concedes in
the edition's apparatus, that "Milton should have delighted in romances."
Annotating the allusions that *L'Allegro* and *Il Penseroso* made to the fabulous
narratives still current in Milton's youth, Warton could disclose the softer,
Spenserian side that the "Calvinist" poet had not managed to renounce.[57] If
Milton's leading role in the political and religious dissent of his time might
with impunity be forgiven because it was overshadowed by his sublime poetry, this was, in Warton's book, a function of that author's anachronistic
position as a lover of romance, a love affair operating as an escape hatch
to another time altogether. "Before the grand Rebellion, these books were
in all hands; and were the source from which young readers especially in
the age of fiction and fancy *nourished the* SUBLIME . . . Milton's strong
imagination might receive peculiar impressions from this sort of reading"
(*Observations*, 1:188; Warton's emphasis).[58]

In Warton's scheme, romance and history *could* be the same. From
the *Observations on the Fairy Queen* on, Warton argued that, however fantastic their contents might appear to the sophisticated inhabitants of an
eighteenth-century Age of Reason, the romances of the middle ages were
in some degree mimetic of the societies in which they were composed.
They were "founded in truth and reality" (*History*, 1:42). Thus, for instance,
Godwin's account, which closely follows Warton's, of how Chaucer would
have "listened" to romances and to minstrels' ballads with "a double interest," "because he knew that, when he went forth into the world, the men of
whom he read, a race that is now extinct, would be the objects of his daily
conversation. The whole world was then romantic, scenic, and sublime. . . .
The mind of man was not yet broken down into a dull uniformity."[59] But in
eighteenth-century literary historicism, it is worth stressing, such accounts
of romance *as* culture coexist in tension with another account, productive of
pathos, in which romance is always already culture's residue—abandoned in
the course of English society's progress through time.

Understood, in these terms, as a casualty of history, romance may be
reconfigured as a mode that is revived in and defined by its *solitary* consumption. It may be reconfigured as the occasion for a reading that is a furtive,
clandestine affair and that withdraws the reader from his time. In this rival
account, the recovered romance is the meeting ground of epochs, but, the rest
of the culture always having moved on, one always has romance to oneself.

Suggestively, Warton's first publication, coauthored by the eighteen-
year-old with his friend Robert Vansittart, was an essay on "snugness." The
subject, the friends asserted in 1746, had ever been a great friend to the

Muses: authors from Horace to James Thomson had depicted that sensation of domestic ease.[60] To many commentators, Warton himself has seemed an aficionado of the snug, a creature of enclosures and interiors and inner sanctums. Richard Mant, the Oxonian who edited Warton's *The Poetical Works* in the posthumous edition of 1802, declared "embower" this poet's favorite word. Confirming Mant's account of Warton's predilection, David Fairer, his modern editor, writes evocatively of how it feels to read *The History of English Poetry*: "The voluminous double-columned footnotes in the *History* have an effect equivalent to opening long-closed secret drawers and peering in at their slightly musty contents." In a 1755 letter, Johnson thought of a kind of homemaking when he thought of Warton. Perhaps referencing Warton's access to the hidden nooks of the Bodleian Library, Johnson wrote of how he imagined Warton ensconced in his "nest of British and Saxon antiquities."[61] Primed by Johnson, one might take a second look at the *History*'s several references to the tapestries of medieval English dwellings—tapestries whose representations of fables of chivalry indicated to Warton "the esteem in which such stories were held" (1:209). Certainly, such nuggets of social history, procured by reading poems as historical documents ("pictures" of "life and manners"), betoken Warton's empiricist commitment to the recovery of facts about how Britons lived in past centuries. But Warton might also have been moved by how this interior decoration licensed the fantasy that medieval people really *could* live inside their books—make a home there. "The very walls of their apartments were clothed with romantic history" (1:209).

   This passage and its counterparts in the other volumes suggest the degree to which readers and readerly experience are spotlighted in Warton's work on authors. The source studies that he pioneered assigned poets places in a discourse of genealogy, inheritance, and derivation—an assignment potentially at odds with the period's growing cult of authorial originality. Such source studies thus had the effect of making readers more consequential entities in history. And one advantage of this Wartonian view that linked the right reading of English to a knowledge of books that the canonical authors had read was that the pursuit of that knowledge appeared to open new possibilities for intimacy with the poetic dead. Pursued as an exercise in sympathetic imitation, source study could bring the eighteenth-century student closer to the ancient poet, the ground for their affinity consisting in their shared receptivity. This may have been one attractive effect of the vignettes that punctuated the new literary historiography of Warton and his allies and in which, as we have seen, the historian conjectured about the poets' formative encounters with the romances of their forebears and imagined a Chaucer, Shakespeare, Spenser, or Milton, during these trysts, receiving unawares the "impressions" that, once stored in his heart, would have nourished his imagination thereafter. These vignettes—portraits of the artist as a young reader—linked rather than separated the scene of reading and the scene of writing, literary reception and production.

Shakespeareans who identified "Shakespeare's library" as the object of inquiry that focused their studies endorsed this view of authorial identity. In his preface to his 1790 Shakespeare edition, Edmond Malone confessed that, despite his editorial pains, Shakespeare's meanings in his allusions and phraseology were not yet completely understood, and explained this short-fall by declaring that scholarship had not yet arrived at that moment "when our poet's entire library shall have been discovered." (The line both admits failure and confesses a still unshaken faith in bibliography's potential—a faith that as soon as the book list is right, meaning will become transparent. In fact, as if meaning to reward Malone's faith, in 1796, William Henry Ireland, whom we encountered in chapter 1, declared that lost library found, informing the public, in his guise as "editor" of *Miscellaneous Papers and Legal Instruments under the Hand and Seal of William Shakspeare*, that he was in "possession of a great part of Shakspeare's Library in which are many books with Notes in his own hand.").[62] Since "library" can designate not just a collection of materials for study, but also the interior architecture housing both that collection and its possessor, there is a hint here, amidst the sober research, of a fantasy centered on being at home with the Bard and so knowing the author from the inside out. Dwelling on Shakespeare's *reading*—rather than, say, his attendance at plays and pageants—served, in addition, to naturalize the authority of print over oral cultures. It dissociated cultural transmission from, for instance, the clamorous and uncozy space of the public stage. Indeed, I want to mark explicitly how often architectural interiors—Shakespeare's library, the apartment walls "clothed with romantic history," or bowers—have loomed into view in my account of the practice and rhetoric of historicism. Eighteenth-century commentators think about architectural enclosure because they have linked cultural transmission to a logic of interiorization that renders literary reading a private affair and enables one to have romance to oneself.

In much of *The History of English Poetry*, the second dissertation on learning's introduction into England particularly, Warton indicates that there were multiple ways in which the praise poems, war stories, love stories, texts of instruction, songs, sonnets, theological arguments, preachers' manuals, jest books, and pleas for patronage that together constituted "English

Poetry" circulated and multiple forums and modes in which this "English Poetry" was received by its audiences. And yet Warton, within the *History*, in his edition of Milton and in his early writing on Spenser, also tells another story about poetic forms of address, one subsequent generations of professors of poetry would promote as the more literary story. This is his story of "romantic poetry." He repeatedly intimates that poetry's *real* history begins only at the moment that "romance" (abstracted from the particular social relations of medieval England, just as it is dissociated from particular narrative instances) is discovered, belatedly, by a Spenser or a Milton—the very notion of its needing to be discovered serving to suggest, in fact, the extent to which Warton is also inclined to airbrush away poems' historic roles in greasing the wheels of social intercourse. In this other story, romance is by definition always *out* of circulation, for its true audience, the one it was truly addressing all along, does not include people who were the contemporaries of its originators. Romance is never in a flourishing state, even at historical moments when books of romances were in *everyone's* hands, "most eagerly and universally studied" (*Observations*, 2:88). A pathos of distance and isolation thus comes to define romance's conditions of address. In those vignettes in the *History* in which the great authors' imaginations are kindled and the sublime is nourished as they claim a direct connection to the past, those authors never read *in company*, either with the dead or with the living. Which is to say that in measure as Warton writes the history of poetry as the story of imagination, he depicts the reception of poetry *as* poetry as though it had to be an act of solitary possession.

In Warton's parlance, Torquato Tasso and Edmund Spenser were alike "romantic poets," and yet each, as Warton takes pains to explain at the outset of *Observations on the Fairy Queen*, writes in the wake of a moment that had seen the classical texts of Homer and Aristotle studied once more and that had, accordingly, seen a "legitimate taste of writing" restored and romance with its illegitimacies and irrationalities displaced (1:1). So positioned, each of these authors perforce regards the romance as do the subjects of George III, the inhabitants of an enlightened, refined, and rational modernity. He too may only "[look] back" at romance "with some remains of fondness" (*Observations*, 1:3). Warton and most of the participants in the eighteenth-century romance revival chose to shape the story of poetic influence to conform to a narrative template first elaborated by their influenced poets themselves. Spenser and Milton, Richard Hurd states, were "seduced . . . even charmed by the Gothic romances." The claim is all the more resonant when juxtaposed with Hurd's brisk account of the typical romance plot:

in that plot, oppressions carried on "by the charms and enchantments of women" are succeeded by "the glory" earned by the knight who resists seduction and avenges the wrongs. Similarly, Tasso, in Warton's comparison, is "like his own Rinaldo," fated to leave Armida and her enchanted garden (1:3). These romantic poets' sojourns in the domain of fancy—their dreaming of Renaissance dreams of what the medieval might have been like—are temporary, as their heroes' sojourns in bowers of bliss are. Their cultures' recantations of romance are already in the cards.

But as Warton also notes in this comparison, the romantic poets tend to keep their "favourite[s]" in their eyes: even as the magic is dissolved and love is disavowed, romance is also intimated to be inescapable, and the romance hero is pictured eternally lingering and looking backward at the moment that he is meant to be completing the rite of passage into wisdom, maturity, and proper virility. When Scott wrote of how tales of chivalry operated on Warton "like a spell," leading him into mazes of digression that put linear argument on hold, he was acknowledging this feature of romance—and diagnosing a bad case of identification in its historian.[63]

In fact, as construed by the romance revivalists, medieval romance was belated even in relation to the medieval Geoffrey Chaucer. The interplay between seductive magic on the one hand and a disenchanted rationality on the other—also an interplay between imaginative pleasure and intellectual duty—was projected back to the fourteenth century. Chaucer had authored "The Squire's Tale," which had enflamed the imaginations of Spenser and Milton, with its "story of Cambuscan bold" and "of the wondrous horse of brass." And yet, repeatedly discovered by inhabitants of the eighteenth century to have been the Cervantes of the fourteenth, Chaucer had also authored the burlesque *anti*-romance "The Rime of Sir Thopas."[64]

The playfulness of tone marking the writings of Warton, Hurd, and Percy makes me think that for them the conclusion that Chaucer's example forced on romances' enlightened historians—that there never was a time when romance was not being driven off the scene—was not unequivocally melancholy. For these eighteenth-century men of letters, one outcome of this account in which romances' time was always already up was an arrangement in which the attachment that these engrossing materials solicited was always made safe by detachment. The central paradox of the epoch's literary history, one that, as we have seen, the literary historians acknowledged and even savored, was that so much of its intellectual labor was expended on behalf of writing whose nature it putatively was to sideline the claims of the intellect. Their *pleasures* as romance readers also included, accordingly, those associated with the experience of self-division. *Other* readers—denizens of a superstitious past; their equivalents, the lower orders and novel-reading ladies, members of the sex that the history of intellectual progress seemed to have bypassed—were associated with an unthinking submission to romance's charms. It was open to the enlightened literary historian both to participate in that ravishment and, by playing the periodization card, stand outside it, a vantage point from which he might enjoy the spectacle of his own enjoyment. If he were seduced by romance, it would be by choice, and by means of an act of historical imagination.

Relevant here is a slippery argument that Hurd set out in *Letters on Chivalry and Romance*. Hurd anticipated Warton's account of the "true lover of poetry" as a solitary being whose reading is disconnected from the external historical world (*History*, 2:463). Although he proposed that "the fictions of poetry" require "popular belief," "a countenance from the current superstitions of the age" (136), Hurd also declared that the bygone Gothic poets were, despite the spirit of that age, "reasonable," or cagey, enough, to give the "Reader leave to be as sceptical and as incredulous as he pleases" (136). It was enough for them that someone else be credulous: "They think it enough, if they can but bring you to *imagine* the possibility" of their fictions (135). "We must distinguish between the popular belief and that of the reader" (136). (As Ian Duncan observes, "The 'naive reader' is a figure projected by these texts for our own indulgence.")[65]

To indulge a foolish fondness for stories of enchantment—to reenact oneself the story of the seduced knight errant and parade, as Warton does, one's susceptibility to being detained by the stories' beauties; or to play, as Hurd does, at being a romance necromancer who has the power to "detain you," his reader, in the "fearful circle" of this "enchanted ground" (113)—was to demonstrate within disciplined romance study the existence of a private space that could accommodate and contain such undisciplined enthusiasms and identifications.[66] Perhaps in writing this chapter in the history of the discipline we should supplement the familiar story of how cool disinterest came to define the limits of a properly aesthetic response with the story of how ardor, that disinterest's opposite, came to know *its* place: that place being a snug sanctuary, in which disciplined responsibility could be temporarily suspended. Later, in the early nineteenth century, the poet, essayist, and anthologist Leigh Hunt would describe the dual perspective afforded the gentleman scholar of romance by declaring that in reading Spenser, "our boyhood is again existing, full of belief, though its hair be turning grey."[67]

Discussing these eighteenth-century literary historians' recovery of Gothic times, Harriet Guest points out how their emphasis on "truths specific to discrete historical circumstances" positioned them in opposition to earlier eighteenth-century ideals of the unity of a republic of taste centered on timeless truths. Where neoclassical theory had aimed to supply (as Johnson put it in the "Life of Dryden") "precepts" that depended on "the nature of things and the structure of the human mind," the romance revivalists, by constructing time as a field of cultural differences, "pluralized truth." As Guest emphasizes, the contextualization of Spenser particularly, as a poet belonging to the *sixteenth* century, and one who thus required *re*introducing to the eighteenth, was the flip side of an argument that repudiated the application to *The Faerie Queene* of the dominant norms of taste—for instance, neoclassical precepts about the unity of epic design. Warton concurred in finding *The Faerie Queene* flawed by that standard, "destitute of that arrangement and oeconomy which epic severity requires" (*Observations*, 16). Spenser's poem related only obliquely to the methods promulgated by Homer and Aristotle and which had been recovered in England by the time of its composition. However, Warton also construed the poem's failure as a classical epic as, in properly historical terms, the very mark of its success as an English romance.[68]

Jonathan Kramnick's argument about the Spenserians centers on the premise that they were deemed an impediment to literature's national dissemination, because, having opted for specialization, they were found "too particular to please." But when Guest outlines how this early literary history disseminated what she dubs a "Gothic aesthetic of pleasurable separateness," she aligns the particularized and the pleasing, just the alignment that Kramnick will not entertain.[69] The historicism that Warton and associates practiced was a venue for their display of professional expertise, but, in committing them to engage with what the classical and public sphere excluded, it could also represent a venue in which a gentleman could self-consciously play truant. It could situate this gentleman in what Johnson in 1758 called "the devious walks of literature."[70]

Warton begins his most famous poem, the 1782 "Verses on Sir Joshua Reynolds's Painted Window at New College Oxford," by calling on Reynolds (the artist whose designs were generally regarded as irreproachably tasteful because irreproachably classical) to put a halt to the progress of refinement. He presents himself a "lingering" votary of the Gothic and says that, despite the example of Reynolds's idealized forms, he cannot help but be "truant to the classic page."[71]

> Ah, stay thy treacherous hand! forbear to trace
> Those faultless forms of elegance and grace!
> Ah, cease to spread the bright transparent mass,
> With Titian's pencil, o'er the speaking glass!
> Nor steal, by strokes of art with truth combin'd,
> The fond illusions of my wayward mind!
> For long, enamour'd of a barbarous age,
> A faithless truant to the classic page;
> Long have I lov'd to catch the simple chime
> Of minstrel-harps, and spell the fabling rime.

This brief excerpt suffices to demonstrate the ambivalence that will be the poem's organizing principle over the next eighty-five lines. One should notice, among other things, how the "treacherous" of the first line and the "steal" of the fifth initially baffle our efforts to determine whether it is the speaker or his addressee who has misconduct to repent. Analyzing this rhetoric, Guest emphasizes that one aspect of Warton's and Hurd's engagement with premodern romance and Gothic manners was a "furtive and feminine opposition to the social and fraternal virtues of public life."[72]

At moments, to be sure, Warton and Hurd conducted their argument about the historical specificity of the elder English poets in terms that seemed to leave unchallenged an older axiology that had granted an unassailable privilege to the classical world's literary achievements. When in the *Letters* Hurd stated—what would now go without saying—that the manners of Gothic chivalry "never did subsist but once and are never likely to subsist again," it was to draw the contrast with "classic manners," which "arising out of the . . . usual situations of humanity" appear archetypal or "natural" (148). The logic that Hurd was recapitulating and then complicating had gone something like this: even if human nature is the same in all times and places, the classical is nonetheless a period more able than the others to approximate universality. Such a concession to classic manners does not contradict Guest's thesis about historicism's pluralizing of truth, but instead clarifies the stakes of the alterist presuppositions that guided the historicist approach to texts from the past. Classicisms of earlier centuries had appropriated ancient styles and signs, "as synecdoches for values that continued to regulate the present," Ted Underwood has noted. By contrast, the ancient signs appropriated when the late eighteenth-century historicists turned to the uncouth but charming materials of Britain's premodern past—to materials founded on "celtick superstitions" and "druidical ceremonies," featuring "our fairies" rather than "the Heathen deities"—"tend to convey prestige by suggesting *distance from contemporary life* rather than dominion over it."[73] Underwood dwells on that new depreciation of the uniform and that new valorization of historical distance from modern manners in order to pursue an argument about the engendering of a modern concept of aesthetic autonomy. In this account, the notion of a plurality of cultures, and, behind that, the notion of time as a field of discrete periods, advance in the long term the separation of "cultural distinction" from other forms of prestige.

As an additional effect of this historicist turn, however, one might also remark how it separates out the heart's convictions from the head's learning. The literary past's alterity "engages the affections of the heart" (I recycle the language Warton uses when he states what the reader of Spenser who had given up on classical regularity might get in return for that renunciation). Classic values, by contrast, solicit "the cold approbation of the head." Hence, as well, Horace Walpole's terms in *Anecdotes of Painting* (1764) as he made explicit the incommensurability of the two accounts of prestige to which Underwood alludes: "One must have taste to be sensible of the beauties of Grecian architecture; one only wants passions to feel Gothic."[74]

EXTRACURRICULAR SUBJECTS

In a complicated manner, one I wish to unpack by way of bringing this chapter to a close, that practice of "feeling Gothic" would become pivotal for the poetry professors' professionalism. It would help provide the auspices for a specifically masculine privacy—a privacy without women—that would lay the foundation for the public literary career. Even as eighteenth-century scholarship treating the Gothic library advanced the disciplinary transformations that would re-create English poetry as a legitimately teachable, profess-able subject, those scholars continued to invest in a notion of literary reading as an after-hours, extracurricular affair, an experience by its nature inimical to the experience of formal schooling. Those investments underwrote the captivating charisma of "romantic poetry." Mediated by Wordsworthian precepts about aesthetic education, those investments would later help shape the doctrine that held that English teaching, if it was possible at all and not a contradiction in terms, needed to be conducted so as to address students' personal experiences and foster students' imaginative play.

It is possible, for instance, to interpret William Shenstone's influential poem *The School-Mistress*—a Spenserian imitation that playfully rewrites the court of the Fairy Queen as a humble village school—along these lines. *The*

School-Mistress can be read as arranging for romance to be pitted against the didactic homilies that were the stuff of the schoolroom—as arranging for romance to put pedagogical schemes back to front. After all, its boy protagonist ("thilk wight" in the quotation that follows) becomes identifiable as the poem's hero and equivalent of the Red-Cross Knight at the moment that, failing to attend to the letters he is meant to be conning on his hornbook, diverted from the text that is meant to be the medium of his socialization, he becomes mesmerized with the romance image backing that text. A pictorial depiction of knight-errantry constitutes his hornbook's reverse side:[75]

> Their Books of Stature small take they in Hand,
> Which with pellucid Horn secured are;
> To save from Fingers wet the Letters fair:
> The work so quaint that on their Backs is seen,
> *St. Georges* high Atchievements does declare:
> On which thilk Wight that has y-gazing been,
> Kens the forthcoming Rod, unpleasant sight, I ween.

Even in the era when the Middle English romances constituted the field on which a new breed of textual bibliographer and textual editor displayed their expertise, romance could still be thought of as a hinge between playtime and schooltime. It helped that it was still the case that abridgements and pastiches of medieval narratives of adventure often supplied the content of the chapbooks customarily given to new readers. That association between the romances and the reading done by those at the cusp of literacy seems to assert itself in multiple accounts, given by literary biographers and others, of the dawning of genius and the discovery of a vocation. As the conventions of the life of the author fall into place, counterparts to Shenstone's truant boy are encountered with increasing frequency: readers who, on the sly, arrange to enjoy secret trysts with romances.

The older reader, particularly the boy reader from the propertied classes, who, unlike his sisters, would receive a formal education, starts to be profiled in these contexts as a figure endowed with a double life. Sent to school, and set in front of one book, his Latin grammar, for instance, he dreams of another, a dreaming inflected by his nostalgia for an earlier period of his childhood. In such profiles, the romances become the symbol of the reader's mental liberty, at the same time that, as objects of memory, and as renewable resources that can be tapped long after childhood, they underpin an account of the self's integrity over time—an account of career development. An odd passage in the wildly speculative chapter of the *Life of Geoffrey Chaucer* that

Godwin entitled "Schoolboy Amusements" condenses these several connections between romance and the development of the individual, as it refers to Chaucer's formative encounter with tales of chivalry and the "visionary scenery . . . on which his boyish thoughts were at liberty to ruminate for ever."[76]

The several stories that James Boswell told in the *Life* of Samuel Johnson as a roaming, secretive reader—"roaming at large in the fields of literature," "as chance threw books in his way, and inclination directed him through them"—set out similar associations. This is especially so in those stories, relayed to Boswell by Thomas Percy, which involve Johnson's engagement with the materials anthologized in the *Reliques of Ancient English Poetry*. "Dr. Percy, the Bishop of Dronmore, . . . informs me, that when a boy [Johnson] was immoderately fond of reading romances of chivalry, and he retained his fondness for them through life; so that (adds his Lordship) spending part of a summer at my parsonage-house in the country he chose for his regular reading the old Spanish romance of *Felixmante of Hircania* in folio, which he read quite through."[77] In his fragmentary autobiography, Walter Scott reminisced about his first reading of the *Reliques* by noting that since he "had been from infancy devoted to legendary lore of this nature" he was at age thirteen all the more elated to discover in the *Reliques* a book that came to him as (in Nick Groom's words) "already a childhood memory." In the *Reliques*, Scott found "pieces of the same kind which had amused my childhood, and still continued in secret the Delilahs of my imagination, considered as the subject of sober research." All through a summer day, those "Delilahs" detained the thirteen-year-old under the tree where he had settled down with his new book, until he was sought after and found still "entranced" in his "intellectual banquet." This is a story of romance captivation and a boy overmastered by a secret vice.[78]

Of course, when the romance reader was a young woman, that coordination would be trickier, the "Delilahs" in Scott's account of his ardent youthful reading suggesting why. Evidence of a girl's indulgence in the desultory, unsupervised, rambling reading was more likely to inaugurate a story of miseducation and loss of reputation than a story of a kindled imagination— consider, for instance Charlotte Lennox's eponymous Female Quixote, who anticipated Johnson in roaming freely and unguided in a library.[79] In the context marked out by admonitory figures like Lennox's Arabella and her many avatars, romance, rather than a designation for the venerable sources of the nation's poetic imagination, was synonymous with the kind of irresponsible prose fictions about love that defined a modern mass market.

Still, women during the last third of the eighteenth century were given plenty of reasons to find the "Gothic manners" that shaped the old romances of great interest, since those manners were often declared the consequence of a feminization of culture. "No sooner was the Roman empire overthrown, and the Goths had overpowered Europe, than we find the female character assuming an unusual importance and authority": Warton's contrast here, in his "On the Origin of Romantic Fiction," is between, on the one hand, the marginalization of women that was the rule in classical culture and, on the other, chivalry, an ethical code that made veneration for women the keystone of public morality. It was thanks to that Gothic legacy, this widely disseminated argument ran, that sexual segregation no longer prevailed in modern Britain, where woman had been enabled to take her rightful rank as the friend and companion of man. Susannah Dobson, translator of the Abbé de Sainte-Palaye's *The Literary History of the Troubadours* (1779) and *Memoirs of Ancient Chivalry* (1784), alluded to this hypothesis about Gothic feminocentrism when she declared that "women, in particular, ought to hold these ancient writers in high esteem."[80] Clara Reeve claimed Warton, Hurd, and Percy as her allies in *The Progress of Romance* (1785), which she wrote as a series of conversations between a classically educated gentleman and two women who successfully talk him out of his conviction of the epic's superiority over the romance while they educate him in the romance's long history.[81] Even so, writers who *as* women wrote from a position already declared private, and whose informal education generally left them without means to trade on the cultural capital of classical learning, could not obtain the kind of frisson from visits to romances' enchanted ground that was obtained by the gentlemen clerics and lawyers who through those visits paraded their truancy from public life and the classic page. By the same token, women who aspired to be taken seriously as intellectuals had powerful reasons for not staging their relationship to romance as a love story.

The most romantic thing about English poetry at Warton's eighteenth-century Oxford might have been, in fact, that its reading as a matter of course happened sub rosa, after hours and after school. Schooltime, after all, was for most schoolboys and all Oxford undergraduates a time defined, by and large, by the toilsome rigors of Latin and Greek grammar and composition—arid learning that was beaten into younger boys, in what was often frankly avowed to be an instilling of manliness. The institutions of bookish intimacy that Oxford's bachelor culture evolved in order to formalize their truancy from that classical regime may well have shaped the terms that Warton used to establish the lovability of romantic poetry. Certainly, there are some re-

semblances between the way that the romance historians theorized and enacted the privatized pleasures of recondite learning and the way that some
of these collegians and those they tutored organized their socializing, loung-
ing, and whimsy. Eighteenth-century Oxford had an unofficial curriculum:
a clubbiness whose chief ingredients were versifying, betting, "good cheer
and good liquor" and, in the first part of the century, the Jacobitism with
which those last two commodities were sometimes linked. (The institution's
official curriculum of classical learning and divinity was, by contrast, notoriously neglected: through the century it was an axiom of Whig journalism
that the university, backward-looking and somnolent, was an impediment
to the advancement of learning.) Oxford also hosted a tradition of secret
literary clubs, their venue not bowers—though Oxford was known in the
later eighteenth century for its gardens and groves—but, for the most part,
the town's coffeehouses and taverns.[82]

Beginning sometime around the 1750s or 1760s Warton was himself a
member of one of these clubs, known as the Jelly Bag Society in honor of
the jelly bag caps (made of linen, striped, and ending in a point) that he and
his companions ritualistically donned for the meetings they convened at
locations that were kept secret. (The story is told of someone who wanted in
on that secret arranging for a showman to beat a drum through the Oxford
streets. Eventually, Warton, "who was always drawn by that sound," appeared at a window, blowing his cover by sporting his jelly bag cap.) The
members' headgear honored a riddling rhyme about why a successful epi-
gram should be fashioned as a jelly bag would be—"Make it at top both large
and fit / To hold a budget-full of wit, / And point it at the end!"—that had
been devised by a founding member.[83]

The tradition that the Jelly Bags carried on dated back to Warton's father
at least: Thomas Warton Senior was University Professor of Poetry by day,
but also circa 1720 a pillar of the Poetical Club that met by night in a back
room at Oxford's Three Tuns Tavern and "motto'd and epigrammatized."
What little is now known about the skullduggery of the Poetical Club derives from a much reprinted and muckraking periodical essay series entitled
The Terrae-Filius, or, The Secret History of the University of Oxford (1719-20) by
Whig journalist and Oxford dropout Nicholas Amhurst. Though his first
essay on this "remarkable cabal" began by insisting that he was not privy
to their doings, Amhurst contrived nonetheless to transcribe the Poetical
Club's constitution—including the articles forbidding members on pain of
expulsion "to discover the secrets of this society to any body whatsoever"
or to "transgress the rules of Aristotle or any other critick"—and later to

provide the minutes of a meeting. Those enabled Amhurst's readers to track
the club's alcohol-fueled progress, in the course of that evening, from "epitaphs and elegies" to "love, smuttiness, and a song." Amhurst's brief in his
essays was to expose the seditious spirit of Tory Oxford (and to lampoon
the notorious Jacobite leanings of Thomas Warton Senior in particular, who
had in 1719 delivered a sermon in which he had equivocated about which
king exactly—George II or the "King over the Water"—should command his
listeners' loyalty).[84] That brief explains his tone of innuendo, the surface effect of an underlying logic in which dalliances with the Muse and flirtations
with the Pretender were appropriately bundled together because they alike
indicated an impaired relation to modern common sense.

The Poetical Club was succeeded in the 1730s by the Triumvirate, a trio
of Pembroke College undergraduates who suspended their classical studies
on a regular basis in order to debate their off-hours reading, a category comprising, according to the biographer of triumvir William Shenstone, "Plays
and poetry, Spectators or Tatlers and other works of easy digestion" imbibed
alongside "Florence wine."[85] Later, as we have seen, came the Jelly Bags, followed, perhaps, by some additional confederacies that have vanished from
the historical record, and then, in the 1790s, by the Society for Scientific
and Literary Disquisition—which was also known, by the undergraduates
whom the society excluded from its company, as the Conclave of Lunatics;
and who had joined together in secret, according to one member, in order
"to indulge in our favourite themes, in the most unrestrained manner, without giving ingress to a single stranger." (As an instance of those themes,
the Lunatic Thomas Frognall Dibdin, whose memoir I have just quoted,
mentions the essay that he read to the society "on the comparative merits of
Dryden's 'Ode on St. Cecilia's Day' and Collins's 'Ode on the Passions.'")[86]
Even as, with the passage of time, Oxford's history of Jacobite politicking
receded into the past, club life preserved a good portion of skullduggery. This
was in part to cite that history and give it its sentimental due, in part because of a formalism according to which secrecy required keeping up for its
own sake.[87] This upkeep served to carve out a space of furtive, pleasurable,
and, to be sure, puerile privateness, in which men whose allegiances were
ultimately to public life could find a respite from ambition and seriousness.
"Waggery" was the blanket term Amhurst used for this in the *Terrae-Filius*.[88]

The secrecy of the secret poetry clubs of eighteenth-century Oxford also
worked to codify some sorts and occasions of discourse—those involving
liquor, bookishnesss, poetry, and the English poets more particularly—as a
medium of snug, same-sex intimacy. The jelly bag caps sported as a sign of

solidarity by Warton and his confederates were, it is important to note, being worn in lieu of their wigs, those symbols of masculine authority and potency that through the eighteenth century would never have been doffed in mixed company. How such secret sharing might have impacted the understanding of English poetry—or of literariness more generally—is intimated in a passage from the 1759 correspondence between Thomas Warton's former schoolmate at Winchester College, the Reverend John Mulso, and his friend the Reverend Gilbert White, who would win fame thirty years later with a parish history, *The Natural History and Antiquities of Selborne.* White had sent Mulso a letter describing the return visit he had paid to Oriel College, Oxford, where both had taken their degrees years before. Mulso's reply, nostalgic for that yesteryear, put the love of literature to work doing proxy duty for other loves: "I am pleased that you have got back from Oxford with a mind impregnated with Poetry, as in former days, and not troubled with Party and Contention. You brought back our old happy Feels over Milton."[89] In Mulso's accounting, at once elegiac and facetious, Miltonic verse stands in for and preserves former, boyish selves that have been left behind.

Its subordination to such ends—and the attendant dissociation of Milton from party and contention (in 1759, still an avant-garde position in discussions of this puritan poet)—might register the terms, self-consciously wistful ones, in which midcentury critics like Warton had been striving to make romantic poetry history. In addition to suggesting the consequences of that periodization, this use of Milton might also suggest how new definitions of literariness were coming to influence and be influenced by the culture's emergent determination to segregate the intimate from the public and play from work. The Wartonian identification of bygone romances as the casualties of history—according to the narrative in which those Delilahs of one's imagination were always fated to be betrayed by the onward march of refinement and reason—had as its compensation the possibility of defining poetry as a bower housing, still, the boy that was.

The ground of the argument that Wartonian historicism made in order to promote romances as, in addition, fit objects for sober study was the premise that these fictions could be read as historical documents, "pictures of real life and manners" and that they possessed public utility for the present accordingly. As others have noted, this rationale for the romance recovery "had the appeal of a paradox"—here "in the wildest imaginative stories" were embedded the hard "facts of social history."[90] That paradox positioned the early literary historian so as to enjoy, impossibly, a coincidence of truth and fantasy, and of public work and private love. This chapter has tried to model an approach to the historicizing of literary history that would acknowledge the seductiveness of those conjunctions. In *Observations on the First Three Volumes of the History of English Poetry*, Joseph Ritson thought to damn Warton as he highlighted the Shandean qualities of his scholarship: "There is some difference," Ritson fumed, "between the History of English Poetry and the Life and opinions of Thomas Warton." Ritson, was not, as it happens, thinking here of how Warton's predilection for meandering digression impeded the linear progress of his history, in the style of Laurence Sterne's *The Life and Opinions of Tristram Shandy*—even though, as we have seen, he might have done. Instead, as he declared in this "familiar letter" to Warton, he was thinking "of another fault which ought to be carefully rooted out; . . . your fulsome and disgusting Egotism."[91] Ritson uses "egotism" here in that eighteenth-century sense that denoted an excessive use of the first person pronoun. But Ritson's distaste for the *History*'s traces of personality and evidences of authorial predilection, his convictions about the unimpeachability of the objective voice, and his doubt (which underlies all these aspects of his response to Warton) as to whether literary history should in fact be written to "gratif[y] the reader of taste," foreclose questions that subsequent history suggests many other adherents of our undisciplined discipline would rather keep open.[92]

CHAPTER THREE

Wedded to Books

Nineteenth-Century Bookmen at Home

My acquaintance with my books has not been confined to their exteriors or to
their typographical peculiarities. They have comforted me after many a weary
day, and have stood often in the place of friends.

A Catalogue of the Collection of Books and Manuscripts Belonging to
Mr. Brayton Ives of New York (1891)

A collector recently bought at public auction, in London, for one hundred and
fifty-seven guineas, an autograph of Shakespeare: but for nothing a schoolboy can read Hamlet and can detect secrets of highest concernment yet unpublished therein. I think I will never read any but the commonest books—
the Bible, Homer, Dante, Shakespeare, and Milton. Then we are impatient of
so public a life and planet, and run hither and thither for nooks and secrets.

RALPH WALDO EMERSON, "Experience" (1844)

BLACK-LETTER LEARNING AND BIBLIOGRAPHICAL ROMANCE

In the previous chapter we began to see how, in its swerve from the classical canon and turn to long forgotten medieval and renaissance sources,
the romance revival that Warton had spearheaded fostered a sometimes
troubling proximity between the defining activities of the scholar and the
collector of rare books. Consult the Bodleian Library's copy of the 1596
edition of Shakespeare's *Venus and Adonis,* for instance, and you will find
a penciled memorandum written by Warton's fellow student of literary antiquities Edmond Malone, dated 1791, that explains that thirty years earlier
Warton had found this book "among a parcel of old iron and other lumber,
and I think he purchased it for *sixpence.*"[1] One can imagine the helpful-
ness of this discovery for the author of the *Observations on the Fairy Queen.*
But in detailing provenance and price Malone's inscription memorializes, as
well, a red-letter day in the acquisitive life of the collector: Malone presents
Warton—and, for that matter, himself—as a figure who enjoys the thrill of
the bargain and the private knowledge of the value of objects that enables

him to take advantage of the ignorance of others. The details of the memorandum make it harder to see the book's acquisition as a mere means to an
end. Was Warton, like the collector whom Walter Benjamin profiles, buying the book to *rescue* it and give it "its freedom" on his shelves? Did he
as he took possession congratulate himself for his ability to give his discovery a good home, where it would be restored to companionship among
its fellows? Maybe. Collectibles often seem to invite the collector to imbue
them with human feelings, even though the collecting of books in particular
seems to entail—often to the exasperation of the activity's critics—acts of
objectification that convert books from authored texts into manufactured
artifacts.[2] These two dynamics and their interlacing will be a central concern of this chapter.

In Warton's day, the very terminology for scholarship helped to blur the
line between the labor of the scholar and the private diversion of the collector. The term "black-letter learning" was the standard designation then for
the researches occupying antiquaries like Warton, representing an equivalent, though with very different implications, of a modern descriptor like
"Middle English literature." In its narrower sense the name of the typeface style developed by the late fifteenth-century pioneers of movable type,
"Black-letter"—when deployed in this extended sense—emphasized the
scholars' investment in the look of the incunables they studied. Playing up
their material-mindedness, this terminology cast this subculture of men of
letters as adepts of bibliographical codes rather than linguistic ones, of the
physicality of the book artifact rather than its textual contents. In this way, it
yoked the black-letter scholars all the more closely to the collectors and the
book dealers who served collectors. Those were the two groups who overtly
had a thing for the physical particulars of the book, its typeface, paper, or
printers' marks—although in their cases those engagements with the book
object were mediated by the recognition that such particulars could also
serve to mark off a particular collectible volume from a crowd of books with
the same contents and make that singular volume something that could be
sold or resold for an elevated price. Starting in the late eighteenth century,
their specialized language of typeface, paper, and so forth served to make
books, "until recently part of an unstructured mass, ... identifiable, desirable,
and marketable."[3] The discipline of descriptive bibliography that would take
up the distinguishing features of book outsides as objects of study was still
in its infancy when Warton died in 1790, and when it made its nineteenth-
century debut in the republic of letters it would suffer in public opinion as a
result of its perceived proximity to the irrational, exuberant, amorous world

of the collector.[4] Not incidentally, in that world, the black-letter book or ballad had by the early nineteenth century taken the place once occupied by the humanist reprint of the classical text. Black-letter had come to represent "the *ne plus ultra* of print possession."[5]

In 1831 an anonymous contributor to the *Bibliographical and Retrospective Miscellany* looked back to this shift with mixed feelings. "At the commencement of the present century . . . a revolution in the minds and feelings of men" was wrought that was "without precedent in the annals of literature," this person writes. In its aftermath "we have seen the sons of rank and fashion contending with tenacious rivalry for the acquisition of a choice library of rare and curious books, which they were then for the first time taught to number amongst the requisite furniture of a mansion." In 1750 Lord Chesterfield had, by contrast, told his son, with pride, "What curious books I have . . . are indeed but few"; he had earlier warned the boy that "due attention to the inside of books, and due contempt for the outside, is the proper relation between a man of sense and his books."[6]

In the 1831 retrospect, the word "curious" strikes one of the notes of reservation. (The suggestion that books are furniture strikes the other.) For many cultural observers, as Barbara Benedict has explained, the *curious* inclinations of patrician consumers appeared symptoms of an "ambition to replace public values with idiosyncratic meanings" and seemed to have "the potential to usurp common culture."[7]

Any collector of rare books has a knack for arranging things so that the particularism of his relation with a specific copy of a text upstages his commonality with that text's fellow readers, who consume the same text but in a more widely available edition. But as this chapter will suggest, there was a widespread leeriness about the patricians' new engagements with, and commodification of, black-letter books particularly. Such engagements seemed to lead them away from the ends that were supposed to be achieved in the gentleman's forming of a private library. Those engagements set them along devious paths, pursuing their whimsies, just at the moment when in other, down-market cultural sectors the numerous purchasers of the "complete libraries" of the English classics—competitively priced reprint series like the one sometimes advertised as *Cooke's Uniform, Cheap, and Elegant Pocket Library* (1794)—were encouraged to view possession of those collections as a way of performing their fellowship with other members of the reading nation. Compounding the collector's reputation for perversity was the fact that the stuff of black-letter learning, deemed out-of-the-way ("rare and curious"), was also considered to be practically

illegible. To nineteenth-century eyes accustomed to Roman type, the typeface of Gutenberg and Caxton seemed cramped, over-inked, and the reverse
of reader-friendly. This seemed not to matter, however. Nineteenth-century
rare book collectors perturbed and fascinated other members of literary
culture not simply with their reluctance to think of reading in idealized,
disembodied terms—witness, as we shall further on in this chapter, the attention expended on their habit of gazing dotingly on book bindings in red
morocco or Russian leather—but also with their reluctance even to think
of reading at all. "Book collectors read not what they buy," the Manchester
physician Dr. John Ferriar complained in a poem first published in 1809.[8]

In this chapter, leaving behind Warton's eighteenth century, I shift focus. Instead of the practitioners of black-letter learning, I look first at the
"the sons of rank and fashion" referenced above and then at some early
nineteenth-century men of letters—Leigh Hunt, Charles Lamb, William
Hazlitt, and Thomas De Quincey, a group who, I aim to demonstrate, campily mimed (despite their rather more limited means) the patricians' displays of bookishness. By these means I trace how deviancies of the sort
that Dr. Ferriar flagged in his poem on collecting, "The Bibliomania,"
proved generative for the romantic-period consolidation of literature as a
love-object.

Thanks to their public reputation for irrational obsession and to the im-
mensity of their purses, the rare-book collectors diagnosed in Ferriar's poem
were, we shall see, minor celebrities within the early nineteenth-century
literary world. Like other sorts of abnormally interesting, uncommon public
figures, those "bibliomaniacs," as we shall call them, excited a blend of re-
pulsion and attraction. The romantic period, as Andrew Piper has reminded
us, is well known for working out a view of literature as something that
"happens in the mind, not on the page."[9] Repudiations of these collectors'
failure to abstract meaning from the realm of corporeal particularity were
thus to be expected, as were, at a moment of widespread uneasiness over
the commercialization of culture, repudiations of the collectors' readiness
to seek their enjoyment in the marketplace. But those repudiations often
went hand in hand with more or less furtive acknowledgments of a deeper
kinship. Literature's soi-disant true lovers both distanced themselves from
the book collectors in the course of their own self-fashioning *and* took inspiration from the publicity surrounding these collectors' extremist form
of devotion to the written word. Furthermore, for every discussion from
the period that proceeds on the premise that the love of literature and the
love of books must be antonyms, one can find another that acts out their

continuities. And, in the publicity generated by the bibliomania, what rare-book collectors were not doing with books—*not* reading—was not as inter-esting as what behind the closed doors of their private libraries they were conjectured to have been doing instead. That publicity offered guidance as to how the literature that one loves might be made more thoroughly one's own and guidance even as to how one might be "wedded to books"—a dream of literary appreciation as snug conjugality that was outlined by the essayist Leigh Hunt in 1820, and that we'll explore later.

Present-day commentators have proposed that we see the bibliomaniac, the book collector who collects to the point of madness, as embodying for early nineteenth-century observers the "bad conscience" both of the era's historical scholarship and of its critics' attempts to regulate the contem-porary literary field.[10] For critics by profession, this amateur's conspicuous consumption highlighted how the period's ever-expanding and accelerating book trade—"commercialism run wild"—at once facilitated the progress of enlightenment and jeopardized it. The bibliomaniac's random acquisitive-ness and enthusiasms for curious books rather than worthy ones highlighted too the critic's own inability ever to transcend wholly the modishness that prevailed in the contemporary book market. The bibliomaniac reminded scholars by profession that the amassing of books is not always the prelude to their reading and that, indeed, with so many books and so little time, some *not* reading might be advisable.[11] (How, without adhering to such a policy, could the new bibliographers of the early nineteenth century even have imagined that they might assemble a systematic and universal history of books, over-plentiful as those were?).

How clear was Thomas Warton's conscience? When in his *Autobiography* (1834) Sir Samuel Egerton Brydges disparaged those persons who, unlike Brydges himself, had yet to recover from "the book-fever" that had had them valuing old books inordinately, he declared "Tom Warton" the excep-tion: Warton, he declared, "knew best how to make use of such books."[12] In fact, the materials I assembled in chapter 2 suggested otherwise: for some readers, Warton's immunity to that book fever during the time when he was recovering "much curious matter of our old literature, then buried in scarce books" might not have been beyond dispute.[13] For them, Warton seemed to emphasize more than downplay the affinities between the scholar and the collector, and to emphasize as well the collector's forte for taking possession. His *History*'s occasional spotlighting of the particularity of a specific copy of a book, its way of giving voice to it as object as well as text, must have reinforced this impression.

But the craziness at issue in the bibliomania had several dimensions. The bibliomania also troubled, and gave definition to, the nineteenth-century presentation of the love of literature as its own, legitimate form of romantic love. In what follows, the bibliomaniac will figure primarily as the bad conscience of—but also an inspiration for—what we may wish to call "companionate reading." This ethos, elaborated through the nineteenth century, both competed and collaborated with the institutions of modern conjugality. It too centered on the fireside virtues (as they were called when human companions were involved) that sustained readers' long-term cohabitation with their book companions. The first epigraph to this chapter, part of the account of himself that a nineteenth-century bibliophile, and Civil War general and railway financier, appended to the sale catalogue of his immense library, brings to view those living arrangements in terms that recall, queerly, the nineteenth century's most clichéd descriptions of home as the protected enclave where men go to recover from working days spent in the marketplace. In that epigraph's reconfiguring of companionate marriage, the library is metonymic of the home, and the books, which are called "friends," are cast as a substitute wife. Though at its nineteenth-century height the bibliomania was associated more with home-wrecking than with homemaking—generating both stories of ruinous expenditures that left collectors and their dependents homeless, and stories of books that, piled up on chairs, tables, and beds, displaced their owners from the houses that they thought were their own—it helped trigger a heightened awareness of books as affective objects and book collecting as a practice that could delimit a space of privacy. The bibliomania also soldered that privacy to the pleasures of possession.[14] This is why the bibliomania keeps looming into view, as problem and promise, when Hunt, Hazlitt, Lamb, and De Quincey, writing about their reading lives, try out and sometimes reject definitions of literary appreciation as a decisively intimate, domestic affair. "But what has a bibliographical romance to do with love and marriage?" asked the Reverend Thomas Frognall Dibdin, the author of the other 1809 text entitled *Bibliomania*.[15] More than you might think.

BOOK KNIGHTS OR BOOK GLUTTONS? THE
PROBLEM OF THE BIBLIOMANIA

The problem wasn't new. Attachments to books had long been held up for scrutiny. Determining the point at which means take over from ends, and the love of literature, in either its old or new sense, becomes book love—or determining the point at which book love in its turn becomes book lust—was a challenge that individuals had been setting themselves as part of their programs of ethical self-governance since the days of the Stoic philosopher Seneca. In essays such as his "Of Peace of Mind" ("De tranquillitate animi"), book owning carried beyond the bounds of moderation—owning more books than you can read—had been represented as the last infirmity of a noble mind. "'It is more respectable,' say you, 'to spend one's money on such books than on vases of Corinthian brass and paintings.' Not so: everything that is carried to excess is wrong"—even "literary pursuits, the most becoming thing for a gentleman to spend money upon."[16] In the late eighteenth and early nineteenth centuries, however, individuals' efforts to monitor their relations to books unfolded against a new backdrop. The arguments against luxury and for "measuring things by their uses" that were key components of the Stoic package were patently trickier to sustain in a culture that was both figuring out ways to vindicate consumerist passions and developing the new aestheticist axiologies that separated off aesthetic value from utility.[17] Partly because I have Dr. Ferriar's medical credentials in view, I am also tempted to say that the late eighteenth-century and early nineteenth-century discourse cataloguing the possible varieties of bookish transgressions has less in common with Stoicism's ethical counsel than with the strange taxonomies of late nineteenth-century sexology.

To be sure, during the romantic period the obsessed human psyche is not yet the diseased human psyche. The full-blown medicalization of collecting by a psychiatric discipline that would read collections as documentation of sexual maladjustment was decades in the future.[18] Even so, when Ferriar evokes the "wild desires [and] restless torments [that] seize / The hapless man, who feels the book disease," or when in 1765 one Louis Bollioud de Mermet sketches the character of a "bibliotaphe"—the sort of book collector who so fears exposing his treasures to the light of day, that he makes of his cabinet a kind of tomb and buries them there—one senses a faint foreshadowing of the strange menagerie of "mixoscopophiles, gynecomasts, presbyophiles, sexoesthetic inverts" that Michel Foucault spotlights in *The History of Sexuality*.[19]

We are perhaps on firmer ground in establishing the historicity of bookish desires when we observe that, compared to Seneca's pre-print day, there was in the romantic period, conspicuously, an awful lot more to buy and read, or to buy and not read. In 1823 the essayist and antiquarian Isaac D'Israeli noted that Seneca's dietetic advice to keep literary pursuits within bounds was all very well, but the Stoic philosopher "had no 'monthly list of new publications'!"[20] And the abundance was compounded, ludicrously, by the fact that there were an increasing number of printed representations of book fools for purchase as well—as the publication in 1809 of not one but two texts entitled *Bibliomania* attests nicely. Many other representations followed these two. Although book collectors were dissociated from reading themselves, famously remaining on the thresholds of their volumes, their follies were nevertheless commonplace topics for the reading matter of others. And although all agreed that this population preferred their books rare, stories of their doings themselves achieved a wide circulation, being taken up by authors very much at ease with the books' mechanical reproducibility and the potential for audience growth that seemed built into the medium of the printed book. In Sir Walter Scott's best-selling *Waverley* novels of the second and third decades of the nineteenth century, the narrators regularly reference the bibliomaniacs whom they claim to discern among their own readers, and who indeed are the bosom companions of the Author of *Waverley* himself. For the sake of this minority audience, they interrupt the diegesis of these historical fictions to editorialize on the astronomical prices that a rare-book dealer might command *now* for the very books that the novels' characters handled *then* so insouciantly. This reflexivity about the book medium can make the reader hyperaware of the disparate methods of valuation that could be applied to the volume currently in her hand.[21]

The indefatigable author of the second of the 1809 books on the bibliomania, the Reverend Thomas Frognall Dibdin (encountered in chapter 2 as a member during his student days of Oxford's Conclave of Lunatics) was single-handedly accountable for a large portion of the bibliomania-themed print deluge. In 1811, in fact, Dibdin reissued his 1809 *Bibliomania*, adding to it both the curious subtitle *A Bibliographical Romance* and some six hundred pages. Extended, it became a silver-fork novel / roman à clef of a kind, a change registering, as Dibdin explained in this second edition's "Address to the Reader," his wish to provide "a *Personal History of Literature*, in the characters of *Collectors of Books*." (With comparable instructional designs on the reader, the new work also interspersed its narration of the courtship that yokes one of its collector-protagonists to the sister of another collector with "notices" of rare old editions—an arrangement that enables Dibdin to weave two stories of desire into one.) This "Bibliographical Romance" was succeeded by (among other things) Dibdin's *The Bibliographical Decameron*, his *A Bibliographical, Antiquarian and Picturesque Tour*, and, in a seeming about-face near the end of his life, his anonymously published *Bibliophobia: or, Remarks on the Present Languid and Depressed State of Literature and the*

Book Trade. In between, Dibdin was occupied cataloguing the great library at Althorp, the country seat of the second Earl Spencer, and also, in 1812, published "Bibliography," a poem in blank verse, in which a young collegian's extracurricular study of the history of printing rescues him from his confusion in bookstores and at auctions, and, it is implied, from a career of vice.[22]

The year 1812 ended up being a banner one generally for those who beat the drum for the bibliomaniacs. In that year newspapers across the land—the *Times*, the *Morning Chronicle*, the *London Gazette*, the *Derby Mercury*, the *Ipswich Journal*, the *Caledonian Mercury*—regaled readers with reports on the Roxburghe sale, the auction of the immense library of the third Duke of Roxburghe, John Ker, sold off by the fifth duke to pay the legal costs that he had incurred in defending in the law courts his right to the title. The "contending book-knights" who sallied forth as bidders for the forty-two days of the sale paid enormous sums for the third duke's rarities, thereby manifesting, according to the self-promoting Dibdin, a "mettle" that his *Bibliomania* had helped foment.[23] What in Dibdin's book counted as "book-heroism"?[24] There was, for instance, the June 17, 1812, day when a bidding war over Roxburghe's 1471 *Decameron* erupted between two grandee collectors, the second Earl Spencer and George Spencer-Churchill, the fourth Marquess of Blandford (cousins, who were recent lords of the admiralty and the treasury respectively). Between them, in front of a large group who were there to look and not buy, they drove up the price of the book to £2,240. On another day of the Roxburghe sale, the rumor circulated, triggered by the only slightly less titanic sums being expended by a certain Mr. Nornanville, that this "man of mystery" was secretly bidding on behalf of Napoleon Bonaparte, at that moment otherwise occupied leading an invasion of Russia, and that "the clusters of Caxtons which were knocked down" in Nornanville's name were to be "shipped off for the imperial library at Paris."[25] Instead, those surviving samples of the output of the first English printer, William Caxton, turned up in the library that the sixth Duke of Devonshire was creating at Chatsworth.

The newsworthiness of these transactions was clearly a function of the high public profile enjoyed by the patrician purchasers, and of the prices they proved willing to pay—most notoriously, for that *Decameron*, which, when it had originally been added to the Roxburghe stores, likely sometime around 1740, had been valued at a hundred guineas. Prior to the "book-effervescence" of 1812, in another Dibdinian phrase, no one had ever before paid a four-figure sum for a book, and never before had a book's seller scored a 2,000 percent profit.[26] But as the *Bibliographical and Retrospective*

Miscellany intimated in the passage about "a revolution in . . . minds and feelings" that I referenced above, another reason that the Roxburghe sale made noise was that it registered emphatically gentlemanly collectors' shift toward "curious books" printed in the black letter, such as those Caxtons, and away from texts whose classical and tasteful bona fides were rather more securely beyond dispute. For the prerevolutionary generation of bibliophiles, humanist editions of Latin and Greek texts, ideally from the press of Aldus Manutius, had been the collectibles of choice. The third duke's Aldine Greek Bible from 1518 sold for only £41, 14s., 6d at the Roxburghe sale, however. And that was a figure that participants and spectators contrasted to the £1,100 given for Caxton's 1471 printing of *The Recuyell of the Historyes of Troye* (in the mid-eighteenth century, stray pages from Caxton's press had been sold by the lot as wastepaper), or contrasted, more shockingly still, to the £477, 15s given for the three volumes in which the duke and their previous eighteenth-century owners had pasted "a collection of old half-penny ballads and garlands."[27] From the seventy-three-page sale catalogue of the third Duke of Roxburghe's library, those participants and spectators would already have inferred that materials of the latter sort were this bibliophile's true loves: "He idolized the talents of *Shakspeare* and *Cervantes*, and collected every thing that could illustrate their works," the bookseller George Nichol stated in the catalogue's preface.[28]

Earlier in his *Bibliomania* John Ferriar had commented on those desires. He too underlines how the new fashions in collecting intersected with the rise of English literary history: he notices the modern collector's tendency when confronting an auctioneer's "dusty lot" to seek out "*English* books, neglected and forgot," and adds, to further illustrate his account of the keen collector as "devious oft' from ev'ry classic Muse," that "dismal ballads, sung to crouds of old [are] / Now cheaply bought for thrice their weight in gold."[29] But Ferriar also implies that as a consequence of the black-letter craze, the uncouth entertainments of an unrefined past and a plebeian present (he mentions "bloody murder, or the yelling ghost" as typical ballad subject matter) had secured an entrée to the gentleman's library. One strike against the black-letter was that this font style from the later fifteenth century remained in the eighteenth century the typeface that printers used for the broadside ballads sold and sung on the streets. Kristian Jensen states that Aldine editions were recognized as "being the first steps towards the formation of a reading public based on taste," but, for contemporary observers, the alternative choice of trophies battled over at the Roxburghe sale betokened the imminent reversing of the progress of refinement.[30] Sometime in the late seventeenth century Samuel Pepys put part of *his* collection of half-penny ballads and chapbook romances between the covers of an album that he equipped with the title "Vulgaria"; the bibliomaniacs of the early nineteenth century contrived matters so that cheap print occupying that category of things held in common and commonplace ("Vulgaria") might simultaneously be categorized as curio and luxury item.

As this conflation of value categories suggests, the political valence of this episode in the history of desire is complicated. On the one hand, we might note the bibliomania's resemblance to another ostensibly upmarket malady like the gout: Dibdin opened his 1809 *Bibliomania* by stating that since England was a charitable nation of hospitals and asylums, his readers were bound to sympathize with the sufferers of a disease that was "almost uniformly confined to the *male* sex, and among these to people in the higher and middling classes of society."[31] On the other hand, the publicity that the bibliomaniacal spectacle of the Roxburghe auction attracted made it a watershed moment in the *mainstreaming* of collecting, crucial to the transmutation that saw an avocation hitherto confined to the upper echelons of the social order become that peculiar institution of middle-class privacy, the "hobby." (The modern sense of the latter word dates, according to the *Oxford English Dictionary*, to 1816.)[32]

Or consider the public relations that Dibdin undertakes with his statement in *Bibliomania* that the low prices given when "old English black lettered books" were put up for sale in the mid-eighteenth century indicates that "this was not the age of curious research into the productions of our ancestors" (40–41). The statement aligns the early nineteenth-century collector's pursuit of those books—zealous in contrast to that of their ancestors—with those books' reading by the early nineteenth-century scholars, perhaps visitors to the patricians' libraries, who produce "useful and profitable works" as they "trace genius to its source." ("To see how Shakspeare has here and there plucked a flower from some old ballad or popular tale . . . [is a study] which stamps dignity upon our intellectual character," Dibdin states further on in *Bibliomania*, persevering in his vindication of black-letter enthusiasms and stressing the symbiotic relation between the historicist's labor and the collector's craze [76].)[33] In Dibdin's account the bibliomania also borrows luster from the heritage consciousness of the period—hence his reference to "the productions of our ancestors." This period's several reprinting and anthologizing projects, the assembling, for instance, of canon-defining, multivolume "pocket" libraries of Britain's literary worthies, presented themselves as realizing the promise embedded in that first person plural

possessive pronoun. Many of the booksellers conducting those projects explicitly claimed to be using cheap print to ensure that the nation's literary
heritage was better held in common—a claim they tendered at the moment
when, in William St. Clair's terms, "a huge corpus of traditional stories, poems, and songs, which had been appropriated into private ownership in the
early years of printing were returned to unrestricted common public use."
Viewing the bibliomania against this backdrop did not work to the bibliomaniacs' advantage. Instead it tended to clarify how the "book-obsession
impede[d] more than it facilitate[d] the circulation of books."[34] After all,
while contemporaries were heralding the universal diffusion of reading
matter, bibliomaniacs savored their volumes' scarcity.

That misconduct made the rare-book collector a case study, to be ana-
lyzed in pathologizing and mock-pathologizing accounts, which listed his
"symptoms." The passion "for the black letter" regularly receives mention as
one of those symptoms—at the end of Dibdin's 1809 list, as if his intention
had been to save the best for last. But you also have a case of the book madness, these accounts inform you, if you crave books printed on large paper,
or printed on vellum rather than paper, or if your pulse races when you
come across a first edition, or a unique copy (one made so by, for instance,
its binding), or a true copy (the designation that in the looking glass world of
book collecting is used for books disfigured by printers' errors). Among the
disorderly desires of the bibliomania, descriptions of those last two symptoms imply, is the anachronistic desire to have a printed copy that one can
conceptualize as if it were a handwritten original. Another of the symptoms,
a preference for volumes whose pages have never been cut, is redescribed
in telling terms by the satiric author of *Bibliosophia; or, Book Wisdom* (1810),
who drolly out-Dibdins Dibdin in the outrageous claims he makes for the
virtues of book collecting and for the relative inferiority of book reading,
that practice distinguishing the "plodding votary of meaning." *Bibliosophia*
praises the delights of the proprietorship afforded by a book whose pages
have never yet become "as free, common, and accessible . . . as the Coffee-
House volumes of a News-paper."[35] If the nineteenth century's confidence
in books' communicative and socializing functions is propped on a (fundamentally ideological) confidence that book matter is something that can
be firmly subordinated to book meaning, bibliomaniacs made themselves
nuisances by shaking up that trust.

As if to undo the effects of their period's reprint enterprises, rare-book
collectors in adhering to this radical particularism cultivated the link between the prestigious literary *work* and the singular, expensive *copy* housing

it. Accordingly, the drive to situate texts in time—to periodize romance, for instance—that had started to prevail in other sectors of literary culture was, among the collectors, superseded by an insistence on locating books in space.[36] This preoccupation with the particular spaces that literary works inhabited went hand in hand with the collector's preoccupation with the library space he himself inhabited. Or so derisive portraits of collectors suggest, casting them as figures fussing over the menace to the symmetry of their shelves that would be realized should any books actually be removed from them. Dispensing with the premise that books were made for reading apparently made it easier to see books as made for arranging and rearranging, often according to idiosyncratic, self-pleasing principles of ordering.

The creation of the enclosed world of the library could be a way to "proclaim that things thought to be in circulation [had] been privatized, to be made available only by the owner's discretion."[37] At the same time, the suggestion that the collector had thus made an end run around the public contexts of literary history could undermine the social cachet that the patrician library enjoyed as a symbol of cultural continuity and stability. This dimension of book collecting is to the fore in Neil Kenny's and Philip Connell's important discussions of the *bibliomanie* and the bibliomania respectively, each of which analyzes how the collectors made trouble for nationalist notions of the literary heritage. Connell, in particular, outlines how bibliomaniacal self-indulgence threatened the ideological sleight of hand that invited Britons to understand others' private properties as part of the common stock of the national heritage and to understand gentlemanly book collecting as an act of patriotic munificence.[38] Jane Austen's Mr. Darcy, who maintains at Pemberley a family library that is "the work of many generations," and who cannot, he says, imagine the "neglect of a family library in such days as these" exemplifies this account of gentry private ownership as gentry public-mindedness: in this view, accumulation across time can ennoble acquisition and remake it as a stewardship that serves larger national and imperial goals.[39] The year of the Roxburghe auction saw Egerton Brydges opening his new edition of *The Peerage of England* with a preface that identified the libraries built up within the country houses of the nobility as "national treasures, becoming a people who are contending for the empire of the world." Dibdin's description of luminaries from earlier historical periods (Thomas More, for example) as prior victims of the book madness has a similar rhetorical effect. Narrating Earl Spencer and the Marquess of Blandford's contest over the Roxburghe *Decameron* as though he had witnessed a medieval combat ("every sword was put home within its scabbard—and not a piece of steel was seen to move or to glitter save that which each of these champions brandished in his valorous hand"), Dibdin insinuated likewise that nineteenth-century book knights carried on the chivalry of their ancestors, rather than, as one might suppose, revealing themselves as super shoppers.[40]

That kind of promoting of cultural continuity also took its meaning from a contrast with the disruptions of revolution and war wracking the European continent. The tradition-revering aristocrat who turned book collector in this period had embarked, however, on a project defined by its proximity to the disorderly energies of revolutionary politics. The hyperactivity of the antiquarian book market during the romantic period was the result of a radical expansion in the number of objects that could be considered marketable cultural trophies. By certain estimates, some twelve million printed books from the late medieval and early modern periods, long sequestered, cascaded into the market following the revolutionary French state's confiscation of monastic and aristocratic libraries.[41] By the first decade of the nineteenth century, agents acting on behalf of English buyers were traveling around Germany in the wake of the French army of occupation and were profiting from Napoleon's confiscations and the economic distress his occupation caused so as to acquire incunabula on especially easy terms. Rare book collecting intersected with war profiteering.

The close relations between the antiquarian book trade and modern mass politics and a modern speculative economy are halfway acknowledged by the gossip, already mentioned, that portrays Napoleon, the quintessential parvenu, and the English nobleman as treading on each other's heels at the Roxburghe sale. But as Connell notes, many of the period's representations of private libraries tend, on the contrary, to present the collectors' acquisitive energies as working to relegitimize traditional social structures: in their domestic libraries collectors were stewards of "national treasures." Such representations downplayed the stratification of the market for literary history—the market for "the productions of our ancestors." "An idea of the literary heritage [had] emerged that, while incipiently nationalistic in orientation, stressed above all the catholicity of the literary past, its socially cohesive function and, more specifically, its capacity to moderate the divisive social energies of commercial society while at the same time stirring the upper classes to a sense of political and social responsibility." The project of promoting "the participation of distinctively aristocratic cultural practices within a broader emergent idea of the literary past as a collective national heritage" could be dicey. It was contingent on the conviction that within the precincts of his library the book collector was reiterating the nationalist themes of a shared public culture.[42] As we have seen, bibliomaniacs made themselves pests by parading their aristocratic credentials and yet departing from this patrician script. There was a political expediency in commentators' reluctance to distinguish with any rigor between, on the one hand, the texts of literary heritage—in new ways following the late eighteenth-century copyright decisions the stuff of a public domain—and, on the other hand, the books containing and illustrating those texts that were to be found in the private libraries of the aristocracy. In its flamboyance, bibliomaniacal foppishness menaced that discretion.

I have been tacking closely in the last few paragraphs to Connell's account of the hegemonic work performed in the romantic period by the concept of literary heritage—a concept that highlights ownership as the crucial feature of the individual's relationship to literary artifacts and casts those artifacts as the belongings that betoken his belonging, his membership within a national community. This account sounds themes that current discussions of cultural politics have made familiar. It explains the nationalist invention of tradition and forging of canons by referring to imperatives of social control, thereby unmasking the politics hidden within those discursive formations. It ascribes to the bibliomaniac, accordingly, a kind of unwitting resistance to the mystified ideological solutions that Britain developed to manage its real social divisions. But if the book madness also raises for romantic-period writers and readers enticing questions about what it means to get intimate with that impersonal thing called a "national heritage," then to nuance our paradigms for how cultural institutions hit home seems advisable. Doing justice to the social meanings of the bibliomania requires attending to the subjective experiences underpinning such meanings and so requires an account of the relation between the self and institutions that instances not just the coercive power structures of the Foucauldian prison, but also those power structures that reside in the family and in sexuality.[43] The rare-book collectors' contemporaries grasped that the tale of possession enacted by those who had caught the bibliomaniacal bug was a story stranger and richer than the history of ownership and capital. They understood that collecting as an amorous activity, as well as a statement about class entitlements and a prop to an ideological ruse.[44] Accordingly, castigation can sometimes be hard to distinguish from indulgence in this period's discussions of the bibliomania. For one thing, those diagnosing the disorder often detect its symptoms in themselves: "Ev'n I, debarr'd of ease, and studious hours, / Confess . . . [the tyrant passion's] lurking powers," writes Ferriar in the first version of *Bibliomania*; he equips this couplet with a footnote describing the treasures "of uncommon rarity" he calls his own.[45]

A reading of the bibliomania for what it tells us about how the nineteenth century managed the relations between economic and cultural capital should not proceed at the expense of acknowledging it as an episode in which *love* went public. Or as a phenomenon that in some contemporaries' descriptions is defined by instances of book *kissing*. I know at least of two stories suggesting that particular definition, each originating from the pen of Leigh Hunt, who in one essay from 1828 describes Thomas Frognall Dibdin "leaping up to kiss and embrace every enticing edition in vellum and every sweetly-toned, mellow-toned, yellow morocco binding" and who in another essay, from 1823, describes having seen his friend the essayist Charles Lamb similarly in flagrante delicto and giving "a kiss to an old folio," which proved, on Hunt's further inspection, to be a copy of Chapman's Homer.[46]

Writing the history of the notion of literary heritage in conjunction with the history of intimacy seems the way to go, as well, if we are to assess what Hunt was doing when, as mentioned earlier, he portrayed himself as "wedded to books." In the 1820 essay on that topic, which appeared in his periodical the *Indicator*, Hunt not only declares his fidelity to his library, the book treasures that in his writings he often describes as liking to have arrayed around him. He also indulges the fantasy that the books in their turn might, forsaking all others, cleave to him alone. He longs for "the usual exclusive privileges of marriage":[47] "Now what a happy thing ought it not to be to have exclusive possession of a book,—one's Shakspeare, for instance. . . . Think of the pleasure not only of being with it in general, of having by far the greater part of it's [*sic*] company, but of having it entirely to one's self; of always saying internally, 'It is my property;' of seeing it well-dressed in 'black or red,' purely to please one's own eyes; of wondering how any fellow could be so impudent as to propose borrowing it for an evening."

Elsewhere Hunt is on record mocking the denizens of the grand private libraries. The mockery is to be expected from someone who, as journalist and onetime founder of a penny magazine, occupied a sector of the book market at a considerable distance from the rare-book trade, and someone who, as an author by profession, had reason to promote the insides of books at the expense of their outsides. But the possessive love playfully enacted in "Men Wedded to Books" suggests, on the contrary, Hunt's attraction to the bibliomaniac's ways of being private with the literary stuff of the public domain. His essay models how the collector's cult of the rare-book collectible could be a useful imaginative resource for a devotee stymied by the ambiguities concealed by that offhand phrase "one's Shakespeare"—useful for a "one" who was conscious of how the expansion of the print market, facilitating the manufacture of the works of Shakespeare in large print runs, made it at once easier for a nineteenth-century individual to have a Shakespearean library and more difficult to claim it as one's *own*. The perplexities I have just outlined are in fact resolved within the fantasy that Hunt's essay works out, and by egregiously bibliotaphic means: "If we could burn all the other copies of our originals . . . this system would be worth thinking of. . . . Nobody could then touch our Shakspeare, our Spenser, our Chaucer, our Greek and Italian writers."[48] (The enlargement of the reading public had multiplied the reprints of "good old books . . . accessible to the purses of poor people," Charles Lamb, Hunt's book-kissing friend, observed in 1825 in an essay in counterpoint with Hunt's: nowadays "we are all readers.")[49] In "Men Wedded to Books" Hunt even ratifies the material-mindedness of the book mad with his reference to the choice of binding, the dress, "black or red," selected to adorn the body of one's book beloved.

Several Hunt essays are about the mundane pleasures in which the writer and his audience are sure to participate equally ("sleep," "the sight of shops," "cream," and "mists and fogs" are characteristic topics). But in "Men Wedded to Books" Hunt complicates this commitment to what is as common as air. On the one hand, he proceeds as though it were a given that his readers know just how he feels and have likewise longed for exclusive possession of their reading matter and so writes about "one" and "our," not "I" and "my." But those pronouns are ironized, since Hunt at the same time is articulating shared pleasures against the solitary, snug pleasure of the collector—a collector whose books, for all that Hunt's essay says about their contents, might as well be made up of blank pages but which serve nicely even so to mark off a personal space from which others may be excluded.[50] This is only one of a series of moments in which the encounter of shabby-genteel essayist and affluent bibliomaniac seems to make them each other's mirror images.

The next section will explore those encounters further with a view to reconstructing how through their commentary on, and sometimes their mimicry of, the proprietary pleasures associated with the bibliomaniac's fine library the essayists pondered just what kinds of private gratifications might be afforded them by the literary tradition, that "national library" for which that space stood. In the *Literary Examiner* essay "My Books" (1823), Hunt fretted aloud about the "jarrings between privacy and publicity" that he felt were an obstacle to his getting any work done in the British Museum's reading room.[51] Lifted out of that context, the phrase aptly designates the challenges to be navigated at a historical moment that associated literature both with intimacy and subjectivity and with an impersonal print culture of reproduction and exchange.

"THE TITLE TO PROPERTY IN A BOOK": INTIMATE POSSESSION AND THE ROMANTIC ESSAYISTS

Of course, Hunt and his fellow essayists are less well known for their biblio-maniacal commentary than for the manner in which in their writings they traded in the lives of, and on their loves of, the Lake poets, their slightly older acquaintance. Periodical essays such as Lamb's "Christ's Hospital Five-and-Thirty Years Ago" (published in the *London Magazine* in 1820) or William Hazlitt's "My First Acquaintance with Poets" (published in Leigh Hunt's journal the *Liberal* in 1823) or Thomas De Quincey's "Reminiscences of the Lakes and Lake Poets" (published in *Tait's Magazine* from 1838 to 1840) are often mined for details about how Wordsworth and Coleridge appeared to the friends who were their first devoted readers. They have been central to the presentation of the essayists as satellites, even parasites, of major authors. (Tellingly, Hunt's first effort at book-length autobiography ended up, on his publisher's advice, appearing under the title *Lord Byron and Some of His Contemporaries* [1828].) For their part these writers often presented themselves—De Quincey, in particular, with a zeal that I'll be examining in this book's final chapter—as the translators and go-betweens who mediated between abstruse genius and a popular readership, electing to ally themselves accordingly with the history of literary appreciation more than with the history of literature. Those commitments, their allegiance to the magazine medium in which they nearly always worked, as well as Hazlitt's, Lamb's, and Hunt's forays into print as anthologists, gave this group a significant stake in contemporary campaigns to enlarge the reading public and a grudging appreciation of the forces of circulation and systematization linked to the printing press.

The history of the essay genre, the form by which this group made their names, runs in parallel with that history of literary appreciation. The essay tends to be organized by its writers' responses to the writings of others. In the early modern period it begins as the genre of text digestion. The familiar essay in the romantic period is self-consciously poised between the authoring of a would-be autobiographer and the assimilative reading of someone who is unabashed about disclosing how the self, chameleon-like, takes its color from its current reading matter. Thus in a *London Magazine* piece that promises in its title to be the vehicle for the author's "Detached Thoughts on Books and Reading," Lamb ends his first paragraph with the claim "books think for me."[52] The subject doing the thinking promptly reverses roles with what was supposed to have been the object of his thought. The poetic quotations and long verse extracts interlarded within their prose, collected as if they were so many souvenirs of what Lamb in "Detached Thoughts" calls their sojourns "in other men's minds," likewise suggest a style of authoring that is pegged to a renunciation of expressivism and an embrace of secondaricity (2:172). The essayist merges "authorial functions . . . with readerly operations."[53] Lamb is thus happy to admit this love of reading, even "at the hazard of losing some credit" where his "originality" is concerned ("Detached Thoughts," 2:172).

The minor romantics' performance of self-marginalization has been productively investigated by present-day scholars, who have shown how, while helping to bestow canonical status on others, the essayists also managed cagily to present their own writings as the "cabinet of minor pieces" that could be admired as a fitting adjunct to English literature's "great national gallery."[54] But, as the previous section began to suggest, the essayists' canon-making and canon-loving enterprises were enriched and complicated in several ways by their engagements with the stuff of the bibliomania. In addition to collecting and recirculating the lives and writings of their poetical contemporaries, they sometimes presented themselves as collectors of rare and recondite pieces of curious learning retrieved from the antiquarian archive. Sometimes, in their praise of *old* books, they berated the reading public for their enthusiasm for books newly published, flagging their own membership in the group of "lovers of old English literature" who in the early nineteenth century were addressed directly by journals like the *Retrospective Review* or Egerton Brydges's *Censura Literaria*. (With startling abruptness, Hazlitt begins one essay with a declaration of antipathy: "I hate to read new books.")[55] Like a bibliomaniac smitten by the black letter, the essayists readily exploited how the book, in addition to being the instrument of public enlightenment that connected its users with their contemporaries, could also sponsor ways of being out of sync.

The essayists also had a vexed relationship to the idealism of the romantic poetry that they helped to canonize. By thematizing in contradistinction to the poets the material dimensions of books and reading, by attending to texts' incarnation, they contrived to allegorize their own position in the literary system. As Margaret Russett has noted, John Guillory's premise in *Cultural Capital* that "canonicity is not a property of the work but of its transmission" has tremendous relevance for the minor romantics, who volunteered themselves as the vehicles that would convey the tenor of high romantic argument and circulate it as cultural capital. But this group recognized that those acts of transmission that constituted their vocation inevitably "produce[d] effects in excess of sheer replication": "this material excess *of the signifier*" engenders, Russett proposes, the space in which the essayists pursue their careers.[56] Russett's discussion suggests why the essayists might have been especially attuned to the physical dimensions of the book—the material vehicle for an immaterial tenor, an ideal form that exists over and above even the words of which it is composed. But complementing this argument about the essayists' readiness to allow literariness to be effaced by the volumes that lodge it, one might also note that they were likewise especially attuned to the affective investments solicited by the book object, the possessibility and kissability that are a book's traits, but not really a text's.

The shuttling between human friends and book friends, and between books and authors, in Leigh Hunt's essay "My Books" provides a signal instance. Here is its opening sentence: "Sitting, last winter, among my books, and walled round with all the comfort and protection which they and my fire-side could afford me . . . I began to consider how I loved the authors of those books: how I loved them, too, not only for the imaginative pleasures they afford me, but for their making me love the very books themselves, and delight to be in contact with them" (136). Having outlined this romantic cycle, in which the companionship of books kindles author love, which in turn takes the lover back to the sensual pleasures afforded by books' physical existence, Hunt moves on first to mapping his authors' locations on his shelves and then muses next on "how natural it was in C.L. [Charles Lamb] to give a kiss to an old folio, as I once saw him do to *Chapman's Homer*" (136).[57] If in my initial mention of book kissing, it seemed proper to differentiate the kiss bestowed out of love of an author from the bibliomaniacal kiss that Dibdin bestowed in homage to fine bindings, this second look at Hunt's reference to Lamb's kiss should complicate matters. Even the fact that Hunt prioritizes that detail about the bibliographical format of Lamb's beloved book—it is an old folio before it is revealed as Chapman's Homer— seems to call the book/author, collector/reader opposition into question. It suggests Hunt's dissent from that logic that would correlate an investment in the material book with a disavowal of its contents.

Others joined him in that dissent. Lamb himself, who appeared in the *London Magazine* in pseudonymous guise as Elia, permitted his readers to overhear him apostrophizing his books in a tender moment—"you, my midnight darlings, my Folios!"[58] Readers may have felt unsure of who exactly Elia, that inveterately autobiographical yet mercurial nonentity, was, but his out-of-the-way antiquarian books—the folio of the drama of Beaumont and Fletcher, whose acquisition is described in "Old China," for instance, or the "jewel" of "Detached Thoughts," Lamb's "Life of the Duke of Newcastle, by His Duchess" (2:174)—possessed a contrasting solidity. As others have noted, such essays rebel against the author function that regulates so much writing within the high-romantic canon.[59] The essayists consistently hide their authorship behind pseudonyms ("the English Opium Eater," "Elia"), and, in Lamb's case, even help circulate premature reports of their authorial eidolon's death. But they do seem to like displaying authors' *stuff.* Thus Elia beckons readers into his (or Lamb's) "little back study in Bloomsbury": to get personal he draws us into a private interior and shows off the arrangement of his shelves.[60] The essayists inventory books, bookcases and other library accouterments, and the clutter they thus evoke is composed of things designed to arouse in men of letters the sensation that Lamb/Elia calls a "tickling sense of property" ("Detached Thoughts," 2:173). They restage the encounters in which they fell in love with literature by remembering the preciousness of particular books' outsides rather than the preciousness of books' insides: the "coarse leathern cover" of the work of Jean-Jacques Rousseau that the young William Hazlitt picked up at a bookstall; or the type, ornaments, wrappers, and frontispieces of the edition of the British poets that Hunt came to possess as a schoolboy.[61] The anecdotes draw them into a strange affinity with the collector of first editions, who reasserts the link between the prestigious work and the singular, expensive copy, in defiance of "a post Gutenberg-consensus [that] makes differently priced editions of a text functionally equivalent."[62] Each group has realized that the "choice of how to bind a book is what binds it to us, the sign of appropriation."[63]

Russett presents the minor romantics as figures who tell us something about the transferential nature of *reading.* Thanks to his starstruck pursuit of a personal relationship with Wordsworth, De Quincey in particular stands for Russett as an object lesson in the failure to respect the boundaries between "representations and real persons, . . . aesthetic response and empirical desire."[64] Personifying the writers they know mainly in textualized form, they infuse the print world with a sense of human presence. But, like other book collectors, they combine that personification with an act of objectification that turns the documents of authorial self-expression into so many collectible objects. This bookishness made their relationship with the world of the thoroughbred Roxburgher book knights edgy, a matter of both affinity and antagonism.

This edginess is apparent in an article in the *London Magazine* of January 1825 that marked the pseudonymous debut of a contributor named "Reverend Tom. Foggy Dribble," and which was entitled "The Street Companion; or the Young Man's Guide and the Old Man's Comfort in the Choice of Shoes." Dribble asserts that he has turned author out of his sense of selfless public spirit, but we need only the opening sentence to conclude that we are reading not a vade mecum but instead the intimate confessions of a fetishist: "From the beginning to the end of this paper, I have never lost sight of what I consider to be the most material object to be gained from a publication of this nature; namely, the imparting a moral feeling to the gratification arising from a taste in leather." "The Street Companion" is, of course, parody—not the record of real research into footwear. (That said, I cannot resist remarking that Dribble's expertise seems to be the feet of actresses, "the thousand little niceties" distinguishing the feet of the ladies who presently tread the stage.)[65] Participating in the identity theft that was commonplace in the roguish magazine culture of the 1820s and appropriating the style and preoccupations of our old friend Thomas Frognall Dibdin, De Quincey, the actual author behind the eidolon, was targeting here Dibdin's latest PR effort for the bibliomania, his *The Library Companion: The Young Man's Guide and the Old Man's Comfort in the Choice of a Library*. This was an elephantine example (at 912 pages) of a genre existing in England since the seventeenth century, the guide to forming a gentleman's library that listed the best authors in the best editions. In Dibdin's version the list is punctuated by his assiduous flattery of his rare-book-owning and rare-book-dealing acquaintance. Dibdin's premise is that through acts of private consumption, his young man and old man might fulfill their patriotic duty and advance the project of national definition. Their book collecting, especially under his guidance, will lead them away from "the mischievous application of superfluous wealth." "From the beginning to end, I have never lost sight of what I considered to be the MOST MATERIAL OBJECT to be gained from a publication of this nature; namely, the imparting of a *moral feeling* to the gratification of a *literary taste*."[66]

A reference to the late king's choice of a library and His Majesty's not inconsiderable skills as a "bibliographer" begins *The Library Companion*. (The previous year that book collection had been given to the nation by George

IV, largesse that expanded the print holdings of the British Museum.) After going on to discuss bibles, histories, biographies, travels, poetry (in ancient and modern languages), and novels, Dibdin concludes with the drama and Shakespeare, in a chapter that appraises the diverse, modern editions of the Bard and also, in a rhapsodic footnote that is eight pages long, *classes*, as he puts it, the thirty First Folios belonging to notable collectors. Earl Spencer's Shakespeare Folio, we learn, is merely of the second class: "There are . . . in the centre of some of the pages a few greasy-looking spots, which might have originally received the 'flakes of pie-crust' in the servants' hall."[67] Viewed otherwise, though, that copy of the First Folio is not defective but rendered all the more auratic—distanced all the more from the mass reproducibility that ordinarily defines the book—by those stains from the pies of yesteryear. This exercise in descriptive bibliography is vintage Dibdin in its Tory conviction that class divides were bridged within the precincts of the aristocracy's ancestral halls and that, even beyond those charmed locales, literature could be the medium for that reconciliation.

De Quincey's parody, "The Street Companion," which in a compressed space mimics quite well how Dibdin's prose can bewilder his readers and set them a-wandering in a mist of black letter, dates, title pages, and colophons, also underlines the elitist, possessive politics at work in passages like the one about the flakes of piecrust. Dibdin's close-up look at the matter of the page renders Shakespeare a family heirloom as it literalizes the period's metaphors of literature as national legacy. Mischievously, De Quincey both plays up that materialism, converting leather binding into leather shoes, and reverses that politics, replacing the gentleman's private library with the pedestrian's public street (the *Street* and not the *Library Companion*). In this manner, he counters Dribble's fetishism, his overvaluing of leather, with a value scheme that sets appreciation at odds with acquisition and possession.

That value scheme is, of course, a setup that, in conjunction with the associated opposition between the ideal and the material, is adopted in much romantic writing on the protocols of aesthetic reception. Think of the essays in which Hazlitt imagines how the student of art can in imagination furnish "the chambers of the mind" with the paintings that he has seen adorning the walls of the country gentleman's seat and how he can also—as Hazlitt puts it in a description of this internalization that uses a literary quotation (from *Hamlet*) to transmute art into literature—bind them "up 'within the book and volume of the brain.'"[68] Equipped with this capacity, Hazlitt's art lover is "richer than the possessor." (Mary Favret notes how these essays on painting define the art lover "as both interloper and interior decorator, furnishing a country estate within his brain and imagining the regions of mind as a country estate.")[69] Or think, to reference a slightly different case, of the axiom that Lamb's Elia cites in "The Two Races of Men"—borrowing it from Samuel Taylor Coleridge, who has borrowed Lamb's books—which holds that "the title to property in a book . . . is in exact ratio to the claimant's powers of understanding or appreciating the same."[70]

This idealist account of aesthetic experience can easily be used to point out a political moral about the intellectual bankruptcy of the nation's property owners, or so it seems when locales other than Lamb's little backroom study are at issue. In "My Books," Hunt declares, to just this effect, that a "grand private library . . . never looks to me like a real place of books" (138): the remark packs that much more punch when we recall how, with the help of figures like Dibdin, descriptions of the libraries of certain showplace homes were widely disseminated during this period and helped make literary reception appear an aristocratic prerogative. When, in his *Autobiography* (1850), Hunt recalls his impressions of the Roxburghe sale, which he, like De Quincey, dropped in on during the late spring of 1812, he reconfirms the spirit of this declaration as he sides with the loser in the famous bidding war for the "unique copy of Boccaccio." Of the two rivals, Earl Spencer (the noble owner of the Shakespeare Folio with pastry flakes) represents for Hunt the "genuine lover of books"; Hunt imagines him returning home from the auction room and "reconcil[ing] himself to his defeat by reading the work in a cheaper edition."[71]

Dissociating texts from the books giving them material form can work to two diverging ends, however: either to elevate reception over mere possession, or to conceptualize a relationship to texts that might be *more* proprietary, because more private, more personal. Marking this distinction makes it easier to acknowledge the frequency with which, as we have seen, that opposition between accumulating books and reading literature comes under pressure within the romantic essay. Collecting (of one sort) can also counter collecting (of another). Doing something more complex than simply castigating the book collector's possessiveness, Hunt's "My Books" in fact goes on to cast the great private library as a site of *imperfect* possession. When thinking of one of those libraries, Hunt finds, he cannot think of the books "and the proprietor together." Hunt is disappointed accordingly with the latest thing in library furniture, the round library table: "Instead of bringing the books around you, they all seem turning another way, and eluding your hands" (138). At Earl Spencer's country seat at Althorp, the books were dispersed among an entire series of libraries that he had had constructed—the Billiard

Library, the Marlborough Library, the Gothic Library, and so on, suggesting that the earl might well have sympathized with that sense of books' evasiveness evoked by Hunt's remark on library furniture. The book collection of Richard Heber—dedicatee of the two 1809 books on *Bibliomania*, the individual who assembled one of the largest collections of early English poetry and drama ever in private hands—was dispersed across eight houses located in England and on the Continent. (It was hardly in his hands at all.) Hence, perhaps, the reference in the Reverend Dribble's "The Street Companion," to how Heber "has a great many old S H O E S ... so many ... that he does not know where to find them when he wants them": a claim located, aptly, in Dribble's footnotes. Such were the embarrassments of riches.[72]

Detectable in the contrast that "My Books" draws between the grand private library and the "small snug place" that Hunt favors himself are traces of a familiar middle-class critique of the faulty home life of the aristocracy (137). Hunt doesn't replace the house with the street as De Quincey does. Instead he implies that in this case, wanting in provisions for inwardness, the house is not a home.[73] The implication is that bookish attachments like his own flourish only when sheltered in small-scale domestic spaces. This is a premise the early nineteenth century British novel made awfully familiar, of course, although fiction makes this point primarily about the emotional unions involving husbands and wives and parents and children and only secondarily about emotional unions involving readers and books.

And yet, as I have been implying, prosecuting this critique of the aristocratic book collector might for Hunt, as for his fellow essayists, serve as a way of deflecting a consideration of how much he and the object of his criticism share. Ina Ferris notes that while early nineteenth-century literary culture placed much emphasis on how "the art of printing" had produced the "flat and open mental spaces through which knowledge could be readily transmitted and reproduced across cultures and periods," that emphasis was countered by an "insistence on worldly locations and pleasures that resisted ideals of transfer and reproduction."[74] The latter insistence crossed class lines in a manner that made the relationship between early nineteenth-century men of letters and the celebrity collectors a volatile amalgam of criticism and identification. When scholars propose that the publicity around the bibliomania shaped the terms in which the formerly elite activity of collecting went mainstream, they often turn to Hunt to make their case. His *Autobiography* shows him contracting the collecting bug as a schoolboy, when he began buying the sixpenny numbers that composed, serially, the "pocket library" edition of the British poets newly issued by the publisher

Charles Cooke. One of Cooke's innovative marketing devices was to print the lists of all the other poets included in this reprint series on the wrappers of each number: the lists nourished visions of future purchases and fueled the repetitive, compulsive, completist desires of the collector.[75] Hunt, who by his own admission bought "over and over again," responded with gusto to the promise that the pleasures of acquisition could be reactivated and reactivated until one got the complete set. He seems as well to have put his own customizing spin on the arrangement—as the *Autobiography* recalls, he "used to get up select sets" of the books, repeatedly splintering the library as manufactured by Cooke so as to remake it anew.[76] But Cooke's edition of *Select British Poets* likely played an additional role in Hunt's affective life. These volumes of English poetry on which Hunt doted figure in his autobiography because they helped to make him his individual, special self, and yet the series in which they appeared is metonymic of the multiple publishing enterprises of collecting and reprinting that during this era confirmed the book's "status as a public good available for concurrent and not exclusive consumption." Thanks to such reprint series, Hunt and his fellow romantic essayists belonged to the first generation who confronted a ready-made canon. They found the classic texts of the literary tradition already collected *for* them, as already recommended reading. This experience is one impetus for their fascination with, and occasional participation in, those phenomena that developed in dialectical relation to the era's multiple modes of "popular re-circulation": the practices of collecting that, as Ina Ferris puts it, "strip the book of its publicness and confirm it as a purely private and material commodity."[77]

"Books thrive on reproduction," John Plotz writes in an account of the contradictions inherent to the very idea of the book collection. Books' replicability and fungibility hold out the "promise that others, spread out geographically and temporally, have experienced, are experiencing, or will experience exactly what you experience."[78] Viewable from one angle as a promise, that shared affect, however, from another angle can appear as an infringement on one's individuality, an infringement discomfiting in the early nineteenth century when book readers were both increasingly responsive to the call for admiration extended by the national literature that they saw as their birthright and at the same time increasingly determined, as the autobiographical writings of the romantic essayists suggest, to see their love of literature as an opportunity for self-expression.

To apprehend how the bibliomania might have helped to strip the book of its publicness, and helped to suggest by extension that English literature might be made one's own, let's return to the statements about the social meanings of literacy embedded in the era's much-disseminated images of gentlemen's libraries. The reader who is the imagined denizen of the spaces conjured up in accounts of noblemen's country seats or books of designs for library furniture, all but crowded out by shelving, globes, busts and figurines of Shakespeare and Milton, has agreed to his conscription into a historical process that is endlessly reiterative.[79] Choosing again what has already been chosen for him, this library denizen honors the works that his ancestors honored. ("I have seen so much of Shakspeare ... in frontis-pieces and on mantle-pieces, that I am quite tired of the everlasting repeti-tion," Lamb is reported to have said.)[80] Yet the period's discussions of how to live with books also negotiated for the gentleman reader spaces, literal and conceptual, in which he might play truant to his responsibilities to tradi-tion. Public men might also have their "cabinet" or "closet libraries": terms that the period used to designate books of less weight, morally and materi-ally, than the well-ordered collections of folios and quartos that were front and center in accounts of sober-sided, gentlemanly literacy. Even the late king, or so we learn when Dibdin opens *The Library Companion*, recognized the need for off-hours reading. Dibdin patriotically reproduces, "from the original document in George III's own handwriting," the book list that the monarch used to assemble what he called "a closet library for a watering place."[81] The seal of royal approval that legitimates this partitioning of the book collection might also be seen as legitimizing a new topography of the reading mind. The category of the cabinet library registers a cultural agree-ment that the interior spaces of private houses needed supplementing, that to ensure the production of an inward-looking subject, extra provision for snugness and the erotics of exclusive possession was required. (In this us-age "cabinet" retains the associations it had in the seventeenth century with arcane and secret treasures.)[82] Consideration of this arrangement leads to another way to identify the sources of the allure, as well as the problem, of the bibliomania. We might say that the bibliomaniac takes the license for self-indulgence and self-stylization associated with the cabinet and closet and remobilizes it within the libraries that supplied patrician public spirit with its notional staging grounds. He scrambles the codes of the cabinet library and the library that is a public stage, using the materials of the print heritage to constitute a special selfhood.

When the romantic essayists played at being bibliomaniacs on a bud-get, they registered this revision of the patrician script for library culture. In those performances, they come across as particularly attuned to how the bibliomania had made the formation of a library, an activity supposed to mark the gentleman, into a site for the kind of unruly libidinal energy at stake in a "craze." The essayists in these performances also bracket the antinomies between collecting and reading, possession and just appreciation on which they elsewhere insist. Their mimicry is accordingly double-edged—adopted to call into question the gentleman's social entitlements, and adopted to mark off the distinctiveness of their own styles of bookish consumption and literary love. The Elia essays and memoirs by his contemporaries sometimes show us Lamb surpassing the bibliomaniacs in their famed capacity for being finicky about the symmetries of their shelves or agitated about the books that went astray and spoiled their sets.[83] Henry Crabb Robinson, for example, marveled in his journal over the fervor Lamb displayed in "banish[ing]" four quarto volumes of Burke from his collection. Explaining why, as Lamb's neighbor, he would sometimes catch sight of books that had been sent sailing over the trees growing in their shared garden, Thomas Westwood suggested that those rejected volumes were "unharmonious on [Lamb's] shelves" and "clashed, both in outer *and* inner entity" with the books Lamb deemed his "household gods."[84] Such high dramas of deaccessioning evidence, campily, the collector's quest for a perfect hermeticism. Lamb's essays often enact the textual equivalent of that deaccessioning. No sooner in "Detached Thoughts on Books and Reading" does Elia declare that as a reader he has no "repugnances," than he begins to parade them, first cataloguing the variety of "*biblia a-biblia*," book impostors "*which are no books*," and then denouncing sweepingly, in the conclusion to his list of antipathies, "all those volumes which 'no gentleman's library should be without' " (2:172).[85] Dibdin's priggish survey of model book collections is matched and inverted by this fastidiousness. A similar inversion—a reverse snobbery—helps animate Elia's vaunted love of the city streets' secondhand bookstalls, locales for bibliographical discovery where the literary heritage has been splintered and reordered by chance.[86]

The destination for the discoveries made there, Elia's little backroom study, is presented in these sources in terms suggesting that Lamb has had his eye on the library shrines that were the showpieces of the elite's country houses. In a still more incongruous way, that comparison with the great patrician library also holds for Leigh Hunt's redecorated rooms at the Surrey jail, which he and his wife, Marianne, adorned with several bookcases full of books, busts of the poets, a portrait of Milton, as well as such nonbookish home comforts as rose trellis wallpaper and a pianoforte.[87] In these two sites, confinement—whether the effect of limited means or, as for Hunt in particular, the effect of the prison sentence for libel he served between 1813 and 1815—becomes a version of the provisions for interiority that are furnished to the gentleman by his cabinet library.

The performance of middle-class private life that Hunt staged from within his prison home base operated as a political provocation, of course. Its impact was in part a function of its difference from the libertinism and domestic disorder that appeared endemic among the upper classes, the household of the prince regent most notoriously. But even after he regained his liberty, Hunt persisted in thinking of walls and books together. As we have seen, "Men Wedded to Books" imagines in *reductio ad absurdum* style the consequences that would follow should one be able to make a seraglio of his library and keep the poets to himself, narrating how the insider in such a situation might imagine the feelings of the outsider: "People might say, 'Those are the walls of the library!' and 'sigh and look, and sigh again' but they should never get in."[88] "My Books" invites Hunt's readers to picture him as literally walled in by his books in his study, in an arrangement— treated less whimsically and more tenderly than the style of space management envisioned in "Wedded"—that makes the components of his collection both the containers and the contained: "I looked sideways at my Spenser, my Theocritus . . . then above them at my Italian poets; then behind me at my Dryden and Pope, my romances, and my Boccaccio, then on my left side at my Chaucer" (136).

When in a later passage of "My Books" Hunt laments "the jarrings between privacy and publicity" that must be endured by individuals who aim to do their reading in the British Museum he appears to have a number of impediments in mind: the "wire-safed," "Museum order" of the books housed there, and the distance between that order and his individual, idiosyncratic principles of arrangement; his worries about appearing bothersome to the formidable-sounding reading-room attendants, who, as others testified, might decide to eject him from the premises. Hunt also gestures in this discussion toward the difference between the British Museum and its counterpart institution in Paris. "They say they manage this better in France" (138), he observes, both citing the opening of Laurence Sterne's *A Sentimental Journey* and acknowledging that the Bibliothèque du roi was the superior institution, distinguished by larger holdings and by its emphasis on public access and public instruction. Its collections had been declared the property of the people when France became a republic in 1792 and, even after the restoration of the Bourbon monarchy, when it ceased to be called the Bibliothèque nationale, it continued to be defined by policies of open access distinct from those enforced at the British Museum. (The letter writer to the *Times* in October 1823 who complained of how the reading rooms at the museum were "hermetically sealed against the majority of those who wish to frequent them" suggests the policies enforced there.)[89] Kristian Jensen has noted that the creation of the Bibliothèque nationale in France effectively altered the meanings of the grand private collections of Britain, before then relatively unproblematic. The competition in the antiquarian book market between its librarians and grandee British collectors like Earl Spencer called into question the relevance of the old view—which had long lent luster to those patrician collections—that "enlightenment was a private rather than a public matter."[90] Even so, as we have seen, the Enlightenment ideal of the universal diffusion of knowledge was itself contested in this era by a willingness to defer to modes of library use that centered on and inspired *local* attachments and that anchored a sense of the singularity and interiority of the reader.

Hunt's association of books and walls and literary affections and snug places at the start of "My Books" makes his comment later on about the jarrings between privacy and publicity experienced in public reading rooms teasingly equivocal. Is the problem with the British Museum as a site for literary appreciation that it is insufficiently public—insufficiently French? Or is the problem that it isn't snug, that it's insufficiently private? Should he actually visit the Bibliothèque, Hunt says, "I should feel as if I were doing nothing but interchanging amenities with polite writers" (138), a comment trading on a very English perception of the French as living too much in public and lacking the capacity for homey, intimate feeling. Hunt's belief that home is the proper scene of reading links him to the John Bull-ish reviewer for the *Edinburgh Review* who in 1820 dismissed the glories of the Bibliothèque, disagreeing accordingly with the book he was reviewing, which had touted them. This reviewer proposed that the true measure of the state of knowledge in a nation was the number of private book collections in the nation's homes, and contended accordingly that Britain, the inferiority of the British Museum notwithstanding, would forever take the lead over France in intellectual matters: "The dearth [in France] of private libraries . . . where men are domesticated with books, and live amidst them, as in their families, cannot be compensated, in practical advantages, by any number of public repositories."[91]

That domestication with books is something that Hunt and his contemporaries sometimes discredited. They did so on some occasions by underlining how such descriptions and the associated concepts of literature as private property and object of gentry stewardship naturalized inequitable

FIGURE 3.1 George Cruikshank, "The Pursuit of Letters," from his *Scraps and Sketches* (1828–32). Cruikshank responds to the Infant Schools movement and the enlargement of the reading public it catalyzed, with this portrait of the new readers of his day—confined to the go-carts used then by toddlers not yet able to walk, but nonetheless managing to overtake the "Letters" they are pursuing. In the background, "Literature," also pursued, exclaims "we shall be run down—be devoured!—there won't be a bit of us left for succeeding ages! the dogs nowadays have such large Capacities!" Photograph: Courtesy of the National Library of Scotland (NLS Ref. 6.759).

class relations; on other occasions they did so writing up fantasies in which they took that domestication in perverse directions or took it too literally— overdoing, as in "Men Wedded to Books," the snuggling up that the trope of domesticity seemed to license. Nonetheless that domestication—such is the charisma of the concept of home—was also a condition to which they sometimes aspired. Few of the era's advocates for literary appreciation were wholly exempt from misgivings about how that appreciation had become the fashion, or about how that fashion and new projects of mass education had in tandem, as Lamb put it, created a new race of "readers against the grain," who were "pant[ing] and toil[ing] with all their might" after the writing of the age (fig 3.1).[92] Despite what in its panic it says about itself when George Cruikshank's cartoon gives it a voice, literature can be recirculated and recirculated without being exhausted by that consumption. But the irrational fear that it could be wholly "devoured" is one reason why the personalizing of literature in this period takes shape as a retreat to the home library, or the out-of-the-way antiquarian archive, or the romantic interior combining features of both sites—why readers wished, if only in imagination, to place literature at a safe distance from the vicissitudes of the public domain.

On June 17, 1812, Hunt and Thomas Frognall Dibdin crossed paths at the Roxburghe sale when each showed up in his grace's late residence on St. James's Square to witness the bidding war over the unique copy of the *Decameron*. The year 1832 saw the pair renew that proximity, in their writings if not physically. In that year of parliamentary reform the Tory Dibdin and the liberal Hunt alike went public with works that seemed to yoke the arrival of modern representative government—an achievement often credited to the power of the press and the expansion of the reading public—with the passing of an era of bookishness.

In *Bibliophobia*, subtitled *Remarks on the Present Languid and Depressed State of Literature and the Book Trade*, Dibdin observes melancholically the slackening of the passions of formerly eager book champions and the disappointing prices recorded at recent auctions.[93] "Books were only the shadow of what they were," his protagonist concludes when he returns from an excursion to London sale rooms and bookshops: "No money was stirring. . . . The Reform had frightened every one away." Dibdin's speculation that "perhaps booksellers, like the Romans, have had their day," sounds to us a familiar note, accustomed as we now are to narratives about the imminent extinction of booksellers, books, readers, and literature—though it has done strange things to my usual scheme for periodizing the end-times to hear that note transmitted to me from 1832 (and in a book).

In his essay from 1832, titled "Men and Books," Hunt sounds a surprisingly similar note as he both takes the measure of a new political modernity and self-consciously rehearses over again the examples of book love that his writings of the previous decade had assembled. Hunt casts himself and his readership as a disappearing race of old "book-men, who love the bodies as well as souls of our books": like Walter Benjamin when he writes about his own collection of first edition books a century later, Hunt is convinced that he belongs to a type for whom (as Benjamin put it) "time is running out." And like Benjamin, leery despite his Marxism about the supplanting of private collections by public ones, Hunt is unsure whether the change in the collector's standing really amounts to progress. Though Hunt, unlike Dibdin, does not identify new forms of representative government as contributing in 1832 to books' loss of their former lovability, he does express trepidation about the pressure exerted by the new democratic ethos of public-mindedness, which already, he states, is breaking up "narrownesses of all sorts, even of the better kind." In the future, he predicts wistfully, modern collegians "will hardly have the *snugness* of the old times."[94]

CODA: FEMALE COLLECTORS AND THEIR
PAPER CABINETS

When Hunt invites his readers to join him in his "small snug place," the personal home he has made among and with books, or when Hazlitt declares books "the most heart-felt, home felt of enjoyments," women are conspicuously absent from these authors' visions of bookish domestic bliss.[95] The romantic period's memoirs of book love, we have seen, testify amply to the sociological and architectural transformations that were by the early nineteenth century making marriage the privileged form of emotional intimacy and making the previously commercial, quasi-public space of the house into a personal sanctuary. We have seen how writers such as Hunt and Hazlitt appropriate the affective repertory generated by these transformations in order to bring print culture home to their readers. But while they do so, they write women out of the home. The relations between the genders are effaced by a "bibliographical romance" that brokers between modern domesticity and the older traditions—of European humanism, for instance—in which bookishness had been the transactional currency of those special male friendships that were valued as meetings of minds.

One component of this bibliographical romance is the fantasies that present the intercourse of these (male) readers with books, their companions for bed and board, as regenerative in a more literal sense than usual. As an advantage of the exclusive possession of books that he touts, Hunt in "Wedded to Books" mentions "the impossibility of other people's having any literary offspring from our fair unique"; he then adds, in a comment that references the important role that anthologizing would play in his working life, that in this way the book-wedded state would save him from "the danger of loving any compilations but our own" (251). When, in "Men and Books," having surveyed the book loves of writers from the past, Hunt exclaims, "How pleasant it is to reflect, that all these lovers of books have themselves become books!" (150), he both seems to state that the fate of bookmen, born of books, is to become books in their turn and seems to valorize this population increase, the multiplication of book objects, as in itself a sufficient rationale for book love. In the twentieth century, Holbrook Jackson gave particularly memorable expression to this fantasy of escape from the human world of reproduction into the artifactual world of print reproducibility: he wrote in his *The Anatomy of Bibliomania* of his "bookmen" as "twice born, first of woman (as every man) and then of books and, by reason of this, distinct and unique from the rest."[96]

Sometimes in their memoirs of book love the romantic essayists represent themselves as hyperactive borrowers and lenders of books, encouraging us to see their collections as perpetually in motion, and less as homes for books than as the boarding houses in which books temporarily take lodgings.[97] But their occasional indulgence of this fantasy of sexless, bookish reproduction suggests their affinity for the alternative account of the collection that Susan Stewart has elaborated—the collection as a site where history may be superseded by classification, an "order beyond the realm of temporality."[98] In this account, the mutability and mortality of the sexual body make it part of the flux from which the ideal collection in its fixity stands aloof.

These fantasies were easier to sustain perhaps because in the romantic period female collectors of rare books—who have been conspicuous in their absence from this chapter—were themselves rare. This fact prompted much fatuous commentary by bookmen. In 1932 Holbrook Jackson was still writing about bibliophily as a masculine passion: "Women are not collectors, nor are they lovers of aught save love and what pertains to it. They are notable readers, . . . but . . . it is only rarely that women have any affection for the books which delight them: *amours de femme et de bouquin ne se chantent pas au même lutrin* (Jackson's footnote supplies the translation: "The loves of woman and of books cannot be sung on the same lyre").[99] The campy innuendo contains a kernel of accuracy. A survey of booksellers' catalogues from the period indeed yields about twenty announcements of the auctioning of a library that was the property of a gentleman for every announcement that involves a book collection assembled by a lady. The disproportion registers in part women's alienation from the institutions of patrilineal inheritance underwriting the library that is the work of many generations, like that at Mr. Darcy's Pemberley. Marriage and property law made the ancestral home a place where men's wives, daughters, and sisters were not at home, so that they inhabited it only on sufferance. The romantic essayists tend to associate female readers, Mary Lamb included, with the kind of consumption, sponsored by the circulating library, that turns books into fungible merchandise.[100] They distinguish those indiscriminate appetites from their own connoisseurship, which takes books out of circulation or at least serves to disengage the particular edition or even copy from the unstructured mass of print products. Furthermore, a female bibliomaniac, should such a being have had the temerity to exist, would have found it difficult to participate in the tavern suppers of the Roxburghe Club, occasions when bad boy bibliomaniacs paraded their foibles and appetites with their toasts to the memories of fifteenth-century printers. Her participation in the social and commercial networks that supported collecting would have impaired her reputation or, minimally, tested her discretion.

In his *A Bibliographical, Antiquarian and Picturesque Tour and Reminiscences of a Literary Life*, Thomas Frognall Dibdin did do homage to Frances Mary Richardson Currer, the "Book-Genius of E S H T O N Hall" (in the East Riding of Yorkshire), whose passion "both for reading and amassing books has been extreme."[101] But even as he linked her, with that reference to her ardor, with his era's bibliographical romance, Dibdin had to tread more carefully than usual, in view of the unmarried Miss Currer's modest aversion to publicity. Despite his best efforts, Dibdin failed, for instance, to persuade her to permit her likeness to be included in his books. In his *Reminiscences* he made do with engravings of the rooms forming her library, reproduced from the catalogue of her collection of fifteen thousand volumes that she had had privately printed in 1831.

To conclude this chapter, I want briefly to consider an alternative forum in which women with intellectual aspirations and leisure time to kill could prove their love for literature: a forum both enabling them to make the print world a more intimate space and enabling them to ally the literary pleasures afforded by that world with the pleasures enjoyed by the collector. One defining artifact of this era's culture of literary appreciation was the homemade manuscript anthology—a compilation of original poetry and prose mixed with hand-copied extracts from published sources sometimes augmented with clippings from newspapers and periodicals; amateur watercolor landscapes (sometimes souvenirs of travels); imaginary portraits of characters from novels or poems (especially Walter Scott's); pastel pictures on rice paper achieving a tremendous level of zoological/botanical accuracy of sea shells, butterflies, and/or flowers; various other specimens of fashionable feminine accomplishments, decoupage and flower and fern pressing included; locks of hair; memorial cards paying homage to the recently deceased. This mixed-media medley, put between covers, formed a book that was often known as an "album," the rubric that the era's vendors of ornately bound blank books favored. Some compilers, however, dignified and customized their books with titles of their own coining—for example, "The Poetical Farrago," "Memorials of Friendship," "Medley, or Scrapbook," "The Leisure Hours Amusement of a Young Lady," "Cabinet of Music, Poetry, and Drawing."[102]

The books were frequently the work of multiple hands and circulated among multiple readers within particular circles of friends. Generally, though, they were presided over by one lady, or pair of female friends or of sisters, who would have handpicked the books' contributors, solicited their "offerings" of original and copied prose and verse, and arranged these pieces and an array of sketches, pieces of decoupage, and souvenirs in relation to one another. Sometimes the owner of the album was more muse than she was editor/curator. A book in this mode could be given as a gift, in which case it would be construed as embodying the aesthetic preferences its contributors imputed to its recipient. To create such books was often to assert the fungibility of the identities of devoted reader and devoted friend. Thus on one leaf of a pocketbook "Memorials of Friendship," dated 1795, the stanza that concludes "The paths of glory lead but to the grave" has been copied out from Thomas Gray's "Elegy Written in a Country Church-Yard" and coupled with the following instruction to Anne Wagner, the book's dedicatee, "When exploring the latent excellencies of this stanza, may memory remind you of your eternal friend, & deeply affectionate sister, Elizabeth." On the first page of her album, Anna Maria McNeill described its contents as comprising "Wild flowers of Poesy, culled from rare exotics, transplanted from the rich soil of genius, by the hand of friends, guided by fancy." (The horticultural metaphor references the literal meaning of the Greek *anthology*, a gathering of flowers.)[103] Content providers who supplied such books with their own poems or selected and transcribed those of others would through such actions have been affirming that, as Hume said in the essay on taste we considered in chapter 1, "the study of the beauties either of poetry, eloquence, music, or painting . . . give[s] a certain elegance of sentiment to which the rest of mankind are strangers."[104]

The reason to include this pastime, highly popular by the third and fourth decades of the nineteenth century, within the account of the literary affections offered by this chapter is that through it hundreds of female votaries of taste gained access to some of the enjoyments catered to within the bibliomaniac's library—the pleasures connected with accumulation and appropriation, for instance, with a creativity detached from the exigencies of originality. The amateur anthologist scales down the book collection to fit within the confines of a single bijou volume. Like the book collector, she brings into being a space whose allure lies in its balancing between exclusivity and sharing, concealment and display. The shelves that present the books to the visitor's eye are crucial to the book collection, but the books arrayed upon them are closed and preserve their secrets. The blank books sold to would-be compilers of albums sometimes came with locks. That feature suggests how these collections could prop up a notion of the interior self, even as—placed atop the parlor table for the entertainment of visitors—they formed the currency of a group's sociability.

Where the rare-book collector, as we saw, shows off his virtuoso ability to reach into odd corners of the print world and obtain copies of the books that can be treated as though they were handwritten originals, the lady assembling her album likewise displays her ability to reformulate print culture's accustomed ordering of the relations of the mass produced and the individuated. In the pages of her paper cabinet, the printed poem that a certain author once *wrote* is turned back into manuscript again. The conversion represents an essential part of its displacement from the realm of public discourse into that of private feeling.[105]

This book object's history intersects at several additional points with the story I've told about the rare book collector's pleasures. Charles Lamb, for instance, who collected and published the verses he had written in ladies' albums, while he was in a contrarian mood decried the popularity of those same collections. The plight of the modern poet, Lamb maintained, had been made worse by "the unfeminine practice of this novel species of importunity." Their "closets and privatest retirements" "besiege[d] and storm[ed] by violence" by troops of lady poem hunters anxious to have celebrity signatures in their books, poets were now expected to versify on demand.[106] The Cruikshank cartoon referenced above was originally part of a book of "scraps" that bound up thirty sheets of such vignettes, sold in the expectation that their purchaser would scissor them out and paste them into a scrapbook of her own. (Presumably, the individual who included "The Pursuit of Letters" in her book of verse and prose excerpts would have *intended* to look as though she were being ironic at the expense of her own avocations.) Prefabricated images like that would, in the most ambitious examples of such books, be interleaved among pages featuring other fancier sorts of cutouts, and showcasing the dexterity with her scissors expected of the accomplished woman of the period. (Some books boast intricately bordered silhouettes, others, collages, like the page composed of tiny paper seashells linked by embroidery thread that has been included in Anne Wagner's "Memorials.") And though cutting out texts and images to recontextualize them in albums "was consonant with women's roles as arrangers of the domestic interior," that skill set actually bridged the female and male spheres of the leisure classes.[107] For the bibliomaniacal gentleman was also wont to approach some books with his scissors and paste pot in hand, snipping out of the less valued books in this group the engraved portrait frontispieces or the maps or, more rarely, the passages of print, that he had selected in order to illustrate another, more highly valued book. He would mount the material he had cut out on leaves that were uniform in size with the pages of that more valued book and bind up the pages together. This practice of extra-illustration, of bringing in illustrative materials *from outside*, is number three in Dibdin's list of the symptoms of the bibliomania. Its consequences are exemplified by the copy of a nineteenth-century *Plays of William Shakespeare*, originally six volumes, that in the wake of its extra-illustration weighed in at twenty-one volumes.[108] (Figure 1.2 in chapter 1 reproduced a tipped-in page from a copy of *Miscellaneous Papers and Legal Instruments under the Hand and Seal of William Shakspeare* that was extra-illustrated by William Henry Ireland himself.)

Book love so practiced shocked, because it betrayed the lovers' propensities for book destruction. Those suffering from this strain of the book disease left trails of dismembered books in their wake: in the 1807 text in which he poses as a Spanish traveler to England Robert Southey commented, "You rarely or never meet an old book here with the author's head in it; all are mutilated by the collectors."[109] (In another way, though, the effects obtained through the cutting and pasting were thoroughly assimilable to the usual bibliophilic dreams. Extra-illustration converted a copy of the book that had been published in large print run—like a *Plays of William Shakespeare*—into a unique association object.) What affiliated the extra-illustrated book with the lady's album filled with copied-out beauties from published authors was their makers' shared insistence on conceiving of the books they bought or borrowed as remaining open to revision and as spurring their own acts of authorship. Notoriously, there is often a willfully tangential quality to the selection of inserted materials in an extra-illustrated book, which, more faithful to the selector's idiosyncrasies than the author's meanings, gloss "terms that even an indexer would skip."[110] The individual who transcribed a stanza of Lord Byron's into an album—as hundreds of participants in album culture did—might take the liberty of changing a "he" in the lines to a "she," the better to lodge a tier of private circulation beneath the consumerist exchanges of the public sphere.[111] Or she might re-present a recopied passage of literature as a garlanded, gilded work of visual art, bordered around with a frame of her designing and painting, so that the piece of poetry would become something to look at as well as something to read.

Yet for all their unwillingness to let authors have the last word, a trait that could betoken disrespect, makers of both these sorts of books have also contrived to prolong their interaction with their reading matter, generally well past the time of reading. That could bespeak a desire for continued involvement. Extra-illustration depends on a kind of close reading, after all: like a philologist, the extra-illustrator weighs every word. The copying out of extracts into one's album, appropriative to be sure, also enhances intimacy with the copied text.

It is possible to view those albums of extracts as documenting, by extension, just how often nineteenth-century readers understood themselves as taking *authors'* parts—not doing battle against authors, as per Lamb's description of importunate ladies besieging and storming, but instead taking authors' sides and doing them service. The manuscript commonplace book of the nineteenth-century Scotswoman Eliza Graeme, for instance, pointedly amasses anecdotes from publishing history that exemplify booksellers' stinginess in their dealings with authors. This reader, who memorializes such raw deals as the fifteen pounds that John Milton received for the copyright of *Paradise Lost*, may in that very action be declaring herself an ally of authors against their oppressors.[112] (This declaration glosses over the fact that commonplacers' habits of transcription could also be deemed a form of illicit reproduction that cheated authors of the copyright payments that were their due.) The inclusion of group portraits of the illustrious authors forming the literary pantheon in some of these books makes them seem the vehicles with which their makers declare their allegiance to the literary tradition—and maybe too more elusively, their sense that readers as well as critics and booksellers were agents of canon making. Thus in the "Medley, or Scrapbook" that a certain Elizabeth Reynolds "published," as her title page cheekily puts it, in 1817, one finds a page of collage that is headed "Flowers of Literature" and that comprises pasted-in pictures of Chaucer, Shakespeare, and Sterne as well as some more surprising choices (Benjamin Franklin, Charles Churchill) and, in the center, a drawing of a book opened to pages featuring copied-out lines of verse by or about each. The memorial page that Miss Reynolds devotes to the poet Mary Robinson has a cutout portrait of Robinson at its center, some of Robinson's verse transcribed on the left-hand side, and "Tributary Verses Addressed to Mrs. Robinson" on the right: pasted-in pictorial ornaments in the shapes of butterflies and birds are scattered across the surface.[113] Such ways of recontextualizing and recycling English literature seem to convert writings by authors into love tokens to authors.

The anonymous scrapbook maker who inserted a pressed fern beside a pasted-in printed portrait of Sir Walter Scott might have aimed to preserve a keepsake of a visit to the Highlands. Or along the lines I have just adumbrated, she or he might have been supplying evidence that where devotion to Scott and his fictional world was concerned, she or he was willing to go the extra mile.[114] Harkening back to chapter 1's discussion of the hierarchy of munificent genius and grateful audience that sometimes structures the scene of literary appreciation, I want to say that this fern to me looks like a gift left at a shrine. What is from one angle a keepsake—an addition to the collection—can from another angle be a votive offering to an authorial saint.[115] The collection documenting a fan's devotions can be a way of keeping and giving simultaneously. The collector's forte for taking possession is sometimes a forte for expending care and affection.

An alternative, and rather more wry, mode of collecting—a mode that doubles as a commentary on the sharedness of a print culture's reading matter—is set out in a certain Miss Mary Watson's "The Scrap Book: Containing a Choice and Amusing Selection from the Standard and Floating Literature of the Last Twelve or fifteen Years Together with an Introduction and Occasional Remarks and Contributions."[116] Like everything else in this book, the words forming the title on the title page have been scissored out from preexisting sources—in this case, an advertisement marketing a printed book—and pasted in. That is the case even with words composing Miss Mary Watson's name, which appear on her title page courtesy of a record of a commercial exchange: to mark the scrapbook as her own, she has clipped a receipt made out to her, dated February 22, 1821, and carefully pasted it too into her volume. The effect of all the little snippets of paper hoarded up and lifted from other contexts is to give Miss Mary Watson's volume the look of a multipage ransom note.

Miss Watson appears to have been keeping within this book a kind of diary of her social engagements, especially ones involving a certain Miss Ross, whose name also appears in the pages courtesy of the detritus of the nineteenth-century paper world. It is tempting to think that with sufficient patience one could piece together the itinerary of the two women's days by studying the fragments of newspaper announcements, advertisements, and handwritten letters that fill the pages of "The Scrap Book." Literary pursuits were clearly central in these lives—at the same time that the nature of Mary Watson's investment in those pursuits is difficult to decipher, with detachment built, as it were, into her very medium. Take, for instance, the Byron page that Miss Mary Watson includes in her book (fig. 3.2), which omits the poetry to concentrate on the scandalous life. The page affiliates her with scores of other album makers, who clipped out engraved portraits of the poet and/or his baby daughter and transcribed scores of his lines, but she also keeps her distance. (For one thing, she organized the volume so that

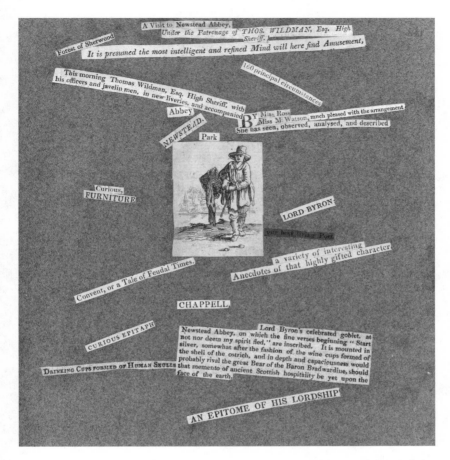

A Visit to Newstead Abbey,
Under the Patronage of THOS. WILDMAN, Esq. High
Sheriff.

Forest of Sherwood!

It is presumed the most intelligent and refined Mind will here find Amusement,

This morning Thomas Wildman, Esq. High Sheriff, with
his officers and javelin men, in new liveries, and accompanied

160 principal circumstances

Abbey

BY Miss Ross
Miss M. Watson, much pleased with the arrangement

She has seen, observed, analysed, and described

NEWSTEAD,

Park

Curious,
FURNITURE

LORD BYRON

our best living Poet

a variety of interesting
Anecdotes of that highly gifted character.

Convent, or a Tale of Feudal Times.

CHAPPELL.

CURIOUS EPITAPH

Lord Byron's celebrated goblet, at
Newstead Abbey, on which the fine verses beginning " Start
not nor deem my spirit fled," are inscribed. It is mounted in
silver, somewhat after the fashion of the wine cups formed of
the shell of the ostrich, and in depth and capaciousness would
probably rival the great Bear of the Baron Bradwardine, should
that memento of ancient Scottish hospitality be yet upon the
face of the earth.

DRINKING CUPS FORMED OF HUMAN SKULLS

AN EPITOME OF HIS LORDSHIP

FIGURE 3.2 A Byron page from Mary Watson's "The Scrap Book: Containing a Choice and Amusing Selection from the Standard and Floating Literature of the Last Twelve or Fifteen Years Together with an Introduction and Occasional Remarks and Contributions" (ca. 1821). The page of printed fragments that Miss Watson, perhaps with the assistance of "Miss Ross," assembles is framed by the words "A Visit to Newstead Abbey" (Byron's ancestral home) and "An Epitome of His Lordship." Photograph: Courtesy of the Special Collections Library, Manchester Metropolitan University. Scrapbook numbered 88 from the Sir Harry Page Collection of Victorian Scrapbooks, Albums and Commonplace Books held at Manchester Metropolitan University Special Collections.

this page was immediately followed by one headlined "A Christian Library," surely a deliberate act of mischief. Then there is the tease of the clipping referring to "160 Principal Circumstances," which promises circumstantiality and the intimate knowledge it brings but doesn't deliver.) In the early nineteenth-century culture of the tasteful excerpt, "picking texts apart" was a tried-and-true way to "draw readers together": such at least was the premise, Leah Price teaches us, of many of the published anthologies of the era, which aspired to form a public by facilitating the reading of a manageable quantity of verse and prose excerpts.[117] What to make, though, of the literalism with which Miss Watson approached the project of picking texts apart?

Earlier in the book she has set floating across the space of the page, without explanatory context, such clipped out, deracinated words as "Books," "Literature," "Read," "Female Literature," and "Art of Reading"—a display of the buzz words of the era that here, as elsewhere in its pages, make her book appear an anticipation of modernist collage. In the history of art, collage is seen as a revolutionary formal innovation because of the directness of its response "to one of the crucial characteristics of modernity, the availability of mechanically reproduced images.[118] The maker of a collage acknowledges her place in a world flooded with representations and collects them to master it. The diaristic quality of "The Scrap Book" bears out a punning claim about books made in Hazlitt's essay "On Reading Old Books": books form "links in the chain of our conscious being . . . [and] bind together the different scattered visions of our personal identity."[119] The pun on "bind" is central to Hazlitt's and his fellow bookmen's bibliographic imagining of the self. Still, these records of Mary Watson's industry with scissors project an account of personal identity in which the binding can never quite offset the scattering.

The collector always collects himself, Jean Baudrillard says: the objects within the collection refer back to the primary term, the collector.[120] In collecting within her scrapbook/diary the detritus of a new world of mass literacy, this female collector reveals an awareness of the ironies of that collecting project that Baudrillard's judgmental portrait of the collector cannot really explain and that Hazlitt doesn't allow himself to ponder. It's by reading again and recycling the literature that everyone reads that we craft our own singular individualities.

PART 3

English Literature for Everyday Use

CHAPTER FOUR

Going Steady

Canons' Clockwork

I hate to read new books.

WILLIAM HAZLITT, "On Reading Old Books" (1821)

To be always reading Shelley would be like living on quince marmalade;
Milton and Wordsworth are substantial diet for all times and seasons.

SARA COLERIDGE, Letter to Hartley Coleridge (1845)

EVERYDAY ITERABILITY

More than once in the *Lives of the English Poets*, Samuel Johnson depicts the
writers whom he anthologizes as readers. Depictions in this mode do more
than register Johnson's embrace of the source study that by the 1770s had
come to center the nascent discipline of literary studies. Johnson imparts a
characteristic touch of melancholy to the new practice of studying "our ancient authours" through, as he put it to Thomas Warton, "the perusal of the
books which these authors had read."[1] In several of the *Lives*, relating the
making of a poet means commencing with a story of the poet's fateful early
attachment to books. In a manner more rueful than celebratory, Johnson
will trace the man's pursuit of poetic fame to the moment when the boy was
captivated by illusions: the anthropomorphic illusions that readers cultivate
when we construe our encounters with the surfaces of representation as
experiences in which we sustain the company of other *people*.

This narrative pattern emerges with the first life in the series. Abraham
Cowley happens on a copy of *The Faerie Queene* left in the window of his
mother's parlor, succumbs to "the charms of verse" and so becomes, "as he
relates, irrecoverably a poet." "Irrecoverably," the loaded term in that passage, suggests that Johnson is halfway inclined to narrate Cowley's discovery of his calling as a story of abasement. In fact, Johnson bowdlerizes here
Cowley's own account of how his reading of Spenser "made [him] a Poet
as immediately as a Child is made a Eunuch." The psychosexual subtext
Johnson thus opts to bury resurfaces in the oddest of the Lives' depictions

of the child's fall into representation, which is found in Johnson's biography of his near contemporary William Shenstone, whose "Life" was one of the last Johnson wrote. After the young Shenstone learned to read, Johnson recounts, he "soon received such delight from books that he was always calling for fresh entertainment, and expected that when any of the family went to market a new book should be brought him, which when it came was in fondness carried to bed and laid by him. It is said that when his request had been neglected, his mother wrapped up a piece of wood of the same form, and pacified him for the night."[2] For the purposes of this chapter, it is significant that this depiction of book love involves not an abrupt crush—the time frame of the sudden and irrecoverable that organized Johnson's narration of Cowley's childhood—but instead the time frame of the routine.

That time frame becomes key when, seventy years after the *Lives of the Poets*, Johnson's anecdote about Shenstone's bedtime routines gets retold, and Johnson's wary fascination with a compulsive reading that goes beyond the pleasure principle gets sentimentalized and, in more than one sense, romanticized. In 1849 this story of the lessons that a mother administers in the dynamics of desire, loss, and mollifying substitution proves newly useful for an elderly Leigh Hunt—the essayist and erstwhile radical journalist we met in the last chapter. During his long life Hunt (1784-1859) was often placed at the forefront of the anthologizing and canonizing enterprises that Samuel Johnson and Thomas Warton had guided in the previous century. Hunt retells Shenstone's story when he introduces *A Book for a Corner*, his compilation of choice excerpts of eighteenth-century English verse and prose. His motive for that retelling confirms an argument Leah Price has made about how anthologists have tended in the paratextual apparatus with which they equip their compilations to downplay, self-effacingly, their own power of selection. Finding it expedient to intimate that "texts transmit themselves" and themselves select their readers, the anthologist, Price suggests, is more apt to locate difference among literature's consumers rather than among its producers. This procedure indicates, she states, how in the final analysis canon-making enterprises are not really about content but are instead centrally concerned with who reads (and who will be deemed to *really* read) and how.[3] Hunt's introduction is structured in keeping with this logic. It is less interested in identifying the kind of poets whose works *A Book for a Corner* collects than it is in pressing the claims of the kind of readers who are able to appreciate them. And hence the infant Shenstone's appeal. Shenstone personifies the target audience that Hunt solicits—the sector of the reading public that is capable of valuing, Hunt explains, "the placider corners of genius."[4] Hunt has assembled "passages from such authors as retain, if not the highest, yet the most friendly and as it were domestic hold upon us during life." And Shenstone, Hunt writes, "is the sort of child we hope to be a reader of our volume"—reciprocating that unfailing "domestic hold" with his own constancy, he is the sort of child able to commit to this lifetime reading plan.

There are two lessons we might extract from these stories of Shenstone's sleeping arrangements. First, the care that Hunt and Johnson take to cast an emphatically Oedipalized situation as the breeding ground for literacy and literary appreciation suggests complexities overlooked in many recent efforts to historicize the concepts of canonicity or of criticism that are the groundwork of our discipline. In Johnson's need to write the story of Shenstone's quirky bedroom rites into the *Lives,* we might see yet another indication that criticism's professionalization of reading cannot easily be disentangled from the history of the emotions, and of intimacy and private life.

The second lesson we might take away from this bedtime story involves the role it assigns to habit. In Leigh Hunt's hands, Shenstone's bedtime routine does not center (as it might have) a fable about the market's power to keep addicted consumers on tenterhooks with its promises of novelty and "fresh entertainment." It becomes, instead, a story of a literary attachment that is distinguished by its steadiness, constancy, and capacity to endure even when the thrill is gone. Hunt makes Shenstone a model reader of *A Book for a Corner* by associating him with a mode of literary appreciation that I will call "everyday love," an affect that is directed at what is already, unobtrusively and unmomentously, familiar, and an affect that counts as genuine precisely because, routine and regularized, it does not belong to any one day but has become quotidian habit.

This chapter is about the reciprocal relations between, on the one hand, that ideal of readerly ethics—and of readerly health—and, on the other hand, the slow emergence in the decades intervening between Johnson's and Hunt's editing projects, of an idea of literature as that which we are always rereading and never reading for the first time. As far as Hunt is concerned, the crucial point of Johnson's anecdote about bedtime routines is that the pacification that books proffer the constantly craving boy never fails. Reassuringly, books are always there for him, even when, markets and mothers failing, they don't show up. And Shenstone in turn reciprocates their steadiness: *he* repeats himself, happily. This, to borrow a pun from the Victorianist Steve Connor, is an account of literature as l-iterature (imagine the *L* as a silent one).[5] In compiling a book for a corner, and lauding, as his subtitle puts it, *Authors the Best Suited to that Mode of Enjoyment,* Leigh Hunt registers a scheme in which literariness is a quality proper only to those books that both *bear iteration* and also *mandate* it. From the mid-eighteenth-century on, the moment when it begins taking on that modern meaning that elevates it above the vast bulk of the market's print products, literature begins to be reconceptualized as a steadying influence on those who love it.

Though rarely acknowledged explicitly, that steadying has been an important source of the appeal exerted by the idea of a literary canon—a motive for seeking the fellowship available from a restrictive grouping of perennially readable great works. Literature's (l-iterature's) hour comes back round with reassuring regularity. The canon is habit-forming. This is not precisely as he would put it, but there is some resemblance between this proposition and Harold Bloom's recent no-nonsense definition of the canonical text as simply the durable, complex text that demands rereading (a definition that is supposed to lend a political neutrality to his project in *The Western Canon* and make it seem as if it were simply transient, fly-by-night reading matter that Bloom disapproved, not multiculturalism or feminism).[6] To situate the desire to reread and desire for l-iterature in history can, however, go some way toward divesting Bloom's definition of its aura of self-evidence. The promotion of habitual rereading that I seek to reconstruct here helped lay the ground for the disciplinary canon. But I am seeking to recover a neglected aspect of that canonicity as I try to demonstrate that the act of reading again that Bloom mandates—and which was ennobled in late twentieth-century literary theory by figures such as Roland Barthes, François Roustang, and Matei Calinescu—does not have stable meanings over time.[7] Rereading's association with, for instance, an augmented cognitive mastery is neither inevitable nor historically constant. This is worth underlining because, as Michael Warner has observed, practitioners of literary studies have a bad track record when it comes to remembering that the "critical reading" for which they advocate in classrooms and mission statements finds its place in the world alongside other, competing ways of processing texts. Rereading so as to have by heart—to make a book one's constant companion—is not always congruent with rereading so as to know better and more deeply by knowing one's own assumptions. And the latter mode is not the only rereading practice that has been embedded within the disciplines of subjectivity.[8]

The recurrent rereadings treated in this chapter do not, in other words, necessarily or simply represent the homage that readers have paid to "complexity"—one term that anchors Bloom's axiology in *The Western Canon* and which casts rereadability as an intrinsic property of select texts, rather

than the effect of a particular set of socially regulated consumption practices. These recurrent rereadings are often, on the contrary, the homage that
readers pay to the sensation of comfort—to the reassuring feeling, for instance, that baby Shenstone gets from books' round-the-clock proximity.
Conceptualized as virtuous habits, these recurrent rereadings are also prof-
fered to view by their adherents as evidence of their regular hours and sober
lives. One may obtain through a beloved book—as Henry Reed, University
of Pennsylvania Professor of Rhetoric and English Literature and William
Wordsworth's American editor did—the means to bind each day to each in
aesthetic piety. A letter that Reed sent to Wordsworth in 1836 shows us how
this influential professional reader set out to share in the recurrent sensations of delight that connect up the days of Wordsworth's life and that are
described in his poem "My heart leaps up / When I behold a rainbow in
the sky." Reed's letter conjures up a home scene organized around Reed's
nightly repetitions of Wordsworth's repetitions: in it Reed attests to reciting
"My heart leaps up" "again and again ... to my one listener," his wife.[9]

By the start of the Victorian era, as Reed's account suggests, readerly reiteration is also aligned with the ceremonies of timekeeping—the regularly
scheduled homecomings, family meals, and gift exchanges—that, as the historian John Gillis claims, first became part of the work of kinship at this moment, when they first provided middle-class families with modern means of
confirming their togetherness through time.[10] Those conceptualizations of
readerly routine register, in sum, something we've been slow to notice about
professional readers' accounts during the nineteenth century of how other
people *should* read and how they themselves putatively did: how often those
accounts were intertwined with discussions of companionate marriage and
of the benefits of domestic timetables and of regular scheduling in social
and mental life.

They were also intertwined with discussions of the human nervous system's propensity for rhythm and repetition. In this era antedating modern
disciplinary divisions, when aesthetics, moral philosophy, psychology, and
medicine remained jumbled together, literary appreciations and medical
case histories could be written by the same authors. The same psychological
principles were mobilized in both neurological and aesthetic speculations.
Those principles linked the editorial apparatuses men of letters supplied
for literary miscellanies both with their prescriptions for long life and with
their scientific descriptions, which hewed strictly to physical principles of
explanation, of how minds worked when brains were on books. The result
of such linkages is that there can sometimes be a curious inflection to the

canon love that these men of letters describe and model. The return engagements with long-loved books that this chapter will portray manifest, on occasion, a devotion that is so engaged as to never miss a beat. One imagines,
for instance, that this was the spirit in which James Boswell undertook the
regimen of annual rereadings of *Rasselas* that he enthuses about in the *Life
of Johnson*: a devotee's recreation in a new register of the Christian liturgical year.[11] But the era between Johnson and Hunt could also, as I have
intimated, accord a surprising amount of respect to affections of a more
everyday, more placid and even torpid cast, affections directed at texts so
deeply familiar that the emotions that they stir barely register at the level
of consciousness. As the proto-psychological writing that I engage here and
in the chapter that follows this one noted frequently, reading might quite
literally be absentminded. It might be an automatic process unfolding like
clockwork. The fact that few of us can remember a time when we had to
will our eyes to move across the page, when our reading wasn't something
that simply happened, was for writers from Erasmus Darwin in the 1790s to
George Henry Lewes in the 1870s a prime example of the automatic way in
which the brain repeats familiar motions, as it shifts from certain physical
sensations and the ideas with which those sensations have regularly been
associated in the past.[12] Working within a medico-moral context that valued
habit as the guiding mechanism of individual identity and social structure,
commentators on reading were, by our lights, surprisingly inclined to view
such reflex actions, despite their mitigation of the will, as testimonials to
constancy.

The correlations between the habitual, the heartfelt, and the reread that
were proposed by this psychology might strike us as wishful. We nowadays think of repetition as rendering affections stale and worry about the
authenticity of retentive feelings. (I'll be exploring that contrast shortly.)
Nevertheless, those correlations inform, in crucial ways, the social norms
for reading that helped produce and institutionalize modern canonicity.
They inform, for instance, Hunt's promotion of those authors who retain
a "domestic hold" on us through life and the rebuke that his introduction
directs at readers who might not wish to be so held. Thinking about everyday love illuminates, in addition, the varying time frames in which the
languages for canonicity have situated literature. Immortality had been one
of these, certainly—and one can easily locate in romantic-period debates
about reading contrasts that oppose "the dust and smoke and noise of modern literature" with "the pure, silent air of immortality."[13] But that inherited
terminology for the timeless is one that during Hunt's lifetime people are

inclined to refine, as they inflect an old concept of eternal fame with new intimacy expectations, and as they make immortality into a more comfortable sphere to visit. Furthermore, as the concluding section of this chapter will suggest, one reason to ponder the iterations of an everyday love of literature is the better to understand how early in the nineteenth century, the novel form, Johnny-come-lately to literariness, could belatedly obtain medico-moral sanction and gain a grudging admission to that category alongside the polite company of the poets. The fact that novels are long—long enough so that even on its first reading a novel can be something you can make a habit of—might contribute to the form's increasing authority for a culture that wanted its standard texts and favorite authors to be steadying ones. Novel reading has had time on its side.

Great books (so classified) are not only socially certified sources of great ideas or artistry. That description doesn't exhaust our transactions with them. The story of inexhaustibly rereadable Great Books is also that of valetudinarians' health regimens, of the compulsory coupledom of a new marriage culture, and of the transformations that reinvented the family and that made a group formerly understood primarily as a unit of economic production into Western culture's primary scene of emotional gratification. Seeking to recover some of those less told stories, this chapter tracks in the next two sections the elaborate efforts readers and publishers made, beginning late in the eighteenth century, to incorporate aesthetic experiences into the continuum of ordinary life. It links the emergence of that new kind of love object, "l-iterature," both to people's new attentiveness to the time scheme that they were only then learning to call "everyday" and to their new conviction that this time scheme—that of the unremarkable, ongoing status quo—was affection's true home. From there I move, in the chapter's fourth section, to some standard works of romantic-period aesthetic theory. I aim to recover from those familiar texts of Wordsworth's and Coleridge's especially some unfamiliar accounts of a low-affect aesthetics, accounts in which the persistence and habituation of feeling are overriding concerns. Section 4's redescription of romantic accounts of the aesthetic relation prepares the ground for the final section's consideration of the novel, the genre that devotes itself to prosy everyday life. Placing the novel in the context of the everyday love that literature seemed to solicit by definition (a new definition) calls attention to the longueurs and long-term obligations with which novel readers by definition cope. One possibility this chapter gestures at in concluding is that to bring those to light may be to apprehend how the novel might rival the lyric as the quintessential romantic genre.

TIME DISCIPLINE AND LITERARY CONSTANCY

It is tempting to imagine that if we could time-travel and take with us an especially sensitive stethoscope, we might as visitors to Britain around the year 1830 actually be able to hear, as if it were a heartbeat, or a kind of bass line, pounding beneath the louder noise of public history, the rhythm that the inhabitants steadily beat out as, turning pages they had turned before, often at the same time of week or year as before, reciting according to schedule the familiar words they had recited before, they conformed to their bookish routines. A kind of low hum might be heard emanating from the nation's domiciles, perhaps soaring into audibility as the several rereading cycles converge, which they seem to do on winter evenings especially. Respectable and happy families at this moment were, historian John Gillis notes, supposed to be those who standardized and synchronized the individual schedules of their members: Gillis quotes as exemplification of this belief a manual of household hints published in 1830 that advises that "in a well regulated family, all clocks and watches should agree" and that every dining room "should be furnished with a good-looking clock; the space over the kitchen fire-place with another, vibrating in unison."[14] What Gillis does not note is that many of these families, as befitted a people of the book, had also devised ways of keeping time and holding themselves together (as families *and* as individuals) with their reading matter as well as their clocks and watches. Our time traveler to Britain in the year 1830 might, I imagine, encounter a soundscape in which pages and pendulums will turn alike in rhythmic unison.

Hark, she might say, once she was in earshot of the beat, they are at it again—going through *The Christian Year* with John Keble; using Wordsworth (as John Ruskin attested he did) "as a daily text-book from youth to age"; reading *The Vicar of Wakefield* through every winter (an annual ritual for the poet John Clare, who, he wrote, preferred in his readerly life his old acquaintances and did "not care to make new ones"); or listening to a *Waverley* novel read aloud every Saturday night "after the candles were snuffed and the fire was stirred" (the custom of the so-called Quaker Poet Bernard Barton, who always on these occasions, his memoirist Edward FitzGerald reported, "anticipat[ed] with a glance, or an impatient ejaculation of pleasure, the good things he knew were coming—which he liked the better for knowing they were coming").[15]

On a second trip, our time traveler might discover that, with the passage of time, the steady hum had got louder. For 1870 would see the entrance en masse into the history of reading of the Janeites: the crowd of eminent Victorians who were determined to make Austenian reading inextricable from the resuming, repeating, and remembering of Austenian reading. A significant part of membership of this group was programmatically committed to the following schedule: "all six, every year." (The phrase is attributed to Gilbert Ryle, who is said to have responded with these laconic four words when asked if he, an eminent philosopher, ever read novels).[16]

The paragon of Janeite constancy, champion at braving the boredom that some might think that schedule would entail, was arguably the prime minister, Benjamin Disraeli. According to the late-Victorian literary critic Adolphus Jack, this gentleman "professed to have read 'Pride and Prejudice' seventeen times." "One wonders no longer," Jack exclaims, "that a statesman who was so often in such company should have found himself on the side of the angels."[17] Who was doing the counting? That Disraeli or somebody else cared enough about his devotion to Austen's novel to keep a tally of the occasions on which it was paid is notable. That there was a reckoning suggests someone keeping tabs on his bookish personal bests. In their dutifulness these rereadings might bear some resemblance to other practices of self-examination and self-regulation that provided the vehicles for the Victorians' habitual performances of "character"—even if in Disraeli's case, we might assume that a touch of waggish superciliousness would have been detectable in the diligence of the former dandy. A more earnest compliance with the institutions of modern rationality appears to have informed many of the rereading routines practiced by Disraeli's compatriots: and those suggest how the norms of sobriety and punctuality whose dissemination Max Weber described in *The Protestant Ethic and the Spirit of Modern Capitalism* penetrated even the innermost domain of personal taste and private attachments, that of solitary reading. The spirit of the age had been subjected to a discipline of clock and calendar time, and the change made itself known through a new zeal for not just working but also amusing oneself by rule.

Disraeli's contemporaries had positioned the statesman "on the side of the angels" in applauding his public repudiation of Darwin's theory of evolution during the 1860 Oxford Debate. Adolphus Jack's description of the prime minister's Janeism suggestively recontextualizes the celebrated phrase remembered from that controversy, transferring it from the scene of politics to the scene of domestic leisure. "Angels" hints at how rereading could for Victorian readers represent another of those occasions, sought out zealously, in which they converted their free time into a moral and spiritual test.[18] But this way of spending time does in one respect differ from the eminent

Victorians' other habitual exertions and programs of self-improvement—
think here of Dickens and/or David Copperfield practicing his shorthand.
These rereadings, which win the devoted reader no credentials or titles, are
not motors for narratives of social climbing or professional success. Odd
compounds of diligence and in-a-rut indolence, they prompt thoughts of
holding patterns and inertia rather than development and mobility. (The
distinction may be just what marks them as part of Disraeli's off-hours and
home life rather than his public life. That the nineteenth-century gentle-
woman does not have off-hours in the same way, has nothing *but* home
life, might explain why protagonists of this period's anecdotes of faithful
reading are, as far as I can tell, almost always male.) Like ritual, as recently
reassessed in anthropology, these rereadings are self-referential processes.[19]
Meaning here lies not in a result but in the doing.

Book history has sometimes sorted out "intensive" reading from "extensive reading" by associating the eighteenth century with the first—the rereading of a few prized texts (usually the Bible and the devotional manuals
that were its auxiliaries)—and the nineteenth century with the second—with
the cursory, scattershot reading encouraged by a culture of cheap print that
invites consumers to scurry from one ephemeral novelty to the next. In this
taxonomic scheme, the nineteenth century's role is to epitomize that second
mode and complete that "epochal shift from Bible to a generalized *biblios*"
that gets under way with the advent of print capitalism.[20] The understanding of secularization that underwrites this periodizing of book history, one
in which a clean break intervenes between a discrete age of faith and a
discrete age of the market, has been complicated in recent scholarship on
the sociology of religiosity. Danièle Hervieu-Léger, for instance, argues that
secularization does not contract religion's sphere so as much reconstruct belief in a manner that fragments and redistributes religiosity. If "sacredness"
is "free-floating" in modern society, she proposes, that means that there will
be religious notes within the rational discourses of consumer culture, even
as it also means, conversely, that religion will bear the imprint of a capitalist
modernity "centered on the individual's right to subjectivity." Keeping this
discussion in mind brings to view what conventional oppositions between
sacred and secular, between intensive and extensive reading, can occlude:
the productive confusions between literary and religious sanctity that com-
prise the post-Enlightenment history of literariness. After all, as William
McKelvy has outlined, the ecclesiastic context was a key site for the late
eighteenth-century "invention of English literature"; this new literary authority was to a great extent shaped by parsons scribbling in their manses.[21]

Keeping this discussion in mind makes it easier too to acknowledge the resemblances—for a start, the shared ritualistic quality—linking devoted readers' returns to beloved old books to the observances of those Protestant communicants whose regular, three-chapter-a-day schedule of Bible readings had long been enabling them to traverse the span from Genesis to Revelations on an annual basis. Indeed, it makes it easier to acknowledge that those two categories of readers are likely to have overlapped.

And yet, even if one declines to mobilize the distinction between intensive and extensive reading as a principle of periodization, there may still be reasons to maintain that a time traveler listening in on the hum of devoted readings in the year 1750 would hear something different from the time traveler eavesdropping in 1830. The later readers, I suspect, would keep better time, go steadier. The reason is not simply that the times would have changed by 1830, but that time itself would have changed. The shift that added everyday love to readers' affective repertory could be described, on the one hand, as the outcome and instrument of a domestication of the aesthetic relation. Certainly, there is evidence for an intensified determination to integrate literary experience into the continuum of everyday experience, of augmented attempts to steep home life in literariness—as though this luxury too, like sugar and tea, were being converted into everyday fare. On the other hand, there is also evidence for an intensified consciousness of the kind of time that gets passed in everyday settings—and a new elevation in the value of that downtime. Indeed, the term "everyday" itself acquired a new semantic shading midway through the eighteenth century. The *Oxford English Dictionary* turns to a 1763 letter written, as it happens, by William Shenstone for its first quotation illustrative of that new usage in which "everyday" is no longer just a synonym of "daily," and no longer simply the designation applied when something recurs every twenty-four hours, but is also a synonym for commonplace, ordinary, or plain. In that new usage "everyday" names (in Stuart Sherman's words) "phenomena—objects, habits, practices—which have become familiar by frequent use over extended time."[22]

Histories of domesticity often look to the middle of the eighteenth century for the origins of that shift that sees families according a new level of attention to their habitual routines, and that sees them, by the nineteenth century, ritualizing them and sentimentalizing them, creating "quality time" (as we would say) from the unexceptional material of everyday mealtimes, bedtimes, and walks. In the history of chronometry and literary form that I cited above, Sherman identifies a precondition for this shift. He outlines how, in eighteenth-century Britain, diary keeping, daily papers, and clocks with minute hands jointly produced a heightened consciousness of time as a continuous sequence of isochronic intervals. This is the temporality Sherman dubs a temporality of "measure," distinguishing it from the temporality over which it came to prevail in the eighteenth century, a temporality of "occasion." The eighteenth century, Sherman proposes, saw new rules for engagement with time that made it visible as a steady continuum.[23] This reconstruction of time also, I think, reconstructed the time frame for devoted readers' literary transactions.

Comparison of the varying ways in which admirers of Samuel Richardson's (very) long novel *Clarissa* linked reading and duration can suggest in a preliminary way what I mean by that—and suggest the alteration that the protocols for affective investment would undergo as a consequence of that reconstruction. Samuel Johnson's admiration of *Clarissa* prompted him to recommend to Richardson, just after the latter had published the novel's third edition, that he equip the novel with an index. *Clarissa*, Johnson insisted in a 1751 letter, is "not a performance to be read with eagerness and laid aside for ever," and accordingly it was fitting that Richardson should supplement "this Edition by which . . . Posterity is to abide" with what will "facilitate its use"—that index that will allow "the reader [who] recollects any incident . . . [to] easily find it."[24] In envisioning the posterity that will abide with *Clarissa* Johnson did not envision it in the form of a reader who will read the novel in toto more than once: Johnson's posterity dips into *Clarissa*, consulting it on occasions of signal need. Johnson apparently did not envision Thomas Babington Macaulay, the Victorian architect of English studies and imperial hegemony who took new, insect-proof volumes of *Clarissa* to India with him in 1834—"Not read *Clarissa*! . . . If you have once read *Clarissa*, . . . you can't leave it"—nor William Hazlitt, a self-confessed, "thorough adept in Richardson" (228).[25] Hazlitt's essay "On Reading Old Books," incorporates a vision of that adept installed in "some old family mansion in the country" and blissfully rereading Richardson "from beginning to end . . . till every word and syllable relating to the bright Clarissa . . . were once more 'graven in my heart's table'" (228).

In the *Éloge de Richardson* that Denis Diderot published in 1766, more staying power still had been ascribed to those Richardsonian words. Describing the reception of *Clarissa*, in terms that carry a slight menace thanks to their emphasis on readers' involuntary, unconscious succumbing to that novel's disciplinary force, Diderot outlined how "the seeds of virtue" that Richardson had sowed in his readers' hearts would, even without their

knowing it, develop in ways that would shape all their future social interactions.[26] This account could be read as Diderot's declaration that, for the
reader who had *once* read *Clarissa*, no refresher courses would ever become
necessary: it makes even Johnson's index redundant. But an alternative account of the novel's habit-forming power is also present in the *Éloge*, as
Roger Chartier indicates in an essay that explores the question of whether
there was a "revolution" in reading practices in the late eighteenth century,
and which discerns in the *Éloge* an innovative vision of the novel as an object
one frequents and one never leaves. ("Thou wilt at all times be the subject of
my reading," Diderot promises the dead novelist.)[27] The identification with a
text envisioned in the *Éloge* is, Chartier states, no longer restricted to the moment of that text's reading; it is of unlimited duration.[28] "What Diderot feels
and what he foretells is something radically new, namely, the text as presence that extends beyond itself, a perpetual existence." That reimagining of
the duration of literary effects drives a wedge between two kinds of literate
subjects—and one wonders whether earlier times would have needed to differentiate admirers who *have read* Richardson from admirers who are readers *of* Richardson, and whose connection with *Clarissa* goes on.

As Richardson insinuated when he had Anna Howe, his heroine's great-
est fan inside the book, preserve for posterity her friend's daily and weekly
schedules, to be a well-disciplined reader of *Clarissa* was also to take to heart
the eponymous heroine's art of time management: "This is another benefit
received from your Clarissa," one of Richardson's earliest admirers, Lady
Bradshaigh, wrote cooperatively to the novelist: "She has also taught me
to keep an account of my time." Earlier (Richardson was repeating himself), a minor character in his *Pamela* had compared the household which
Pamela runs following her marriage to a "good eight-day clock": "no Piece
of Machinery, that ever was made, is so regular and uniform, as this Family
is."[29] Pamela, like Clarissa, was ahead of her time: as I have intimated, in
the nineteenth century such rhythm methods could define real households
as well as fictional ones. In both locations they were valued for advancing the cause of domestic economy and also the perpetuation of domestic
affection. Commenting on how the new emphases on clocked and calen-
dared time and standardized scheduling advanced a ritualization of family life, which in turn was supposed to stimulate familial togetherness,
John Gillis explains that during Victoria's reign "the family was put into
cultural production, representing itself to itself in a series of daily, weekly,
and annual performances that substituted for the working relationships that
had previously constituted the everyday experience of family life."[30] In this

context, loved books served as one medium of these everyday reaffirmations of togetherness (think of the Reeds in Philadelphia getting surprised by Wordsworthian joy every evening like clockwork). At the same time, loved books were also on the receiving end of a parallel sort of steady and steadying affection.

I am attempting here to map that zone of cultural history where the history of literariness meets up with the history of affective life and the history of domestic timekeeping. But maybe there is no reason to confine us to *domestic* timekeeping. In the 1820s, denizens of Oxford and Cambridge universities began to call their salubrious daily walks their "constitutionals." A loaded term, thanks to its linkage of the health of individual bodies and the health of bodies politic, "constitutional" suggests the role that the idealization of steadiness also plays in bachelor domains—the academic disciplines—that have been defined by and valorized according to their distance from homes.

We are used to identifying the long eighteenth century as a turning point in the history of affective life: the time when kinship ceased to be based, first and foremost, on consanguineous ties; when definitions of kin that instead privileged affinal ties combined with a new account of the affections produced by domestic cohabitation, a convergence that produced "the modern family"; when matrimony came to the forefront of public discourse on amorous experience and when it came decisively to monopolize, as well, the culture's accounts of lifetime companionship, of people who were and would remain a good fit. I wish to add a twist to that historiography: maybe that reinvention of conjugality as long-haul intimacy—as well as the creation of the idea of the marriageable type—proceeded in tandem with the reinvention of literature and the reimagining of the duration of literary effects. "A lively imagination creates a sympathy with favourite authors, which gives to their sentiments the same power over the mind, as that possessed by an intimate and ever present friend," the moralist and novelist Elizabeth Hamilton observes in 1810. The way that Hamilton concludes the sentence suggests that the ever-presentness of that imaginary friend is crucial for her: "Hence a taste for reading becomes to females of still greater importance than it is of to men."[31] This is reading as a kind of cohabitation. The suggestion is, in effect, that authors who will always be on their minds train young ladies for married life, with husbands who will likewise incessantly claim mental time and space. In his 1804 *Letters to a Young Lady on a Course of English Poetry*, John Aikin uses similar language mediating between the durational order of canonical literature and the durational order of conjugality.

He segregates the poems that he does not want to see as "the favourites" or "closet companions" of the "Young Lady" whom he addresses from those poems that he declares, in effect, better marriage material—that poetry that will leave the young lady "possessed for life," Aikin states, with a source of "elegant entertainment."[32]

THE ANTHOLOGY AND THE ALMANAC

As this example of a young lady's aesthetic education suggests, at the turn of the nineteenth century the ideal of the lifelong companionate marriage, itself a construct of books, began to reorganize other social expectations, including those involving books. We have already seen, at the opening of this chapter, signs of how that ideal inflects Hunt's program in *A Book for a Corner*, which anthologizes "such authors as retain . . . the most friendly and as it were domestic hold" upon readers (v). Hunt's expectations of literature are worth making explicit. Literature is to give people the emotional content for everyday life at every stage of their life cycles. It both benefits from and assists in the sanctification of that everyday ordinary time—time as cycle, time as unremitting and regular measures—that in Hunt's day was becoming the sanctioned time of private affection. To enhance his readers' sense that the authors whom he excerpted "sympathize with [them] through all portions of [their lives]" (v), Hunt in fact arranged the anthology's contents so that "the first extract is a Letter addressed to an Infant [a poem by the bluestocking Catherine Talbot], the last the Elegy in the Churchyard [by Thomas Gray], and the intermediate ones have something of an analogous reference to the successive stages of existence" (v). Nowadays we may scarcely notice how all the literary diaries and poem-a-day calendars that sit atop our desks likewise urge the claims of this socio-temporal order, so often has literariness been pressed into this kind of service since Hunt's era. Beginning in the last two decades of the nineteenth century, publishers of volumes such as, for example, *Birthday Echoes from the Poets: A Selection of Choice Quotations Arranged for Every Day in the Year* (1886) promise recipients of these books that they will be able (in the customary phrase) to "go through the year" with "the poets" or, more intimately still, with *an* author who is a particular favorite (a role assigned by these volumes, mostly the manufacture of Hatchards Publishing, to, variously, Chaucer, Shakespeare, Milton, Cowper, Burns, Keats, Scott, the Brontës, the Brownings, George Eliot, Dickens, Hardy, Kipling, Longfellow, Whittier, and Brett Harte—not an exhaustive list). These "remembrancers" and birthday books—whose selections are arranged so as to constitute a "daily text book," as the subtitle of *The Hemans Birthday Book* explains (*A Selection of Beautiful Passages from the Poems of Felicia Hemans, Arranged as a Daily Text Book*)—bind the individual's cultivation of the literary sensibility to the practices she uses to mark off the progress of the year and to remember anniversaries and appointments. They bank on the association of literariness and perdurable attachments.

Victorian publishers' recognition that dailiness itself could be an object of their marketing conditioned even their handling of the Bible, motivating their mutation of immutable holy writ. The term "textbook," the *Oxford English Dictionary* instructs us, took on a new, specialized meaning circa 1861, as a designation for "a book containing a selection of Scripture texts, arranged for daily use or easy reference." As this definition clarifies, the Victorian readers who aimed to read Felicia Hemans or, as in Ruskin's case, to "use Wordsworth," "as a daily text-book" made large claims for the seriousness of their devotion.

Let us linger with Hunt so as to examine up close one progenitor of these volumes: his *The Literary Pocket-Book; or Companion for the Lover of Nature and Art*. One of Hunt's earliest anthologizing projects—in fact, an odd compound of anthology with almanac, historical primer, and London guidebook—*The Literary Pocket-Book* was published in five consecutive installments from 1819 to 1823, which suggests that one ought to backdate the Victorian birthday books' aspiration to fuse the canon with the almanac to Hunt's romantic moment. Present-day scholars who have engaged Hunt's project have been interested principally in the section of "Original Poetry" that comes near the end of the first volume: John Keats's sonnet "The Human Seasons" had its first printing there. Hunt's introduction, however, is less excited about that "Original Poetry" than about the *Pocket-Book*'s "nomenclatures"; for these, he notes, go beyond the information about, for instance, "hackney-coach rates" that was incorporated in most contemporary almanacs, so as to include, among other lists, a "Chronological list of eminent persons in letters, philosophy, and the arts" that runs from Trismegistus to Mary Wollstonecraft and Madame de Staël. The latter account of time as sequence is within the *Pocket-Book* counterbalanced by a "Calendar of Nature"—a description of the progress of the seasons and nature's varied appearances through the year, which presents time as a cycle.[33] This calendar too is touted in Hunt's introduction (2), which also spells out Hunt's hope that, primed by the notations in the diary section that mark the birthdays of men of "ORIGINAL genius," the purchaser of *The Literary Pocket-Book* may be tempted after "he turns, for his ordinary memoranda, to the Diary," "to make some little homage in the course of the day to the memory of a favourite writer or artist,—to drink it after dinner or turn to his life or works" (2).

Over the course of the eighteenth century, almanac and pocket-book makers had established a certain set of print protocols to make visible time's uniformity (the empty spaces of identical dimension, one succeeding the other as the almanac's user proceeds methodically through the book). They number, accordingly, among the discoverers of "homogeneous, empty time."[34] In the *Pocket-Book*, as literariness is adapted to this format, its daili-ness becomes visible too. Hunt allies not only the selections of "Original Poetry," but also a larger literary tradition, with time's measured regularity. Such a scheme—like the scheme for a *Muses' Almanack* floated in 1823 by Thomas Hood—builds bridges between personal experience (the domain of familiar intimacy and everyday routines) and public time, subjective time and literature's.[35]

It would not be unreasonable to deride this scheme as *kitsch*. After all, ac-cording to Franco Moretti, kitsch originates with the desire to "domesticate" aesthetic experience and to render art the material from which households are constructed.[36] Conceding that should not, however, get in the way of acknowledging the indications that for Hunt, this bridge building was con-tinuous with his radical republicanism. He declares at the outset his demo-cratic desire to supply "intellectual power" "a Court Calendar of its own" (1). Pointedly, the *Pocket-Book* excludes the notations of royal birthdays and dates of accession to the throne that were standard in the almanacs of his contemporaries. In 1819 Hunt's invitation to his readers to rewrite the year according to their own private, bookish meanings would have recalled the example of the French revolutionaries' refashioning of their calendar not quite twenty years before.[37] Hunt's diversion of almanac time to new ends also links his volume directly to a near-contemporary publishing experi-ment by a fellow radical, William Hone's *The Every-Day Book* (first published in weekly numbers from 1825 to 1826), a miscellany of folklore, secret his-tory, curious literary anecdotes, records of seasonal temperatures, and po-ems. Hone manages somehow, while jumbling all that material together, to cite Hunt's *The Literary Pocket-Book* liberally as well. The subtitle to *The Every-Day Book* declares it an "everlasting calendar of popular amusements, sports, pastimes, ceremonies, manners, customs, and events, incident to each of the three hundred and sixty-five days" and recommends it for "daily use and diversion" (fig. 4.1).

One can indeed go through the year with Hone's book, one day after the next, and begin the cycle anew on New Year's Day. And Hone's explanatory

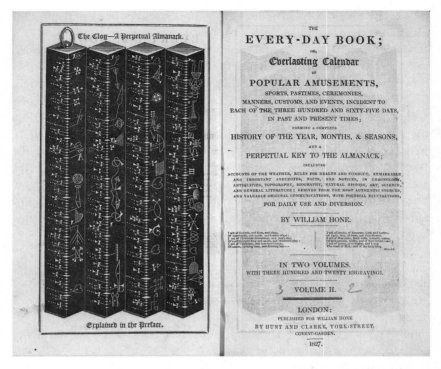

FIGURE 4.1 Frontispiece and title page from volume 2 of William Hone's *The Every-Day Book* (1827). As Hone explains, the frontispiece depicts the stick, known as the "clog" or "perpetual almanack," that formerly was "in common use with our ancient ancestors." The notches on the stick denote the phases of the moon and the pictorial carvings symbolize the saints' days. Photograph: Courtesy of the Thomas Fisher Rare Book Library, University of Toronto.

address mentions, in particular, the "kind feelings" that are engendered by the "excellent poetry [interspersed] throughout the work." (This category includes, for instance, Wordsworth's "Influence of Natural Objects in Calling Forth and Strengthening the Imagination in Boyhood and Early Youth" and Keats's "Ode to a Nightingale," the latter supplied by Hone on the pages of his second volume that he dedicates to February 23, marked as the date of Keats's death in Rome.) Hone resorts to a poet to make his point about that soliciting of feeling: "As [William] Cowper says, . . . 'a volume of verse is a fiddle that sets the universe in motion.'"[38]

It is easy to overlook this political dimension of the fusing of literariness

with everydayness—the challenge to class hierarchy embedded in this policy of vulgarization. (*The Literary Pocket-Book* "saunter[s] between the polite
and the plebeian" in ways that, as other descriptions of Hunt's Cockney
informality have stressed, often infuriated tradition-minded commentators.)[39] The analytic difficulty that this mode of romantic anthologizing
poses for the twenty-first-century critic is that its impulse to make literariness familiar is now itself become excessively familiar. After all, the
descendants of the *Pocket-Book* and *The Every-Day Book* represent a major
branch of the contemporary book trade. Available in every museum gift
shop, those poem-a-day calendars and literary diaries and address books
currently share shelf space with twee, pretty, pastel knickknacks (cute cat
books, fridge magnets, and coffee mugs stenciled with cheery mottoes), all
those things that are marketed to women especially as the very currency of
their long-term, cozy togetherness. Consumer culture in late capitalism has
long since deviated from the state of affairs depicted by the historian John
Crowley, who describes how the orientation to the comfortable was "an innovative aspect of Anglo-American culture" in the late eighteenth century,
and the province of an intellectual vanguard who felt it had to be taught and
learned.[40]

Pledged to familiarity, kitsch repudiates the distanced relationship to
phenomena that is valued in orthodox accounts of the aesthetic transaction.
Of course, recovering the historicity of the love of literature has, throughout this book, meant tracing a counterplot to those orthodox accounts of
the development of aesthetics, since these tend to make, not attachment,
but detachment their end point. The retroactive Kantianism of the orthodox
account predisposes it to highlight disinterested judgments wherever they
can be found. It occludes therefore the aspects of romantic-period aesthetic
theorizing that helped to legitimate readers' investments in reiterability, and
which at this point I want to engage in depth. For the original consumers
of Hunt's kitsch—the first beneficiaries, more precisely, of Hunt's impulse
to make literariness an everyday matter—differed from their modern-day
equivalents in a signal respect. When romantic-era readers made their literary transactions into a forum in which they reunited with the friends with
whom they were to go through the year and through life, they found support in the aesthetic theorizing of their time. If romantic-era readers turned
to favorite authors as they sought to position themselves within "temporal
convoys,"[41] several accounts of aesthetic experience that conflated the pleasures of reading with the pleasures of remembered, refelt feeling promoted
those temporal connections. My next section examines those accounts.

THE AESTHETICS OF ASSOCIATIONISM:
GOOD VIBRATIONS AND KINDRED EMOTIONS

Romantic-era critics' readiness to promote the domestication of the aesthetic relation can be seen, in fact, as the logical adjunct of their commitment to an empiricist model of mind and of their interest in how the impressionable, receptive minds that empiricism predicated found themselves moved during the process of reading. With imaginative writing valued primarily as a conduit for the communication of feeling, the perennial subject for the critic working in the second half of the eighteenth century and first half of the nineteenth was "emotions caused by fiction," the latter being a blanket term for imaginative writing. (The phrase is in fact one of the section titles of Henry Homes, Lord Kames's *Elements of Criticism*, which was published in 1762 and was still being pressed into service in American colleges a century later.) Let me begin this section by delineating the terms in which emotions caused by fiction were most often engaged, since these also shaped the framework in which readers were meant to think about their emotions *for* fiction.

As modern commentators often note, critics during this period by and large sidelined the questions about the unities and decorums that had earlier preoccupied neoclassical critics. The psychologically focused discussions that these writers pursued instead took two forms. Both were informed by a description of the brain, obtained from earlier philosophers of mind such as John Locke, David Hume, and David Hartley, as an echo chamber of vibrations and oscillations, and informed too by an account of cerebration as consisting largely in a reactivation that riveted associations formed, even haphazardly, in the past. Sometimes critics focused on the author's mental state during the activity of composition, aiming to piece together—according to the principles of mental correspondences outlined in that "doctrine" of associations—the itinerary of imaginative wandering followed by an author who was carried away by his own conceptions and passions or who threw himself into a character's. (The latter process, it was emphasized, depended on the author's personal acquaintance with "such associations as a person actually under that passion would be likely to make.")[42] At other times, these later eighteenth-century writers and their nineteenth-century successors addressed the psychological and physiological states induced by the activity of reading, aiming to delineate the associative excursions, "this vibration of the mind in passing and repassing betwixt things that are related," that the readers of an author would embark on in their turn.[43] Those excursions might begin with the ideas—the denotative meanings—regularly linked to the words on the page. But they would also invariably, it was conceded, extend and augment those meanings and amalgamate them with readers' own imaginings. Valued as "reverie," the private castle-in-the-air building that the language of a text prompted in the reader was regarded as a defining component of aesthetic experience.[44]

Hence Joseph Priestley in his 1777 *Course of Lectures on Oratory and Criticism*, a book which aims—reworking the ground that Lord Kames had already tilled—to demonstrate how "the doctrine of the association of ideas" might account for "the striking effect of Excellencies in Composition." (Priestley prints in this volume the lectures he gave a decade before at Warrington, the dissenting academy that often figures in histories of the literary studies curriculum.) In Lecture 12, Priestley mentions the contribution that "the discreet use of fiction and works of the imagination" might make to the project of cultivating the heart and determines that the trickiness such a project entails lies in the fact that "the heart is instructed chiefly by its own feelings."[45] The feelings represented in texts, Priestley is saying, do some educating of the reader's heart; but the greater workload is carried by the feelings that the heart feels—or, more often, which it rediscovers and reenacts—in responding to those representations. (The representations themselves might well be considered merely as means to this end.) In this scheme, what endowed the elements of a piece of writing with their power to trigger emotional effects was the cluster of contexts, called up by way of association, in which they had appeared to the reader in the past. The raison d'être of poetry, the critic Francis Jeffrey declared in a typical statement in the 1809 *Edinburgh Review*, "is to awaken in our minds a train of kindred emotions, and to excite our imaginations to work out for themselves a tissue of pleasing or impressive conceptions." That "train of . . . emotions" that swept up the reader would have her retracing mental itineraries traced before, whether in previous encounters with other texts or in the course of experiences that were evoked anew by the world of her book.[46]

Priestley's statement about audiences' auto-education—"the heart is instructed . . . by its own feelings"—suggests two important aspects of the psychologistic discussion of the belles lettres that prevailed at the close of the eighteenth century and opening of the nineteenth. It suggests the extent to which a description of the emotional, imaginative process that a poem's diction, imagery, and rhythm triggered within a particular readerly psyche (the critic's own) might also, in this period, count as a valid description of the poem. Writing from the end of the eighteenth century and beginning of

the nineteenth rarely affirms our present-day expectation that a proper critical stance depends on distinguishing the poem, as an objective structure,
from individuals' experience of the poem while reading it. Interpretation—
though never far from our present-day sense of what reading is, or at least
"a reading" is—is not its aim. This criticism from the age of associationism
downplays assessments of the aesthetic object in and for itself, while it plays
up the *reader's* subjective experience of that object. Within that subjective
experience, moreover, the process of recollection often appears to outweigh
in importance the acquisition of new information.[47]

Another aspect of this psychologistic discussion of literary matters worth
highlighting is the readiness with which it acknowledges that large areas
of mental life are, or quickly become, unconscious and automatic.[48] The
sentimental education that reading is said to sponsor when "the heart is
instructed . . . by its own feelings" is not exactly a scene of consciousness-
raising. In describing association's workings, Kames declares that "one passion is often productive of another," a declaration that omits the person
"having" the emotions from the picture, implying that emotions are not
quite the person's to command.[49] The phrase "train of kindred emotions"
in Jeffrey's description of a response to poetry has similar implications. As I
have just suggested, romantic-period critics' accounts of these mental operations that readers perform in reading gave pride of place to remembrance
of readings past. But it is noteworthy that the sort of recollecting that in this
context reading is believed to trigger verges on being what Henri Bergson
would later call "habit memory." This remembering is less a cognitive operation than an automatic physiological reflex, a "process of serial stimula-
tion that occurred through the senses and inside the body."[50] Setting out
something like this contrast in an aesthetic treatise of 1753, Joseph Warton
(brother to Thomas) declared that, although the "understanding feels no
pleasure in being instructed twice in the same thing," "the heart is capable
of feeling the same emotion twice, with great pleasure." For Warton, the
heart's capacity to keep on keeping on explained the greater rereadability
of the eclogue, a poetic form engaging that organ, in comparison to that of
didactic poetry that necessarily, and to its disadvantage, targeted its readers'
understandings.[51]

The philosophers of mind and medical practitioners whom literary critics
consulted through the eighteenth and nineteenth centuries often found in
the activity of reading a model for consciousness's operations in all manner
of situations. Reading was suited for that exemplary role precisely because
habit makes it a quasi-reflex action, an activity that, confronted with the

sight of script, we are engaged in almost before we know it. Habit enables the reader's naturalizing of the initially arbitrary connection between the verbal sign and what it imports. So associated in our "habit memories" are the several motions of several muscles that make up the action of reading that—reading with facility, finding this mental process as automatic as the physical processes of walking or breathing—we no longer have the where-withal to pull them apart. My favorite example of this commentary on how reading comes naturally and involuntarily occurs at a moment in the philosopher, poet, and physician Erasmus Darwin's *Zoonomia* (1796): Darwin has his audience read the words "PRINTING PRESS" and then queries us whether we have attended to the shape, size, and existence of the thirteen letters or whether the motion of our retinas has not produced, instead, the idea of the "most useful of modern inventions."[52]

Cued by such descriptions of consciousness's automatist proclivities, literary critics of the period endowed habit with great explanatory power. Thus when Priestley, for instance, sought to explain to his audience why be-holders of a play feel sympathy when confronting scenes of "ideal" (unreal) distress, in which the passions are "unavailing," he identified the power of habit as the cause. The passions are roused, blindly, and mechanically, when-ever "suitable circumstances are presented," he notes, and the association of certain passions with certain circumstances overrides reason's objection that these things are merely representations, so that "if we read and form an *idea* of the scenes there exhibited, we must *feel* in spite of ourselves."[53]

Criticism also *valued* the power of habit. This is more surprising. As is well known, the section of John Locke's *Essay concerning Human Understanding* that first put the association of ideas on the agenda of the philosophy of mind finds Locke intent on alarming his readers. His topic there was our suscep-tibility to madness. To launch his investigation of how this "Connexion in our Minds of *Ideas* in themselves, loose and independent one of another" becomes a matter of "custom" for the mind, Locke discusses the insanity to which such connecting of ideas leads. "*Ideas* that in themselves are not at all of kin, come to be so united in some Mens Minds, that tis very hard to separate them, they always keep in company, and the one no sooner at any time comes into the Understanding but its Associate appears with it . . . the whole gang always inseparable shew themselves together." This clustering of ideas repeats and repeats. The anxiety close to the surface in this section of Locke's *Essay* is also in part the one at issue when we speak of someone as a slave to habit. His gang of ideas threaten individual self-possession. But late eighteenth-century and early nineteenth-century belletristic writers took a different tack while they applied Lockean premises about the association of ideas to aesthetic matters. Archibald Alison, for instance, asserts in his *Essays on the Nature and Principles of Taste* (1790) that it is "in this powerless state of reverie, when we are carried on by our conceptions, *not guiding them*, that the deepest emotions of beauty and sublimity are felt."[54] Romantic-period critics redeemed the workings of association from Locke's charge that the automatic nature of associative thought estranged us from our reason and will.

In large part, they did so by highlighting associations' capacity to "bring us *back* to the starting-point from which we have diverged."[55] These writers promoted aesthetic experience precisely *as* experience that summoned anew the secondhand materials that had been previously lodged in the mind. The doctrine of the association of ideas enabled writers on belles lettres to celebrate reading as a means by which readers returned home to themselves, as Jeffrey's reference to the "*kindred* emotions" that poetry awakens suggests.

Freighted with this account of aesthetic experience as homecoming, criticism represents one more context that made the lifetime reading and re-reading plans sketched in the previous section of this chapter make sense. Prevailing critical formulations invited the bookish to imagine that they might have stored their pasts *inside* their favorite books or—to shift metaphors—invited them to understand their reading matter as a mirror with a memory. In his *A View of the Pleasures Arising from a Love of Books* (a series of letters addressed, as Aikin's 1804 *Letters* had been, "to a lady") the Reverend Edward Mangin declared that "few things are more palatable than the pleasure communicated by this mirror-like property which books have." (So, much later, Charles Dickens's hero David Copperfield reminisced about his long-ago childhood reading with his nurse Peggotty and said of his return to those books: "I find it very curious to see my own infant face, looking up at me from the Crocodile Stories.")[56] Hazlitt discussed this property at length in "On Reading Old Books," the essay in which he punningly portrays books as "bind[ing] together the different scattered visions of our personal identity" (221). That reunions with "old books" represented, in this manner, a forum in which readers might monitor the continuity of their lives over time was, Hazlitt believed, one reason for old books' superiority over new. In the *Edinburgh Review* essay I quoted above, Francis Jeffrey denied any real power of pleasing to new poems that depended on novelty to be striking. Jeffrey proposed reserving praise for those new poems only that "propagate throughout the imagination that long series of delightful movements which is only excited when the song of the poet is the echo of our familiar feelings."[57]

I like the looping syntax that entangles Jeffrey in this depiction of literature as a space of self-memorialization. He is, in essence, stating that, during encounters with the estimable poetry that we love, our feelings are moved by what echoes our feelings. The looping mimes the reverberant flip-flopping between cause and effect, and reality and representation, that from the mid-eighteenth century on fascinated the philosophers of mind who were the most influential exponents of the doctrine of associations. Back in 1749 in *Observations on Man*, David Hartley had evoked that flip-flopping with phrases such as "the same perpetual recurrency of vibrations." In mental life as depicted in the *Observations*, ideas and feelings are said to both draw strength from associated ideas and feelings and impart strength in their turn. Hartley's inspiration, David Hume, had treated this topic via a different idiom (no "vibrations" or "vibratiuncles" in *A Treatise of Human Nature* [1739-40]), but with similarly vertiginous effects. For Hume, capturing the story of persons' psychic operations meant doing justice to the spiraling fashion in which sensations and ideas, the emotions that the person feels and the emotions that the person merely recollects or reads about, will—though related as originals are to copies—nonetheless trade places perpetually. Hume's description of psychic operations brings to view a principle of reverse mimesis in which the representational film ordinarily dividing idea from object may be endlessly broached. As a matter of course, he explains, the idea of a passion may be converted "into an impression, and acquire such a degree of force and vivacity as to become the very passion itself."[58]

The account of psychic life and its rhythms that Hume and Hartley delivered affords emotion a life support system. So supported, feeling never, as we might expect, fades irreversibly into memory. It is never *merely* habitual because it is always on the verge of making a comeback. Our usual premises about the affective entropy that comes with the passage of time are obstacles here. They make it hard for us to acknowledge how readers in the past might have identified the essence of feeling with its reiterative practice—an identification both facilitated by and facilitating their habitual exercises of literary leisure. Philosophy in this mode repeatedly raises the distinctions between emotions engendered by experience and emotions caused by the fictions that merely simulate experience only to put them aside. It does the same with the distinctions between emotions one feels and emotions one only recollects.

The principles that these philosophers outlined are generally considered pivotal for the affective revolution of the late eighteenth century. They underwrote the interest in sympathy, that capacity to "feel other people's feelings" that, with far-reaching political consequences, late eighteenth-century Europeans learned to construe "as the sign of humankind's essentially social nature."⁵⁹ Modern commentators have noticed, all the same, the conservatism of this account and the resilience it bestows on the status quo. Jerome Christensen, for instance, has described Hume's program as a philosopher and historian as hinging on his desire to reduce individual and historical experience to a "continuous present" that might be sustained by the "various devices of repetition." When Hume describes the self and the social formation, Christensen has stated, he tends to arrange for questions about beginnings and terminations to be canceled "under the dispensation of an ongoing maintenance."⁶⁰ Strange things do happen to temporal sequence in the associationists' universe, as a direct consequence of the associationists' attentiveness to the force of habit. And that same strange time frame, which Christensen calls a "continuous present," is also at issue when commentators used associationism to ponder the nature and duration of literary effects, the time frame in which "emotions caused by fiction" subsist.

This becomes apparent if one takes a second look at, for instance, Jeffrey's description in the *Edinburgh Review* of the raison d'être of poetry, this time through the lens supplied by Christensen's analysis of Hume. One notices, then, that having cast estimable poems as reminiscent ("the echo of our familiar feelings") Jeffrey goes on to challenge commonsense propositions about time's linearity. For he also casts those estimable poems as proleptic, remarking how they "strike root and germinate in the mind, like the seeds of its native feelings." Jeffrey's own flip-flopping rhetoric in this piece of criticism—poems in his scheme both echo and implant feelings, and the feelings themselves are both deep-rooted and just germinating seeds—aptly suggests, in fact, the tautology that is customary in most discourses of canonicity, in which the best poetry is deemed the best (iterable) because it is familiar, and in which it is familiar (iterated) because it has been deemed the best. Jeffrey, in other words, has done more than internalize Hume's account of habit as second nature. He has also anticipated Steve Connor's discussion of iterability and l-iterature. Jeffrey's rhetoric resonates too with a definition of the everyday tendered by the twentieth-century philosopher Maurice Blanchot—"what we never see for a first time, but only see again, having always already seen it by an illusion that is, as it happens, constitutive of the everyday."⁶¹

Received accounts of romantic aesthetics do not prepare us all that well for this associationist critic's affiliation of literariness with the familiarity that we "only see again," any more than they prepare us for the kitschification of the literary tradition promoted by Hunt's *Pocket-Book* or for the lifetime reading plan outlined in his *A Book for a Corner*. The romantic understanding of art, it is usually said, prioritized the breaking of habit, not its reinforcement. Definitions of romanticism regularly cite the poets' antipathy toward the emotional torpor induced by the routinized and customary. (Pedagogically many of us model ourselves after this romantic profile. If, as Warner states, piety about critical reading forms "the folk ideology" of professional literary studies, piety about defamiliarization plays a supporting role. We often say that we aim for our classes to shake up our students and make them *un*comfortable—as though we conceived of the literary experiences we administer as a kind of electroshock therapy jolting them into intellectual health.)[62] And it is not simply the role repetition is granted within this scheme—the fact that associationism underwrites a notion of aesthetic pleasure as "thriv[ing] . . . on copies and replicas"—that challenges received wisdom.[63] Another problem is the elongated time frame that associationism invokes, thanks to its concern with habituated responses and steady states.

At first glance, nothing could be more different from aesthetic experience than the associationists' "perpetual recurrency of vibrations." Suddenness and all-at-once-ness are the classic hallmarks of aesthetic experience. Aristotle's *Poetics* linked it to sudden fear. Longinus contrasted the sublime— brilliant moments of high-intensity incandescence; gusts and thunderbolts in his meteorological terms—to those lesser, monotonous concerns of composition that had to be developed "by slow degrees" through the "whole texture" of the work. With similar effects, descriptions of literary form have long identified it with what is emphatically transient. Catherine Gallagher outlines, for instance, how New Critical identifications of the poem as a momentary arrest of an epiphanic perception and structuralism's elevation of synchrony over diachrony alike work to sever literariness from sequence and aesthetics from duration.[64]

The conventional identification of romantic aesthetic theory as the consummation of an earlier discussion of the sublime in fact occludes some aspects of this theory's distinctive dispositions toward time and duration. (Definitions of romanticism that forget the novel's increasing authority during the period also contribute to this blind spot—as we will see later.) Even the celebrations of spontaneous feelings that are so frequent in romantic poetics can be seen as working not in opposition to, but in consort with, discussions of habitual pleasures.

Of course, Samuel Taylor Coleridge famously linked William Wordsworth's achievement in *Lyrical Ballads* to the way his verse remedied the repressive effects of custom: *Biographia Literaria* identifies Wordsworth's genius with his capacity to make the reader see afresh "forms, incidents, and situations, of which, for the common view, custom had bedimmed all the lustre."[65] But in fact Wordsworth's preface to *Lyrical Ballads*, though it founds "all good poetry" on "the spontaneous overflow of powerful feelings," floats more than once a notion of literature as an occasion for and creator of steadying attachments.[66] It predicts the reception scenario that Wordsworthians such as Henry Reed and John Ruskin—who each, as we saw, pressed Wordsworth's verse into everyday service—would make a necessary adjunct to literariness. Thus the suggestive terminology of the passage in the preface in which Wordsworth strives to specify the role that poetry ought to play within the network of discourses surrounding it. Having depicted the "man of science" as one who seeks "truth as a remote and unknown benefactor," Wordsworth goes on to demote that man in comparison to the poet, who, by contrast, makes truth present as "our visible friend and hourly companion" (606). He makes proximity crucial to the personalization that differentiates readers' relation to the poets from their relation to other sorts of benefactors. With that odd adjective "hourly," he associates poets' beneficence with the regularity and repetitiveness of time's fixed measures.

Wordsworth's reference to around-the-clock reader friendliness chimes with other formulations the period coins to valorize literature's soliciting of perdurable attachments. Many of these have been forgotten because they are so difficult to square with now-conventional accounts of the development of aesthetic theory. Who remembers now, for instance, that one author after another during Wordsworth's lifetime mentioned something that was called "a parlour-window book" and pressed that phrase into service as a moniker for the kind of book that itself solicited perpetual recycling? Montaigne, with whom the phrase originates, had half in earnest deprecated the prospect that his *Essays* might "only serve the Ladies for a common moveable, a Book to lie in the Parlour Window" and proposed jokingly that he "be preferred to the Closet" (meaning the study) instead. But later writers often claimed for themselves just the standing Montaigne disdained. To be that book that is never returned to the bookcase but instead left out in the open, the "parlour-window book . . . left lying about, . . . as a source of constant recreation," could define the ambition of many of Montaigne's successors—William Hone included, whose preface to *The Table Book*, the 1827 follow-up to *The Every-Day Book*, I have just cited, and Leigh Hunt, as well, whose *A Book for a Corner* was "(not to say it immodestly) intended to live in old parlour windows" (2).[67] This aspiration relates more closely to the high-romantic tradition than we might suspect, and its traces are discernable in genres beyond that of the familiar essay, the form that Montaigne would share with Hunt. When, as Hazlitt recounted in his story of bygone literary friendships, "My First Acquaintance with Poets," he and Coleridge breakfasted together in the "old fashioned parlour" of the inn at Linton in Wales in 1798, they found a worn-out copy of Thomson's *The Seasons* that was lying "in a window-seat." That the poetry had found this home struck the romantic poet, Hazlitt reports, as an instance of "true fame."[68]

That this location for literariness was also the space of habit—that a "visible friend and hourly companion" might be *taken for granted*, as the object of that kind of intimacy that gets absorbed, invisibly, into the continuum of daily life—merits underlining. Despite the way we draw the battle lines of the period, the canonical texts of romantic aesthetics can yield just what critical writing that overtly drew on associationist psychology can: an account of literary experience as a kind of school for healthy habits. Intent on tracking Wordsworth's and Coleridge's opposition to empiricist models of the human mind (their disputes with Locke, Hume, and Hartley), romanticists frequently overlook just how often nonetheless these two appear to have heeded the lessons about the mind's propensity for repetition and its pleasure "in the same emotion twice" that were showcased within the physiological and medical writings subscribing to just these models. The poets read the physicians—the poets' reputations for idealism notwithstanding—and, indeed, recent commentators on the preface to *Lyrical Ballads* have noticed just how often Wordsworth echoes contemporary medical writings as he redefines the nature of the poet and of poetry.[69]

At this moment, the Brunonian system of medicine linked health to the maintenance of the proper proportion of excitability in the human organism and made the physician responsible for managing his patients—and his patients' passions—so that they might avoid both under- and overstimulation. The poet whom Wordsworth profiled in the preface is assigned a similar medico-moral project.[70] This poet's authority over the well-being of readerly bodies is a function of how poetry—as redescribed within the preface—balances a commitment to the excitements that sets readers' pulses racing with a commitment to low-intensity, long-lasting affects—the sensation of comfort, for example. What to make of the preface's recurrent references to permanence and durability—to how a poetry drawing on rural life, where "passions . . . are incorporated with the . . . permanent forms of nature," might be "a class of Poetry . . . well adapted to interest mankind permanently" (597, 595)? Or what to make of that need to situate "spontaneous feelings" in an intricate relation to "habits of mind" that we obey "blindly and mechanically"? Wordsworth's portrait of the artist in the preface depicts a creature of healthy habits. His poet is endowed "with such habits of mind . . . that, by obeying blindly and mechanically the impulses of those habits, [he] shall describe objects, and utter sentiments" in a way that will of necessity enlighten any audience which is in turn, and reciprocally, "in a healthful state of association" (598). Wordsworth too is interested in the conditions under which participants in literary culture might go steady.

I use that term in ways meant to suggest romantic attachment—and indeed we might think of Wordsworth, as we thought of Leigh Hunt, as being another romantic "wedded to books." (In the autobiographical *Prelude* Wordsworth declares his constancy: "The books which then I loved the most / Are dearest to me now," though a passage in *Prelude 5*, which I'll discuss in this book's final chapter, calls that constancy into question.)[71] At the same time I am equally determined to use the term "going steady" to designate a condition of physical well-being. Those two senses were not always kept apart. In the last two decades of Wordsworth's life, phrenologists on both sides of the Atlantic took to detecting marriageability in the configurations of individuals' skulls, locating there not only "organs of amativeness" (whose ostensible existence proved that romantic love came naturally), but also organs of adhesiveness (the cause of marital fidelity, according to George Combe, and national allegiance).[72] We should not assume that the poets always shared our presupposition that to somaticize reading is to criticize it.[73] When Wordsworth and Coleridge took up the issues of emotional constancy and routinized passions that psychologically minded critics such as Jeffrey were making central to discussion of "emotions caused by fiction," they aimed to profile a reading body that, in exemplary fashion, would be on an even keel.

In *Biographia Literaria*, Coleridge expressed alarm over the bad effects on the individual's memory wrought by the "perusal of periodical works" (1:49), articulating a commonplace in medical discourse about the magazine reader. For instance, Benjamin Rush (American physician and a founder of Dickinson College on the Pennsylvania frontier) warned that reader in 1812 of the debility that would be produced by the suddenness of "the frequent and rapid transition from one subject to another" that her reading matter encouraged.[74] This passage in the *Biographia* is there in part to be counter-pointed by commentary on the rereadability of what Coleridge, intent on carving out and consolidating the category of literariness, calls "essential poetry" (1:23). That literary category comprehends "not the poem which we have *read*, but that to which we *return*" (1:23; Coleridge's emphasis).

Coleridge similarly identifies the value of Cervantes's *Don Quixote* with the reiterability that prompts its "admirers [to] . . . open the book on those parts which they best recollect, even as we visit those friends oftenest whom we love the most" (2:187) The time frame in which this encounter between friends unfolds is odd—there is no imagining a first reading here, so intent is Coleridge here on dissociating *Don Quixote* from narrative excitement. Its admirers, he declared, "feel the disposition to go back and re-peruse some preceding chapter, at least ten times, for once that they find any eagerness to hurry forwards" (2:187).

Solicitous about readers' overexcitable nerves, Coleridge divides literary appreciation from the pleasures of novelty. At the same time, however, his medical advice also doubles as moral judgment: he would expel from literary culture those readers who might be inclined to feel in the wrong way. The word "genuine" in the following passage indicates as much: "Our genuine admiration of a great poet is a continuous *under-current* of feeling; it is every where present, but seldom any where a separate excitement" (1:23; Coleridge's emphasis). Admittedly, Coleridge is of two minds about the conditions of familiarity that underwrite such mild, steadying feelings. Just as typical in the *Biographia* are passages like the one that laments the loss of aura effected by the rapid growth of the reading public and wider diffusion of literature. Books in "times of old" were "as religious oracles," but with their increase in numbers they have descended to "the rank of instructive friends" or, worse, of "entertaining companions" (1:57). Aesthetic experiences, Coleridge is lamenting, have been diffused to the point of banality. In her study of the affects that are awkward to accommodate to conventional accounts of aesthetic emotions, Sianne Ngai speculates that "something about the cultural canon itself seems to prefer higher passions and emotions," by which she means eruptive moments of upheaval, rage or fear or grief. She muses that the ongoingness of certain "moods"—entirely opposed to the suddenness of Aristotle's catharsis or Longinus's sublime—appears to disable the texts that those moods drive "from acquiring canonical distinction."[75] Coleridge's ambivalence about familiarity, about the take-it-for-grantedness that is the fate of modern literature, may register his acceptance of this axiology. But what Coleridge also demonstrates in the *Biographia*—in his guise as a theorist of canonicity, a theorist of "reading old books," we might say, thinking of Hazlitt, rather than as a theorist of aesthetics—is that the very idea of a canon involves a structure of feeling that values lasting literature for its round-the-clock proximity.

In another health-conscious passage of the *Biographia*, Coleridge touted as a defining property of poetry its "exciting [of] a more continuous and equal attention" than that solicited by "the language of prose" (2:15). His solicitude about readerly overexcitement determined his ranking of literary genres. This was true of Wordsworth as well, as his discussion of meter evinces. Passages of his preface to *Lyrical Ballads* seem to evoke a hydraulic model of poetic action and stress reduction, a model in which the metrical repetitions that distinguish poetry from prose perform a crucial function. For Wordsworth, Susan Wolfson has noted in her reading of those passages, the repetitions of poetry—its rhymes and rhythms—represent a "self-regulation generated by the passionate mind itself."[76] Metrical composition tempers the excitements that might carry poets and readers beyond the proper bounds, as it introduces "the co-presence of something regular, something to which the mind has been accustomed . . . in a less excited state" (609). Having set up this model, Wordsworth goes on to link such repetitions within the work to repetitions *of* the work. He endows meter with the capacity to confer rereadability on literary representations: "Words metrically arranged will long continue to impart . . . pleasure" (609). The fact that even the most emotionally wrenching scenes of Shakespeare never, Wordsworth declares, "act upon us as pathetic beyond the bounds of pleasure" is to be ascribed to "small but continual and regular impulses of pleasurable surprise from the metrical arrangement" (610).[77] This praise bestowed on poetry's and poetic drama's rereadability comes precisely at the novel's expense. Wordsworth follows up this comment on the reiterable pleasure of Shakespearean pathos with an appeal to the "Reader's own experience of the reluctance with which he comes to the re-perusal of the distressful parts of *Clarissa Harlowe*" (610).

Pronouncements like this doubtless confirmed Hazlitt's belief that the Lake Poet was not to be trusted on the topic of "the Novelists" and their "passages relating to common life and manners" (226)—a complaint Hazlitt issued in "On Reading Old Books" just before declaring his desire to read Richardson all over again. However, there are signs, Wordsworth notwithstanding, that during the romantic period prose fiction—and especially, as the next section will propose, prose fiction committed to the longueurs and recursive rhythms of common life—was beginning to absorb the remedial functions that he and Coleridge had ascribed to poetry's metrical repetitions. During the romantic period, as we have seen, associationist psychology's account of habit as integral to the constitution of the mind began reshaping accounts of the nature and duration of literary effects. In ways we tend to overlook, canonicity was correlated to texts' fitness for that role of "hourly companion" and their capacity to put an audience in touch with that temporality that takes shape as an unbroken series. It makes sense that under that new arrangement, one in which literature was supposed to merge the cyclical rhythms of our everyday holding patterns, novels would have an edge.

VOLUMINOUSNESS: ON GOING STEADY WITH NOVELS

It is no surprise, either, that the novel is central to the discussion of "Voluminous Authors" and the particularly "intimate . . . familiarity" that voluminous authors inspire that the essayist Mary Russell Mitford (1787–1865) includes in her *Recollections of a Literary Life* (1851). The issue Mitford's essay engages—which is the nature of the pleasure that the reader takes when living with a book long in itself or when embarked on the reading of a large collection of works of the same class or by the same author—is one deemed of little moment by novel theory of a narratological bent. The varying degrees to which works claim their readers' time have been inconsequential for a critical scheme that declares, as Catherine Gallagher explains, "the relation of parts to each other [to be] the relevant question": adherents of this scheme find, after all, that the "internal patterning of *The Last Chronicle of Barsetshire* may be set down as concisely as that of *The Turn of the Screw*."[78] Mitford, however, does notice claims on readers' time. She makes the familiarity bred by voluminous authors' protracted unfolding crucial. She also identifies it as one cause of the success, during her lifetime, of a sequence of new series fictions. The novels of James Fenimore Cooper, she comments, "extended to fifteen volumes the adventures of Leather-Stocking, until every reader offered his hand to greet the honest backwoodsman as if he had been a daily visitor." On Mitford's testimony, the linked novels composing Honoré de Balzac's *La comédie humaine* were more successful still. So potent proved their reality effects, Mitford confesses, that she actually asked a friend whether "Horace Bianchon, whom I had just found consulted for the twentieth time in some grave malady, were a make-believe physician or a real living man."[79] Mitford does not explain her interest in this character, but it does seem apt that Bianchon's repeated reappearances should be a function of his medical qualifications—in addition to being par for the course in series fiction, the fictional mode that prolific novelists set up so that, in one linked novel after another, they could subject the same invented world to recurrent reexamination.

Mitford's reference to the repeated calls on Bianchon's expertise may register a growing consensus about the therapeutic effects ascribable to the reading of voluminous authors. Perhaps the especially prolonged aesthetic encounter at issue in the novel, that bulky form, had become a medicinal quality. Dino Franco Felluga's research indicates that around the second decade of the nineteenth century a milestone was reached in the novel's ascent toward cultural legitimacy. At that point, medical tracts and reviews alike began "repeating the idea that certain novels could function as preservatives rather than poisons."[80] Certainly, the warnings about the deleterious effects of novel reading that had been issued since the early eighteenth century (warnings about the reader's erotic overstimulation or about the jangling of her nerves caused by her exposure to manipulative, suspense-filled plotting) did not disappear in the nineteenth century. To pathologize the novel, an increasingly popular form, continued to serve as an indirect means of condemning the changes in the composition of the reading public precipitated by mass literacy. And yet there is a notable overlap between the romantic poets' promotion of meter as a principle of regulation and balance and as a mechanism for the healthy discharge of emotion and the increasingly frequent discussions in the nineteenth century of novel readers' ways of going on with a form whose distinguishing characteristic is to go on.

Relevant here is a story that in the early nineteenth century migrated from literary biography to the medical writings of Benjamin Rush, whose engagement with it helps account for his current title as the "father of bibliotherapy." In the final five years of his life, also the final five years of the eighteenth century, William Cowper, confirmed invalid and mad poet, had alternated between walks with his caretakers along the seashore, where, his memoirist reports, his spirit was soothed by "the monotonous sound of the breakers" and, on days of inclement weather, by a routine deemed equivalent. As others read aloud, Cowper revisited books he had previously encountered, particularly the "voluminous" novels of Samuel Richardson and later of Frances Burney. His interesting patient, his kinsman John Johnson explained, expressed "peculiar satisfaction" whenever their therapeutic routine involved "a production of fancy of more than ordinary length."[81]

Might we connect the novel's gradual ascendancy in the generic hierarchy to the proposition that, to maximize well-being, every reading should represent a resumption of an earlier, interrupted reading? The very existence of the series format that Mitford mentions testifies to the public's willingness to ratify such a proposition. And we have only to note Richardson's place in Cowper's therapeutic regimen to realize that those norms for steady, ongoing engagement were at issue in the novel's eighteenth-century history as well.

In ways that extend beyond his sometimes too-evident concern with his own literary immortality, perpetuity did interest Richardson deeply. In *Clarissa*, this interest shapes the elaborate arrangements the heroine makes to live on after death, in her literary remains. It shapes, as well, the efforts Jack Belford makes to convert this literary executorship into a lifetime reading plan. Combining Clarissa's letters with Lovelace's, Belford precipitates the shift that makes the novel in its closing volumes not just Clarissa's story but also the story of the making of *Clarissa*: he edits the same text that he also (anticipating Diderot) will "reperuse with melancholy pleasure to the end of my life."[82] (This scheme for emotional self-management centers on Belford's resubmitting himself to the delicious pain that arises from his feelings about a suffering female.) Belford moves smoothly from feeling for Clarissa to feeling for *Clarissa*, in a move that places the emotions that he feels and the emotions that he remembers on a continuum. Hume's and Hartley's accounts of the mind's vibrations in passing and repassing between associated ideas might have been tailor-made to make sense of the emotional dynamics at stake when *Clarissa* stages its own rereading.

But I am most struck by how associationist psychology's charting of the mind's routine ways of rewinding time illuminates the peculiar relationship to narrative order and narrative completion that Richardson's works share with other voluminous fictions of the period. His novels can look intent on eluding the consequences of their sequentiality. Productions of an author notoriously reluctant to leave off, each seems less to end than to replay itself. I would claim this even for *Clarissa*, which conforms to a grim narrative logic leading its protagonists step-by-step to the grave, but which also entertains, equally grimly, a notion of time as something that can be rewound or put on hold. Hence, for instance the sense of déjà vu, of a time loop, that its readers feel as, seven volumes in, following the heroine's rape, the members of the Harlowe family resume their letter writing and resume the invigilation of the heroine's sincerity that gave them—since the matter was never susceptible to definitive proof—so much to write on in the novel's inaugural volumes. This proclivity for the reprise is indulged, as well, in the seventh volume of *Sir Charles Grandison*, which sees Sir Charles's ward Emily Jervois situated in exactly the lovelorn position previously occupied by the heroine

Harriet Byron—likewise sickening with hopeless love for the hero, explicitly identified and identifying as "a second Harriet." This introduction of a facsimile edition of a character already met, and these circular movements that make endings not closural but generative of more beginnings, have formal consequences that approach the better-known challenges to linearity and closure posed by Laurence Sterne's *Tristram Shandy*. Think of the latter's procrastinations and digressions—of the intricate balance of "digressive and progressive movements, one wheel within another" that is supposed to render Tristram's book a kind of perpetual motion machine that he can keep "a-going" ad infinitum.[83]

These prolix means of compounding voluminousness and of keeping books on a "life-support system" speak to a discrepancy between the eighteenth-century voluminous authors' understanding of novel reading and the narrow mandate ascribed to that activity in modern-day criticism. That criticism envisions readers reading for closure, for revelation and then resolution. But where process is "more important than completion," readers also "read for continuation": they read to carry on both without ever leaving off and after reading off.[84]

Also worth emphasizing are the pains that the century's voluminous authors took to incorporate into their fictions scenes of everyday reception—how, at the level of content, those fictions mirrored proleptically the dailiness in which they were incrementally and reiteratively consumed. Consider, in *Grandison*, the evening gatherings in the "cedar parlour" at Selby House that the heroine's friends, "the venerable circle," incorporate into their schedules so as to read over her letters, and with which they notch off the steady passage of the days. (Thomas Macaulay's letters home from India are likewise addressed to "the venerable circle," registering how Richardson's fiction supplied him the ground on which, from a distance, he might reconfirm his intimacy with his sisters.)[85] Or consider the cedar parlor's equivalent in *Tristram Shandy*, which describes the fireside at Shandy Hall as a scene of habitual conversation and habitual whistling—the latter being, of course, Uncle Toby's reflex reaction whenever Walter's discoursing takes a turn that threatens the conviviality to which the place is dedicated. Part of what makes these fictions voluminous is their determination to give this ordinary pottering and piddling their due. In adding to the novel's formal repertory the background hum of everydayness (prose fiction's equivalent to Wordsworth's "co-presence of something regular"?), eighteenth-century writers endowed the form with a way to register steady temporal succession independent of plots' twists and turns. They also weighted the genre in new ways toward everyday actions that have never not been going on (it is impossible to imagine a first whistling of Lillibulero) and toward the interactions of people who have never not been familiar to one another.

In a recent essay that likewise explores readers' feelings about the rhythms of recurrence and connects them to the novel's achievement of canonicity, Franco Moretti credits a handful of romantic-period novelists—Jane Austen, above all—with ushering in during the second decade of the nineteenth century a new narrative hierarchy: a slowing down of narrative that promotes those moments of pause that intervene between the turning points of plots. Moretti's elision of most of the fictional output of the eighteenth century is one shortcoming of his account of how novelists learned to imagine the meaning of a life as "dispersed among countless minute events" and how they resolved accordingly to "keep the narrativity of life under control."[86] (Austen's nephew-memoirist insisted, after all, that "all that was said or done in the cedar parlour was familiar to her." One way to specify her achievement is to say, perhaps, that it hinged on extracting the feel of continuous everydayness that *Grandison* conveys from Richardson's eighteenth-century prolixity—that this was what enabled Austen to carry a newly compacted novel of daily life into the nineteenth century.)[87] But Moretti's insights into a romantic-period overhaul of the novel's relationship to time do helpfully explain the transformation of attitudes toward the health of the novel reader discernible in this era. In Moretti's account, Austen, Goethe, and Walter Scott relegate the unheard of and the untoward, earlier fiction's strange, surprising adventures, to the background of the novel form. They relocate to the foreground the more modest happenings—the walking, talking, eating, shopping, and, also, reading—that in their repetitions "give regularity to existence." In their hands, accordingly, "fillers"—the prosy materials that are reluctant to narration—triumph over plot.[88]

Thus, for instance, *Emma*—which I want to attend to briefly, for a couple of reasons: both because Austen there implements that shift so self-consciously ("there is no story whatever," was how Austen's sister novelist Susan Ferrier reported on *Emma* when it appeared in 1816, and Ferrier *liked* the novel)[89] and because later in the nineteenth century this Austen novel became pivotal for the definitions of steady, wholesome reading matter this chapter's discussion of canon love has been examining. Austen centered *Emma* on a set of characters who are more or less boxed in by their daily rounds and routines and whose relationship to the frequentative tense is particularly ardent. They constitute, accordingly, a social world in which a lot can be taken for granted, a feature of their environment that for the individual inhabitant is alternately comfortable and irksome. Primed by Felluga's discussion of the novel's romantic-period assimilation to notions of therapeutic reading, one might notice especially the valetudinarian routines that define Mr. Woodhouse's experience of time during the year in which the plot of *Emma* unfolds. Over the course of his extended life—extended by gruel, regular hours and checkups, and a policy of keeping his daughter on a short tether—our heroine's father has apparently worked out a full-fledged theory of scheduled sociability, outlined by the narrator in the following passage: "Mrs. and Miss Bates and Mrs. Godard, three ladies almost always at the service of an invitation from Hartfield, . . . were fetched and carried home so often that Mr. Woodhouse thought it no hardship for either James or the horses. Had it taken place only once a year, it would have been a grievance."[90] If Mr. Woodhouse experiences some qualms of conscience in contemplating how his arrangements for whiling away his evenings at home unceasingly send his coachman and his horses out of the house, he appeases them with an appeal to habit—that queer arithmetic in which augmenting the number of repetitions of an action makes its performance less burdensome.

Whether this routine is "thought . . . no hardship" by James himself is not specified. But the aspiration to equanimity that motivates Mr. Woodhouse's enthusiasm for routine is not his alone. All Highbury has a knack for transmuting potentially disruptive novelties—"Harriet Smith's intimacy at Hartfield," for instance—into already "settled thing[s]" (26). A sort of legerdemain enables whatever newness infiltrates this world to be routinely whisked out of view. This cast of characters is always moving in circles (we glimpse them making their social "rounds," taking "turns" around the Hartfield shrubbery, visiting the local haberdashery "six days out of seven" [200])—and it is noticeable how good almost all are at never breaking stride. Austen places almost as much emphasis on the process by which this fictional world reverts to stasis, the "stationary movement" that is the everyday, as she does on complying with her narrative obligation to make things change.[91]

Thus it takes only a few rounds of morning visits, and so only a few revolutions of the village gossip cycle, for the news of Emma and Knightley's engagement, momentarily astonishing, to represent, instead, exactly the eventuality that everyone had always "foreseen" (468). Even Mr. Woodhouse at the end has it in him to bounce back from the alarming prospect that he will soon gain another son-in-law. Helpfully, when the news breaks, Mrs. Weston is at hand to represent this marriage "in its most serviceable

light," which is to say as "settled." "The idea was given: time and continual repetition must do the rest" (466), *Emma's* narrator says as she reports
on this process of shock absorption (perhaps registering the influence of
an associationist psychology that, as we have seen, cast such a process of
familiarization as exactly what minds do best). Earlier, the sudden revelation of Frank Churchill and Jane Fairfax's secret engagement had in similar
fashion entered the category of things to be taken for granted: Mr. Weston,
Mrs. Weston, and Emma "talked it all over together" and then Mr. Weston
"talked it all over again with Emma, in their walk back to Hartfield" (401).
The repetition ("all over again") is key to the course correction that returns
everyone, comfortably, to the beaten path.

The wonderful thing about how *Emma* handles its central courtship plot
is that Austen contrives to narrate what will be discovered to have been a
foregone conclusion in such a way that, nevertheless, that concluding revelation of love comes as a shock. In fact, Austen's heroine spends much of
the novel's last volume astounded by events. "Every moment had brought
a fresh surprise," we are told (411): a statement that might have originated
in just the kind of fiction, one dashing from one coup de théâtre to another,
that, in Moretti's presentation, Austen is meant to have rejected. Emma is
surprised, above all, by a sudden acquaintance with her own feelings: "It
darted through her, with the speed of an arrow, that Mr. Knightley must
marry no one but herself!" (408). Against the odds, Austen makes this world
of stick-in-the-muds yield a narrative of love. And the virtuoso element of
this achievement is that she pulls this off not by matching Emma with Frank
Churchill—who comes into this world from the outside, the carrier of the
disequilibrium that gets the story going—but instead by matching her with
the insider who was never not there, who by rights should be considered a
fixture of the background against which narrative events will take place.
"I have done with expecting any course of steady reading from Emma,"
this Mr. Knightley declares in the book's opening pages (37), as he ponders,
along with her former governess, this heroine's spotty educational record.
But Emma, who would like to fancy herself a dreadful flirt, is ultimately
revealed as a paragon of steadiness, who has been loving this same man all
along.

The rereadability of *Emma* itself—the idea that it is a book to which the
reader should commit herself for the long term so as to pick it up again and
again—was a commonplace of the twentieth-century critical tradition. The
consensus around Austen's works generally has been that only with repeated,
increasingly probing readings can we honor the lesson she inculcates about

the complexity of other people. In the case of *Emma* in particular, if our first-time reading reenacts Emma's misreading of her world (this heroine's hermeneutic laziness, her quixotic insistence on construing people's lives according to cheesy romantic conventions), that is just what mandates the second reading, the reading that we undertake armed with foreknowledge of the relationship of Frank and Jane. Only by repeating with a difference will we reenact this heroine's moral education.[92] Professors of literature get a wonderful ego boost from Austen when she appears to be ratifying our insistence to our students that they distance themselves from their interpretive habits and become self-conscious rereaders: *Emma* can seem tailor-made for *us*.

And yet there are signs that Austen's endorsement of the ethos of critical reading is less than thoroughgoing. I suspect her of a soft spot for other motives for rereading: the kind actuating Emma's nephews, for instance, who asked "every day for the story of Harriet and the gipsies" and protest the slightest deviation "from the original recital" (336). It seems noteworthy, for instance, how enmeshed in routine this novel's proposal scene is. Knightley's customary daily call on the Hartfield household is protracted when Emma suggests that they take "'another turn'" around the shrubbery and then, as they walk, he declares himself (and finds, delightfully and redundantly, that the affection "he had been asking to be allowed to create if he could was already his!" [432]). Austen pointedly delivers the happy dénouement in a scene that—since the shrubbery also hosts Mr. Woodhouse's daily constitutionals—is indelibly associated with quotidian habit and so with the kinds of repetitions that, redundantly, do not make a difference, rather than with the kinds that do. In this episode at least, wisdom is not distanced from but rather associated with the kind of unassuming, passive agency to which individuals' immersion in the recursive everyday limits them.[93]

The second section of this chapter suggested that in the Victorian period, as in academic novel studies at present, the notion that the essence of Austen reading was Austen *re*reading had an almost official standing. Indeed, the notion had been ratified from the top. Sir Walter Scott's three readings ("at least") of *Pride and Prejudice*, which Scott tallied up in his diary in 1826, became part of public consciousness after 1844, thanks to their approving mention by Robert Chambers in the article on Miss Austen he prepared for his *Cyclopaedia of English Literature*.[94] (Within the Victorian-period annals of Austenian reception, first-time encounters with the Austen novel seldom come to view, as if Victorian literary culture as a whole shared Highbury's preference for already "settled" things.) But to do justice to the framework in which, in the nineteenth century, Austen's canonization (and the novel's) proceeded, and the framework in which these investments in Austen's reiterability were made, we need to take seriously how novelists' claims to value rested on something more than their capacity to produce in their audience a new self-critical attention to their interpretive procedures. Deploying their representations of everyday iteration in order, as Moretti claims, to damp down the excitements of plot, novels at the same time cued the audience to their own desire to be permanent residents of the real-life equivalents of those scenes.

They succeeded. As I noted in this chapter's second section, by the middle decades of the nineteenth century, Austen's fictions had joined Scott's *Waverley* series as objects of those regularly scheduled rereadings through which lovers of literature confirmed their devotion. Communion is not the whole story here, however. The precise way in which some Victorian gentlemen kept the Janeite faith can seem less an expression of love than the expression of the solicitude of a Woodhouseian valetudinarian scheduling regular appointments with his physician. The "eminent persons" whose opinions of his aunt's novels J. E. Austen-Leigh catalogued in his *Memoir* include in their number a certain Lord Holland, who, whenever afflicted by the gout, would take to bed and have his sister read aloud from "one of Miss Austen's novels, of which [we are told] [Lord Holland] never wearied."[95] Meanwhile, at Cambridge, the University Chair of Sanskrit, Edward Byles Cowell, had formed the habit of reading Miss Austen each night "after his Sanskrit Philology [was] done"; Cowell's former pupil in Persian, the poet Edward FitzGerald, reported (a touch acerbically) that Cowell found that the novels *composed* him, like, FitzGerald said, "Gruel."[96]

In this therapeutic context, encounters with novels appear to have been understood less as events and more as means of re-steadying time and restoring routine in events' wake. Thus, perhaps, Thomas De Quincey's 1824 declaration that "the Bore" is a "weighty office . . . necessary in every well-regulated novel, as a constitutional check upon the levity of the other characters."[97] De Quincey meant to take a slap at Scott, sneering at routinization *in* the *Waverley* series (as per Moretti's comments on the ascendancy of novelistic fillers) and at the routinization *of* the *Waverley* series (a couple dozen narratives of historical change over eighteen years). But this statement about the formulae for novelistic equanimity and about boring characters' utility in keeping novels on an even keel illuminates a feature of the wider culture of the novel in the nineteenth century. With that word "constitutional" in particular, it illuminates what the admission of some well-regulated novels

to the category of timeless literature might have owed to a faith in the cura-
tive effects of big books that, as they give one more of the same, maintain
good habits. Reading routines like those of the Janeite Sanskrit professor
place the desire for edification and the desire for inertia, fidelity and obsti-
nacy, pleasure and tedium in a delicate balance. This homeostasis is another
version of what it means to be wedded to books.

CODA: CANON LOVE AND THE CONVALESCENT

The Woodhouseian quality of those reading routines, the determination to
go on *after* the thrill is gone, the determination to go on with the novel
because commentators on the genre, physicians and critics alike, had reassuringly certified that indeed the thrill *had* already gone: all this, if we gen-
eralize from the situation of the novel in the nineteenth century to that of
literature more generally, points to a somewhat disquieting kinship between
the lover of literature and the valetudinarian. And certainly, through the
century, as architects of the discipline of English studies affirmed readers
in the desire to go steady and to saturate the everyday with literariness, the
health needs of the reading public did get invoked regularly. In concluding,
I want briefly to turn back to the figure with whom I began, the anthologist,
to refine this point about how canonizing discussions of imperishable literary works—discussions confirming the iterability that made them books for
all seasons—overlapped with moralists' and medical men's promotion of the
ethical and physiological benefits of family time and regular hours.

The most famous Victorian practitioner of the anthologizing enterprise
shaped earlier by figures such as Samuel Johnson and Leigh Hunt was
Francis Turner Palgrave (1824–97). His *The Golden Treasury* of English verse
(1861), covering the span from the Elizabethans to the Romantics, is said to
have sold ten thousand copies a year for a century. In the preface to its first
edition, Palgrave tacitly recapitulates arguments about the brain, attention,
and time that informed medical culture's promotion of healthful habit. The
explicit topic of the passage in question is the difficulties that he had been
obliged to surmount in ordering the entries in the anthology. Strict chronology as a principle of arrangement had its dangers in a book of *The Golden
Treasury*'s sort, Palgrave cautioned, because "the English mind has passed
through phases of thought and cultivation so various and so opposed during these three centuries of Poetry, that a rapid passage between old and
new, like rapid alteration of the eye's focus in looking at the landscape, will
always be wearisome and hurtful."[98] Palgrave's allusion to the perceptual

disorders thought to be wrought by railway travel and the attendant experience of speed (railway brain) is a reminder that under the aegis of modernity's temporal order it became possible, as usages recorded in the *Oxford
English Dictionary* confirm, for people, as well as clocks and machinery, to
find themselves "mistimed." The adjective designated digestive disturbances
and sleep disorders—the arrhythmic ailments that might be counteracted by
bedtime routines like the Janeite Sanskrit professor's.[99]

Victorian culture was highly aware of the risks that individuals and societies ostensibly ran whenever they pursued excitement and departed too
abruptly from a steady state of equanimity. Nineteenth-century ideas of
English and of the canon love it would promulgate were shaped by that
risk aversion. Thus in 1848, in his inaugural lecture at Queen's College,
an occasion often heralded as a founding moment in the discipline of English, Charles Kingsley prescribed the study of English literary history as a
means of forestalling in young people (women particularly) those "sudden
and irregular revulsions of affection for different schools of writing" that
he evoked by imagining an unschooled reader, of errant feelings, who, un-
checked, would rush promiscuously from Pope to Byron to Scott to Wordsworth to Shakespeare.[100]

In 1860, the year before *The Golden Treasury* appeared, Palgrave published
in *Macmillan's Magazine* an essay decrying the contemporary period as an
era when "everything is to be read, and *everything only once*; a book is no
more a treasure to be kept . . . if deserving that intimacy." The beef that he
has with the reader of 1860—who is someone unable, Palgrave claims, to
"read even novelties more than once"—is that, unlike his counterpart in
1760, he is a figure with commitment issues. Canon love demands a capacity to remain in relationships for the long haul and thus a willingness, especially, to reread. Thus the peroration with which Palgrave concludes his
essay, in which, over and against that reader who reads everything once, he
applauds the reader who will read "mainly the best books, and begin again
when the series is ended."[101] The "fittest readers" of *The Golden Treasury* as
imagined by Palgrave in that anthology's preface the following year also repeat themselves. Dodging in this preface the burden of individual judgment
and trying to make his editorial decisions as anthologist seem the outcome
of an already established consensus, Palgrave declared that "the Editor will
regard as his fittest readers those who love Poetry so well, that he can offer them nothing not already known and valued" (5). Curiously, Palgrave
here announces his collection's redundancy—in the course, however, of promoting poetry as a love object whose value is intertwined with its capacity

to keep commanding love even when "already known" and so its capacity to immunize the reading population against irregular revulsions of affection. Poetry's fittest readers value it precisely as what is at all times present, their genuine admiration (like that Coleridge discussed in *Biographia*) therefore constituting a continuous feeling, and "seldom any where a separate excitement."

As Palgrave's writings amply indicate, the idea of a literary canon has been mobilized both as a resource ushering a populace into health-giving unanimity and community and as a mechanism for establishing hierarchical differences among readers—for diagnosing some readers' failings. But moving between the theory of canon love and its practice—the routines of everyday love by which readers kept aesthetically, emotionally, and physically fit—as I have aimed to do here raises some disconcerting questions. At what point do the commitments demanded by and supporting the idea of a canon become evidence that the reader is in a Woodhouseian rut? How does one distinguish fidelity to "the best that has been thought and said" from the mental inertia and automatism of a creature of habit? The children of Matthew Arnold—whose 1869 definition of culture as "the best" thinking and saying I have just cited—appear to have been inspired by their father's annual return visits to Austen's fiction when they coined their nickname for him. They called him Mr. Woodhouse.[102]

Is canon love an identifying trait of the slacker? Wondering whether this is the case leads me back to the romantic essayists, Charles Lamb and William Hazlitt, each of whom in his time edited anthologies. Lamb, Thomas Noon Talfourd reported in a memoir of 1838, had contrived to miss out altogether on the *Waverley* novels, "preferring to read Fielding and Smollett and Richardson, whose stories were familiar, over and over again, to being worried with the task of threading the maze of fresh adventure." Lamb's determination to read in circles is a suitable trait for the author of an essay on "The Convalescent," which enumerates among the sick man's privileges his oblivion to life's usual "call[s] to activity."[103] And yet it is an open question in Talfourd's biography whether Lamb's way with books is being recommended for emulation, or whether this equanimity that takes Lamb beyond the pleasure principle is meant to irk those less fastidious readers who have, after all, managed to break with routine and read Talfourd. The same problem—in part one of tone—is posed by Hazlitt's "On Reading Old Books," a treatment of book love that begins, curiously, with a declaration of hate: "I hate to read new books. There are twenty or thirty volumes that I have read over and over again, and these are the only ones that I have any desire ever to read at all" (220). One cannot help but wonder how *any* fellow lover of old books would ever come to be reading Hazlitt's essay, and reading it, to compound the irony, not in a book but in a magazine, the medium that in furbishing ever fresh novelties had become a byword for unhealthy reading.

Though Hazlitt's essay is shadowed by a subtext story of loving and leaving (peppered with oblique references to the termination of old friendships and to his inability now to match the ardors of his youthful reading), it is framed primarily as a testament to his constancy. He proposes that this constancy to old books makes him the antitype to female readers, who judge of books, he says, "as they do of fashions . . . admired only 'in their newest gloss'" (220). This comparison taps a long history of negative representations of female reading—in particular, innumerable descriptions by Hazlitt's contemporaries of the novel addict who is always upping her dose. It indicates how in this essay the pleasures of the imagination are wedded to the pleasures of social calculation. Not increasing his literary acquaintance is Hazlitt's way to increase his cultural capital. As he touts his fidelity to the self-same volumes and ability to dispense with new ones, and as he manages thereby to set appreciation and acquisition at odds with each other, he attests to his distinction.

This chapter, however, has proposed that attending to the stratagems that advance social mobility does not get us far enough. It doesn't take into account the aspirations to *immobility* that center the steady reader's chosen mode of self-fashioning—and this reader's way of incorporating old books into those periodic practices that help people experience time as a steady state. And so I've traced the affective logic that Hazlitt and others exemplify when, domesticating the aesthetic relation, they begin to redefine literature as an object of everyday love.

But the more I ponder Hazlitt's self-representation or Thomas Babington Macaulay's parading in his private correspondence of the Richardson obsession that runs in his family—or descriptions of Lamb's refusal of the *Waverley* novels or of the Sanskrit professor's Janeite routines—the less everyday, the more indeterminate, their everyday looks. I feel puzzled by the tonal instability, the odd compound of sentimentality and self-mockery marking these reports on the rereading routines that the nineteenth-century man undertook in his off-hours. The aspirations to immobility are perhaps the problem. Invalidism has been read—because it shifted individuals out of "medicine's narrative of promise" and ensconced them "within a more stationary, nonlinear space"—as a strange sort of nineteenth-century protest movement. "As an apotheosis of inertia, the invalid tapped into

and expressed deep-seated societal doubts . . . about progress and mobility, . . . master narratives of [the] culture."[104] People's investments in the
rereadability that fits particular books for their lifetime reading plans, indeed their investment more generally in ideas of a love that will last a lifetime, share in this dissenting quality. Maybe the tone of mockery I have
found in these reports, the parading of readerly crotchets, is a preemptive
strike against other people's ridicule. It might be a move motivated by these
constant lovers' awareness of the bias against repetition that was becoming so ingrained in post-Enlightenment culture and central to its norms of
masculinity.

It is notable that even as Hazlitt trades on descriptions of the fashion-
conscious female reader as addict, his own disinclination to change his old
books for new looks like an addiction, in its own right, to sameness. This
is steadiness, sure, but in a different, less healthful mode.[105] The ambiguity
seems calculated. Hazlitt makes his canon love, his affection toward texts
that he necessarily shares with others, into the ground of his individuality,
and this entails a doubleness in his self-representation of his readerly life.
From one angle, Hazlitt may look to be a paragon of fidelity. From another,
he appears to be converting a virtuous monogamy into a modern perversion.

PART 4

Dead Poets Societies

CHAPTER FIVE

Canon Love in Gothic Libraries

What a mighty difference is there between the existence of one of our old baronial ancestors, who could not read, but as he sate over his winter fire, solaced his spirit with the lays of a wandering minstrel, and of him who has at his command all the intellectual splendour, power, wit, the satire, the joyous story, the humour, the elegance of phrase and of mind, the profound sentiment and high argument of such men as Chaucer, Spenser, Ben Jonson, Shakspeare, Beaumont and Fletcher, Milton, Dryden, Addison, Steele, Pope, Sam Johnson, Goldsmith, Cowper and the noble poets of the present day. . . . Why there is more delight in one good country library, than any one mortal life can consume.

> WILLIAM HOWITT, "Enviable Position of the English Country
> Gentleman as regards All the Pleasures and Advantages of Life," in *The Rural
> Life of England* (3rd ed., 1844)

Capital makes it possible to appropriate the collectively produced and accumulated means of really overcoming anthropological limits. The means of escaping from generic alienations include representation, the portrait or statue which immortalizes the person represented . . . ; and memorials, the tombstone, the written word, aere perennius, which celebrates and "hands on to posterity," . . . the commemorative ceremonies in which the group offers tributes of homage and gratitude to the dead, who are thereby shown to be still living and active. Thus it can be seen that eternal life is one of the most sought-after social privileges.

> PIERRE BOURDIEU, "The Aristocracy of Culture," in *Distinction:
> A Social Critique of the Judgment of Taste* (1984)

QUOTATION COMPULSION

Samuel Taylor Coleridge, glimpsed in the previous chapter promoting the rereadability of "essential poetry," did not always insist that such repeat encounters with texts should result from a reader's conscious choice. Sometimes he would instead concur with those contemporaries who were happy to believe that a reader's marriage to his books could (like marriage to a person) be a matter of unconscious constancy and everyday routine. On these occasions Coleridge appears to have recognized the expediency of defining readers' homage to literary staying power as something *un*willed. The chapter of

Biographia Literaria that winds up the book's assessment of William Words-worth's poetry thus makes a curious claim about that verse's effects on read-ers of "elevated powers." These readers have told Coleridge, he says, that al-though they might consciously admire other authors' writings much more, "from no modern work ha[ve] so many passages started up anew in their minds at different times, arising without reference to the poem in which they are found."[1] The verb choice—"started up"—lends an eerie feel to Coleridge's description of this involuntary recall of Wordsworthian verse.

Indeed, in representing Wordsworth love as a matter of unbidden mem-ories and of insidiously invasive quotations, Coleridge has to strange ef-fect associated his readers of "elevated powers" with a case he discusses elsewhere in the *Biographia*—that of a peasant girl who during a nervous fever mechanically reproduces the Latin, Greek, and Hebrew passages she has overheard her employer, a learned pastor, enunciate during his stud-ies. (The girl, who has become a sort of embodied record of those stud-ies, gives Coleridge an example of the imprintability of the memory, which preserves latently a verbatim record of the sensations impressed upon it; her history thus launches a rhapsodic discussion of the "imperishability of thought.") Individuals who had bits of poetry, in particular, stuck fast inside their heads featured often in the psycho-physiological writings published during Coleridge's lifetime. Dr. Erasmus Darwin's *Zoonomia*, for instance, had as an illustration of the human propensity to repetition its case history of an "Ingenious and elegant young lady of 17," who, during the periods of reverie that followed her convulsions, and while remaining unconscious of her surroundings, had "repeated whole pages from the English poets."[2] In his 1789 essay on the "Influence of Habit and Association," Dr. John Percival discussed the exasperating way that errant scraps of verse could, along with random snatches of tunes, steal into the individual's mind and stay there. He described these recalcitrant bits of verse as "troublesome guests" outstaying their welcome, a strange personification that recalled the terms that John Locke's "Of the Conduct of the Understanding" had used a century earlier to discuss such mental quirks as hazards endemic to the association of ideas. To narrate the buffeting that the will takes when the mind falls captive to familiar routines of its own creating, the early psychologists often found it useful to associate that buffeting with the verse that people have (as they say) by heart.[3]

Percival's and Darwin's case histories illustrate abnormal psychologies, as does Coleridge's story of the compulsively reciting peasant girl of Göt-tingen. When discussing the staying power of Wordsworth's verse, however,

Coleridge seems to have broached the topic of involuntary quotation—and the unwilled fidelity to poetry that it instances—for a different purpose. When Coleridge mentions the hold that those stray Wordsworthian passages have over the worthiest readers, he describes literary receptivity in terms that clash with any understanding of aesthetic experience that would make such experience useful to one's social maneuvering. The involuntarily recalled or recited literary quotation that betokens a reading habit gone haywire is the antithesis of the literary quotation that is used as an ornament, helping to gussy up writing or conversation, or wielded as a proof of a reader's ownership of cultural capital. That may be the point. John Keats wrote in an 1818 letter that poetry had better come as naturally as "the Leaves to a tree" or not come at all.[4] There were powerful social pressures—in a culture in which literary enthusiasms were increasingly becoming near-compulsory components of polite people's identities and in which fashionable texts could appear to be extorting lip service from all—that dictated that someone like Coleridge would find it desirable to extend Keats's "axiom" so that it applied to poetry love as well as to poems. Poetry love too should come naturally—but how might one tell that it had? In this context, Coleridge may well have concluded that "readers of extraordinary powers" would appear all the more admirable when portrayed as lacking power over those powers. In his account of the hold that these Wordsworthian passages have over their readers we might discern a reproach to more deliberative, pragmatic ways of navigating the nineteenth-century culture of literary taste.

For Coleridge, there was, in other words, some strategic expediency to demonstrating how uncalculated, unconscious and thoroughgoing readers' internalization of the Wordsworthian text could be, even if it meant that these members of the poet's public ended up sounding *possessed*. His description ascribes agency to those striking passages that "start up anew" and "arise." It takes agency away, by contrast, from the readers of the passages. Their minds appear merely the screens on which poetry is enabled in almost spectral fashion to reappear. If in this instance readerly passivity counts as reassuring evidence of literary power, it is, however, also well known that Coleridge elsewhere took a dim view of any reading that was less than entirely mindful. Should it even be called reading? Not in the case of the addicted clientele of the circulating libraries, he had already declared in a long sardonic footnote appended to chapter 3 of *Biographia*. Those readers' mode of amusing themselves with the novels that they hire is, he states, as mindless and mechanical an activity as—and what follows is a list of the many annoying forms he has seen other people's bad habits taking—"swinging or swaying on a chair or gate; spitting over a bridge; smoking; snuff-taking; tete a tete quarrels after dinner between husband and wife; conning word-by-word all the advertisements of the *Daily Advertiser* in a public house on a rainy day, etc. etc. etc." (1:48–49n). (*Other* people's bad habits, so they are cordoned off from his literary autobiography proper by being treated in the notes at the bottom of *Biographia*'s pages—but the penultimate reference to the domestic doldrums of conjugal life was likely informed by firsthand experience.) The equally extravagant sentence that precedes that list sees Coleridge thinking once again about the uncanny things that happen when readers surrender to textuality. Here, however, Coleridge, dealing with *novel* readers rather than "readers of extraordinary powers," renders that state of possession in a grotesque idiom. He represents the circulating libraries' clientele as an undifferentiated collective in thrall to an elaborate machinery engineered to bring about their mass zombification: "a sort of mental *camera obscura*, manufactured at the printing office, which *pro tempore*, fixes, reflects, and transmits the moving phantasms of one man's delirium, so as to people the barrenness of an hundred other brains afflicted with the same trance" (1:48n).

In this draft theory of mass culture as a work of deception and dark enchantment, Coleridge likely had an eye on gothic novels especially. The mode's popularity in the face of critical strictures that condemned its deviations from the accepted standards of novelistic probability was frequently bemoaned by conservative commentators. For them it seemed proof of the cultural decline that was, they opined, the inevitable corollary of the book market's expansion. (At the peak moment for the mode, 1795, gothic novels accounted for 38 percent of all novels published in Britain: the figure registers the retailing successes of entrepreneurs such as William Lane, whose national network of circulating libraries provided him with ready-made markets for the volumes churned out at his Minerva Press.)[5] Coleridge's footnote in the *Biographia* thus indexes a wider pattern of commentary that aligned the readership *of* the gothic novel with the victims of magical delusion represented *in* the gothic novel. That the addicted reading public kept coming back for more of these potboilers, even as their stock-in-trade shocks and mysteries appeared increasingly clichéd, seemed to the disenchanted few evidence that the wills of their countrymen and women had succumbed to nefarious acts of mental manipulation.

It is more accurate to say, however, that the gothic fiction of Coleridge's lifetime straddled both of the *Biographia*'s accounts of how texts are kept in readers' minds: this description of a zombie-like addiction to novels and that comment on the eerie staying power of Wordsworthian verse. Gothic fictions give every evidence of indulging this same superstitious veneration of writings' uncanny powers, especially poems' powers, to possess the memory of the reader and also to survive both the disappearance of their original contexts and the deaths of their authors.

Here are some examples of those powers. A "sentence of dreadful import" read "involuntarily" (though never read by us) despite the heroine's best efforts to obey her father's strictures and burn his papers without looking at them. Letters of lambent flame that appear suddenly on a castle wall and terrorize into repentance the villainous usurper who believes them to be the products of celestial penmanship (fig. 5.1).[6] Inscriptions on walls and windows or carved into tree trunks by unknown hands.[7] Moldering manuscripts on the verge of becoming illegible and dilapidated books that seemingly open of their own accord to particular pages and that appear thereby to have foreseen their readers' arrival. Enigmatic fragments of writing frequently numbered among the materials that the early gothic novel used to produce in its characters and readers its defining mood of anxious dread.

The evocation of a fictional world that is dense with signage is one measure that the gothic mode adopts so as to insinuate to its protagonists the spooky news that they are not alone and that instead invisible agents orchestrate their fates and possess their minds. Words can haunt as much as apparitions do. (Emily St. Aubert, heroine of Ann Radcliffe's 1794 *The Mysteries of Udolpho*, finds it difficult to dismiss that "sentence of dreadful import" from her thoughts, and hundreds of pages on we find that, like a "troublesome guest," it retains possession of her imagination, "starting up anew.") Acknowledging the strange powers with which words could be freighted, the gothic accompanied its defining interest in the hallucinatory psychology involved in ghost seeing, or the belief that one is ghost seeing, with an interest in the hallucinatory phenomenology of reading. And this fictional mode had a case of quotation compulsion of its own, pillaging the canon of English poetry for tags of mood-enhancing verse that it could redeploy as chapter epigraphs and arranging for those quotations to attend, as well, on its bookish heroines' reveries and inspire the verses that they in their turn might compose in homage. If you are the heroine of a *Tale of Other Times, A Gothic Story*, or *A Romance Interspersed with Pieces of Poetry*, you will feel that you are not alone. You will feel oppressively conscious of uncanny, importuning presences around you, in part, the suggestion is, because you dwell amidst a dead poets' society and because the poets' words, somehow reverberating across time and space, are faintly distinguishable too among

FIGURE 5.1 Frontispiece from an anonymous gothic chapbook, *The Monks of St. Andrews, or Castle of Haldenstein: A Romance* (ca. 1808–27). At the story's end, this ghost will be revealed as the rightful owner of the castle and as very much alive and well. Using a "chemical preparation" to form those letters of flame, Alphonso is able to play upon the superstition and guilt of the enemy who, years before, had attempted his murder. Photograph: Courtesy of the Lilly Library, Indiana University, Bloomington, Indiana.

the other human tones, the half-audible whispers, sobs, and sighs, that you fancy you hear mingled with the wailing of the wind. In a conceit that will be reencountered over the course of this chapter, the very air that the gothic heroine Emily St. Aubert breathes is pervaded in this manner by the murmurings of antique story and song. For a start, having left her native France for Italy, she will discover a taste for "classic story . . . descend[ing] to the peasants of [that] country" (421), who have made the "verses of Ariosto" and "the melancholy sweetness of Petrarch" (177) the bases for their songs and who in doing so have extended the solitary voice of the author into a generalized, communal one.[8]

This chapter investigates the bookishness of this strain of romantic-period fiction: the peculiar way it combines its discussions of possible returns from the afterlife with lessons in literary appreciation. It will concentrate on Radcliffe's works, those cross-generic hybrids of prose narrative and lyric poetry, and also on the many novels that after the early 1790s and through to the second decade of the nineteenth century took her ultra-imitable successes as models. This fiction provides a vantage point from which to investigate the spooky side to the love of literature. The upshot of the canon-making projects of the eighteenth century studied at the start of *Loving Literature* was, as we have seen, that antiquity was established as the touchstone of literary achievement. By extension, devotion to such achievement became in more pronounced terms than previously an affiliation linking, even ghoulishly, the living and the dead. Gothic novelists make visible the necromantic possibilities that their contemporaries discovered lurking in that affiliation. Sir Walter Scott learned about those possibilities from the Radcliffean gothic, which also supplied him with many of his plot structures. The identification of Chaucer offered by a character in Scott's 1826 novel *Woodstock, or The Cavalier* captures nicely the gothic dimensions of Scott's representation of canonicity. Who is Chaucer? Not a hunter, as this character's unlettered interlocutor has supposed from the sound of the name, but instead, he is instructed, "one of those wonderful fellows . . . who live many a hundred years after they are buried and whose words haunt our ears after their bones are long mouldered in the dust."[9] Canonicity, this description implies, is a supernatural phenomenon.

Recent scholarship on romantic canonicity has reconstructed how gothic novels furnished commentators of the era with the negative example that they needed as they set out to define the boundaries of literature proper.[10] In the episodes from gothic writing that this chapter treats we can glimpse the novelists themselves taking an interest in the literary immortality from which they were barred. Themselves sub-canonical, gothic fictions flaunted their pious canon love. They presented reading, as we shall see, as an act of filial mourning, at once a poignant remembrance and an anxious propitiation of the cherished ancestors to whom a modern reading public were indebted for their cultural heritage. As these novelists quoted from the canonical poets and through that quoting confirmed poetry's staying power, they registered the travails entailed in bearing the literary dead.

The idioms of filiation and consanguinity that were, as we shall see, deployed elsewhere in the culture as literary texts came to be reconceptualized as bequests from the ancestral dead, and as English literature became a kind of family trust, are dramatized by gothic writers. Their dramatization can help us apprehend the desirous aspects of literary history, and the guilt-ridden aspects too. It can make it easier to discern the notes of mournful feeling, superstitious awe, and ancestor worship that often infuse their contemporaries' accounts of their attachments to English literature. Gothic novels advance the domestication of the literary relation that has been at stake in previous chapters of this book. At the same time they also complicate that domestication: their plotting broaches, though finally only to close down, an account of home as a locus of animosity as well as a haven of loving feeling and an account of the family as an institution founded on violence and rapine. Accordingly they acknowledge darker emotions.

HAUNTED READING

Thomas Warton's histories of romance appear sometimes to have been studied, selectively, by gothic novelists on the lookout for picturesque customs from the middle ages or Renaissance that they might insert into their texts in the hope of lending their settings the patina of antiquity. This group, however, paid little heed to how often Warton in those histories, interpreting the past as a good Protestant should, had stressed the contrast between the "present diffusion of literature" and the scarcity of books and readers in those Gothic times when the church jealously monopolized learning. Instead, blithely bracketing Warton's narrative of modernization, the authors of these gothic romances anachronistically projected onto premodern times the polished literary pursuits of the late eighteenth century. Their heroine, conventionally distinguished by her sensibility and mental refinement, is in many episodes glimpsed with a volume of verse in her hand. The Petrarch-loving heroine of Mary Robinson's 1792 *Vancenza, or, the Dangers of Credulity*, set in fifteenth-century Spain, is even equipped with a pocket-book

in which she can transcribe the inscriptions that have engaged her attention and which she reperuses to nourish her pensive melancholy.[11] Literary
enthusiasms extend beyond the protagonist and down the social ladder to
encompass secondary characters: the servants, for instance, who, when ordered to keep watch overnight for smugglers, banditti, or ghosts, pick up tat-
tered romances of chivalry to fill the time. Modern critical discussions of the
gothic mode have tended to emphasize the other, more strenuous actions
its characters undertake—the breakneck escapes from their oppressors that
take them through subterranean passages and along vertiginous mountain
paths, the explorations of long deserted buildings in which they must surmount the superstitious fears engendered in them by others' reports of preternatural happenings. Critics generally neglect the scenes in which, to use
the idiom of these novels, these characters are portrayed as being "wrapt by
the visions of fancy" and "hurried along by the current of a poet's imagination." But an interest in how it feels to read, in the psychological states that
readers enter and exit, is a defining trait of the early gothic novel.[12]

Sometimes, of course, when the gothic authors have us read over the
shoulders of those characters who have taken up a book to kill time or
withdraw their minds from painful contemplation of their distresses, they
thereby put on hold the stories *of* those distresses. The author who deploys
this kind of metatextual reference is, it is fair to say, simply being a tease.
She uses a cheap trick to keep us even longer on the rack of suspense. On
other occasions, however, ones that I eventually will consider in some detail,
a character's reading is cast as integral to the narrative's movement toward
its resolution.

On these occasions a character's entrance into the chamber that a household sets aside for its reading and writing signals the launch of a genealogical plot. The secret cabinets of gothic libraries house, among their books,
the documentary raw material from which narratives of reproduction and
succession will subsequently be pieced together: testaments left behind
by dead fathers; long-lost certificates of marriage; and, of course, musty,
scarcely legible manuscript memoirs and confessions. *Udolpho* even has that
portrait miniature of an unknown lady, which Emily discovers concealed
within a bag of coins (104)—and which, some five hundred pages on she will
belatedly learn is a likeness of her now-deceased paternal aunt. The library
is for the gothic mode a standard launching point for that storyline whose
dénouement reveals family secrets, reestablishes disrupted family lines, and
restores to the orphaned protagonist the property that has been her birthright all along.

Hence, for instance, the opening of *The Mysterious Warning* (1796), a so-called German tale by, in fact, the Englishwoman Eliza Parsons, one of the workhorses of the stable of authors at Lane's Minerva Press: "No sooner had the struggling soul escaped from the clay-cold body of Count Tenaud, than his eldest son . . . hastened to the library, and open[ed] the secret cabinet where his late father usually deposited his papers of consequence."[13] Visits to castle libraries, described in detail, and searches of the various cabinets and escritoires they house will recur across the novel's four volumes, which trace the adventures of the son who is disinherited by the will stored in the secret cabinet of the book's first sentence. (This will is finally proved a forgery, just as the "mysterious warnings" of Parsons's title—uttered by a spectral voice that seems to come out of nowhere—have from the outset intimated that it will be.) Another visit to a castle library forms the opening episode of Parsons's earlier German story, *The Castle of Wolfenbach* (1793). When, defying the local peasantry's wild stories of supernatural happenings at the castle and of its "bloody floors, prison rooms, and scriptions . . . on the windows to make a body's hair stand on end," Parsons's heroine sets to exploring the edifice, she discovers a dark prehistory of family violence and a secret that she must keep. When the castle caretaker, old Bertha, asks our heroine about what she has seen within those apartments that all agree are haunted, Matilda's response therefore conveys only part of the truth, quite airily: "An excellent library . . . I intend to sit there very often and shall borrow some books." Matilda's entrance into those apartments, where the "books and implements for drawing" that she spots atop the tables have convinced her "the inhabitants were alive," launches a plot that in due course will see Matilda's parentage discovered, confirming the young woman's "pre-sentiment that [she is] no base-born unworthy offspring."[14] Matilda's comment on the excellence of the castle book collection—which strikes an odd note, calling to mind the metropolitan culture of polite taste just as readers are meant to be getting absorbed by Black Forest horrors—is perhaps best understood as Parsons's arch acknowledgment of the library's utility to such gothic plotting. The opening to *The Castle of Wolfenbach* registers how books, along with moldering manuscripts and strange (in)"scriptions," serve gothic fiction as essential props for its protagonists' projects of memory and mourning, the projects that reestablish the terms on which the generations will be linked and on which the living will relate to the dead.

Those projects, and their ramifications for the gothic novelists' interactions with their period's canon of dead poets, will concern us later. Let us note now, though, that, often, when gothic characters behave as libraries prompt them to and pick up a book, they either are, or feel, haunted. One site in which Radcliffe's Emily remembers the dead and, sensing the presence of unseen specters who attend on her nostalgic reveries, receives assurance that departed spirits also remember her is the library of La Vallée. This is the home in the south of France in which her story begins and in which, her rights of inheritance having been resecured, it ends. Returning to that home after the first of her absences, unnerved to find herself amidst "melancholy memorials of past times" (92) and "almost fancy[ing]" that she sees the dead who populated that past, Emily eventually—and, I am arguing, almost inevitably—finds her way to the library and then to a book.

> Her courage for a moment forsook her, when she opened the door of the library; and, perhaps, the shade, which evening and the foliage of the trees near the windows threw across the room, heightened the solemnity of her feelings on entering that apartment, where every thing spoke of her father. There was an arm chair, in which he used to sit; she shrunk when she observed it, for she had so often seen him seated there, and the idea of him rose so distinctly to her mind that she almost fancied she saw him before her. . . . She walked slowly to the chair, and seated herself in it; there was a reading-desk before it, on which lay a book open, as it had been left by her father. It was some moments before she recovered courage enough to examine it; and, when she looked at the open page, she immediately recollected, that St. Aubert, on the evening before his departure from the chateau, had read to her some passages from this his favourite author. The circumstance now affected her extremely; she looked at the page, wept, and looked again. To her the book appeared sacred and invaluable, and she would not have moved it, or closed the page, which he had left open, for the treasures of the Indies. (95)

In an influential essay, Terry Castle argues against the long popular notion of Radcliffe as a proponent of "the explained supernatural" who dogmatically resolved the mystical and marvelous to natural causes. This drawn-out, dreamy passage suggests why Castle states, instead, that ghostliness suffuses even the sections of Radcliffe's fiction that at first glance appear to be written in the "natural" idiom of eighteenth-century domestic fiction. Radcliffe renders home, Castle observes, as a site of the "uncanny, a realm of *apophrades*"; "To be 'at home' is to be possessed by memory, to dwell with spirits of the dead."[15] Importantly for my purposes, Radcliffe also renders home as a site of book love. To be at home with the spirits of the dead is also to remember those dead dwelling with their favorite books. The description of Emily's return to the library of La Vallée thus represents the book left behind by St. Aubert's death as an essential prop to his daughter's rite of mourning. And it is not just for the reader *inside* Radcliffe's book that reading matter functions in this way. By the end of the novel Radcliffe's audience discovers that the novelist had assumed all along that Emily's bereaved situation was likewise its own. The final sentence, in which the narrator breaks the frame of the fiction, shifts out of narrative to a vocative grammar, and acknowledges that audience's presence, reveals that Radcliffe has all along addressed *The Mysteries of Udolpho* to someone who was and is a "mourner," and who, as a result of his reading, an activity now assimilated to a generalized program of elegiac consolation, may have been—the narrator presumes to hope—"beguiled of one hour of his sorrow" or even "been taught to sustain it" (672).[16] Should this sorrowful reader return to the passage from the novel's first volume we have just been discussing he will discover staged in this episode *in* the text his own relation *to* the text and discover that the orphaned Emily has been held up before him as an idealized proxy.

Radcliffe's description of Emily's anxious and awestruck sensations inside La Vallée's haunted library presages a pattern in subsequent scenes, both in *Udolpho* itself and in the works of Radcliffe's many imitators. In his 1796 *The Monk*, for instance, in an episode that balances between plagiarism and parody of the Radcliffean original, Matthew Lewis has his orphan heroine, Antonia, return to her mother's chamber shortly after her mother's death. Antonia remembers that "Elvira's little Library was arranged there, and . . . that She might possibly find in it some Book" with which to occupy the time hanging heavy on her hands. The moment Antonia concludes her reading of the text that she lights upon there, and which Lewis forces us to read over her shoulder, the grisly ballad imitation "Alonzo the Brave, and Fair Imogine," the chamber door's sudden opening reveals her dead mother in spectral form—a plot turn palpably shaped by Lewis's determination to literalize and materialize what Radcliffe had tended, discreetly, merely to insinuate. (Lewis gives his audience "real" ghosts, complete with shrouds.)[17] Or let us consider another scene of reading from a later episode in *Udolpho*, involving Emily's manservant Ludovico, who has been ordered to stand watch by night locked up in a room thought to be haunted. The chapter begins with Ludovico borrowing a book that a fellow servant has retrieved from the dark, damp corner of the library of the chateau (551) and quickly becoming absorbed in one of the "old Provençal tales" it collects. The narration breaks off abruptly just after the narrator tracks Ludovico's growing conviction that while he has been reading some unknown being has joined his solitude. The tale followed to its conclusion and his book laid aside, Ludovico raises his eyes and, the narrator tells us in a virtuoso bit of psycho-narration that mimes the feeling of haunted reading, he "almost expected to meet other eyes, fixed upon his own" (557). The chapter that succeeds this one shifts the scene to the morning that follows Ludovico's watch, when his friends open the locked chamber in which he had read and discover that now no one is there. (At the novel's conclusion we will hear about the smugglers who have been exploiting the secret passage that opens into this chamber, but at this stage Radcliffe's readers can only speculate about this creepy quid pro quo whereby the ghost's surmised apparition seemingly requires Ludovico's disappearance in exchange.) Here bookish activity is again described as a half-inadvertent necromancy that embroils the reader with revenants.

The episode casts in relief what is uncanny about the act of reading. Radcliffe's audience is reminded of how they too have enlisted in a process characterized by periodic disappearances and apparitions, in which the book as object, the thing of paper that one grasps in one's hands, ceases to be a material reality as one comes to be engrossed by one's text, while the images and ideas that this book contains seem to spring into embodied existence in their turn. Educated by such episodes, readers of, as well as in, gothic fictions learn to associate the textual and the spectral. Reading comes to be elevated above everyday habit for the reader who follows the lead of these books that determinedly make it strange again. Reading can give you the shivers.

The narrator's reference in the earlier episode of *Udolpho* to how St. Aubert's book appears to his daughter more valuable than "the treasures of the Indies" and her reference in the later episode to how Ludovico's fascinating Provençal tale "had captivated the careless imagination in every rank of society, in a former age" suggest an additional point. In these episodes of gothic phantasmagoria the pages the characters behold are often conceptualized as their legacies, either familial or cultural. Within these narratives that are so often geared to resecuring lines of succession and legitimizing the intergenerational transmission of property, even the time of reading is bequeathed to the reader by the dead. The gothic mode insistently locates reading within a strange time of posthumousness.[18]

In these novels the dead have all sorts of methods for ensuring that they will get a reading. The disinherited hero of Parsons's *The Mysterious Warning*, mentioned above, learns this in several episodes, perhaps most eerily in the sequence in the novel's first volume in which, launched into a wandering life in foreign lands in the wake of his disinheritance, he comes across a ruined castle and takes refuge there alongside a mysterious misanthrope whose occupancy is of longer date. This solitary tells our hero that he resides there alone, though our hero thinks he hears the cries of "some person distressed and confined," and he tells him that he is not the owner of the castle, while nonetheless conducting his visitor into "what he called his library . . . [where] the glasses in many places were broken, the books all tumbling in disorder, and so covered with dust, that they were scarcely discernable." Following this hermit's sudden death, Ferdinand enters that library once more and, "opening one drawer, he met with a manuscript . . . [;] his eyes caught the words: *'The stranger, who calls himself Ferdinand.'*" Ferdinand's shivery sensations at encountering his own name indicate that the manuscript (in fact, the "Memoirs of one Baron S***," an inset tale which Parsons thereafter has us read over Ferdinand's shoulder) possesses the eerie powers with which gothic novelists often endow the texts inside their texts.[19] Reading is the action by which Ferdinand confirms his interpellation and confirms that persons can be "caught" by "words." This text seemingly boasts the telepathic capacity to see its reader coming.

That invisible hand that, especially in gothic fictions of a more didactic bent, is charged with ensuring that the plot will finally demonstrate innocence's triumph over vice will indeed often contrive to lead the protagonists to particular pages, even despite their intentions. In Radcliffe's *The Romance of the Forest* (1791), the heroine finds, in a hidden chamber of the ruined abbey she temporarily calls home, the eerie traces of a prior occupant, including a manuscript much decayed with damp. She attempts to read it immediately, "but the part of the manuscript that she looked at was so much obliterated that she found this difficult, though what few words were legible impressed her with curiosity and terror."[20] (In this novel as much as in *Udolpho*, Radcliffe takes an interest in how verbal fragments sometimes start up into independent life and, as though composed of magic words, take hold of a reader.) Adeline's perusal of this crumbling manuscript is eventually protracted over four chapters, both in a showy demonstration of Radcliffe's power to keep us readers in suspense (peering over Adeline's shoulder, as it were, and dying to read on), and the better to explore the psychological states into which a reader enters—the "strong illusion of fancy," for instance, that makes an event that was set down in writing in the past seem to this reader "at this moment present" (132).[21]

Bit by bit, we learn that these pages written in "discolored and almost obliterated ink" (127) record, diaristically, the final days of a prisoner who after a long confinement was murdered in the chamber in which Adeline discovered the manuscript. At the close of *The Romance*, when we have straightened out the lines of filiation and established this writer's relation to his reader, we realize retroactively, with Adeline herself, that the manuscript left behind by this unfortunate prisoner was the last testament of her real father. Radcliffe has mobilized still another fantasy about the power that a text might have to forge a connection with—to foresee—its reader. "Oh my children . . . Ye know not my wretched state," the prisoner wrote. He then detected the wishfulness in which he had indulged in thinking that his children might ever be the audience to his writing: "Ye cannot know it by human means. . . . My pen can call no friends to succour me" (132). That the particular reader for whom this writer longs does beat the odds and find her way to the "very chamber where her parent had suffered" (346) bespeaks the power that paternal pens often command in these fictions.[22]

As gothic novels explored those powers, they also offered their contemporary audience guidance about what it might mean to be at home with English—at home with an illustrious literary antiquity. Developed, in ways that the next section will briefly sketch, in close relation with the later eighteenth century's reconception of the English canon, and highly conscious of the new cult of the antiquarian book that grew up in concert with that reconception, the gothic mode modeled the mixed feelings that this canon could inspire in those to whom it is supposed to stand as their birthright. This chapter is working its way toward an account of those mixed feelings. To get there, let us think first about the mode's own bibliomania—and the intertextual weave of the fictions, their echo effects, and the particular soundtrack those echoes provide for the fictions' inheritance plots.

"HALLS ECHOING TO THE SOUND OF REMOTE GENERATIONS": LITERARY LEGACIES

Practitioners of the gothic mode seem to enjoy thinking about how, housed within the deserted libraries that seem requisite architectural features of this mode's châteaux and abbeys, a book can survive for ages without anyone lifting up its cover—and yet still be available to the readers who might just happen along and select it from the shelf. Its sheer durability makes the material book an apt emblem for the mode's defining interest in the ease with which the barbarisms of other times can resurface in civilized modernity. In 1803 a writer named Sarah Wilkinson exploited that symbolic power in her *The Subterraneous Passage: or, the Gothic Cell*. Left to her own devices in a derelict room in the ancient French castle where she has been held captive since her abduction by banditti, Wilkinson's heroine attempts to remove an engaging-looking volume from the dusty bookshelves, only to knock down several of the books surrounding her selection. Light streams through the gap opened up on the shelf, and Lady Emily finds that the shelving has concealed *a door*: her entry into an underground passage, which she begins to explore, conjecturing correctly that "something dreadful and mysterious was connected with that part of the edifice."[23] After many travails, Lady Emily succeeds in finding the concealed apartment to which the passage leads, the Gothic cell of Wilkinson's subtitle, and discovers there, near starvation, a certain Bertha Dubois, sister-in-law to the employer of the banditti, who, determined to appropriate Bertha's property, has held her captive there, reporting her dead, ever since his fratricidal murder of her husband more than five years before. Lady Emily's own suffering at the hands of this same Dubois, who soon forces her into a loveless marriage, repeats that of the older woman—as per the plot convention that the gothic mode developed to suggest the persistence across the generations of female subjugation and patriarchal coercion. The entrance into the library allegorizes her conscription by this established storyline.

Within the gothic mode generally, the dusty, long unread book, whose longevity casts into relief the truncated life expectancy accorded to mere humans, gives symbolic form to these uncanny repetitions of an undead past that will not go away.[24] At the same time, a more cynical reading of the gothic novel's bibliomania is possible. One might also consider the improbable prevalence of old book collections among the furnishings of ruined castles in fictions such as Wilkinson's or Eliza Parsons's as a telltale sign of their texts' bad conscience, since, in their formulaic conventionality, such gothic fictions do not exactly look as if they have been created by authors. They strike one as books made from other, recycled books.

Gothic novelists do not exactly discourage this impression that their texts might have originated in their commonplace books. But since their heroines determinedly "seldom look into novels" (a posture of bad faith that Jane Austen's narrator notices in her burlesque gothic, *Northanger Abbey*), the debts that Parsons and Wilkinson might owe to Radcliffe, or that Radcliffe might owe to Charlotte Smith, are left unacknowledged.[25] Instead, notoriously, the novels highlight their writers' acquaintance with the kind of book collection brought to view by the epigraph to this chapter, in which William Howitt, name-dropping, enumerates the canonical (and all male) company that the country gentleman keeps in his library. (The writers announce this acquaintance, even though as producers of wares hired out in circulating libraries, they would surely be gate-crashers at the country gentleman's party.) The quotation compulsions that I have already mentioned result in the frequent reappearances within these romantic-period texts of scraps of older, classic verse. The beauties of Shakespeare are favored candidates for transcription into the texts of the novels, a treatment that converts what was often originally dramatic dialogue into short bursts of lyric utterance. Shakespeare's words generally mingle with those of other staples of the late eighteenth-century booksellers' compilations of beauties and "compleat libraries of English poetry"—with the words of John Milton and James Thomson, for example, or of the newer graveyard poets, Thomas Gray, William Collins, and Robert Blair. These classic lines also mingle, perhaps contributing to readers' sense of the texts' clamorousness, with original verse: the lyric effusions that poetical-minded heroines and heroes jot down so as to record moments of reverie, or that they have discovered inscribed upon a tree or a rock or on the wall of an ancient building, or that they have committed to heart because the lines were often recited by an absent beloved. Even *The Subterraneous Passage*, a chapbook of a mere thirty-six pages whose frenetic pace leaves little time for pensive melancholy, allots space to an original poem.[26] In the passage from Parsons's *The Castle of Wolfenbach* I cited above, the catalogue of the castle's horrors includes "scriptions, they say, on the windows to make a body's hair stand on end."[27] We know that, with its generous allotment of "[in]scriptions," crowded with inset verse quotations and chapter mottoes, the typical gothic text often resembles that castle.

The fictions' first audiences appear to have taken in stride the contradiction that the convention I have been describing creates. The contents of these books are framed, from the title pages on, as "German tales" or as exposés of the horrors of the Italian Inquisition, but at every turn readers encounter in their pages familiar snippets of English literature in, variously, the form of the ornamental verse epigraphs that headed up each chapter, or as part of the narrator's discourse, or as material prompting the characters' own exercise of literary taste. In *The Romance of the Forest*, for instance, set by Radcliffe in seventeenth-century France and Switzerland, the heroine manages to carry on with her belletristic pursuits during the story's rare intervals of calm: at such moments Adeline contrives both to study "the best English poets" (82) and to write poems of her own, including an homage to *A Midsummer Night's Dream* (284-85). In these manifestations of her bardophilia, the heroine of *Romance* seems to act out the longings for canonicity of the fictional mode in which she appears. For our own part, we readers of, rather than in, the gothic navigate our texts in a mental state resembling the "confused remembrance" (*Romance*, 114) that a Radcliffe heroine like Adeline or Emily St. Aubert experiences as, for instance, entering a long deserted chamber, she contemplates the weirdly compelling portrait lodged there, whose lineaments seem so familiar.[28] Readers who have already formed an acquaintance with the best English poets will, as they peruse these pages, participate in the protagonist's sense of déjà vu. Gothic texts programmatically intermingle the strange with the familiar. They are set in a world elsewhere, of bygone superstitions and preternatural events, and yet they also feature enlightened protagonists who apprehend their experiences much as a modern reader would and feature quotations from much-anthologized and reprinted verse that this modern reader will already have read. Put otherwise, these novels insistently keep open the lines of communication with the canonical dead—even as they explore the possibility that the unquiet spirits of those who died by misadventure and who have not been properly buried or mourned will return to haunt the living.[29]

To describe the effects created by the reappearance in the pages of gothic fictions of those already known quotable quotes we might also recall the numerous episodes that dramatize characters' sensations as they listen to the echoes that resound through a landscape or ruined castle. Exposed to "the varied and distinct sounds which disturb the silent desolation of a half-deserted mansion"—as Sir Walter Scott put it in describing Horace Walpole's originary gothic setting, the eponymous Castle of Otranto—characters find that "superstition" becomes "contagious."[30] In these conditions the living cannot help but begin thinking that they have been joined by the dead. Echoes send the individual's own words back to her, but these acoustic environments also prompt the anxious listener to wonder where her own voice ends and another's begins.[31] With analogous effects, poetry is throughout this fiction associated with echoes as well. It is made the accompaniment to isolated individuals and single voices.[32] The gothic novelists appear as a group to have determined that through its inclusion of scraps of classic verse modern fiction could acquire something of the aura that Scott identifies when, discussing Walpole's success in the scene setting of *Otranto*, he comments on how old Gothic buildings, unlike modern imitations, raise our awe because they "have echoed to the sounds of remote generations and . . . have been pressed by the footsteps of those who have long since passed away."[33]

Particularly in Radcliffe's novels or those novels that adhere closely to Radcliffe's example, the protagonists' own verses are often presented as responses to, or sympathetic reverberations of, words already read or heard—the words of *A Midsummer Night's Dream* in the example from *The Romance of the Forest* referenced above, but, more often, the whispered communications of the genius loci, the kinds of "shadowy forms" that are summoned in another poem of Adeline's, the sonnet titled "To the Visions of Fancy." These shadowy forms "attend on the lonely hours" of aesthetically responsive individuals and "chase [their] real cares with [their] illusive powers" (35). As Adeline's lines confirm, in the story this sonnet tells of its own coming into being, poetry in gothic fiction is often in the *air*—not incidentally the medium out of which specters are likewise thought to materialize. "The Mariner," a ballad that Emily St. Aubert writes following her escape from Udolpho, moves in eleven stanzas from a budding romance to the deaths of both the eponymous sailor and his true love, and then, as Marshall Brown has put it, in its concluding two stanzas "dissolve[s] story" into "persisting resonances":[34]

> Oft, at the calm and silent evening hour,
> When summer-breezes linger on the wave,
> A melancholy voice is heard to pour
> Its lonely sweetness o'er poor Henry's grave!
>
> And oft at midnight airy strains are heard
> Around the grave where Ellen's form is laid;
> Nor is the dirge by village-maidens fear'd
> For lovers' spirits guard the holy shade. (*Udolpho*, 464)

The recontextualization of canonical poems that these novels effect assimilates that poetry to the eerie music of unquiet spirits.

The prose fiction that effects this spectralization of poetry also gestures, through the same measures, toward its familialization. Even as gothic fictions highlight the secrets of the child bed and arrange for the unfolding of narrative to bring about the clarification of these obscured bloodlines and unknown family origins, those epigraphs keep persistently in view the source texts of modern literary history. It is as if those fictions were anxious to clarify their own literary legitimacy and as if they believed doing homage to the evergreen memory of their forefathers would achieve that end. The argument, which was advanced by Warton and other antiquarian scholars of the late eighteenth century, that the romances of the Middle Ages formed British culture's imaginative wellspring is thus one these novelists take to heart. They mobilize it when they present their *own* books as romances (not novels) and as though they were the modern translations and/or imprints of rare incunabula or medieval manuscripts, newly redeemed from long centuries of obscurity. A prefatory advertisement thus informs us that *A Sicilian Romance* (Radcliffe's second novel, published in 1791) ushers into the public realm a "solemn history" that unfolded long ago in a deserted castle in Sicily, and which has been preserved hitherto only in an old manuscript housed in the library of the friary neighboring the castle. Mary Robinson's narrator tells us that the "mournful manuscript" that is the basis of *Vancenza* has been deposited in "the library of the University of Naples, where possibly it remains, a *sad record* of the fatal consequences of a MISTAKEN CREDULITY" (2:337). These pseudo-editorial authenticating devices produce a strange proximity between gothic novels—cheap fictions produced for the circulating libraries—and the bibliographical antiquities that, as we have seen, were valued so highly and ferreted out so eagerly by both the romantic period's book collectors and its historians of poetry. "The discovery of an old book, always seems to me like the revival of some forgotten Being from the grave," Egerton Brydges wrote to Thomas Frognall Dibdin in January 1812, congratulating him on his achievement in *Bibliomania*.[35] Brydges's terms cast the study of old books as a solemn necromantic activity that should give the shivers to those who undertake it. They also suggest that the traffic between literary historicism and gothic fictions took place on a two-way street.

In the mid-eighteenth century, as criticism came to pivot around a newly emphatic account of the value of literary antiquity, source studies and etymologies became more prominent in critical practice. The reading of old books with the assistance they afforded was esteemed precisely as a means through which the present generation might assert and retain its affiliations with the generations preceding it. "Shall we not endeavour to secure to future generations, entire and unchanged, their birthright in Shakespear, in Milton, in Addison, and Swift?" the Anglo-Irish lecturer Thomas Sheridan had asked in 1756 in his *British Education*, registering with that reference to Britons' birthright the impact of this reorientation of criticism.[36] Sheridan posed the question just after he gloomily reminded his readers that the "prodigal and spendthrift successors" of the great men of the classical past such as Virgil, Horace, Cicero, and Livy had "squandered away their language as well as the many other treasures bequeathed to them by their frugal ancestors." His intimation was that circa 1756 British authors were being similarly betrayed by their posterity, and that this betrayal would in their case be calamitous, because, as Sheridan warned throughout *British*

Education, the English language, unlike Latin, had neither been established on "solid foundations" nor fixed by "certain rules." Sheridan's strenuous efforts to make English language and literature central to the nation's curriculum and to claim for English the prestige then monopolized by Latin and Greek have given him a high profile among recent historians of English studies. Intent on making personalization as well as professionalization part of that history, I am struck by how artfully this passage of Sheridan's transmutes collective historical phenomena into a family saga (complete with frugal fathers and prodigal sons) and reframes persons' engagements with texts so as to shift them into the terrain of intersubjective relations. This architect of eighteenth-century literary studies here appears willing to play on the public's guilty feelings—and his willingness to do so should be granted a historical effectivity of its own.[37] He suggests the affective pressures—the demands for family loyalty, for instance—that the concept of the literary heritage can carry along with it.

In the wake of the later eighteenth century's new enterprises of canon formation, "poetic succession," Ian Duncan states, ceased to be merely "a trope of legitimation among poets themselves" and became instead "the property of an expanding reading public, and highly lucrative to booksellers."[38] Duncan's terms are suggestive for both the family saga that Sheridan sketched and those sagas that unfold in innumerable gothic novels. The allusion in his statement is to a development that this book referenced at its start: the boost that the Law Lords' decisions that copyright should be of limited term gave to the enterprise dedicated to reprinting those old works of English poetry that, out of copyright, had entered that new juridical space that would eventually be named the public domain. There was nothing new, as Duncan acknowledges, about invoking a metaphor of "legitimacy" to authorize a work of literature. John Dryden, for instance, had included in his preface to the *Fables* of 1700 a discussion casting Milton as the poetical son of Edmund Spenser and Spenser in turn as a scion of the Chaucerian family tree. Those genealogies exemplified Dryden's self-canonizing premise that "we"—meaning *we poets*—"have our lineal descents and clans as well as other families": they shored up a "notion of a connective past with composite authority."[39] However, as we saw earlier, the canon of English poetry was being reconceived in the midcentury, in the decades following the copyright decisions of 1774 particularly, as the "gift" that dead authors bequeathed to the British "people." Dryden's trope of genealogical inheritance, of a gift from the dead, came accordingly to be a way to identify *readers* as well as poets. (The trope is strangely literalized by the standard bit of gothic plotting in which a protagonist's story is put on hold while she serves as audience to what will turn out to be the story of her parents and does so while lodging in a building that, unbeknownst to her, she is next in line to inherit.) This trope made the most *legitimate* reading the one that proved the reader's continuing, filial attachment to those who had gone before.

If, as the gothic novelists suggest, the old family trees of literary history also came to be charged in this era with a new affectivity, this may have registered, as well, how family itself was changing, thanks to the "affective intensification of the family space" that occurred in the eighteenth century. To illuminate the new resonances the genealogical trope acquired then, we might recall Michel Foucault's account, from which I have just quoted, of how in the eighteenth century, as the nuclear family superseded the extended kin network of earlier centuries, the family "intensified in comparison with the functions it formerly exercised in the deployment of alliance." When it made up part of the language of legitimation that poets used to establish their relations to predecessors, the genealogical trope referenced the traditional duty of family members to ensure that the names and memories of the older generation live on after they die. After the eighteenth century, such remembering, in new ways, was the reader's charge. And the genealogical trope becomes more richly productive of psychological effects, and more burdensome, once received into a culture intent on sacralizing companionate marriage and filial affection, once the family has become, that is, as Foucault indicated, a hotbed of Oedipal angst and the "obligatory locus" of "affects, feelings, love."[40]

To consider how the old family trees of literary history could take on new meanings when written into the late eighteenth-century novel, let us turn to the gothic library that provides the opening scene of Charlotte Smith's *Emmeline, the Orphan of the Castle*. Smith's novel from 1788 is historically important as an early example—one that Radcliffe doubtless studied before she launched her career in the following year—of how scenes in which all that "breathe[s] a certain solemn and melancholy stillness calculated to inspire horror" could be incorporated within the already established formats of sentimental fiction.[41] This novel also modeled influentially how a prose narrative could be "interspersed with pieces of poetry" (to cite the subtitle Radcliffe affixed to her *Romance of the Forest*).

Emmeline is plotted so as to deliver proof after proof of its eponymous heroine's natural good breeding, making the concluding disclosure of her legitimacy something of a redundancy. To fascinating effect, Smith launches this familiar plotline of virtue rewarded and birthrights restored with a par-able of canon formation. Thus in our first glimpse of Emmeline, the orphan whose story is launched when she is "found" in Mowbray Castle by its putative owner, her uncle Lord Montreville, she is portrayed exploring the "once noble" castle's ruined library, where books "of all ages" are likewise to be "found"—some, however, "so injured by time that the most indefatigable antiquary could have made nothing of them." The young girl salvages those few that are not yet beyond repair, "Spenser and Milton, two or three volumes of the Spectator, an old edition of Shakespeare, and an odd volume or two of Pope," cleaning off the dust that has covered them, and removing them "into the housekeeper's room: where the village carpenter accommodated her with a shelf, on which, with great pride of heart, she placed her new acquisitions." Through further researches among "all the piles of books, some of which lay tumbled in heaps on the floor, others promiscuously placed on the shelves," she eventually "complete[s] several sets."[42] It is a bibliographical rescue mission, chiming with the projects undertaken by the bookmen who were at this moment traveling to the Continent's monastic libraries there to confront the dust and confusion of centuries. Completing the sets, Emmeline sets straight the "lineal descents" that define the familial order of the English canon.

The episode revivifies the metaphorics of literary legitimacy and legacy developed by the poets, while redeploying it in a new generic context. It prefigures, as well, the manner in which throughout this novel Smith will align questions of literary history, genre, pedigree, and the disposition of property. *Emmeline*'s dénouement involves the discovery (repeated in various forms in multiple gothic fictions of the 1790s) that Emmeline's uncle, eager to increase his fortune and acting on long-standing envy of his brother, had at the time of her father's death in Italy contrived to suppress the truth about her heritage. Lord Montreville self-servingly permitted others to believe, wrongly, that this brother had never married the mother of his child and had died intestate: the sexual reputation of Emmeline's mother was sacrificed to advance his ambitions and enable him to claim his brother's property. (Over the course of her story Emmeline will likewise be traduced by enemies who make it their business to construe dubious appearances to her disadvantage, in the hope of convincing the world that she is following in her mother's footsteps.) When in the novel's fourth volume Montreville's greed and envy are brought to light, the orphan of the castle is revealed as its rightful owner. Poetry is directly aligned with the documents that establish Emmeline's legitimacy and so disclose Montreville's crime. After two "embroidered caskets" that had long been the charge of an old family retainer at

Mowbray Castle are at last put into Emmeline's hands, she finds inside one of them two certificates of her parents' marriage, one signed by the Catholic priest who had married the pair when they first eloped to the Continent, the other by the Anglican clergyman who had repeated the ceremony a few days before Emmeline's birth. But the collection of family papers—"silent memorials" of the dead—also includes letters from her paternal grandmother, the correspondence "between her father and mother during the early part of their acquaintance," and, written in the same hands, "several pieces of poetry, elegant and affecting."[43] The family whom Emmeline has never known, including the mother who died giving birth to her, have contrived to secure themselves a posthumous reading. Their poems are their memorial, as is their child.

Alongside the suggestion that Emmeline's existence has somehow demanded the demise of both her mother *and* her father, one senses an understanding of poetry, routed through the idiom of the authorial gift and the authorial sacrifice, in which poems are things purchased by poets' lifeblood. In gothic fictions, it seems, poetry and parenthood each involve high mortality rates, a phenomenon brought home to readers and orphan daughters alike. And in fact Emmeline has additional reasons for feelings of guilt. She has for most of the novel wrongly believed, as many gothic heroines will in the quarter century following the publication of Smith's novel, that "there was a mystery in her birth dishonorable to her parents"—the phrase that *Udolpho*'s narrator uses to name the anxieties that haunt Emily St. Aubert after she inadvertently sees more of her dead father's papers than she was meant to and finds that that sentence of dreadful import has fastened upon her mind (650).

Mary Robinson's *Vancenza* also assigns the poetry of a dead parent a crucial role in the belated revelation of the backstory that explains a heroine's birth. At the moment when, as will become evident later, she is on the verge of reenacting the tragic story of seduction, abandonment, and shame that was previously the lot of her unknown mother, Elvira, a foundling brought up in the castle of Vancenza, makes a discovery when she looks closely at a casement window in the castle. She finds inscribed there, evidently by someone wielding a diamond ring, a poem comprising thirty lines in five stanzas (imagine the hand cramps endured by its writer). The third person narrator of *Vancenza* has already established Elvira's poetry love. From the start we have known, for example, that Petrarch is this fifteenth-century Spanish girl's "favourite" author. Still, this narrator takes pains to indicate that for the heroine these lines are extraordinarily affecting. "Something unfelt before seemed to take possession of all her faculties; the tenderness of love, the sympathy of sorrow. . . . She read the lines over and over with the most earnest solicitude" (2: 276). For good reason, as it turns out, Elvira takes this poem personally. The novel's dénouement reveals that the poem, whose speaker laments being "betray'd by love" (2: 275), was composed by her mother, who did not survive the pregnancy that was the sequel to that betrayal.[44] Almost as thoroughly as Smith, Robinson intertwines poems and legacies, ancestors and authors, reverent reading, filial piety, and feelings of guilt.

AT HOME WITH THE DEAD: NATIONALIST NECROMANCY

In this manner the novelists evoke what was in fact a widely shared impulse in their era—"to route anxieties about literature, community, and cultural heritage through the dead."[45] The political theorist Martin Thom has, for instance, described how at the close of the eighteenth century the coming into being of a new world of nations, constructed on the ruins of the Enlightenment, "brought the dead, forever murmuring, among the living."[46] With the ascendancy of nationalist principles across Europe, and a new emphasis on the separate destinies of peoples, rather than their lateral relations, came another shift, famously traced by Raymond Williams in *Keywords*. The later eighteenth century gradually jettisoned the framework in which "culture" had named a process of cultivation that unfolded through social and commercial exchange, as in the ancient concept of the *translatio imperii et studii*, and which had linked "culture" to the lateral diffusion of artifacts and institutions.[47] Instead, "culture," as substantive noun rather than process, became the bounded collection of arts and ideas that was transmitted, as "heritage," in a vertical descent from each bygone generation to its successors, and that was localized in a particular plot of classic ground or literary landscape. In late eighteenth-century Britain specifically, that new scheme is elaborated in tandem with accounts that make the distinctiveness of the national character hinge on the inhabitants' willingness to center collective life on the project of doing proper reverence to their ancestral dead.

Thus just two years after Smith published *Emmeline*, Edmund Burke was in *Reflections on the Revolution in France* casting Britain as the antithesis of Jacobin France precisely on the grounds that in his country the ways of the dead remained a living part of social life. British nationhood was for Burke a "partnership," not only, as the social contractarians might have it, "between those who are living, but between those who are living, those who are dead, and those who are to be born." In France, by contrast, the French had "murdered" their dead and appeared to Burke to be able and willing to take the next step and murder their living priests and king.[48] The genealogical metaphor, explored in *Emmeline*, as we have seen, that makes the history of writing into a tradition and remakes the history of writers as a history of an uninterrupted family line also underpins Burke's redefinition of British nationality as a matter of inbred, filial sentiments. In *Reflections* Burke redefined the British nation as a web of kinship relations, in a theory of statecraft that unabashedly identified governance with the harnessing rather than the suppression of libidinal energies. "To be attached to the subdivision, to love the little platoon we belong to . . . is the first principle . . . of public affections." The *Reflections'* central claim was that "it has been the uniform policy of our constitution to claim and assert our liberties, as an *entailed inheritance* derived to us from our forefathers, and to be transmitted to our posterity."[49] That inheritance comprised family heirlooms. His country's liberty, Burke explained, was a *noble* freedom, possessing "its gallery of portraits; its monumental inscriptions; its records, evidences, and titles"—all such furnishings as were proper to Gothic halls.

Notwithstanding his sympathy in the first part of the 1790s with France's democratic project, Burke's political opponent, William Godwin, came up a decade and a half later with something closely approximating Burke's sense of a body politic constituted through its remembrance of the dead. Godwin's memorial scheme was outlined in his *Essay on Sepulchres* (1809), which argued that the final resting places of the dead should constitute the stations of a national pilgrimage circuit, and which to that end proposed, as Godwin's subtitle put it, "Erecting Some Memorial of the Illustrious Dead in All Ages on the Spot Where Their Remains Have Been Interred." The *Essay* assigned dead literati a place of privilege among the "illustrious dead," on the grounds that they had, as Godwin stated, benefited humanity far more than had military or naval heroes. Homer, Milton, Shakespeare, Chaucer, Sir Philip Sidney, Lord Bacon, all received mention there, candidates for the séances that Godwin imagined undertaking before their tombs, in which he would summon their "ghost[s]" and "satisfy the ardour of [his] love." (Because of that orientation to literary achievement, Godwin perforce navigated in the *Essay* between an account of how national identity might be founded on the dead—whose physical remains are interred in particular hallowed spots of ground—and a more freewheeling celebration of books in general, which the *Essay* construes as authorial remains of a more portable kind.)[50] Recent scholars who have considered the *Essay* have seen Godwin as a prophet of the literary tourism of the later nineteenth century and of the grave visiting it so frequently involved. (In the next chapter I shall have more to say about the tinge of gothicism distinguishing this enthusiasm for touring, as the preferred idiom had it, the "homes and haunts" of the British authors, but for now let us simply note how often the grave, understood as the dead author's final dwelling place, figured on these touristic itineraries.) Poets' Corner in Westminster Abbey was too official and public a place to sustain the communions Victorian readers desired. When they took to the roads as tourists, they fanned out well beyond the metropolis, in part out of their sense that the most sentimentally satisfying memorial practice would be one that, as Nicola Watson puts it, "locate[d] the author within a place . . . conceived of as organically connected both to the physical person and to the literary corpus."[51] Those touristic desires to localize and personalize relations with beloved dead authors seem to be foretold in Godwin's *Essay*.

The *Essay* proposed as key to their national identity the fact that living British readers would find it easier than other peoples to think of themselves as "mingling," in such especially snug, intimate, and affectionate terms, with dead writers. Godwin congratulated himself for being the "native of an old country." He dismissed the globe's "new" countries as sites where the remoter generations had passed away "without leaving a vestige behind," and where the inhabitants were able accordingly to "converse only with the generation of men that now happens to live." His homeland, he maintained by way of contrast, represented a place where "on whichever side I turn I find some object connected with a heart-moving tale."[52] His nation was saturated with literariness. If this representation anticipates, as Watson proposes, the kind of theme park literary nationalism promulgated by present-day tourist boards, the conditions of existence in Godwin's "Old Country" also recall and write large the echo chamber in which the Radcliffean gothic fiction of the 1790s tended to install its protagonists: those haunted landscapes where heroes and heroines are fated, whether or not they know it at the time, to experience close encounters with their ancestral pasts and where, as we have begun to see, dead poets are the resident genius loci. We should note, as well, that the subgenre of nineteenth-century poetry that emerged to chronicle poets' visits to poets' graves shared with gothic fiction this trope of the still-reverberating poem. Thus the speaker of Robert Montgomery's 1832 "At the Tomb of Gray" savors his haunted state when he observes that at this graveside, "The air is eloquent with living thoughts, / And fine impressions of

[Gray's] favour'd muse; / While Inspiration, like a god of Song, / Wakes the deep echoes of his deathless lyre."[53]

In her discussion of the *Essay on Sepulchres* Julie Carlson maintains that Godwin thought of the dead whose veneration he promoted as his "brother-men," and not as parental figures.[54] In this respect, his familialization of the literary dead diverged from that discernible in a novel such as *Emmeline*: I have been suggesting here, after all, that such gothic fictions worked with their era's new critical discussions of literary antiquity to endow dead authors with some of the mysterious authority that parents have exerted within the Oedipal household, the authority of those who preexist us. But aspects of Godwin's self-portrait within the *Essay* do make him resemble those gothic heroines—Emily St. Aubert, Emmeline Mowbray—who, when they regain their homes, their tribulations at last concluded, are welcomed by "pleasing shades . . . with a thousand tender and affecting remembrances" (*Udolpho*, 671). Godwin's announced desire in the *Essay* is both to be at home with the dead—visiting them, he insists, in the exact places where they reside *now*, and not in the houses where they *once* lived or where they died— and to arrange for the dead to be at home with him. He wants a relation that is close: "I would have them 'around my path, and around my bed' and not allow myself to hold a more frequent intercourse with the living, than with the good departed."[55] Too close for comfort? Maybe. "Why should Milton and Shakespear . . . die?" another passage asks. "Perhaps yet they shall not wholly die . . . some spirit shall escape from [Milton's] ashes, and whisper to me things unfelt before." The reference to a whisper brings dead bards awfully near.

As has often been noted, the cultural construction of nationness that engaged so many thinkers of the late eighteenth and nineteenth centuries centered overwhelmingly on celebrations of the nation's hoariness, not its youth.[56] Burke's counterrevolutionary account of England as a genealogical community unified by its reverence for its forefathers and William Godwin's description of his good fortune in inhabiting an old country that is littered with authorial graves each make this evident. They suggest the centrality of memorial rituals to the period's pedagogy of national belonging. ("What Burke and the romantics tend to suppress," by contrast, as Marlon Ross has commented, "is the *machinery* of modern nationalism, the fact that it functions like a series of interlocking cogs, fueled by coal and capital, rather than like a patriarchal tribe, motivated by the instinctual love of kin that spreads out into loyalty for the national kind.")[57] "Through literature we are able to feel the kindling spirits of the mighty dead," one W. J. Alexander stated in the inaugural address he gave in 1887 upon assuming a professorship of English literature at the University of Toronto, resorting to a quasi-gothic idiom as he promoted his academic subject. That idiom can be encountered, as well, in the handbook *History of English Literature*, written by another nineteenth-century English professor, that was widely used in universities across the British Empire for decades following its initial publication in 1853: its author, William Spalding, Regius Chair in Rhetoric and English Literature at the University of Edinburgh, states that literature calls "up before us, by an innocent necromancy, the perished world in which our forefathers lived."[58] Statements of this sort are not unusual in the writings of the Victorian professoriate, but it does not follow that we should rush to dismiss as empty rhetoric the notes of superstitious awe and ancestor worship audible in these early vindications of disciplinary English studies. The scenes of reading that we've been encountering in our survey of gothic libraries might well prime us, instead, to notice how such statements go beyond the requirements of a straightforward didacticism. The works of dead authors are presented not simply as set of meanings to be learned but also as things to be mourned and loved and even (as Spalding's reference to "necromancy" implies) reanimated through those passionate efforts. The strong affective dimensions of the programs of study here commended derive from a notion of authors as kin. Framed in this way, the curriculum resembles that verse inscription that the heroine of *Vancenza* discovers on the castle casement and which prompts her rereadings and "most earnest solicitude."

Cultural nationalism proposes that the canonical works of the literary tradition can be a reader's ticket of admission to a perennial Englishness (claimable even by readers situated in the colonial dominions where Alexander taught and where the edition of Spalding's handbook from which I have quoted was published). At the same time, that nationalist account of community as something erected on the nation's burial ground likely raised the emotional stakes of readers' literary transactions and freighted them with new pressures. We might recall here too chapter 3's discussion of how late eighteenth-century library design was informed by an effort to make the scene of reading into a site where readers would repeat the preferences of their ancestors and where, by that means, their individual acts of reading could be subordinated to what Samuel Johnson in prefacing his edition of Shakespeare called "the continuance of esteem," and what Jonathan Kramnick, glossing that preface, has called "the historical spirit of common English"—the "immemorial perpetuity of response, the praise of readers across the expanse of time and location." In such a site the reading of Shakespeare would not simply ally you to a community of fellow Shakespeare lovers. That community of love would come to the present from the past.[59] The reception scenarios that the gothic novelists stage and which this chapter has highlighted foretell the pressures that such an arrangement creates.

Certainly, as we have been seeing, the gothic novelists make heavy weather of reading. Hence the way in which, to recapitulate for a moment, Radcliffe's novels assimilate the encounter with poetry to the encounter with an apparition; on both occasions one braves an "incursion" from an alien, unseen world.[60] Hence the presentation of reading as the mournful probating of an inheritance (a portrayal that resonates with the terms in which cultural nationalism reimagines the reader as a national subject), and hence in *Emmeline* and *Vancenza* the coupling of dead parents with dead poets—figures whom orphan daughters come to know principally by reading their literary remains and whose sacrifices for their progeny will be only partially repaid by the reverence of such readings. In probing such reception scenarios, we have also been tracing the aftereffects of the reorganization of the relations of the living to the dead that Philippe Ariès described in the closing chapters of *The Hour of Our Death*. There Ariès outlined how, in the eighteenth century, as affectivity, formerly more widely distributed, came to be concentrated on a few "exceptional, irreplaceable and inseparable" individuals within the conjugal family, the Anglo-American notion of the afterlife was reconceived. Ancient ideas about the beyond were replaced by "a new and anthropomorphic image," a heavenly home, which was "the earthly home saved from the menace of time, a home in which the expectations of eschatology are mingled with the realities of memory."[61] Prior to this eighteenth-century development, apparitions had been frightful calls for conversion. But as mourning took over from conversion as the major event in individuals' spiritual histories, the meanings of ghosts expanded. (They expanded too in concert with that shift that saw homage to literary fame become a necrotouristic activity—the confirmation of "a personal, sentimental relation between the physical remains of the poet and the literary pilgrim").[62] The gothic fictions from the eighteenth century's end register those changes while they send their protagonists ricocheting among spectral populations of various, not entirely distinguishable, kinds. There are, to start with, the fearsome apparitions, who, gothic narrators caution, may simply be psychological projections, not "real" ghosts at all; but there are also the sort of "pleasing shades" figuring in the conclusion to *Udolpho*, who define the space of home while they function as benignant guardian spirits and travel-weary daughters' welcoming committees; and, in addition, there are those differently pleasing shades, whose deathless words and living thoughts reverberate through the air to form the soundscape of a national homeland. While describing how the afterlife was reorganized to accommodate the intimacy expectations of the living, Ariès intimated that there was a downside, and this too is something that late-eighteenth-century gothic fiction documents. The dead now presented themselves as needy, importunate figures, with "emotional demands."[63]

BROKEN ENGLISH, OR, THE POEMS IN GOTHIC NOVELS

It seems characteristic of the tributes that gothic novelists make to canonical poetry's cultural prestige, characteristic too of how they underscore that canon's anteriority, that in the 1810 Minerva Press novel *The Nocturnal Minstrel, or, The Spirit in the Wood* Milton and Shakespeare get the very first words. In the bookish universe of the romantic-period gothic novel, their oeuvres represent the great source texts. The title page of this novel by Eleanor Sleath is ornamented with an epigraph from Milton's *Comus*—

> Can any mortal mixture of earth's mould,
> Breathe such divine enchanting ravishment?
> Sure, something holy lodges in that breast
> And with these raptures moves the vocal air,
> To testify his hidden residence!
> How sweetly did they float upon the wings
> Of silence, through the empty vaulted night;
> At every fall smoothing the raven down
> Of Darkness, till it smiled.

And lines from the opening of *Twelfth Night* supply the epigraph for its first chapter:

> That strain again!—it had a dying fall;
> Oh, it came o'er my ear like the sweet South,
> That breathes upon a bank of violets,
> Stealing and giving odour.

Of course, at work in this selection of epigraphs (which Sleath ascribes simply to Milton and Shakespeare, sidelining their dramatic dialogue) is the hope that the two British bards, in escaping time, might *give* to the living.

Their words are resurrected here to endow this novel, a member of a down-market genre, with literariness and legitimacy. But Sleath has arranged to endow her quoting (or misquoting) with additional dimensions, in keeping with the smart self-reflexive commentary on literariness and literary immortality that, as this chapter has suggested, is pervasive in the gothic mode. So, when we look closely at her first chapter, Shakespeare's and Milton's words also appear, haunting presences, as though they have *stolen* into the characters' minds, infiltrating their fictional world so as to set the narrative in motion. When we move past that initial motto, the next words we encounter are a line of dialogue assigned to the heroine. "Oh, how enchanting are those notes!" Gertrude, Baroness Fitzwalter, says to her companions, as though echoing Duke Orsino's line and as though she too had been listening to his palace musicians, or as though she were a Comus who had caught the strains of the Lady's song.

The subject on which the baroness speaks is, in fact, the mysterious music that has been heard in the woods surrounding her castle on the Scottish borders.[64] Like an echo, the music frustrates all efforts of location. Sleath's text thus begins by collapsing the distinction between its inside and outside, its contents and the paratextual matter situated at its edge. It shows us that poetry is no observer of boundaries. Many pages in, the "divinely sweet" music will be traced to its origin, and the identity of the nocturnal minstrel will be discovered: the baroness's husband, falsely reported dead months before the novel's opening, but really in hiding (in the wake of his participation in Perkin Warbeck's failed revolt against Henry VII, the baron had been declared an outlaw). The web of associations that this discovery brings into view links a character's mournful fidelity to her beloved—"I have thought, that, in approbation of the resolution I have long formed of devoting my days to widowhood and the remembrance of a husband's love,—some benignant—some approving spirit hovers nears me"—with something we would like to think of as more impersonal, which is readers' fidelity to Milton and Shakespeare. It links both feelings to the phantasmagoric. For, as one might expect, the eerie possibility the novel flirts with, in defiance of the skepticism of a rational, rather modern-sounding third person narrator, is that the music has no earthly point of origin.[65] It is as if the lines that supply the epigraph also, as strings of magic words, had raised the specter—or even as if they were the specter.

Are the presiding spirits of English literature friendly ghosts? Near the end of the *Essay on Sepulchres*, Godwin used spooky terms to celebrate the spirits' secret ministry. "I cannot tell what I should have been, if Shakespear or Milton had not written. The poorest peasant in the remotest corner of England, is probably a different man from what he would have been but for the writings of Shakespear and Milton."[66] The influence that the poets exert on the individual in modern times, Godwin goes on to explain, is so far-reaching as to affect even those who have never heard Shakespeare's or Milton's names: the inspiration "passes from man to man, till it influences the whole mass."[67] Even more explicitly than *The Nocturnal Minstrel*, the *Essay* implies an account of literature that locates it within a numinous realm; Milton and Shakespeare here have the omnipresence of deities. The account of the origins of collective life evoked by this passage is a bit scary. There is not much in the way of public spirit, or social contract, or even agency here, but instead a fetishism that makes *texts*, not living people, into the actors and the authors of collective life.

In 1913 in *Totem and Taboo* Freud argued that the veneration of the dead was always freighted with an unconscious current of hostility or distrust toward them. The unconscious wish for the death of those we love represented for Freud the "classical example" of the "ambivalence of human emotions." Disavowed and projected outward, that hostility was transmuted into the conviction that the dead harbored ill feelings towards the living. Hence among the so-called primitive peoples whom Freud describes in *Totem and Taboo* that strange psychological operation that converts figures who were beloved when living into malevolent specters that their survivors fear to meet. "It is no longer true that they are rejoicing to be rid of the dead man; on the contrary, they are mourning for him; but, strange to say, *he* has turned into a wicked demon ready to gloat over their misfortunes and eager to kill them." An alternative defense against the unconscious satisfaction that human beings take in the deaths of others was to intensify one's affection for the dead—an intensification that is also, in this scheme, the token that reveals that some hostility was being "shouted down." (This is why the domestication and sentimentalization of the dead that Ariès chronicles should not be seen as terminating these psychodramas, even if at first glance this Freud essay places those mainly in more "primitive" and "infantile" times.) In this manner, Freud explained, "Two completely opposing psychic structures, on the one hand fear of demons and ghosts and on the other hand veneration of ancestors" derive from the same root.[68]

The plotting of gothic fiction seems custom-made for parsing this tangle of opposed feelings, as literary critics have long noted. Hence heroines' propensity to mistakenly conclude that the men who threaten them are their real fathers, and hence the arrangements that make terrifying, specter-infested domiciles serve as the way stations on the journeys that these characters undertake to find out their parentage and regain their homes. Freud's argument has additional resonances for the materials this chapter has been surveying. Some of these have been articulated by Joseph Roach in a discussion that roots the eighteenth-century development of a canon of English classics within a context defined both by new sorts of secular reverence and by print's reshaping of social memory. Roach provocatively yokes the groundwork of modern English studies with archaic cultural fears: "Canon formation serves the function that 'ancestor worship' once did," he writes, and continues, "Like voodoo and hoodoo, the English classics help control the dead to serve the interests of the living."[69] This proposition, especially when taken in tandem with *Totem and Taboo*, suggests a way to read the *Essay on Sepulchres*. It invites us to identify Godwin's self-abasement before the powers of the literary dead in the passage I just quoted, his announced conviction that Milton and Shakespeare author their readers and even their nonreaders, as that exaltation of fearsome ancestors that Freud links to the father complex of the neurotic. We might hear in Godwin's language a shouting down of hostility or a cherishing that is meant to serve as a disarming or propitiation. Similarly, while tracking how the gothic novel stages the reading of literary remains, we have encountered more than a few traces of "the ambivalence of human emotions." Even as they pay homage to the literary canon, these novels play down the traditional ideas about the serenity of the dead and the dead's transcendence of earthly turmoil that had long shaped the notion of posthumous fame. Hearing the still vital voices of people who were alive in the past is, after all, an experience distinct from encountering their ghosts. When the gothic emphasizes the second over the first it modifies the idioms of eternization that the literary canon is supposed to mobilize.

I remarked above that the dead within gothic fictions have all sorts of ways, extending across the generations, of getting themselves read. This makes them different from the dead who *wrote* gothic fictions, works generally deemed disposable, as these authors when living likely knew all too well. Often read to pieces, a gothic chapbook—Sarah Wilkinson's *The Subterraneous Passage*, for instance—is in the twenty-first century much rarer than the biblio-treasure for which the patrician book collectors of 1812 battled at the Roxburghe auction.[70]

Often in gothic fiction, as we have seen, the dead, to secure themselves that reading, possess the power to draw their heirs to the very spots where their written testaments have been left behind or where their physical remains lie unburied. Somehow such connections with these predestined readers can be forged without the assistance of the living. This fiction also posits the existence of words that can haunt, with the power to fasten on readers' memories, even against their wills. But this is only part of the story this fiction tells about the fortunes of magic words from the past. The voices of the dead are often preserved only imperfectly, in crumbling manuscripts. Their power is hostage to the vulnerability of physical objects that are the prey of mildew and mold, or which, like bones, are in the process of moldering away to dust. To conclude this chapter, I want to trace briefly how a similar doubleness conditions the presentation of the poems within gothic prose; I mean thereby to underscore one last time the notes of ambivalence detectable in the literary appreciation this fiction models.

In Walter Scott's gothic account of the dead poet, encountered near the start of this chapter, Chaucerian poetry transcends material circumstance. It prevails against time and continues to "haunt our ears." Like the music of Sleath's nocturnal minstrel, Chaucer's words are somehow in the air, ethereally unlocatable but omnipresent. But alternative locations for poetry, that genre of choice for the representation of postmortem speech, are also proposed in the gothic novels we've been surveying—and so, accordingly, are alternative definitions of poetry. Gothic fictions also call attention to poems' constraint by their material embodiment, by language's physical properties. Or they lift poetry out of context and by that means invite readers to view it as a relic, charged with pathos accordingly. In the next chapter I shall be examining how nineteenth-century literary culture taught the discipline of English studies to mourn poetry's passing, how it continued projects launched by Thomas Warton and Thomas Percy that made "true poetry" something apprehensible only across a temporal chasm. But the present account of how the gothic novelists trope on their period's accounts of literary immortality and on poetry's privileged access, as poetry, to that immortality would be incomplete without my noticing how the novelists also imply that in some sense the dead poets for whom we all are mourning, their utterance shaky or impeded, speak at best a kind of broken English.

Let me, so as to explain those statements and wrap up this account of the ambivalent way sub-canonical gothic literature contemplates literary kinds whose canonicity is more assured, discuss briefly two related characteristics of the poems in the gothic novel. Like the ghost of Alphonso the Good, which returns to his ancestral home, the Castle of Otranto, generations after his death, in the shape of a giant helmet, hand, and sword, when poetry (re)appears in the space of prose fiction it is very often in fragments. The gothic tends to present poetry in piecemeal form. It marks it off as language that has been severed from its context of origin. This is obviously the case with those chapter mottoes, extracted from the eminent British poets, and confirming the novelists' fidelity to the literary tradition. Typographical convention—the typesetting that sets the epigraph afloat in white space, the fact that the jagged right-hand margin of verse becomes more conspicuous when the verse heads up a block of right-justified prose—helps define the lines that form the motto as set off and broken off. Consequently, this bit of verse all the more evidently operates in the manner that Susan Stewart has associated with quoted language in general. If it speaks "the voice of history and tradition," the quotation also appears, Stewart observes, "as a severed head, a voice whose authority is grounded in itself."[71] Because it is supposed to serve in part as the material token or talisman that evidences an otherwise suspect author's aesthetic bona fides, the poetic epigraph, the bit of a poem repurposed in a work of prose fiction, is understood to be an object of interest not simply for what it itself says, but as much for how it looks—it looks like poetry—and as much for the authorial ascription that accompanies it ("Shakespeare," "Milton," "Gray," "Collins"—those names to conjure with). The epigraph makes language thing-like, so that it displays itself rather than communicating a particular content.

In this manner these quoted verse extracts help provide prose fiction with the vehicle for a highly self-interested commentary on poetry as poetry: for, in the absence of other meanings these poetic pieces might possess in the context in which they originated, the meaning that *is* theirs simply by virtue of belonging to the class of poetical utterances becomes all important. "As dividing form, genre . . . tends toward elegy and melancholy because it exists by itself and accentuates its own absence," Paul Magnuson observes, suggesting how it is that this abstraction of the poetical can operate as an engine for the production of poignancy.[72] The fidelity to which the quotation compulsions of gothic writers testify is, as the writers sometimes seem to know very well, of a compromised nature. Quotation entails the subordination of composition to transmission, for it puts the individual's pen in the service of others, but it is also an act by which a perfect original is dismembered. Epigraphs are also then the melancholic tokens of that poetry that has disappeared: they are a kind of epitaphic writing. What supports such a funereal alignment is the fact, in addition, that the poets *inside* gothic novels generally conceive of paper as only one among many surfaces on which to write. As we have previously glimpsed, on some occasions their poems are also *written on*—meaning *incised into*—other materials, including stone, though often window glass as well.

An inheritance from the sentimental fictions of the mid-eighteenth century, inscription poems, verses that are supposed to have come into being by these means, abound in gothic fictions.[73] Of course, because these verses explicitly speak only out of their situation, they are in some ways the antitheses of the ultra-portable quotation that is pressed into use as a chapter motto: instead, this is language that cannot "hope to achieve the immaterial, abstracted status of the infinitely transmissible text,"[74] because the proxy reader inside the text is made conscious from the start of how temporally and physically constrained her engagement with these words will be.

But in other respects, to align the epigraphs that are at the edges of the gothic novel with these poems found inside it, in the books' secret chambers or their cloisters cut off from the world, makes sense. For inscription poems also, and more or less by definition, blazon their status as writing, their constitutive scriptiveness—and yet at the same time this emphasis on writing's materiality, on the fact of the characters having been fashioned through the wielding of the diamond ring or the chisel, accentuates the absence of the hands that undertook that task. This absence is especially evident in those instances of the inscription poem in which a first person speaker commemorates himself or herself in anticipation of an imminent death. Thus the "Inscription in an Hermitage," carved by an unnamed agent on a marble tablet in the monastery garden frequented by Matthew Lewis's monk, is both an address to an unknown future reader and the self-authored epitaph of the first person speaker, the hermit who has left the world and who, in a mental leap into the future, foreshadows in his lines the death that will make that departure even more complete.[75] In the stanzas, already glimpsed, inscribed on the casement of the Castle of Vancenza, Mary Robinson's lyric speaker both references a "now" that can be understood as contemporary with the moment of inscription—as in the opening couplet, "The chilling gale that nipp'd the rose / Now murmuring sinks to soft repose"—and references a future moment in which this "I" will no longer exist, yet will somehow still deploy the grammatical first person:

> Perchance, when youth's delicious bloom
> Shall fade unheeded in the tomb
> Fate may direct a daughter's eye
> To where my mould'ring reliques lie;
> And, touch'd by sacred sympathy,
> That eye may drop a tear for ME! (2:275)

The readers of Eliza Parsons's *The Castle of Wolfenbach* confront comparable entanglements of absence and presence when at last, with the daring heroine, they light upon the "scriptions" that number among the castle horrors. One of the inscription poems that are discovered incised into the window glass of the secret chamber reads, for example, "I am dumb, as solemn sorrow ought to be; / Could my grief speak, my tale I'd tell to thee." A trace, this writing testifies to a human presence, but in minimalist, self-negating terms. It does not communicate, but evidences the incommunicable. The tracing of another sort that accompanies it compounds the effect: a "shape of a hand . . . trac'd in blood, which seemed to have flowed in great quantities" is "plainly marked" on the floor of the room in which the inscribed poems are found.[76] The presence of the handprint, like that of the words etched in the glass, merely accentuates the other disappearances that this site of inscription has witnessed.

The mysteriousness of the inscription poems of *The Castle of Wolfenbach*, like those in *The Monk* and *Vancenza*, grants them considerable power. The unknownness of that hand and the inaccessibility of the backstory behind the words are arresting. (This is the case, as well, with the sonnet penciled on the wall of La Vallée's little fishing house that Emily St. Aubert discovers as *The Mysteries of Udolpho* opens [7–9]: its author unknown, it appears out of the blue—as though it takes a startling incursion from poetry's otherworldly realm to inaugurate a novel's plot.)[77] But that power is often inextricable from a sense of desperation and desolation, especially in those verses directly addressed to a reader by a "Me" (the word that, capitalized, concludes each of the five stanzas in the poem of Robinson's we were just considering, in an arrangement that gives the poem a particularly needy feel). The pathos that in some examples of the inscription poem attaches to this first person voice is a function of its solitary, forlorn condition—this unknown poet wrote because he or she was alone and craved a social context. But because the reader arrives on the scene too late to provide that longed-for contact, this writing becomes the sign of its own impotence. Indeed, because for this very reason the "I" is so difficult to identify, lyric utterance comes to converge here with prosopopoeia—meaning that these poems seem not only or primarily to be the vehicles in which a human voice is precariously preserved, but also seem poems in which poetry comes to life itself, though only to speak about its own mortal condition, speak on its own behalf about what it is like to be poetry.

Inscription poems both are about states of privation and exemplify such states. These texts' durability—written in stone, written with a diamond—is coupled with, rather than balanced against, their long neglect. "The broken physicality of verse aligns poetry more than any other literary genre with corporeal disintegration" writes Diana Fuss. "In its isolated, fragmented, and unnatural form, poetry resembles a Yeatsian 'rag and bone shop.' "[78] This resemblance, which often comes to the fore when poetry is written into gothic prose fictions, is key to the poetry pity and scorn shadowing the novels' poetry love.

CHAPTER SIX

Poetry at Death's Door

In love, unlike most other passions, the recollection of what you have had and lost is always better than what you can hope for in the future.

STENDHAL, *De l'Amour* (1822)

OBITUARY PAGES

Since the dawn of the literary era, readers have been getting ready to bid literature a final farewell. At the start of the twenty-first century, there is no shortage of anticipatory obituaries for literature, if at the same time there is little consensus about what precisely we will be mourning when it ceases to be. When scrutinized, the list of the departed or departing reveals itself as markedly various. Close reading (which, allegedly, no one practices anymore), the canon (which, allegedly, no one reads anymore), poetry (ditto), departments of English, a sense of history, of heritage, of the aesthetic, brick and mortar bookstores, books in general—all are said to labor under death sentences.

There are pressing reasons for the present sense of beleaguerment. The corporate interests that increasingly shape policy within university administrations regard the study of the humanities as at best a quaint anachronism, too attached to and defined by the past to have a future. In a wired world, the printed book, to which the identity of humanistic study has long been tied, appears to occupy an increasingly marginal position as a medium of creativity or knowledge making. This is not the place to rehearse once more these many challenges. Nor does this chapter (or book) enlist in the "Erotic Rearmament Campaign"—Daniel Cottom's witty term—that some practitioners of English studies have mounted in order to respond to them. These scholars mean to model a new critical idiom that forgoes the skepticism requisite during the last age of ideology critique and which is accountable, instead, to the affective attachments that reading creates. This critical idiom is occasionally presented as though it might help literary studies survive its current legitimation crisis.[1] In this chapter, however, I identify a reason to be cautious about the claim that love might save us. This is the very frequency with which since the romantic period declarations of love for literature have been framed in elegiac terms. Before signing up for a return to the love of literature, we need to reckon with the numerous historical associations that predispose us to feel in our hearts that literature is never more lovable than when at death's door.

This chapter engages those pleasures of melancholy, as it considers some romantic readers' investments (later some Victorian publishers' investments) in the proposition that loving literature goes hand in hand with losing literature. It explores an idiom that both helped bring the abstractions "literature" and "English" into social being and persistently associated the literary with the afterlife and poets in particular with the absent dead. Building on chapter 5's account of gothic fictions' alignments of reading with filial mourning and lyric utterance with perturbed spirits, it examines how nineteenth-century adherents of the love of literature portray themselves as beghosted and center their literary reverence on revenants.

Poets especially look wraithlike in these portrayals. At the turn of the nineteenth century, poetry was in more hands than ever before, thanks to rising literacy rates, increased press runs, and multivolume editions offering the public "the British Poets" at bargain prices. The paradox that launches this final chapter is that at this same time poetry was being associated in new ways with the distance between the living and the choir invisible of the dead. Some classic romantic-period accounts of poetry's subjection to time can be seen accordingly as prefiguring the now frequently heard lament that, with "the literary . . . disappearing from literary study" (since nowadays departments are about sociology, history, religion, and "everything except literature"), poetry and poetry reading especially must be slated for extinction.[2]

After it considers the strange time frame of posthumousness in which the discursive rearrangements of the late eighteenth century installed poetry, this chapter rounds back on materials from chapter 1, to look once more at one of the principal discursive instruments through which literary genius was brought home to the reader: biographical writing.[3] My primary case study here will be Thomas De Quincey's biography of William Wordsworth—though I will also consider how and why De Quincey's *Reminiscences* recapitulates James Boswell's *Life of Johnson.* I conclude by engaging a second medium that was developed for the memorializing of the literary past: anthologies of romantic poetry that were "photographically illustrated," published by a series of Victorian publishers in the 1860s, and which, I shall argue, used photography as a machine for periodizing.

Those books' announced purpose—to harness up-to-date technology so as to locate poetry readers in almost face-to-face proximity to the homes and haunts of the literary past—illuminates how the earlier tradition of literary biography too had defined itself technophilically, with reference to new and improved intimacy effects. These were the terms Boswell, for instance, had mobilized when touting his fidelity in preserving Johnson's conversation for posterity. In commenting on the "clearness of narration and elegance of language" with which Johnson's *Lives of the English Poets* had "embalmed so many eminent persons," Boswell is claiming the same power—one enabling the biographer to put readers in the presence of the very person himself—for his *Life* too.[4]

When John Durham Peters comments on the modern credo that emotional communion will be achieved through our perfection of media technologies, he highlights the pathos, the acute sense of imminent disconnect, that is the invariable counterpart and reflex of such convictions. "Dubious signals from the dead" are the very stuff of communication for modernity, Peters explains, for the modern idealization of "communication as a bridge" that brings the parties together "always means an abyss is somewhere near."[5] The explanation hints at how in the historical media regime in which literature in the modern sense of the term came to be it was overdetermined that literary reception would be described in an idiom that suggested the mourning of the absent dead and the conjuring of their ghosts.

WEEPING TO HAVE

In 1805 in book 5 of *The Prelude* Wordsworth reworked a line that a sonneteering Shakespeare had addressed to a person he loved (or so Wordsworth as a romantic reader of the sonnets was predisposed to believe). Wordsworth made it encapsulate his feelings about books he loved. In sonnet 64, Shakespeare's speaker had reported on how ruin had taught him "that time will come and take my love away" and then in the sonnet's volta had added: "This thought is as a death which cannot choose / But weep to have that which it fears to lose." Likewise schooled by ruin, Wordsworth borrowed Shakespeare's language of grief for the first verse paragraph of *The Prelude*, in order to grieve for, in effect, Shakespeare and Shakespeare's language. The grief is for deaths foretold. We "cannot choose but feel," Wordsworth wrote, in the first echo of the sonnet in the passage, that in the future books will perish: as the earthly garments for our souls, books have no future because the time is coming when "immortal being / No more shall need such garments."[6] The faith in the soul's immortality articulated here, the certainty that the end of all earthly things will be the sure prelude to the soul's resurrection, does not altogether preclude mourning, as Wordsworth makes clear in the second echo of the sonnet—this time, by contrast, an echo that ensconces Shakespeare's words inside quotation marks: "Man / As long as he shall be the Child of Earth, / Might almost 'weep to have' what he may lose" (book 5, lines 23–25).

The quoted phrase captures the mixed feelings making up Wordsworth's book love. The opening of *The Prelude*'s book of books dwells with some anxiety on the gap between book objects' earthy physicality and the intellectual spirit with which these objects are freighted. The ultimate unviability of these compounds of matter and mind—"shrines so frail" (book 5, line 48)—means that their presence feels like absence and that possessing them feels like a dispossession.[7] The quotation that preserves Shakespeare's words (words conveyed to Wordsworth by means of books) is a stay against this sense of imminent loss, a loss that will get only more pronounced in the next section of *Prelude 5*, when Wordsworth will turn to a dream prophesying a coming deluge that will drown the world. The irony, however, is that this quotation from Shakespeare also gives that loss a language. That quotation—Wordsworth's bookishly mediated account of his melancholic attachment to the books which he "weep[s] to have"—also gives me a way to name the particular kind of melancholic, achy affect that centers this chapter.

Wordsworth's investigations of his own feelings have long had a paradigmatic status for literary studies. As several scholars have shown, Wordsworth's premises about the affective intensities of childhood and about the growth of the mind helped, from the nineteenth century on, to shape understandings of the literary curriculum and vocation.[8] The lines of prophecy that end *The Prelude*, in which Wordsworth, addressing Coleridge, declares that "what we have loved / Others will love; and we may teach them how" (book 13, lines 444–45) remain, for instance, eminently quotable in the speechmaking that attends on graduation ceremonies or on those public, hortatory occasions when professors of literature are variously called upon to own up to their love lives or are derided for not having them the way amateurs do.[9] Such occasions often require participants to acknowledge the romanticism, in a double sense, of instruction in English.

The lines about weeping to have from *Prelude 5* represent, by contrast, a more infrequent choice of motto. One problem is that Wordsworth's mournful feelings there appear out of keeping with their occasion. As David

Simpson notes, this avowed "disquietude" about books' endangered state is odd coming from someone who "had had access to the treasured collections of college, public, and some private libraries and who could look to well-preserved and cherished editions of Virgil and Homer as evidence for the powers of great poetry over time and change."[10]

Still, some readers anticipated this sort of disquietude. Indeed, in the *Life of Johnson* (1791), Boswell had already reported on how he got over it. The report is part of Boswell's account of a conversation held on Good Friday, 1778, in which he and Johnson considered death, resurrection, and the afterlife as the sphere in which friends separated by death would be reunited. A mutual acquaintance, Hugh Blair, the Presbyterian minister and Edinburgh University lecturer whose preference for literary love over literary admiration we encountered in chapter 1, felt uneasy at the thought of what he would leave behind at his own death—"his house, his study, and his books." Johnson, on being told of this uneasiness, dismissed it, on the grounds that the individual's consciousness would be retained in the passage to the afterlife and that we might therefore be assured of carrying our books in our heads. Boswell demurred. He recounted how as a young man, he once in a melancholy mood was distressed to think that he would ultimately depart this life into a "state of being in which Shakespeare's poetry [did] not exist": "A lady whom I then much admired . . . relieved me by saying, 'The first thing you will meet in the other world, will be an elegant copy of Shakespeare's works presented to you.' Dr. Johnson smiled benignantly at this and did not appear to disapprove of the notion" (*Life of Johnson*, 963). His literary faith bolstered by the lady's, Boswell was able to imagine a celestial book manufactory furnishing heaven's occupants with elegant editions that would be all spirit and yet would still be books. Though Wordsworth for his part could or would not indulge that vision, Boswell's reported conversation does help us get a fix on the tangle of mixed feelings that opens *Prelude 5*. Boswell's trademark callowness is helpful (one reason this chapter will later return to his author appreciations) in giving so much away about the conflicting impulses, the dynamics of displacement and substitution particularly, that help organize the elegiac feelings that he and Wordsworth each direct toward beloved reading matter. Good Friday, the start of the interval in the Christian calendar during which Christ's death is yet to be canceled out by Christ's resurrection, is likely to have set Boswell musing on the odds of his own salvation. Given the context, expressing fear for the fate of Shakespeare's works operates as a diversionary tactic: proleptically mourning literature's subjection to time, Boswell manages to evade the issue of his own mortality. Those mournful feelings thus have a self-reflexive dimension, in ways that underline for us once again how people's affections for works of literature can be directed as much toward objects internal to the individual psyche as toward objects that exist outside it—for those affections involve both memories of particular episodes of reading and memories of the younger selves those episodes enrolled.

The follow-up to the passage in *Prelude 5* in which Wordsworth grieves for the frailty of books ups the ante compared to what has come before. It makes such displacement of anxiety more evident still. The report on his friend's apocalyptic dream that Wordsworth gives next has the dreamer-friend learning from a mysterious Arab of coming danger, a "deluge now at hand" (book 5, line 99). It seems that the stone and shell that the Arab is carrying—objects that, entranced by dreaming's delusory logic, the friend does not doubt to be books, "Having a perfect faith in all that passed"—must be preserved against the coming flood (line 114). This is the Arab's heroic mission. He is a Noah for bibliographers. And yet his stated plan, which is "to bury those two Books" (line 103)—a plan which may be read as a variation on that course of action that sees people in times of peril bury their money and treasure for later retrieval—is shot through with ambiguity. Burying so as to preserve looks identical to burying so as to entomb, to lay to rest forever. The burial that Wordsworth's dreamer hastens to assist might itself enact a sentence of death.

There are additional ways in which motives seem muddled in this book of *The Prelude*. The oppositions between matter and mind and, by extension, physical book and immaterial text that had been set out in book 5's opening and that had prompted Wordsworth's initial regret for the book's remoteness from the human mind seem to break down as Wordsworth proceeds to recount the dream of the Arab. Mortality seeps, as he proceeds, from the material platform of the book to the textual content that it contains. The "shrines so frail" of line 48 become the "poor earthly casket" of line 164. It becomes increasingly apparent that, like us when we lament that literature nowadays exists on borrowed time, Wordsworth finds it difficult to pinpoint just what kind of impermanence he is mourning.

Is the impermanence his own? A later passage in this book, for instance, identifies as another cause for Wordsworth's sadness "even unto tears" the fact that certain unattributed poems that formerly entranced his boyish self now are "dead in my eyes" (book 5, lines 570, 574). That poetry, it turns out, had a limited shelf life, so that its reading at present no longer feels to Wordsworth like an encounter with persons but instead has the uncanniness of a visit to "a theatre / Fresh emptied of spectators" (lines 574–75). On one level, Wordsworth reports this sensation simply to document the improvement of his literary taste since adolescence—as the continuation of the verse paragraph makes clear. But, intriguingly, in opening that report he also chooses to cast the experience of falling out of love with pieces of literature he had once had by heart as an experience of *their* de-animation and decease. My fourth chapter, describing the love of literature as an everyday, steadying attachment, exhibited a Wordsworth who took a more upbeat view of the reiterability of poetry's pleasures and linked those pleasures to the stabilizing power of habit. Yet in *Prelude* 5's account of the reading life a loving inextricable from losing comes to the fore. The difference is in part a function of the developmental logic governing *The Prelude* and of the terms in which, in keeping with that logic, poetry's standing has been identified with that of childhood. One suggestion that *Prelude* 5 floats as it analyzes the state of Wordsworth's literary affections is that the raptures that have attended on poetry are in fact predestined to fade, as the maturing individual moves further and further away from the intensities of childhood experience. ("Whither is fled the visionary gleam?" asks Wordsworth's "Intimations Ode"—his miniaturized version of *The Prelude*'s self-portrait—as it sets out the framework in which nineteenth-century culture would come to apprehend the relationship between infancy and adulthood.)[11] And if, as in the more optimistic account that *The Prelude* in toto also offers, one's former ardor for poetry persists over time, it is principally as an object of remembrance—retained, just as a kind of inner child is retained, as the archaic contents of a historically layered self. In this account, poetry may be understood as "working to return its readers to earlier, child-like states of emotional absorption," but an awareness of loss still shadows the joy of that reconnection.[12]

I shall return intermittently in what follows to the influence that these developmental accounts crystallized in the romantic period still exert on people's understanding both of literary history (since Wordsworth's operative premise is that the life of human culture parallels and recapitulates the life of the individual) and of their lives as readers—and in this chapter's conclusion will briefly scrutinize the nostalgia that these accounts infuse into that understanding. Let me notice now, by way of winding up this discussion of Wordsworth's loving and losing of poetry, that there remains one more sense in which poetry's parlous condition is at stake in book 5 of *The Prelude*. Four years before drafting it, Wordsworth in the course of prefacing *Lyrical Ballads* had already sounded an apocalyptic note that rings familiarly while it registers another motive for mourning poetry: its endangerment by a debased popular culture's indifference to classic texts. The situation described in the preface might represent still another reason why in *Prelude 5* Wordsworth writes obituaries for poetry: "The invaluable works of our elder writers, I had almost said the works of Shakespear and Milton are driven into neglect by frantic novels, sickly and stupid German Tragedies, and deluges of idle and extravagant stories in verse," he had claimed in 1800.[13] As this mention of a menacing deluge of commercialized print suggests, the stone and shell that are preserved/buried in book 5's dream of a coming flood serve Wordsworth's agenda all the better, and are all the more appropriate as symbols for a threatened intellectual heritage, because they number only two. That they are in short supply (a rarity that ensures their preciousness) distinguishes them from book commodities whose principal characteristic is their over-plenteousness.

It is worth underscoring that in the romantic period, the moment when people were just beginning to accommodate themselves to cohabiting with the canon, the lament that the literary past—literature in general—was about to be lost stood in a complicated relationship to contemporary writing on the book's perturbing ubiquity in commercial modernity. "While books had by the turn of the nineteenth century been a constant of Western cultural life for over 1,500 years, what was new around 1800 was [this] imminent sense of too-muchness," Andrew Piper observes. A fear that individuals' identities were at risk of being dissipated under the weight of the printed word accompanied this sense of bibliographical surplus.[14] And, as we have seen, the terms in which Wordsworth articulates his lament for the imminent loss of literature both register such perturbations and exorcise them. The lines from *The Prelude* I have paused over carry out this double duty by, variously, imagining books' disappearance and so annulling the menace of their ubiquity, entangling literature's fate with books' fate and also disentangling it, and positioning literature's devotee both to save and to kill what he loves.

POETRY AND ANACHRONISM, OR, THE PLEASURES OF HISTORICAL SENSATION

Through this enactment of ambivalence, the lines resonate with the larger cultural patterns traced in earlier sections of this book. As we saw earlier, from the mid-eighteenth century an uneasiness wrought by the widening of the market for cultural products and a recoil from books' resulting ubiquity in popular culture had reshaped the criteria of canonicity. In this sense, the institutions of modern literariness came into being as, paradoxically, a reaction against modernity. Chapter 2's discussion of Thomas Warton's historicism suggested along such lines how during Warton's lifetime the project of canon formation represented to some extent a sentimental reeducation during which British readers learned to cherish, or learned from other, expert readers that they were supposed to cherish, the *antiquity* of English writing. Learning to value "our elder poets" properly meant jettisoning an older account of the progressive shape of literary history, which even in the early eighteenth century had still been construed as the story of how literature rose above its uncouth, Gothic origins and improved with time. Historical distance made the works by Spenser, Shakespeare, Milton, and, later, Chaucer that were the principal beneficiaries of this transvaluation of literary antiquity difficult and inaccessible; but that historical distance itself sponsored these same works' membership within the glamorous category of restricted culture, much as it made them deserving of learned treatment. Remoteness from contemporary manners and existing social standards became the hierarchizing principle of a newly autonomous cultural field. Engagement with those works was thus presented as engagement with what Thomas Warton's brother Joseph had influentially promoted as "the most poetic species of poetry," as well as with (in Samuel Johnson's phrasing in the preface to the *Dictionary*) "wells of English undefiled."[15] The desire for a canonical English that could claim the qualities of Latin and Greek in likewise standing apart from the language of commerce motivated Britain's expert readers—textual critics, antiquarians, anthologists—as they insisted in new ways on texts' status as historically distant period pieces and as they devoted a new energy to retrieving old texts from obscurity.[16]

In tandem, such transformations account for the strange relationship to time that the canonical work inscribes as a canonical work, when read via the emergent protocols of literariness. By 1805 all sorts of readers might have had the works of Milton to hand, thousands of times as many as ever did during our elder poet's lifetime, but these several causes had also conspired to make *Paradise Lost*'s historical anteriority the crucial fact in its reception. Though reprinted on pages that are lying right before you, canonical verse is, by definition, the object of a backward glance. It comes into view at its vanishing point. Like the specter as discussed by Jacques Derrida, such poetry's modes of existence and presence confound our usual sense of what it is for something to be and be there.[17]

When in a 2002 essay Ted Underwood canvasses the new arrangements for the distribution of cultural prestige that defined the literary era and suggests how a new emphasis on the distance of the literary past supported those arrangements, he repeatedly highlights the importance of the literary conjuring of ghosts. Underwood derives the archive for his argument from the poetry of Ossian (the third-century Highland bard for whom the eighteenth-century James Macpherson served in the 1760s as ghostwriter) and Ossianic imitations by figures such as Anna Seward, Felicia Hemans, and Samuel Taylor Coleridge. As he explains, the ancient bard is defined within this corpus of romantic poetry in two ways. The bard converses with ghosts, misty figures from a yet more ancient past who communicate to him their tales of other times: "I hear, at times, the ghosts of bards, and learn their Pleasant Song" Ossian/Macpherson states in *Songs of Selma*. The bard doing that conversing is himself self-consciously ghostly: in the next sentence of *Songs* Ossian/Macpherson describes his own voice as though it issued from the tomb, an eerie survival from another time, which remains, he says, "like a blast that roars, lonely, on a sea-surrounded rock, after the winds are laid." In this second guise, the poet is, Underwood states, a figure "aware of the way time is turning [him] into [a] monument."[18] That first trait secures the resemblance between the ancient bard and the modern reader. The second secures the resemblance between the ancient bard and the modern poet— and registers accordingly the poet's aspiration to auto-canonization.[19]

In Underwood's account, specters furnish poets with means of representing the historical relation—of acknowledging the sense of alterity that the past evokes at a moment increasingly preoccupied by accounts of historical time as a discontinuous series. Romantic poets, he states, "fix their gazes not on monuments of the remote past but on the gulfs of estrangement that separate those monuments from each other and from the present."[20] In this manner they make good on the promise that the reception of literature, the encounter with canonicity, will sponsor in the reader the poignant "pleasure of historical sensation"—which Underwood, like Trevor Ross and Jonathan Kramnick, has advised us to recognize as a "class feeling."[21] Wordsworth's worry, articulated in the preface to *Lyrical Ballads*, that mass culture would soon make our elder poets history is thoroughly entangled with this feeling.

One more factor requires acknowledging: the pathos enriching the pleasure of historical sensation. In a statement that suggests the close relations between the romantic period's new preoccupation with literary history and an emergent "culture of subjectification," Isaac D'Israeli wrote in his *Dissertation upon Anecdotes* of 1793 that because "our hearts have learnt to sympathize," "we" look to the past, not as a "dull antiquary" would, but "as a son and a brother would turn over his domestic memoirs."[22] In describing this lesson in sympathizing, D'Israeli applauded a personalizing of the literary past that effectively recast it as autobiography and made it less something that one learned about, and more something that housed the occulted sources of the individual's identity, something that one remembered. He also conflated affectivity generally with family feeling more narrowly. D'Israeli's description of a new, heartfelt reading habit thus registers how a new Burkean idiom of national heritage was, in the aftermath of the upheavals of the 1790s, beginning to link the nation's virtues and values with its intimate zones, its spaces of affective attachment and identification. In D'Israeli's call for "sympathy," there is also a glimmer of that practice of personification, discussed in my opening chapter, that would bind up the value of texts with the value of vulnerable and mortal persons.

The peculiar pathos of literary reading derives from the tension between that wish for identification and the wish to experience the discontinuities of historical time. The aspiration to relation and (self-)recognition announced in D'Israeli's *Dissertation on Anecdotes* might formerly have been accommodated by classical and humanist forms of history that stressed the past's usefulness and vitality as a collection of exemplars for the present and based themselves on a uniform and nonprogressive temporality. But, as Ina Ferris has noted, that aspiration came to be blocked in the wake of a romantic-period rewriting of historical process as linear progress.[23] Thinking about the literary relation as a relation that could never quite traverse the divide between the living and the dead, meant, almost by default, thinking about it as a relation convening a reader and a ghost. D'Israeli's insistence on the tenderness of that relation underscores how the imperatives of an age of sensibility guided this reconstitution of the literary past.

In the era spanning Thomas Gray's "Elegy," Charlotte Smith's *Elegiac Sonnets*, and the tribute lyrics that Felicia Hemans set at the gravesides of dead poets, poetry was increasingly defined as a vehicle of mourning. From the mid-eighteenth century on, the elegiac had vastly expanded its purview. This happened, for instance, as night thoughts on death and loco-descriptive poems converged, blurred the lines between the countryside and the cemetery, and made the natural world in which the poets took up their positions feel like a larger graveyard "inscribed deeply with evidences of past life"—as in Geoffrey Hartman's account of how Wordsworth characteristically manages lyric address so as to speak as one of the dead and as the spirit of the place.[24] It happened, in addition, as poetic demonstrations of private grief, whose unseemliness had worried early eighteenth-century commentators, acquired a new legitimacy in texts that painstakingly staged their relation to the literature of the past: elegy became during the last two decades of the eighteenth century the designated genre for literary reflexivity, as Esther Schor has proposed. Signaling their allegiance to an idea of poetry as made from other poems, elegists came to foreground allusions to bygone predecessors, made explicit the links between bookishness and grieving, and, by such means, made British literary history appear, in Samantha Matthews's words, "a line of graves and monuments."[25]

At the same time, through a strange act of personification, one that at once animated its object and relocated it at death's door, poetry was in this era increasingly defined as mourning's *object*. In the gothic novels of Ann Radcliffe and her imitators, as we have seen, the verse fragments from Shakespeare, Milton, Collins, Gray, and others that are put on epigraphic display end up feeling like counterparts to the disembodied voices that echo through the halls of ruined abbeys and castles. Decontextualized and floating free of its origins, that quoted poetry can likewise seem as if the site of its provenance lay beyond the grave. In other contexts, the romantic poem proposed its own subjection to history and hence its mortality, by presenting itself as a member of a "distressed genre": the term that Susan Stewart has coined to capture how during the eighteenth century, modern print culture's remediating and repurposing of oral, folkloric forms such as the ballad or fairy tale remade those forms as historical artifacts, "speaking objects" that spoke primarily and poignantly about their own dated condition.[26] In chapter 2, we saw how romance evoked a special tenderness from the early literary historians because it was defined a priori as a casualty of history, always destined to be abandoned in the course of the reading nation's progress. William Hazlitt began his 1818 lectures on the English poets with the gloomy, inauspicious observation that "the necessary advances of civilization . . . are unfavourable to the spirit of poetry." "Poetry cannot travel out of the regions of its birth, the uncultivated lands of semi-civilized men," Thomas Love Peacock declared not long after: Peacock deployed the same stadial model of cultural history as Hazlitt had in the *Lectures* but abstained from the regret that Hazlitt indulged, while ignoring as well evidence of how it was now newly open to nineteenth-century practitioners of poetry to compound their tales of *other* times with tales of the distressed state of poetry in *these* times of advanced civilization. (Thus the gesture toward the impossibility of the poem that we are reading at that very moment which opens Walter Scott's *The Lady of the Lake*: an unnamed speaker, himself impossible to locate in historical time, begins by asking, "O minstrel Harp, still must thine accents sleep?") Such tales of distress have represented one reason why to multiple commentators from the romantic period onward the persistence of poetry has seemed to mark out a problem of anachronism.[27]

That view of poetry as inherently ghostly is also confirmed by the history of lyricization as Virginia Jackson has traced it—a history that over the last two centuries and a half has seen various poetic genres rolled into one ("the lyric"), has seen various modes of poetic circulation effaced "behind an idealized scene of reading . . . identified with an idealized moment of expression," and has seen "the lyric [emerge] as the one genre indisputably literary and independent of social contingency" and as "discourse immediately and intimately addressed to the reader precisely because it is not addressed to any one at all."[28] This sounds like the transcendence and timelessness traditionally ascribed to poetry by its practitioners and devotees, but Jackson's point is, on the contrary, that "the more ideally lyric poems and poetry culture have become, the fewer actual poetic genres address readers in specific ways," and that it is that ratio that "is responsible for our twenty-first-century sense that poetry is all-important and at the same time already in its afterlife."[29] The era spanning Thomas Percy's 1764 *Reliques of Ancient English Poetry* and John Stuart Mill's 1833 "What Is Poetry?" was, Jackson contends, the crucial inception period for the *longue durée* history of lyricization. It launched the particular practices of interpretation, consumption, and pedagogy that have produced a lyricized idea of poetry in the abstract out of a variety of verse forms and practices of cultural circulation—and that have thereby produced "an abstract genre accessible to all persons educated to read lyrically in the place of verse exchanged by people with varying degrees of access to one another who may have read according to their own historical referents."[30]

Though her focus is primarily on a later period, Jackson's account of a long-term shift from poetry as "cultural practice" to poetry as "pathetic abstraction" and "spectral ideal" is suggestive for thinking about why romantic-period readers sometimes seem to be loving literature (another "pathetic abstraction") to death. This suggestiveness is owing in part to her savvy acknowledgment of the emotional rewards that have been smuggled into the argument that, variously, no one reads poetry now, or that hardly any one read it properly then, or that there was never any particular reader who was intended to read it at all (John Stuart Mill had, of course, proposed in 1833 that "the peculiarity of poetry . . . lie[s] in the poet's utter unconsciousness of a listener"). "The payoff for agreeing" with such propositions, Jackson observes, "is that what has been turned into a ghost can be brought back."[31]

GHOSTS AND THE LIFE OF THE AUTHOR

This section, focused on De Quincey's and Boswell's ways of aligning the memorializing of authors (even living ones) and the raising of ghosts, seeks to explore in more detail the emotional rewards and pitfalls that attend on placing poetry—and literature more generally—at death's door. When I have given versions of this chapter as a talk, colleagues have sometimes confessed afterward that as starry-eyed undergraduate English majors in the 1980s they felt befuddled by fellow students' choice to specialize in creative writing, befuddled over how those students contrived to miss the messages, which they themselves heard loud and clear, that literature was a past, not a future, and that authors were dead not alive.[32] Waxing confessional in my turn, I will admit that one reason I find the *Life of Samuel Johnson* and the essays for *Tait's Magazine* (1834–40) making up De Quincey's *Reminiscences of the Lakes and the Lake Poets* compulsive and yet uncomfortable reading has to do with my realization that there have been moments in my history as a reader when I would have wanted what Boswell and De Quincey wanted: to find out where books came from, to go to great lengths to turn my reading into a human transaction.[33] That they present soliciting the friendship of authors as a process dependent on something like good study habits—they are keeners, both—is another ground for this discomfiting sense of a resemblance.

Others have looked to these texts by Boswell and De Quincey for evidence of a late eighteenth-century / early nineteenth-century shift in the relations between biographer, subject, and reader. Biography emerged from this shift as a modern market force defined by its capacity, widely acknowledged and frequently resented, to repackage the literary author for popular consumption. By the time De Quincey took up for *Tait's Magazine* a project that he had designed on a self-consciously Boswellian plan, it was clear, furthermore, that the relations between the biographical subject and the biographer were as competitive as they were collaborative, and that the biographer was winning the competition.[34] The nineteenth-century public's appetite for writers' lives tended to outrun its eagerness to consume writers' works. This was demonstrated by the disparate nineteenth-century fortunes of Boswell's and Johnson's writings, Johnson's own *Lives* included, and, in particular, by the fact, likely appreciated by De Quincey, that Boswell's portrait of Johnson *was* Johnson for nineteenth-century readers. (The medium— the intervening third party who, as biographer, takes charge of another's literary legacy—had overtaken the message. No editions of collected works of Samuel Johnson were published between 1825 and the early twentieth century.)[35] Julian North has written compellingly of how, exacerbating that marketplace rivalry between poetry and lives of poets, De Quincey in addressing the audience of *Tait's* tended to stress how his sympathy with a popular readership set him apart from those poets who were his subjects. *He* was willing for those readers' sake to decode the "Delphic obscurity" that attended on Wordsworth's sublimity even if, as he insinuated, Wordsworth himself was not.[36]

In what follows, however, I am less interested in analyzing biography's and poetry's respective positions in the literary field than in thinking about what Boswell and De Quincey can tell us about literary reading and appreciation during the romantic period. Their biographical writings also bear witness to how the emergent institutions of canonicity invited readers to attempt to suture two rather different things—subjection to literature and friendship with the literary genius. My question involves why during this attempt it was useful to these two lovers of literature to represent their love as a beghosted condition.[37]

In letters he sent in 1803 to Wordsworth, whom he had read but not yet met, the teenaged De Quincey attempted to establish his credentials as an acolyte and a Boswell (*his* Johnson, however, rejected him, so that De Quincey ultimately inverted his predecessor's story: "I witnessed a case where a kind of idol, had, after all, rejected an idolater that did not offer a splendid triumph to his pride").[38] The letter from August 6, 1803, identifies as a qualification for this role De Quincey's devotion to *Lyrical Ballads*: "I feel that, from the wreck of all earthly things which belong to me, I should endeavour to save that work by an impulse second to none but that of self-preservation." This letter's apocalypticism likely informed, Margaret Russett suggests, the book-burial dream in *Prelude* 5, which Wordsworth would draft in early 1804.[39] De Quincey meant here to assert his lover-like readiness to make sacrifices for the beloved, but this disclosure of his strong feelings reads as self-aggrandizing as well. The disclosure insinuates the prospect that authors might be in readers' debt. And De Quincey conveniently overlooks the fact that print culture affords few opportunities for acts of individual heroism that will actually make a difference for literature's fate. Whether a single copy of *Lyrical Ballads* is plucked from flame or flood makes only a little difference to the canonical survival of *Lyrical Ballads*. In bracketing the irrefragably collective and impersonal nature of the institution of literature, De Quincey contrives to forget that readers in a print age always read in company. The letter suggests some of the obstacles encountered when one construes readerly relations to texts within the terms that belong to the intersubjective domain of relations between persons. It simultaneously suggests the conjunction of possessing and losing enacted in De Quincey's love of literature, a conjunction that the *Reminiscences* would three decades later thematize more self-consciously. This conjunction is enacted, as well, in the *Life of Samuel Johnson*: the work with which Boswell Johnsonised all the land.

The pains that Boswell sometimes took to insinuate Johnson's distance even when Johnson was present—ascribing, as we shall see, a kind of non-contemporaneity to his contemporary—complicate a claim that Mark Salber Phillips has made about how new norms of proximity were adopted across a wide swath of historiographic genres at the turn of the nineteenth century. For Phillips, literary biography and literary history came to qualify in the romantic period as exemplary historiographic genres precisely because they modeled for more traditional forms of history writing an intensified, distinctively inward and affective engagement with the past. They brought it close. Phillips locates biography in the forefront of the effort that Thomas Babington Macaulay called for in the famous *Edinburgh Review* essay of 1828 in which he advocated for a new kind of history writing—the effort to "make the past present, to bring the distant near, . . . to invest with the reality of human flesh and blood beings whom we are too much inclined to consider as personified qualities in an allegory."[40] In Boswell's own promotion of the immediacy effects his mode of life writing offers we can glimpse an anticipation, "photo-prophetic" even, of the excitement that early in the nineteenth century would be generated by the promise of total recall held out by new representational techniques—more precisely, by techniques that promised that the way to authenticity was to abandon mimesis altogether by abandoning a mediating level of signs.[41] The *Life of Johnson* proposes "life"—its provision of "the live" and "real time"—as its selling point, thereby pointing ahead to the preoccupations with lifelike reproductions, indexical traces, and conflations of representation and referent that by the 1820s and 1830s would variously inform historical dioramas, William Henry Fox Talbot's sun pictures, and Charles Waterton's new science of taxidermy: "I cannot conceive of a more perfect mode of writing any man's life, than not only relating all the most important events of it in order, but interweaving what he privately wrote, and said, and thought; by which mankind are enabled as it were to see him live, and to 'live o'er each scene' with him, as he actually advanced through the several stages of his life. Had his other friends been as diligent and ardent as I was, he might have been almost entirely preserved" (*Life*, 22).

But such claims are in a dialectical relation with Boswell's tendency to preserve, as well, past moments that were even at the time defined by a sense of an absence: the moments in his interactions with Johnson when he saw the living author as if through the wrong end of a telescope or as a figure with one foot in the grave. Because Boswell takes this view, the death of the author is in the *Life* far from being a punctual, singular, or terminal event. Instead for Boswell the author is first and foremost a person leading a posthumous existence.[42] Even more insistently than De Quincey's *Reminiscences*, Boswell's *Life* suggests how such a representation of the author could prove essential to the personalization that transmuted readerly admiration into love, even as it installed the barrier of death between living readers and dead authors.

Notoriously, the *Life*'s primary project, the monumentalizing of Johnson, had as its side effect the creation and maintenance of another literary figure, a certain James Boswell.[43] Prior to the deferred point when those two stories unfolding in the *Life of Johnson* (the life of Johnson and that other drama that has Boswell as its hero) intersect, prior to the point, that is, at which biographer meets his biographee, Boswell had been reading the *Rambler* essays for some time. For this reason, Johnson was for him from the start a figure possessed of a larger-than-life monumentality—as much Dr. English as Dr. Johnson, I want to say, returning to my earlier speculation about the undergraduate major that would have been pursued by a late twentieth-century Boswell. Through Boswell's reading Johnson became possessed of the qualities that Boswell captures when, in a passage that characteristically attends not simply to Johnson but also to Boswell's own powers of imagination, the biographer outlines how his reverence for the Rambler "had grown up in my fancy into a kind of mysterious veneration" because he had been figuring to himself the "state of solemn elevated abstraction, in which I supposed [Johnson] to live" (*Life*, 272). Of course, literature—as well as the canon (as John Guillory has taught us)—is defined by its abstraction, its perpetual evasion of materialization in any finite list of texts, its skewed relationship to presence as well as the present. This last phrase about Johnson's "life" in "a state of solemn elevated abstraction" evokes that skewed relationship. It suggests Boswell's adherence to a curious "two-bodies theory" of literariness, as though what were true for monarchy were also true for literature, as though the latter too were something divided between a natural, mortal body and the enduring essence of a *corpus mysticum*.[44] Boswell would soon meet Johnson in the flesh. Nevertheless, as though he were aiming not to reconcile but to maintain the division of the spiritual from the physical,

of the overarching category of the literary from that category's actual repre-
sentatives, abstraction and absence remain central to his writing.

This is so, even as Boswell represents himself as engaging in the activities
of literary tourism and souvenir hunting that were meant to make the so-
called standard authors he had known only on the page proximate, present,
and real. "London authors . . . are to me something curious, and, as it were
mystical," Boswell characteristically observed in his journal on February 3,
1763, ten weeks into his London sojourn, and after spending an evening at
the theatre during which Oliver Goldsmith occupied the seat directly behind
him.[45] Michael Holroyd has stated that "it is clear that people only became
real to Boswell when he could see and hear them, when he could enter
their world."[46] Boswell's gestures toward an unreal "state of abstraction"
are a counter-indication. For Boswell, it would be more accurate to say, real
authors simultaneously resided both in the real London and in some other
invisible, numinous domain. This other domain might be the space of literary antiquity and tradition into which two years later he would install the
still-living Voltaire, in a letter to that author that was meant to flatter but
that probably botched the job, "When I first heard of you, I heard of a man
whose works had been long existing and being no chronologist, I imagined you really one of the Ancients."[47] For Boswell, it is a conundrum how
Voltaire can both be his contemporary and still be Voltaire the famous author. Conundrums of just this ilk are, however, at the heart of this devotee's
faith in literary fame as a version of an afterlife.[48]

In reporting on his cultivation of the openings for intimacy that have
allowed him to get personal with the authors, Boswell simultaneously underlines his bookish, mediated relationship to just these experiences. De
Quincey's relationship to the period's historiography of presence is similarly
paradoxical. De Quincey was an enthusiast of the anecdote. He endorsed
how that form both promised the nineteenth-century public that information could feel like intimate knowledge and traded on the possibility that
intimate knowledge might be convertible into information. He believed, accordingly, that "the interest which attends *the great poets*"—by contrast with
"a great philosopher, a great mathematician, or a great reformer"—was the
more to be treasured when mingled up with "household remembrances."
(Names such as Archimedes and Galileo are associated only with a "frosty . . .
feeling," De Quincey states at the start of the first essay on Wordsworth. By
contrast, Shakespeare and Wordsworth are "*household* image[s] . . . hallowed
by a *human* love.")[49] But De Quincey's practice did not match up with his
theory. He postponed intimate knowledge. More than four years elapsed
between the moment in 1803 when, in response to his acolyte's fan mail,

Wordsworth invited him to Dove Cottage and the moment De Quincey accepted the invitation and arrived there to meet him. When he gets round to telling the readers of *Tait's Magazine* how the poet looked face-to-face, that sight that he himself had, he states, long and fervently wished for, he characteristically tells readers, as well, how a page of a *book* looks—and not a book about Wordsworth, but one about Milton. De Quincey had first been anxious to obtain this particular volume, Jonathan Richardson's compilation of notes on *Paradise Lost*, on account of the likeness of the seventeenth-century poet it contained: "Judge of my astonishment when, in this portrait of Milton, I saw a likeness nearly perfect of Wordsworth, better by much than any which I have seen, of those expressly painted for himself." The essays' selling point, on which De Quincey insists often, is the fact that their author is Wordsworth's contemporary. De Quincey has inhabited the same time frame and even the same house as Wordsworth: he has been in the habit of seeing "the real living forehead" of Wordsworth "for more than five-and-twenty years."[50] But through that reference to how the living nineteenth-century poet channels his defunct seventeenth-century predecessor, a reference that makes Wordsworth *Milton's* contemporary, De Quincey insists on the impossibility of Wordsworth ever having been simply present in his presence.

De Quincey like Boswell lived in his real life and not just in the paper world of books the dream of contact that motivates every literary tourist. Julian North describes his enterprise in the *Reminiscences* thus: "Both Wordsworth and Coleridge were introduced as disembodied presences, tracked down, embodied, and observed in detail amongst their immediate family and friends. The genius was thus placed within a private context, relocated within the human, fleshly realm and judged according to his intimate social relations."[51] But De Quincey also subscribed, I am suggesting, to that two-bodies account of literature which both sees tradition incarnated in living flesh-and-blood and sees it as transcendental communications from the Beyond. That paradox inflects the manner in which he records the moment in 1807 when, as he recounts it, he believed himself and his companions to have at last "reached our port" and realized that he was "less than a minute" away from meeting Wordsworth "face to face." Just at this moment De Quincey launches into a digression: it has the effect, like his account of the Milton portrait, of denying Wordsworth's contemporaneity:

> Coleridge was of opinion that, if a man were really and *consciously* to see an apparition . . . , in such circumstances, death would be the inevitable result; and, if so, the wish which we hear so commonly expressed for such experience is as

thoughtless as that of Semele in the Grecian Mythology, so natural in a female, that her lover should visit her *en grand costume* ... presumptuous ambition, that unexpectedly wrought its own ruinous chastisement! Judged by Coleridge's test, my situation could not have been so terrific as *his* who anticipates a ghost—for, certainly, I survived this meeting.[52]

The contagiousness ascribed to death in this anecdote, the fact that such contagion, in an uncanny reciprocity, blurs the boundaries between the acolyte and the object of the acolyte's worship, the fact that Wordsworth's fate is not made explicit but that we are told in a rather deadpan manner that De Quincey survived—all are noteworthy. Paul Westover suggests that for nineteenth-century sightseers visiting "living authors . . . was . . . an analog to visiting canonized dead authors at their gravesites";[53] the anecdote confirms this.

But De Quincey's digression also feels all the more bookish, careening wildly away from the promised immediacy, once we cotton on to the possibility that the effects of ghost-seeing might here have come to be at issue precisely because De Quincey has sought at this point to rewrite the most famous scene in the biographical tradition: Boswell's description in the *Life* of how, in 1763, Samuel Johnson at last met his true biographer. Even though Boswell in this scene was able at last to exercise the powers as eyewitness that lend him his authority, in this meeting with Johnson in the flesh Johnson was perceived, first, as a literary figure. The literary allusion preserved in the passage describing that meeting makes the latter point for me: "Johnson unexpectedly came into the shop; and Mr. Davies having perceived him through the glass-door in the room in which we were sitting, advancing towards us,—he announced his aweful approach to me, somewhat in the manner of an actor in the part of Horatio, when he addresses Hamlet on the appearance of his father's ghost, 'Look, my Lord, it comes.'" (277) Johnson enters the *Life* already ghostly, which is also to say he enters the *Life* already literary. In preparing the ground for that entrance into the bookshop and his book, Boswell goes beyond the solicitude about the specifics of place and time that will certify the literary biography's status as a work of nonfiction. Pointing to the work of his imagination, he is concerned with something more than the facts that will put his readers into proximity with Johnson as he actually was.

In Boswell's biography the alignment of Johnson and the apparition of dead king Hamlet partakes of a larger pattern: in associating his biographical subject with an opportunity to learn of capital-*L* literature from the horse's mouth, so to speak, Boswell simultaneously associates literature with news from the beyond, from the afterlife. Of course, when in the *Life* he restages the scene in Davies's shop Boswell is in part telling the joke at the expense of his younger, wide-eyed, quixotic self. (And the bathos of De Quincey's "certainly, I survived"—as though we had been wondering about that—adds a jokey dimension to his restaging of the acolyte-author encounter too.) There is nonetheless a serious side to Boswell's need to see the author as a figure at death's door, and it has to do with his desire for reassuring news about the hereafter. With literature representing, in effect, an anteroom of that undiscovered country from whose bourne no traveler returns, the author is for Boswell an object of theological curiosity. The corny moments in which we glimpse Boswell maneuvering Johnson into the conversations that Boswell thinks will best represent the author to posterity often seem occasioned by Boswell's subscription to just such premises. June 1763, for instance, as the *Life* records, sees Johnson and Boswell conversing of "belief in ghosts" (287). In an earlier passage in the *Life* in which Boswell first restrains himself from quoting *Rasselas* and then goes on to indulge in just one more quotation, the passage he selects is the debate between the Prince and Imlac as to whether it is reasonable to maintain "that the dead are seen no more" (242). As if already measuring his living companion for his canonical coffin, Boswell recounts a visit that Goldsmith and Johnson paid to Westminster Abbey and records the latter's speculations as to whether his remains will mingle with those interred in Poets' Corner (528).[54] In that conversation from 1778, already mentioned, in which Johnson's benignant smile confirms Boswell in his faith that there will be copies of Shakespeare in heaven, Boswell likewise credits Johnson with inside knowledge of the matter.

However informed by private psychological quirks, Boswell's yearning for Johnson's assurance that there will be life after death and books after death, a yearning that he balances with a vision of his friend as embodiment of a literary past that will be mourned in the future, confirms some of the observations I have been making about the collective framework in which the category of the literary was comprehended by 1791. This point may be clearer if we go back to that quotation from *Hamlet*, overdetermined on several counts. As others have noted, through this quoting Boswell installs himself inside a gratifyingly Oedipalized literary space. On the lam from his father's house in Scotland, a guilty Boswell is eager to dramatize himself as a young Prince Hamlet. But implicitly the quoting also taps lore about Jacobean casting practices that identified the role of Hamlet's ghost with the Bard, that exemplary national poet, himself. Entering as Hamlet's ghost, Johnson enters in the role Shakespeare was said to have played when he appeared on stage, providing a doubling of images of spectral authorship that Boswell obviously relishes.

Through the eighteenth century and romantic period Shakespeare was depicted time and again as both English literature's chief expert on the afterlife and as the afterlife's denizen. For De Quincey, for instance, "the supernatural world, the world of apparitions" was the "one great field of [Shakespeare's] power." "Genius has ever had a predilection for such imagery," wrote Nathan Drake in 1798, in his essay defending poets' deployment of invisible spirits: "No poet, adopting a machinery of a similar kind, has wielded it with equal effect. Among the Italians it is too frequently addressed solely to the imagination . . . ; conducted, as by Shakspeare, it powerfully moves the strongest passions of the heart." A spectacular example of this spectralization, unabashed about abstracting Shakespeare's authorship from any specific writings and so associating him instead with a generalized literariness, occurs in a certain William Pearce's 1778 *The Haunts of Shakespeare*. Pearce's volume includes a sonnet in which the "sweet shade" laments *in propria persona* Garrick's retirement from the stage. Its title poem transplants Shakespeare from the metropolitan stage to a landscape of gothic melancholy and recounts, in the third rather than first person, how Shakespeare wanders through ruined castles, where he raises ghosts: "On a night such as this, when the village was still / Wou'd he rove the deep forest, or silver tip'd hill / . . . / When darkness a mantle more shadowy spread, / With spirits he'd roam, and converse with the dead."[55] Harp in hand, this Shakespeare is a version of James Beattie's Minstrel (protagonist of the poem tracing "the progress of genius" that Beattie had published in 1771) or of Macpherson's Ossian—a lonely figure who appears to be the last of his kind.

This spectral Shakespeare's solitude, the counterpart to the condition of the solitary reader of Shakespeare's printed works, distinguishes him from the literary worthies of an earlier tradition. In the earlier eighteenth century, "Dialogues of the Dead" had, for instance, pictured the dead as engrossed by their clubby fellowship on Parnassus and mulling over the latest news of mundane affairs. To a certain extent, late eighteenth-century literary culture had set to rehousing those immortals. As the conceptual setting for the literary tradition, Parnassus was partially replaced at this time. In its place we find something resembling a family crypt or resembling that depopulated solitude in which we might find a ghost-raising Shakespeare, or an

Ossian, or, more generally, that paradigmatic lyric speaker, who, as J. S. Mill insisted, is utterly unconscious of a listener. That replacement, never entirely completed, suggests how the idiom of eternization through which the transhistorical dimension of literary texts was understood might have been transfigured in Boswell's day so as to open up new possibilities for pathos.

There are reasons to think that from its inception the enterprise of literary canonization began in England as an adjunct to a primarily mortuary discourse. Filling their texts with details about authorial interment and memorialization, the seventeenth century's inaugural literary biographers and anthologists—figures like William Winstanley and Gerard Langbaine—cast themselves as taking up where antiquarians had left off. Recording epitaphs and inscriptions carved on tombs and monuments, antiquaries race against time as the stones crumble around them, and so, transcribing those memorial writings in their turn, did the first historians of English poetry.[56] Such Restoration and early eighteenth-century historians took care to cast their books as equivalent to pyramids and sepulchers, the material means of preserving for perpetuity the memories of the dead. They thus underwrote an early modern understanding of fame as the deathless second life that the poet gains through bodily death (fig 6.1). But this second life, immortality in memory, does not coincide exactly with the situation of a lonely ghost like Shakespeare/King Hamlet, or the Ossianic ghost, or the ghost that Boswell says he saw when he first looked at the living Johnson. The difference suggests an important shift in the affective charge of romantic historiography, as well as the impact on the emergent discipline of new concepts of historical change and of the historical period.

For one thing, the revenant's call on the feelings of those it haunts derives in part from its belatedness—that it returns from a world that is no longer present.[57] "Ghostly apparitions . . . are quite distinct from the persistence of the dead through fame; hauntings are not about the dream of occupying a place in the memories of future generations," Stephen Greenblatt writes in his book on Hamlet's ghost. On the contrary, Greenblatt notes, the ghost is a figure of *intimate need*, a spectral voice that "is not for strangers."[58]

The intimate need is that of the living mourner who has endured a loss. It is also, crucially, the ghost's intimate need. As Greenblatt stresses in his reconstruction of the affective uses of the doctrine of purgatory, the doctrine licensed the thought that the living could have an ongoing relationship with an important segment of the dead, "and not simply a relationship constituted by memory." For those dead souls in purgatory, who continued to exist in time, "there were things that the living could do"—such as pray

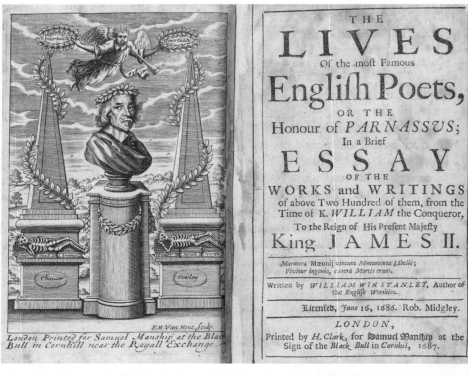

FIGURE 6.1 Frontispiece and title page from William Winstanley's *The Lives of the Most Famous English Poets* (1687). Combining a goddess of fame, pyramids, and skeletons crowned with laurel wreaths, the frontispiece typifies how timeless fame could be imaged at the start of the eighteenth century. Winstanley translates the Latin motto on his title page as follows: "The Muses Works Stone-Monuments outlast. / 'Tis Wit keeps Life, all else Death will down cast." Photograph: Courtesy of Western Archives, Western University.

and give alms.[59] Souls in bliss by contrast did not require anything from the living. Greenblatt implies—in part simply by making Shakespeare the end of his story—that with the Reformation rejection of the doctrine of purgatory and the end of the church's jurisdiction over people's negotiations with the dead, this proximity and emotional reciprocity between the living and the dead were lost. There may be different terms, though, that we can use to tell the story of what changed when in the eighteenth century stories of ghosts lost their ecclesiastical and theological functions. (They perhaps never did so entirely: many Victorians were eager to revive the theological concept of an intermediate state).[60] Maybe what later people learned that they could do for the dead is to believe in them, by believing in the idea of ghosts, even when ghosts did not appear.

This brings me back to Boswell, a figure very interested in probing his own powers of belief. We might think of how, in his *The Journal of a Tour to the Hebrides*, Boswell represented himself as seeking out the storied sites that would give him reason to preen himself on his visionary powers and susceptibility to "atmosphere." (The specter-seeking Shakespeare of Pearce's *The Haunts* has, in this respect, Boswellian traits.) In his diary Boswell defined himself as the proud possessor of a "vivacious fancy," and deployed the "vivacious" in that self-description in an almost literal sense:[61] as this chapter's earlier scrutiny of the language of the *Life* established, for instance, recounting Johnson's entrance entailed for Boswell recounting, first and foremost, how what was absent could take on *life*—could even *grow up*—in Boswell's imagination.

To assess the epistemological dispositions that Boswell's imaginative practice required, we can turn to Terry Castle's work on the fate of superstition and specter-seeing in the age of enlightenment. Blurring the boundary that narratives of enlightenment set up to divide a traditional credulity from a modern skepticism, Castle describes how the spirit world is, through a strange recoil, displaced at the end of the eighteenth century into the intimate space of the mind itself—relocated from "the external, objective, and theologically structured world to the internal and psychologically haunted world of personal experience."[62] A newly romanticized epistemology equates imaginative activity with ghost-seeing and casts reading, particularly, as a phantasmagoric process in which the reader sees figures and scenes in her mind, subjecting herself as she falls into the world of her book to a spectral parade of mental images. This epistemology accords little importance to the opposition between credulity and skepticism; instead, it advocates for the mental state of suspended disbelief and promotes this disposition over the certainty—and the lack of sensibility—that would prematurely terminate or forestall the pleasures of construing such fictions as if they were not fictional.

Specter-seeing in this manner became an occasion directing attention to the things that beholders could do with their feelings—and do in defiance of a disbelieving world. In December 1762 Boswell pondered comparable issues in a diary entry in which, first, he thinks about how his passions prompt him to pursue what his judgment knows to be of little value, then thinks about the case of a man (perhaps himself) who fears ghosts in the dark, although "he is sure there are none," and then thinks about the imaginative pleasures of stage illusion. "It is very difficult," Boswell writes, "to be keen about a thing which in reality you do not regard, and consider as imaginary. But I fancy it may do."[63] Perhaps preening himself on his ability to surmount that difficulty, Boswell moves with a telling readiness in this passage between considering the possibility that the dead are not yet gone and considering drama's ability—with an imaginative audience's assistance—to enforce the sense that its fictions are present.

Why would Boswell's *Life*, even as it parades its objectivity, its capacity to preserve Johnson as human flesh and blood, invoke ghosts at a moment when to do so is to invoke—as a mental object—that which blurs the distinction between subject and object? Why does personifying Johnson as literature itself ("Dr. English") go hand in hand with seeing him, in the proleptically elegiac terms that have been at stake throughout this chapter, as already one of the spirits of the departed? In addressing these questions we have come to a better understanding of the other problematic that this chapter, with those preceding it, has engaged: how in the age of sensibility literature became a personal matter. When they had redefined their transactions with texts along those new lines of inclusion and relation, readers learned to claim new powers. Thinking about ghost-seeing—and doing so during an era when ghosts are not seen but may be believed in—is a means of theorizing the love of literature as in essence a love whose object is internal to the psyche of the lover.[64] In underscoring the self-referentiality of his project, Boswell's allusions to ghosts also serve to remind his readers that the subject of a biography is indebted to the biographer for the latter's efforts to imagine him into reality. The secular premise that the dead have no presence among the living other than that which the living imagine for them can work to make the living awfully important. The memorial context in which poetry was situated in the nineteenth century, Samantha Matthews states, invited "the reader to respond to the book as he or she would read and contemplate the poet's grave." For readers one charismatic aspect of this "posthumous imaginative contact" was how it gave "animating power and ultimate authority" to *them*.[65]

The strategizing and magical thinking we undertake to understand authors as ghosts in whom we have opted to believe advances the project of personalizing our relationship to literature because it establishes the conditions for a "correspondent kindness"—that definition of love we encountered earlier in Johnson's *Rambler* 64. In this situation the obligation lies on both sides, and readers too have benefits to confer. That elegiac dynamic assumes and produces distance, but it also effects a kind of social leveling, offsetting the separations of producers and consumers that have become a structural feature of print culture. The compound of aggression and piety involved in casting the author as ghost and then going on to believe in him, of divesting him of presence and then reparatively restoring it, remakes literary transactions as human relations—as aspects of a common emotional culture.

HOMES AND HAUNTS AND SPIRIT PHOTOGRAPHY

In the Victorian period volumes devoted to writers'"homes and haunts" swelled the ranks of the literary biographies that in the eighteenth century had launched the project of humanizing readers' literary transactions. Titles like *Pilgrimages to English Shrines* (1850), *Poets' Country* (1907), and *Where Ghosts Walk: The Haunts of Familiar Characters in History and Literature* (1898) used the materials of writers' lives and "views" of locales associated with writers' works to model a more robust form of literary appreciation than that afforded by the consumption of ordinary biographies. They promised that the passivity of admiration might be supplemented with a more active exchange, which would represent "a more intimate and exclusive relationship" than "mere reading" could deliver.[66] In insisting that one could not know Scott's poetry, for instance, without an acquaintance with "his" heaths and mountains, these books modeled how readers might go the extra mile to prove their devotion.

They also modeled how readers might continue those pilgrimages that retraced an author's steps all the way to the edge of his grave. The collective effect of these texts' representations of authors in situ was also to remake Great Britain as a literary landscape: author by author, haunt by haunt, they superimposed upon the nation's mundane topography a patchwork of scenes sanctified by their bookish associations, thus continuing the monumentalizing scheme of William Godwin's *Essay on Sepulchres* while reviving the "necromantic" bent of Godwin's style of author veneration. As they set readers traveling, these topographical texts imagined the shades of the poets as in motion themselves, as periodically passing into the domain of the living to revisit the scenes they loved and "to refresh themselves with their old delights." During a walk through forest scenery "nothing seems so natural," declared William Howitt, the first writer to use "homes and haunts" in a title, than to "imagine" the "presence" of Shakespeare, Milton, and Spenser, "joined with the kindred spirits of a later day—Scott, Byron, Shelley, Coleridge, Hogg, and the like,—their religion, their passions, their doubts, their philosophical mysticism all now blended down into a heavenly nobility and union of heart and desire."[67] With that last clause about kindred spirits—testimony to how genius constitutes a breed apart—Howitt also betrays something both of the behind-the-scenes work of idealization that is necessary to bring the abstraction "literature" into being and of the central role that ideas of death and the afterlife play in that work.

This chapter—and book—concludes by considering a set of Victorian books that built on the "homes and haunts" tradition at the same time that they used new media to underscore poetry's subjection to history and time. Beginning in the 1860s, sometimes in violation of copyright, a series of book-sellers contrived to reissue the works of certain romantic poets—Wordsworth and Scott in the examples that will focus this brief discussion—in books that were, in the phrase that became standard, "illustrated by photography": sumptuously bound and gilded volumes whose ostentatious materiality registered the Victorians' readiness to convert memories into mementoes—tangible, possessible, and commodifiable. In many ways, the enterprise of remembering romantic poets on these terms, and of making them *matter* in more than one sense, seems wrongheaded. The confirmational capacity ascribed to photography by its early advocates—photography's way, as indexical sign, of seeming to verify the genuine, concrete existence of the topographical sites that literature commended to notice, be they Wordsworth's Tintern Abbey or Scott's Loch Katrine—seems misapplied, especially when aligned with Wordsworth's verse, celebrated most often today for hymning unseen powers. (Indeed, in an 1846 sonnet the elderly Wordsworth deplored the contemporary enthusiasm for "Illustrated Books and Newspapers.)[68] But rather than outlining how this Victorian remediation of the romantic poetic imagination was mistaken, let's ponder what it accomplished and consider how this Victorian deployment of photography's materializing power conditioned the Victorians' construction of the romantic period as a period. The periodizing gesture these books enact is charged with pathos, in ways that serve to confirm the elegiac dimension of the love of literature. The books cannot help but remind their readers that the romantics were born, wrote, and died in the pre-photographic era that Louis Daguerre's and William Henry Fox Talbot's marvelous inventions brought to an end.

The books' claim is to have brought poetic discourse up-to-date. "We submit the present work to the public as a step in the right direction and as evidence on the part of the publisher of a desire to assist in authenticating literature by the splendid achievements of modern art": thus the fulsome prefatory language of one of A. W. Bennett's photographically illustrated tomes.[69] Photography, that medium promising the transcendence of mediation (readers have before them, that preface asserts, "the genuine presentment of the object under consideration"), promises as well an elimination of temporal distance.[70] An account of the history of media that currently shapes much discussion of the book's fate in the digital age is already discernible here and underwrites the claim that the poetry book illustrated by photography can redeem poetry from obsolescence. In this account one medium naturally supersedes another; each new medium is deemed distinctive for mediating less, bringing its user closer to actuality, than its predecessor did.[71] Photography will, its Victorian devotees insist, transport the literature of the last generation into the future. But at the same time, photography's effect in the volumes at the center of this section is equally to consign poets to the realm of ghosts.

Scott and Wordsworth had of course themselves already pondered the posthumousness of poetic utterance. Each had grappled in his own right with how the new concepts of literary antiquity and the historical period complicated that enterprise of speaking with the dead and as the dead that of old had defined the project of poetry. Showing himself to be a good student of their writings, a literary pilgrim on a Lake District tour marveled in 1838 over the fact that he had actually clapped eyes on Wordsworth while alive (the poet, it is worth underlining, would not die until 1850): "How odd it seemed to knock at a neighbour's door and inquire, 'Where does *Mr.* Wordsworth live?' Think of rapping at Westminster Abbey, and asking for Mr. Shakespeare, or Mr Milton!"[72]

In the Victorian poem that comments best on this double vision, Robert Browning's "Memorabilia" (1855), the speaker begins with the exclamation "Ah, did you once see Shelley plain?" and then trails off in ways that bathetically and wryly acknowledge the futility of the very desire that memorabilia should satisfy: "Well, I forget the rest." The poem speaks to Victorian belatedness:

> Ah, did you once see Shelley plain,
> And did he stop and speak to you?
> And did you speak to him again?
> How strange it seems, and new!
>
> But you were living before that,
> And you are living after,
> And the memory I started at—
> My starting moves your laughter!

> I crossed a moor, with a name of its own
> And a certain use in the world no doubt,
> Yet a hand's-breadth of it shines alone
> Mid the blank miles round about:
>
> For there I picked up on the heather
> And there I put inside my breast
> A moulted feather, an eagle-feather—
> Well, I forget the rest.

The story that unfolds, stutteringly, in the third and fourth stanzas casts Browning's "I" as a victim of bad timing, as well as a bad memory. He comes onto the scene tardily, having (as the final two stanzas suggest) missed out on glimpsing the eagle in flight, able to recover only a trace of the sublime. The poem might also speak, obliquely, to the romantics' own bad timing, their tragically abridged lives, and their poignant status as the last generation to live and die before the invention of photography. In this manner the poem might speak, as well, to the disparity between the plethora of opportunities Browning's Victorian readers feel that they have had to see contemporary authors *plain* and the dearth of opportunities they have had to thus see Shelley. This interpretation of "Memorabilia" received support in 1886 when the poem was reissued in *Selections from the Poetical Works of Robert Browning, with photographic illustrations by Payne Jennings*. One of the photographs touted in that title is matched to the third stanza of "Memorabilia" and pictures a distant vista of a moor—betokening Jennings's rather literal-minded approach to his task. However, when we contemplate the image more closely, we realize that the landscape scene is also a scene of reading. It includes a female figure with a book, though the camera has been so positioned that we can neither decipher her features nor her book's title (fig. 6.2). Is the book one of Shelley's authoring? The same image that satisfies readers' desire to substantiate reading and *see* also points up the limits to our vision. Through its juxtaposition of a book you can't see and a face that, looking at that book, doesn't see you, the art historical genre of the painted reader, Garrett Stewart has remarked, triggers old separation anxieties as it replays "the return of the repressed moment when your mother's voice first went silent to you."[73] Payne Jennings's photograph might affect its beholder similarly.

This balancing of gain and loss, of contact and separation, defines the photographically illustrated poetry book. The Victorian photographer is on

"*I crossed a moor.*"   *Memorabilia.*

FIGURE 6.2 "Memorabilia." Photograph by Payne Jennings in the photographically illustrated compilation *Selections from the Poetical Works of Robert Browning* (1872; rept. London:
Suttaby, 1886). Photograph: © The British Library Board (C.60.e.2, opp. p. 194).

the one hand represented as realizing the romantic poet's visionary and
mnemonic aspirations. Illustrations secure for the poet the admiration that
is his due, ensuring that the reader, as one preface asserts, will appreciate "fully Wordsworth's wonderfully true descriptions of the beauties of
Nature."[74] *Our English Lakes, Mountains and Waterfalls, As Seen by William
Wordsworth,* whose preface makes this pledge to Wordsworth's readers, also
requisitions for an epigraph lines from the ninth book of Wordsworth's *The
Excursion.* In this new context the lines intimate that photography itself
might fulfill the longing that the poem's speaker expresses for a means of
recording and extending the perfect moment. "Ah! that such beauty, varying
in the light / Of living nature, cannot be portrayed, / By word, nor by the
pencil's silent skill; / But is the property of him alone / Who hath . . . in his
mind recorded it with love."[75] The camera's work is cast, in the arrangement
outlined here, as ancillary to an ongoing history of the progress of poetry.
It assists (as Helen Groth puts it) "the poets' search for signs of the eternal amidst the transient forms of historical time."[76] This characterization

of photographic illustration also reminds us that photography is sometimes said to have "originated . . . from a tourist's desire for a better quality souvenir";[77] Fox Talbot's experiments with photochemical paper date to the longing he felt, honeymooning in a Swiss hotel, for a way to fix the images of Lake Como that he saw taking shape in the scene projected by his camera obscura. Indeed, books such as A. W. Bennett's 1868 *Scotland Her Songs and Scenery, as Sung by Her Bards and Seen in the Camera* or Stephen Thompson's 1870 *Venice and the Poets; with Photographic Illustrations* at once package souvenirs and, touting their serviceability as travel guides, establish the itineraries that sightseers of the future will follow. Readers who turn over the pages of the 1876 *The Loved Haunts of Cowper* bring "to remembrance," publisher and photographer William Samuel Wright asserts, "all the varied scenes around which such a charm has been thrown [by the topographic verse of William Cowper] and can 'to the loved haunt return' again and again, knowing that we are enjoying photographic faithfulness; and while we view them, as in a mirror, our fancy can easily picture the poet roving amidst their quiet beauty, or entering one of those buildings so often frequented for his sake."[78] The reader interpellated by Wright's words is possessed by a roving dead poet (speaking his very language, as Wright does when he arranges for his words to give way to Cowper's). At the same time, this reader is imagined as haunter in her turn, someone who in returning to her memories of Cowper's *The Task* reenacts as an armchair tourist itineraries that retrace Cowper's own. This reception scenario casts readers as travelers who will prove their poet love and the strength of their identification by arranging to see as, and where, the poet saw.

Carol Armstrong and Helen Groth are certainly correct to detect in the project of word-image combination pursued in these books the tacit admission by photography's nineteenth-century aficionados that photography could not stand alone and that only circumscription within a textual surround could grant respectability and canonicity to the upstart medium. To partake of the reassuring timelessness of art, photography needed poetry. The words that, as captions, served to anchor a photograph to a code of legibility and so make that trace of contingent moment meaningful could also—when they were fragments of famous poems—transform ordinary shots of ordinary scenery into valuable mementoes.[79] And yet there are also signs that the poetry book "illustrated by photography" was not so much paying tribute to poetry—not so much walking in the "golden footprints" of the poets—as announcing poetry's obsolescence.[80] As Celeste Langan and Laura Mandell have argued, it is characteristic of the romantic poem to reflect on poetry's transformation by the soundless medium of print, to deploy the figure of the last minstrel, for instance, so as to reflexively contemplate its own place in the history of media technology.[81] The photographically illustrated volumes that house these romantic poems about silenced song are evidently resolved to give graphic form to this history of media change and media supersession. That resolve explains their flagrantly cluttered, multimedia state. If these pages keep calling attention to their own material instantiation and so making it difficult to read through the letter to the spirit (really making it difficult to read *period*), it is in part because they pointedly resurrect every old trick in the typographer's book. Though determinedly modern, the latest thing, these poetry books are also museums. Their pages are display spaces for passé print modes and inscription systems: the black letter and rubrication of old incunabula, as on the title page of A. W. Bennett's edition of *The Lady of the Lake* (fig. 6.3); or a typeface that reintroduces a Victorian readership to the long *s* of the eighteenth century; or a lithograph reproducing Wordsworth's handwriting (fig. 6.4).

Relocated within these media museums, the romantic poem is made to seem untimely, a relic or "distressed genre." This, however, happens as these books promote the opposite effect: the photographic illustration's materializing of the poet's vision also promises to make romantic poetry—or at least romantic poets—more present. This packaging of the poem invites the closest of readings: for the camera's objectivity assured the reader that, as an 1892 volume in this tradition puts it, "the self-same pictures may have attracted the poet's eye" and that "the same flowers that charmed the poet's gaze spring up by hedgerow and streams and in the cottage gardens."[82] The *shared* seeing brings author and reader closer. Nonetheless this closeness has the curious quality of mediation that De Quincey exults in when he elides the living Wordsworth and the dead Milton—to recall that episode in the *Lake Reminiscences* that earlier exemplified the mixed feelings composing the elegiac idiom of poet love. The photographic illustration's promise of an immediate relationship to the poet's vision doubles as the vehicle by which that emotional communion becomes a dialogue with the dead.

Photography's often remarked capacity to establish an instantly retroactive view of experience of course compounds these mournful qualities. Through the eyes of the photographer, "the now becomes the past," Susan Sontag once declared. For Roland Barthes, "the Photograph is without future (this is its pathos, its melancholy); in it, no protensity [capacity for duration], whereas the cinema is protensive, . . . simply normal, like life."[83] The Victorians thus discovered in their cameras machines for periodizing. They

The Lady of the Lake.

Sir W. Scott, Bart.

SCOTT'S TOMB AT DRYBURGH.
PHOTO., G. W. WILSON.

London:

A. W. BENNETT, 5, BISHOPSGATE ST. WITHOUT.
1865.

FIGURE 6.3 Title page from A. W. Bennett's photographically illustrated edition (1865) of Sir Walter Scott's 1810 long poem, *The Lady of the Lake*, with a photograph of Scott's tomb by George Washington Wilson. The rubrication familiar from the early days of printing was revived by Bennett and used on this page both for his imprint and for Scott's title. Photograph: Courtesy of the Robertson Davies Library, Massey College, University of Toronto.

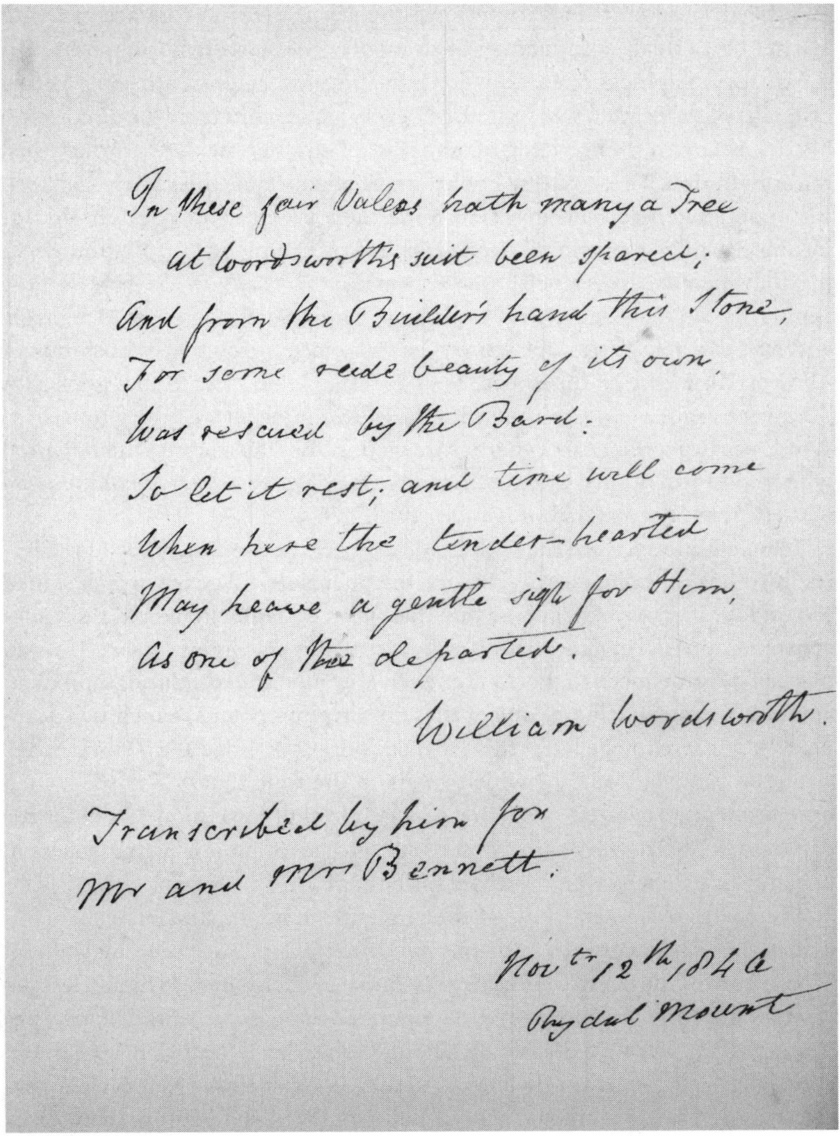

In these fair Vales hath many a Tree
    at Wordsworth's suit been spared;
And from the Builder's hand this Stone,
For some rude beauty of its own,
Was rescued by the Bard:
To let it rest; and time will come
When here the tender-hearted
May heave a gentle sigh for Him,
As one of the departed.

                    William Wordsworth.

Transcribed by him for
Mr and Mrs Bennett.

                    Nov.ʳ 12ᵗʰ, 846
                    Rydal Mount

FIGURE 6.4 Lithographed facsimile of a handwritten transcript by William Wordsworth of one of his inscription poems ("In these fair vales hath many a tree"), used as a frontispiece for *Our English Lakes, Mountains and Waterfalls, As Seen by William Wordsworth, Photographically Illustrated* (published by A. W. Bennett in 1864). Photograph: Courtesy of the Robertson Davies Library, Massey College, University of Toronto.

mobilized these machines to perform the act of division that according to Michel de Certeau is fundamental to modern Western historiography. For the historiographical operation, de Certeau states, begins with the positing of a rift, of "a death," which is then "everywhere reiterated in discourse"; history becomes a chronology composed of discrete periods through just that reiteration. These poetry books' internalization of the modern histori-cal imperative may help overdetermine their investment in death—in, for instance, using the camera's pencil of light to retrace the epitaphic writ-ing that memorializes poets' mortal remains. *The Lady of the Lake* volume begins, as we have seen, with a photograph of Scott's tomb at Dryburgh, and *Scotland Her Songs and Scenery* has its close-up of the tombstones of Alloway Kirk (setting for Robert Burns's "Tam O'Shanter")—the gravesites that were regular stops on the itineraries of nineteenth-century tourists.[84] Wordsworth's tomb at Grasmere is imaged in the illustration which, paired with the "Intimations Ode," concludes *Our English Lakes, Mountains and Waterfalls, As Seen by William Wordsworth* (fig. 6.5).

In an additional tie to the gothic side of literary devotion, many of the lyr-ics this book anthologizes are, in fact, the poems that Wordsworth designed as lapidary inscriptions, poems that double as epitaphs thanks to their self-conscious pondering of writing's divorce from the living voice. Thus in place of a frontispiece to the book, we have, as mentioned, a lithograph of an autograph transcription of one of these inscription poems, which will reap-pear on a printed page later: this is "Inscription, Intended for a Stone in the Grounds of Rydal Mount," which refers to the time that will come "when here the tender-hearted / May heave a gentle sigh for Him / As one of the departed."[85] Wordsworth did not see his own grave, but it is uncontroversial to claim that he wrote and rewrote his epitaph.

Strange as it is to conceive of the graveside scene in Grasmere that con-cludes *Our English Lakes, Mountains and Waterfalls* as one "seen by William Wordsworth," the overtly mortuary discourse of such a page is finally less ee-rie than the enigmatically empty, depopulated appearance of the landscapes portrayed by the majority of the photographs. For a Victorian readership especially, beneficiaries of a new National Portrait Gallery, and collectors of cartes de visite of famous faces of living authors, the authors themselves would have been almost tangible in their absence from these volumes. As far as I know, none of the photographically illustrated poetry books features the portrait frontispiece that was conventional in Victorian bookmaking, an omission that reinforces one's sense that the romantic authors are, in these volumes, confined to the past, defined precisely as the unseen occupants

WORDSWORTH'S TOMB, GRASMERE CHURCH-YARD.
p. 183.

FIGURE 6.5 "Wordsworth's Tomb, Grasmere Church-Yard," photograph used at the end of *Our English Lakes, Mountains and Waterfalls* to illustrate Wordsworth's "Ode [Intimations of Immortality]." Photograph: Courtesy of the Robertson Davies Library, Massey College, University of Toronto.

of a pre-photographic era. They haunt those pages, however. For also ee-rie in these books is the discovery that some of these empty landscapes in fact include tiny figures regarding the vistas that we regard too. These figures are seen from a distance (like the reading woman in the illustration to Browning's "Memorabilia"), often only from behind. In some ways they are readable as fellow devotees of the poetry, already on the spot. In other ways, though, the reader is primed to think, wistfully, that, if she strained hard enough, she might recognize the poet himself in one of these wraith-like figures. The devotional practices that the images in these poetry books mobilize are, however, those of a love that is aware of itself as projection.[86] The subtitle for the A. W. Bennett volume, *As Seen by William Wordsworth*, installs Wordsworth anachronistically in the position of the photographer, the individual behind the apparatus who has brought the scene to light. But the devotee whom the volume interpellates knows very well that, so located, the poet can only be a ghost.

CODA: LOST LOVE

This chapter has suggested that the mournfulness involved in the belief that poetry or literature is at death's door often entails a diversion of pathos from another place. As we have seen, Boswell's anxieties about his chances of salvation are diverted into worry about the endurance of Shakespeare; De Quincey's determination to imagine *Lyrical Ballads* as though it were in harm's way (so that he can save it) is construable as a bookish equivalent to Munchausen syndrome by proxy. I should concede therefore that there is likely some projection of my own in the foregoing account of how the reader/beholder of *Our English Lakes, Mountains and Waterfalls* might have *missed* Wordsworth—might have savored the bittersweet sensation that she had just missed seeing him in that landscape—even as the book promised through photography to make the world of his poems newly proximate.

For it is worth underscoring that the séance-like attempt to summon Wordsworth's shade that I have delineated would have been enacted against a backdrop constituted by the more robust afterlife that Wordsworth's educational ideas and verse were coming to enjoy by this time in the Victorian schoolroom. In ending with the photographical illustration of poetry in the 1860s and 1870s *Loving Literature* has arrived at the decades when it began to be especially plausible to narrate the progress of poetry as a success story: knowledge of literary history had after 1853 been installed at the heart of the competitive examinations for the English Civil Service, new university chairs in English literature had been founded in response to that development, the Education Act of 1870 had created both a new program of compulsory state schooling and a new machinery of teacher training, and self-declared lovers of literature had taken on a large share of the instruction involved in both. Indeed, as English literature made the transition from pastime to school subject, one salient proof of poetry's power to endure could have been found in the way that Wordsworth's autobiographical verse not only became an object of study but also came to define this study's method and telos. The ideas of moral development and social cure that it had set out came to define what it meant to possess a literary vocation.[87] By the 1880s the Wordsworthian child, who exults in its powers of imagination and is "yet glorious in the might / Of untamed pleasures," had become a standard-bearer for campaigns against those utilitarian definitions of public education that would have restricted English to instruction in language and grammar.[88]

Thus in 1921 the authors of the Newbolt Report, *The Teaching of English in England*, who saw the English class as the key to a needful humanizing of the school curriculum, turned explicitly to *The Prelude* and *The Excursion* for a ⅃ refiguration of their mission in defense of the pupil's imaginative freec⌐ ⱻ. They also, however, betray some of the tensions at stake in canon love, the individual's romantic choice of what has already been chosen for her, when over the course of two pages they move from Wordsworth's anticipation of the English Association's conviction that the ends of education were best served by securing for the young an *intimacy* with "poets and romancers" to the admission that Wordsworth himself had advocated for "true education" and not "book learning"—"the transmission, not of book learning, but of the influence of personality and the experience of human life." Their Wordsworthianism sponsors a wishful vision of a schoolroom encounter with poets and romancers that would somehow *not* be mediated by books. This vision betrays a worry—that to *assign* reading to pupils is to spoil it and is to kill rather than to nurture intimacy—that has often vexed the very people who do that assigning. Promoting children's study of imaginative literature as intimate "contact with great minds" thus goes hand and hand in the report with worrying about how if entrusted to the wrong sort of teacher literary study will be reduced to "conventional appreciations, historical details, and the minute examinations of words and phrases." Here, and in a later comment that warns that teachers must "not come between their pupils and the authors they are reading," the early twentieth-century Newbolt authors substantiate Stanley Fish's late twentieth-century description of anti-professionalism as a version of a "traditional Protestant" distrust of forms, "in favor of a spirit that the letter of forms is always threatening to kill."[89]

This makes me wonder whether to think of English as being in its afterlife has sometimes worked, in a perversely consoling way, to distract us from the mundane embarrassments and compromises entailed in the subject's institutional success. It might have been easier for some late Victorians to think melancholically of romantic poetry as having faded away than to dwell on how frequently and unremittingly it was dinned into their ears— say, as a consequence of the fact that Her Majesty's inspectors of schools had made "We Are Seven" the object of Standard II (eight-year-old) pupils' mandatory exercises in memorization and recitation.[90] Some of those embarrassments and compromises derive, that is, from the tricky, though entirely routine, work of making the program of a sentimental education accommodate the requirements of discipline and student assessment—just the work that reminds us, peskily, that our passion for reading matter, rather than coming naturally, requires a particular set of cultural codes and conventions to support it. But if a counterbalancing investment in an idea of poetry as (in Virginia Jackson's terms) a "pathetic abstraction already in its afterlife" helps sustain a notion of literature as looming above and untainted by the machinery of its transmission, the emotional payoffs that notion involves also have their costs. For a start, as Jackson observes, this idea of poetry at death's door predisposes its adherents to *miss* poetry in another sense of the term "miss." It can make one inattentive to the poets around us in the here and now.

In a related way, the very success that the late Victorian and early twentieth-century proponents of "English" enjoyed in their efforts to put literary pedagogy at the center of the state school curriculum might have compounded the tendency to understand the love of literature as necessarily following an elegiac script in which loving leads to losing or in which adorability increases as the object of our adoration moves closer to death's door. That success in the school setting meant that literature came to be more closely linked to childhood and youth at the moment when these phases in the life cycle also came to be understood, in part thanks to Wordsworthian and De Quinceyan models, ever more insistently through those narratives of a lost Eden that commit adults both to mourning their younger selves and to mourning the transience of those selves' romances. In this context, literature—or, to be more precise, feeling for literature, though, as we have seen, the two are inextricable—takes on some of childhood's qualities of lostness and gone-ness and sealed perfection.

Hence the frequent undertone of nostalgia in the complaints that current and former PhD students in English make about how the training in criticism and theory to which they must conform smothers the love of authors and of reading that had brought them to their graduate programs in the first place. To call them nostalgic is not to say that the complainants don't often make good sense when they query the definitions of rigor with which the discipline of literary studies has sometimes saddled itself or when they notice the programmatic and uncritical way it has celebrated critical reading. And yet their complaints also betoken how one tried-and-true method that professionals and would-be professionals have long had to define themselves *as* professionals is by ascribing charisma, authenticity, and a capacity for true feeling to amateurs, to the as-yet unschooled who are "yet glorious in the might / Of untamed pleasures."[91] "*Joy*: remember that feeling?" Martha Banta asked in a 1998 Editor's Column for literary studies' flagship journal *PMLA*, adopting a Wordsworthian idiom to describe how the Modern Language Association members ought to feel when they read literature: "If you do not, try to regain it. If you never had it, then you ought not to be in this business."[92] "There was a time when to my thinking, every word was a flower," Hazlitt wrote in 1822, using the "Intimations Ode" as a framework in which to narrate his reading life, and, in keeping with this elegiac script, longing not so much for a lost love as for lost loving.[93]

Acknowledgments

This book and its author have benefited from the wisdom, generosity, and energy of many—a group of friends and colleagues who have earned the right to say, with Dr. Johnson, that they "have read like Hercules." Thank you to Timothy Campbell, James Chandler, Ian Duncan, Andrew Elfenbein, Ina Ferris, Penny Fielding, Nancy Glazener, Kevis Goodman, J. Paul Hunter, Virginia Jackson, Paul Keen, Karma Lochrie, Christina Lupton, Michael Macovski, Adela Pinch, Leah Price, Stuart Sherman, Janet Sorensen, Patricia Meyer Spacks, Alison Syme, and Paul Westover. I regret tremendously that the late Susan Manning is no longer with us: one reason why is that I would have liked to give her both my thanks and this book. Several of the people whose names I have just listed combined their feats of heroic reading with feats of heroic writing, writing letter after letter supporting my applications for the fellowships and travel grants that helped *Loving Literature* get written. It is a pleasure to salute them in that capacity too and acknowledge how very well, over many years, I have been sustained by their collegiality. Many other people contributed to this book by organizing panels at conferences, by inviting me to their campuses to lecture, by attending those lectures and asking searching questions, and/or challenging my premises, and/or sharing confidences. This group includes Amanda Anderson, Steve Arata, Brian Corman, David Collings, Alex Dick, Simon During, Joel Faflak, Mary Favret, Marcie Frank, William Galperin, Denise Gigante, Geoffrey Galt Harpham, Sonia Hofkosh, Heather Jackson, Theresa Kelley, Jayne Lewis, the late Peter Lindenbaum, Sandra Macpherson, Charles Mahoney, Laura Mandell, Peter Manning, Mary Helen McMurran, Richard Nash, Nicola Nixon, Matthew

Ocheltree, Mary Ann O'Farrell, Daniel O'Quinn, Joanna Picciotto, Andrew Piper, Wolfram Schmidgen, James Simpson, Jack Stillinger, Katie Trumpener, Chip Tucker, Cynthia Wall, William Warner, Nicholas Watson, and Arlene Young, and audience members in many locales whose names, in several cases, I never learned.

I have also been fortunate in receiving institutional support for this project. The National Endowment for the Humanities, the National Humanities Center, the College Arts and Humanities Institute at Indiana University, the John Simon Guggenheim Memorial Foundation, and the Institute for Advanced Study in the Humanities at the University of Edinburgh all supplied me with the resources, time, and, best of all, boosts to my confidence that I needed. At the University of Toronto, the Connaught Fund and a Chancellor Jackman Professorship endowed by the Hon. Henry N. R. Jackman have supported my research in myriad ways and most recently made it possible for me to hire two gifted research assistants, Julia Grandison and Melissa Patterson, who brought sharp eyes and immense amounts of critical acumen to the penultimate version of the manuscript. While this book was in its final stage of production, I moved from the University of Toronto to Harvard University. I am grateful to Harvard's dean of arts and sciences for the additional research support that helped defray the costs of proofreading and indexing. I wish to thank Simon Reader for the enthusiasm and ingenuity he brought to those tasks. At the University of Chicago Press, Alan Thomas encouraged me to be brave and, with his impeccable sense of timing, knew to push me at the moments when I most needed pushing. Randolph Petilos has fielded my many questions with his customary patience and aplomb. Jennifer Rappaport has been the most scrupulous and patient of copy editors.

Earlier versions of materials now in chapters 3 and 4 appeared in the *Romantic Circles Praxis* volume "Romantic Libraries," edited by Ina Ferris (February 2004) and in *Bookish Histories: Books, Literature, and Commercial Modernity, 1700–1900,* ed. Ina Ferris and Paul Keen (Basingstoke, UK: Palgrave Macmillan, 2009), and I am grateful for permission to reuse those materials here.

That this book about how and why English professors bring their work home did not in the end prove home-wrecking speaks volumes about the paragon-like patience and good humor of Tom Keirstead, whom I continue to love even more than I love literature.

Notes

INTRODUCTION

1. Lorraine Daston, "Whither Critical Inquiry," *Critical Inquiry* 30, no. 2 (Winter 2004): 363.

2. William Clark, *Academic Charisma and the Origins of the Research University* (Chicago: University of Chicago Press, 2008), 7.

3. See Andrew Ross, "The Mental Labor Problem," *Social Text* 63 (Summer 2000): 1–31. Ross describes how the new knowledge industries of digital culture have followed artistic and academic traditions in dissolving the lines between labor and leisure: workers in those industries likewise subsidize their own enterprises as they accept a "'discounted wage' out of 'love for their subject'" (22). For the longer history informing that arrangement, see Clifford Siskin's discussion of the romantic period's rewriting of work as love: *The Work of Writing: Literature and Social Change in Britain* (Baltimore: Johns Hopkins University Press, 1999), 112–18.

4. See Carol Atherton, *Defining Literary Criticism: Scholarship, Authority and the Possession of Literary Knowledge, 1880–2002* (Basingstoke, UK: Palgrave Macmillan, 2005), 38 (citing John Churton Collins's 1887 "Can English Literature Be Taught?"). See also Gerald Graff, *Professing Literature: An Institutional History* (Chicago: University of Chicago Press, 1988); John Guillory, "Literary Study and the Modern System of the Disciplines," in *Disciplinarity at the Fin de Siècle*, ed. Amanda Anderson and Joseph Valente (Princeton, NJ: Princeton University Press, 2002), 19–43; and on the mystique of the amateur Marjorie Garber, *Academic Instincts* (Princeton, NJ: Princeton University Press, 2001), 3–52; and Daniel E. Harney, "Amateur Modernism: Literary Responses to Professional Society" (PhD dissertation, University of Toronto, 2013).

5. A. S. Byatt, *Possession: A Romance* (New York: Random House, 1990), 62.

6. *Dead Poets Society*, directed by Peter Weir (Touchstone Pictures, 1989). Unfolding along similar lines, Mr. Keating's lesson plan for the next class meeting requires these students to tear the introductory chapter of their poetry textbook out of their books.

7. *The Teaching of English in England* (London: H. M. Stationery Office, 1921), 150.

8. Lauren Berlant, "Feminism and the Institutions of Intimacy," in *The Politics of Research*, ed. E. Ann Kaplan and George Levine (New Brunswick, NJ: Rutgers University Press, 1997), 150; Dean Bakopoulos, "Straight through the Heart," *New York Times Book Review*, March 24, 2013, 27.

9. Eve Kosofsky Sedgwick, "Gender Criticism," in *Redrawing the Boundaries: The Transformation of English and American Literary Studies*, ed. Stephen Greenblatt and Giles Gunn (New York: Modern Language Association of America, 1992), 296.

10. Ian Hunter, *Culture and Government: The Emergence of Literary Education* (Basingstoke, UK: Macmillan, 1988).

11. The National Home Reading Union, founded in 1889, was a network of friends, church

groups, and "Pleasant Sunday Afternoon groups," extending across the British Empire and held together by a monthly magazine that issued prescriptions about worthy reading. Meetings took place in the houses of individual members, which enabled the union to present itself as continuing traditions of family reading. See Robert Snape, "The National Home Reading Union, 1889-1930," *Journal of Victorian Culture* 7, no. 1 (January 2002): 86-110.

12. Peter Novick, *That Noble Dream: The "Objectivity Question" and the American Historical Profession* (Cambridge: Cambridge University Press, 1988). See Guillory, "Literary Study," on how the persistence of belletristic models within late Victorian/early twentieth-century English studies offset philology's self-consciously modern embrace of the norms of scientificity.

13. This is one way in which *Loving Literature* deviates from John Guillory's *Cultural Capital: The Problem of Literary Canon Formation* (Chicago: University of Chicago Press, 1993), to which I am otherwise indebted. Focused on the school as agent of cultural reproduction, Guillory equates the history of cultural capital with the history of the curriculum and engages the embrace of English literature by the eighteenth century's dissenting academies as the first of his case studies. But even when considering the later eras in which English literature's disciplinization is a fait accompli it may be unwise to assume that one might tidily reduce the cultural work performed by the school system or even by the concept of English itself to a single function. The boundary confusions I pointed to in opening this introduction militate against such certainties, and even now author societies, tourist boards, popular lecture series, book clubs, journalism, and *Masterpiece Theatre* all have a stake in the questions the professorate likes to consider its own. See also Nancy Glazener, *Literature in the Making: A History of U.S. Literary Culture in the Long Nineteenth Century* (New York: Oxford University Press, forthcoming), which traces literature's "populous public life" and reconstructs its position at the intersection of education, sociability, and entertainment.

14. Arguments for this periodization, in which the age of sensibility outlasts the romantic period, may be found in Adela Pinch, *Strange Fits of Passion: Epistemologies of Emotion, Hume to Austen* (Stanford, CA: Stanford University Press, 1997); and Christopher C. Nagle, *Sexuality and the Culture of Sensibility in the British Romantic Era* (Basingstoke, UK: Palgrave Macmillan, 2007).

15. Simon During, "Out of England: Literary Subjectivity in the Australian Colonies, 1788-1867," in *Imagining Australia: Literature and Culture in the New New World*, ed. Judith Ryan and Chris Wallace Crabbe (Cambridge, MA: Harvard University Committee on Australian Studies, 2004), 4. See also his "Literary Subjectivity," *Ariel: A Review of International English Literature* 31, nos. 1 and 2 (January-April 2000): 33-50.

16. For divergent accounts of the place of personification in present-day critical practice, see W. J. T. Mitchell, "What Do Pictures 'Really' Want?" *October* 77 (Summer 1996): 71-82; and Amy Hungerford, *The Holocaust of Texts: Genocide, Literature, and Personification* (Chicago: University of Chicago Press, 2003), 57-66.

17. For instance, Paul Keen demonstrates that struggles over contending definitions of literature continue through the romantic period: although a concept of imagination has subsequently come to demarcate the distinction between Enlightenment and romanticism, for Wordsworth's and Coleridge's contemporaries the scope of "literature" had not been narrowed to aesthetic expression exclusively. See *The Crisis of Literature in the 1790s: Print Culture and the Public Sphere* (Cambridge: Cambridge University Press, 1999), 2.

18. James Boswell, *Life of Johnson*, introd. Pat Rogers, ed. R. W. Chapman (Oxford: Oxford University Press, 1980), 1363, 272.

19. [Thomas Green], *Extracts from the Diary of a Lover of Literature* (Ipswich, UK: John Raw, 1810), 53, 240, 195.

20. During, "Literary Subjectivity," 39.

21. During's list of the relations that demarcate the literary is worth quoting at length: "Writing that will be read in the future against journalism which will not; writing to be voiced against writing to be silently consumed; writing which records and administers versus writing which en-

tertains and instructs; writing which enters the market versus writing which remains in the files of various institutions or is preserved privately; writing which has 'authors' versus writing which is anonymous; writing as act against writing as reflection" (*Foucault and Literature: Toward a Genealogy of Writing* [London: Routledge, 1992], 223).

22. The first of the *Lectures on English Literature from Chaucer to Tennyson* by Henry Reed, appointed professor of rhetoric and English literature at the University of Pennsylvania in 1835, is interrupted by an aside in which Reed expresses exasperation over the "mischief" wrought by the "vapid, half-naturalized term 'belles-lettres'": "The term had an appropriateness for much in the literature of France, but translate the words and transfer them to English literature and how inane is such a title so applied" (5th ed. [Philadelphia: Claxton, Remsen, and Haffelfinger, 1878], 34).

23. Trevor Ross, *The Making of the English Literary Canon, from the Middle Ages to the Eighteenth Century* (Montreal: McGill-Queen's University Press, 1998).

24. Reid is quoted in J. C. Bryce's introduction to Adam Smith, *Lectures on Rhetoric and Belles-Lettres* (Indianapolis: Liberty Fund, 1985), 30.

25. Thomas De Quincey, "Lake Reminiscences, No. 1," in *The Works of Thomas De Quincey*, ed. Grevel Lindop, vol. 11, *Articles from* Tait's Magazine *and* Blackwood's Magazine, *1838-41*, ed. Julian North (London: Pickering and Chatto, 2001), 61.

26. This metacritical investigation of the institutions of literature began with Raymond Williams's *Culture and Society, 1780-1850* (London: Chatto and Windus, 1958). Significant recent studies working this vein and not yet referenced include Chris Baldick, *The Social Mission of English Criticism, 1848-1932* (Oxford: Oxford University Press, 1983); Brian Doyle, *English and Englishness* (London: Routledge, 1989); Jonathan Brody Kramnick, *Making the English Canon: Print-Capitalism and the Cultural Past, 1700-1770* (Cambridge: Cambridge University Press, 1998); George Justice, *The Manufacturers of Literature: Writing and the Literary Marketplace in Eighteenth-Century England* (Newark: University of Delaware Press, 2002); Andrew Elfenbein, *Romanticism and the Rise of English* (Stanford, CA: Stanford University Press, 2009); Robin Valenza, *Literature, Language, and the Rise of the Intellectual Disciplines in Britain, 1680-1820* (Cambridge: Cambridge University Press, 2009); and Jon Klancher, *Transfiguring the Arts and Sciences: Knowledge and Cultural Institutions in the Romantic Age* (Cambridge: Cambridge University Press, 2013).

27. See Gauri Viswanathan, *Masks of Conquest: Literary Study and British Rule in India* (New York: Columbia University Press, 1989); and Alok Yadov, *Before the Empire of English: Literature, Provinciality, and Nationalism in Eighteenth-Century Britain* (Basingstoke, UK: Palgrave Macmillan, 2004).

28. See Franklin E. Court, *Institutionalizing English Literature: The Culture and Politics of Literary Study* (Stanford, CA: Stanford University Press, 1992), 168. The gender politics I have evoked also seem implicit in Trevor Ross's and David Simpson's presentation of the history of literariness as an episode in a broader feminization of culture: Simpson, for instance, sees literary studies as overly beholden accordingly to a "lexicon that is dominantly feminized: intuition, exceptionality, sympathy, empathy, lived experience and so forth" (*The Academic Postmodern and the Rule of Literature: A Report on Half-Knowledge* [Chicago: University of Chicago Press, 1995], 103). Such characterizations risk shoring up gendered dichotomies rather than investigating their construction or contestation.

29. See Pierre Bourdieu, *Distinction: A Social Critique of the Judgment of Taste*, trans. Richard Nice (Cambridge, MA: Harvard University Press, 1984), as well as *The Field of Cultural Production: Essays on Art and Literature*, ed. Randal Johnson (New York: Columbia University Press, 1993).

30. Jonah Siegel, *Desire and Excess: The Nineteenth-Century Culture of Art* (Princeton, NJ: Princeton University Press, 2000), 96.

31. Guillory, *Cultural Capital*, 30.

32. Amélie Oksenberg Rorty, "From Passions to Emotions and Sentiments," *Philosophy* 57 (1982): 159-72.

33. Samuel Taylor Coleridge et al., *Letters from the Lake Poets: Samuel Taylor Coleridge, William Wordsworth, Robert Southey to Daniel Stuart* (London: West, Newman, 1889), 81. Presumably, Dahomey's involvement in the slave trade—whose abolition is under way when Coleridge writes—is what Coleridge has in mind when he holds off on granting this African nation a stake in Milton's poetry.

34. Daniel Boyarin, "Placing Reading: Ancient Israel and Medieval Europe," in *The Ethnography of Reading*, ed. Jonathan Boyarin (Berkeley: University of California Press, 1993), 19.

35. Cf. Kramnick, *Making the English Canon*, 241.

36. The vocabulary of *preference* links the domains of aesthetic evaluation and of sexuality, but, as Marcie Frank proposes, we should remember that these preferences are "exercised within confines loosely described as available options, and more rigorously understood as social and psychic conventions": "Fighting Women and Loving Men: Dryden's Representation of Shakespeare in *All for Love*," in *Queering the Renaissance*, ed. Jonathan Goldberg (Durham, NC: Duke University Press, 1994), 325.

37. Boyarin, "Placing Reading," 33n21.

38. René Wellek, *The Rise of English Literary History* (Chapel Hill: University of North Carolina Press, 1941), v; emphasis in the original.

39. Zadie Smith, "Love, Actually," *Guardian*, November 1, 2003, http://www.guardian.co.uk /books/2003/nov/01/classics.zadiesmith.

40. David Denby, *Great Books: My Adventures with Homer, Rousseau, Woolf, and Other Indestructible Writers of the Western World* (New York: Simon and Schuster, 1996), 371, 370.

41. Daniel Cottom, *Why Education Is Useless* (Philadelphia: University of Pennsylvania Press, 2003), 51.

42. See April London, *Literary History Writing, 1770–1820* (Basingstoke, UK: Palgrave Macmillan, 2010), for a study of the cross-generic negotiations engaging late eighteenth- and early nineteenth-century literary historians.

43. David Hume, *A Treatise of Human Nature*, ed. Ernest Mossner (Harmondsworth, UK: Penguin, 1969), 343.

44. Richard Hurd, *Letters on Chivalry and Romance*, ed. Edith J. Morley (London: Henry Frowde, 1911), 148.

45. Thomas Warton, *The Correspondence of Thomas Warton*, ed. David Fairer (Athens: University of Georgia Press, 1995), 53.

46. Julie Carlson, "Hazlitt and the Sociability of Theatre," in *Romantic Sociability: Social Networks and Literary Culture in Britain, 1770–1840*, ed. Gillian Russell and Clara Tuite (Cambridge: Cambridge University Press, 2006), 159-60.

47. Denby, *Great Books*, 61.

CHAPTER ONE

1. Kenneth Haltman, "Reaching Out to Touch Someone? Reflections on a 1923 Candlestick Telephone," in *American Artifacts: Essays in Material Culture*, ed. Jules David Prown and Kenneth Haltman (East Lansing: Michigan State University Press, 2000), 76.

2. Sherry Turkle, "Diary," *London Review of Books*, April 20, 2006, 36-37.

3. The distinction between canon and list is explored by Laura Mandell in "Putting Contents on the Table: The Disciplinary Anthology and the Field of Literary History," *The Poetess Archive Journal* 1, no. 1 (2007), http://www.nines.org/exhibits/Putting_Contents_on_the_Table.

4. Throughout this book I will by and large be excluding theatre from consideration. One justification for this exclusion is that theatre's relationship to the "live" differs radically from that of printed texts. As Elkanah Settle noted in 1698 the reader who can "form a personal idea" of a character, either "historical or romantick"—so that he takes that favorite with him "from his Closet to his Bed"—will at the playhouse have a different experience: "When you see the hero or heroine,

or any other darling in a play, tis the person of the Actour or Actress ... both the Hero and the Heroine are no more to you than the Betterton and Barry" (names of Restoration players); "You want that darling personal Idea, which the reading only can give you" (*A Farther Defence of Dramatick Poetry* [rept. New York: Garland, 1972], 54–55). Starting in the 1770s booksellers marketed multi-volume compilations of reprinted "British Drama" and "English Theatre" that in several respects resembled their canon-making collections of British poetry but, crucially, these lacked the lives that made poetry an authored discourse. The editions of the drama, Michael Gamer notes, were often based on prompters' copies, so that they were as much records of performances—or scripts for future home or school theatricals—as documents of literary achievement. See Gamer, "Oeuvre-Making and Canon Formation," in *The Oxford Handbook to Romanticism*, ed. David Duff (Oxford: Oxford University Press, forthcoming).

5. Michel Foucault, "What Is an Author?" in *Language, Counter-memory, Practice: Selected Essays and Interviews*, trans. Donald F. Bouchard and Sherry Simon (Ithaca, NY: Cornell University Press, 1977), 126; Leah S. Marcus, "The Silence of the Archive and the Noise of Cyberspace," in *The Renaissance Computer: Knowledge Technology in the First Age of Print*, ed. Neil Rhodes and Jonathan Sawday (London: Routledge, 2000), 22, 23.

6. Cited in Paul Keen, "'Uncommon Animals': Making Virtue of Necessity in the Age of Authors," in *Bookish Histories: Books, Literature, and Commercial Modernity, 1700–1900*, ed. Ina Ferris and Paul Keen (Basingstoke, UK: Palgrave Macmillan, 2009), 45.

7. Samuel Taylor Coleridge, *Biographia Literaria*, ed. James Engell and W. Jackson Bate, 2 vols. in 1 (Princeton, NJ: Princeton University Press, 1983), 1:12. Subsequent references are to this edition and appear parenthetically in the text.

8. I quote from the title page of Thomas Hayward, comp., *The British Muse, or, A Collection of Thoughts Moral, Natural, and Sublime, of Our English Poets*, 3 vols. (London: F. Cogan and J. Nourse, 1738).

9. William Oldys, "Preface, Containing an Historical and Critical Review of all the Collections of This Kind That Were Ever Published," in Hayward, comp., *The British Muse*, 3:xx. *The Beauties of Poetry Display'd, Containing Observations on the Different Species of Poetry, and the Rules of English Versification, Exemplified by a Large Collection of Beautiful Passages, Similies [sic] and Descriptions* (Dublin: J. J. Hoey, 1757).

10. "Use" has emerged as a key category for scholars seeking to pinpoint the specificity of early modern habits of reading: see Bradin Cormack and Carla Mazzio, *Book Use, Book Theory, 1500–1700* (Chicago: University of Chicago Library, 2005); and William H. Sherman, *Used Books: Marking Readers in Renaissance England* (Philadelphia: University of Pennsylvania Press, 2008).

11. Oldys, "Preface," *British Muse*, 3:xv.

12. Authorial self-expression is downplayed in this format, as it is, quite disconcertingly, in the seemingly more author-centric books "of beauties" that in the 1770s and 1780s were best-selling staples for the book trade. The compilers of, for example, *The Beauties of Swift* do not present such a volume as a forum in which the spotlighted author will be monumentalized or venerated. Instead, their selections reduce an author's texts to quotable quotes. See Daniel Cook, "Authors Unformed: Reading 'Beauties' in the Eighteenth Century," *Philological Quarterly* 89, no. 2–3 (Spring 2010): 283–308.

13. Philip Sidney, *Defence of Poesie*, cited in Trevor Ross, *The Making of the English Literary Canon, From the Middle Ages to the Late Eighteenth Century* (Montreal: McGill-Queen's University Press, 1998), 70. Subsequent references to Ross's book appear parenthetically in the text.

14. Thomas F. Bonnell's *The Most Disreputable Trade: Publishing the Classics of English Poetry, 1765-1810* (Oxford: Oxford University Press, 2008) describes how eighteenth-century British booksellers argued for modern poems' equivalence to ancient Greek and Roman classics.

15. Mandell identifies Hazlitt's *Specimens* as the first poetry collection to resemble closely the modern disciplinary anthology (the second, 1825 edition, especially, which for copyright reasons

omitted all the living authors Hazlitt had included in the first): "Putting Contents on the Table," 3, 15.

16. Samuel Johnson, preface to Shakespeare, *The Oxford Authors: Samuel Johnson* (Oxford: Oxford University Press, 1984), 420. In this book's final chapters, I consider how this transvaluation of literary antiquity brought about a state of affairs in which it really was the case that the best poet was a dead poet.

17. *Spectator* 309 (February 21, 1711), cited in Ross, *Making*, 217.

18. James Boswell, *Life of Johnson*, introd. Pat Rogers, ed. R. W. Chapman (Oxford: Oxford University Press, 1980), 979. Cited in Ross, *Making*, 296; and see also 182-86. Subsequent references to Boswell's *Life* are to this edition and appear parenthetically in the text.

19. Douglas Lane Patey, " 'Aesthetics' and the Rise of Lyric in the Eighteenth Century," *S.E.L.* 33, no. 3 (Summer 1993): 602-4. Cf. Neil Rhodes's account of the eighteenth-century chapter in the history of the discipline of English: "With the arrival of belles lettres from France—the form itself suggests a feminization of the subject—in comes the concept of 'society' . . . together with the matching concepts of taste and politeness which are formed in part by the passive reception of the printed book" (*Shakespeare and the Origin of English* [Oxford: Oxford University Press, 2004], 203).

20. Sherman, *Used Books*, xvi.

21. Simon During, *Foucault and Literature: Towards a Genealogy of Writing* (London: Routledge, 1992), 223.

22. David Marshall, *The Frame of Art: Fictions of Aesthetic Experience* (Baltimore: Johns Hopkins University Press, 2000), 4. "What defines a work of art [within the Kantian scheme] is its status as an object to be 'contemplated' and contemplated 'disinterestedly' . . . without regard to the personal interests or possessiveness or the desires of the perceiver": M. H. Abrams, "Art-As-Such: The Sociology of Modern Aesthetics," cited in Marshall, *Frame of Art*, 3.

23. Marshall, *Frame of Art*, 4-5.

24. Denise Gigante, *Taste: A Literary History* (New Haven, CT: Yale University Press, 2005), 3, 2.

25. David Hume, "Of the Standard of Taste," in *Selected Essays*, ed. Stephen Copley and Andrew Edgar (Oxford: Oxford University Press, 1993), 150. There is an echo of the Earl of Roscommon's "Essay on Translated Verse," line 96, in Hume's paralleling of the choice of an author and choice of a friend. (See *An Essay on Translated Verse* [London: Jacob Tonson, 1684], 7, *Early English Books Online*, eebo.chadwyck.com.myaccess.library.utoronto.ca.) Tellingly, however, in Roscommon's poem the figure who is instructed in the choice of author is not assumed to be a reader but instead another author, preparing a translation, in a relation of emulation and rivalry with the original. By the time Hume adapts the line, however, it can be taken for granted that the encounter with the author/friend is not the spur for new composition but instead an occasion for literary appreciation.

26. Edmund Cartwright, unsigned review of *Lives of the Poets* in the *Monthly Review* (1782), in *Samuel Johnson: The Critical Heritage*, ed. James T. Boulton (London: Routledge, 1971), 269.

27. Hume, "Of the Delicacy of Taste and Passion," in *Selected Essays*, 12-13.

28. John Dryden, *Prose, 1688-1691*, in *The Works of John Dryden*, ed. Edward Niles Hooker and H. T. Swedenberg Jr., vol. 17, ed. Samuel Holt Monk (Berkeley: University of California Press, 1971), 58; William Godwin, "Of an Early Taste for Reading," in *The Enquirer* (London: G. G. and J. Robinson, 1797), 34.

29. Elizabeth Carter, Letter to Elizabeth Montagu, October 26, 1759, in *Letters from Mrs. Elizabeth Carter to Mrs. Montagu, between the Years 1755 and 1800*, ed. Montagu Pennington, 3 vols. (London: F.C. and J. Rivington, 1817), 1:67-68; emphasis in the original.

30. Aristotle, "Friendship," book 8 of *The Nicomachean Ethics*, trans. David Ross, rev. J. L. Ackrill and J. O. Urmson (Oxford: Oxford University Press, 1998), 194.

31. Aristotle, *Eudemian Ethics*, in *The Athenian Constitution, The Eudemian Ethics, On Virtues and Vices*, trans. H. Rackham (London: Heinemann, 1952), 395.

32. Ricks's review for the *Boston Sunday Globe* was quoted in a Harvard University Press advertisement in *PMLA* 115, no. 4 (September 2000): 902. I owe the second quotation to Laura Quinney, "Poisonous Frogs," *London Review of Books*, May 8, 2003, http://www.lrb.co.uk/v25 /n09/quin01_html.

33. The separation of authors and readers is also shored up in new ways by a gender binary. The shifts in the tables of contents as one moves from the poetry miscellany to the anthology are telling in this regard. Mrs. Leapor and Mrs. Behn provided content for *The Beauties of Poetry Display'd* but go missing from the later anthologies whose author-centeredness makes them more conducive to canon love. The fact that women authors seem to vanish when the anthology collects poets rather than poetical sentiments ready for appropriation and reuse is one reason to question Trevor Ross and Douglas Lane Patey when they equate the romantic autonomization of the cultural field with that field's "feminization."

34. William Duff, *Critical Observations on the Writings of the Most Celebrated Original Geniuses in Poetry* (London: T. Becket and P. A. de Hondt, 1770), 339; Edward Young, *Conjectures on Original Composition*, quoted in Dustin Griffin, *Literary Patronage in England, 1650-1800* (Cambridge: Cambridge University Press, 1996), 281.

35. Goethe, *Wilhelm Meister*, cited in David Allan, *Commonplace Books and Reading in Georgian England* (Cambridge: Cambridge University Press, 2010), 195. Freya Johnston's account of Johnson's ambivalence toward condescension has informed this chapter: see *Samuel Johnson and the Art of Sinking, 1709-1791* (Oxford: Oxford University Press, 2005).

36. Trevor Ross, "Copyright and the Invention of Tradition," *Eighteenth-Century Studies* 26, no. 1 (Autumn 1992): 3, 24.

37. Justice Yates, *Speeches or Arguments of the Judges of the Court of King's Bench . . . in April 1769; in the Cause Millar against Taylor* (Leith, UK: William Coke, 1771), in *The Literary Property Debate: Seven Tracts, 1747-1773*, ed. Stephen Parks (New York: Garland, 1974), 57.

38. Lord Camden's speech, Thursday, February 24, in *The Pleadings of the Counsel before the House of Lords in the Great Cause concerning Literary Property* (London: C. Wilkin, J. Axtell, and J. Browne, n.d.), in *The Literary Property Debate: Six Tracts, 1764-1774*, ed. Stephen Parks (New York: Garland, 1975), 34.

39. On the shift in the uses of the gift, see Andrew Piper, *Dreaming in Books: The Making of the Bibliographic Imagination in the Romantic Age* (Chicago: University of Chicago Press, 2009), 121-25.

40. Lewis Hyde, *The Gift: Imagination and the Erotic Life of Property* (New York: Vintage, 1979), xiv.

41. Samuel Richardson, *The History of Sir Charles Grandison*, ed. Jocelyn Harris (Oxford: Oxford University Press, 1986), 3 parts in one, part 1, vol. 1, letter xxvii, 145; letter xxxix, 211; letter xxxiii, 167.

42. Thomas De Quincey, "Samuel Taylor Coleridge," in *The Works of Thomas De Quincey*, ed. Grevel Lindop, vol. 10, *Articles from Tait's Edinburgh Magazine, 1834-38*, ed. Alina Clej (London: Pickering and Chatto, 2003), 306.

43. Virginia Woolf, *The Essays of Virginia Woolf*, ed. Andrew McNeillie, 4 vols. (London: Hogarth, 1986), 2:463.

44. Margaret Visser, *The Gift of Thanks: The Roots, Persistence, and Paradoxical Meanings of a Social Ritual* (Toronto: HarperCollins, 2008), 70, 209.

45. *Rambler* 64, October 27, 1750, in *The Yale Edition of the Works of Samuel Johnson*, vol. 3, ed. W. J. Bate and Albrecht B. Strauss (New Haven, CT: Yale University Press, 1969), 344. Subsequent references to Johnson's *Rambler* essays will be included in the text and will be to essay number and page numbers from this edition.

46. Jane Austen, *Jane Austen's Letters*, ed. Deirdre Le Faye, 3rd ed. (Oxford: Oxford University Press, 1995), 250. For more on Austen's relationship to author love see my "Jane Austen and

Genius," in *A Companion to Jane Austen*, ed. Claudia L. Johnson and Clara Tuite (Oxford: Wiley-Blackwell, 2009), 391–401.

47. Jane Austen, *Sense and Sensibility*, in R. W. Chapman, ed., *The Oxford Illustrated Jane Austen*, 6 vols. (Oxford: Oxford University Press, 1933), 1:92. For the lack of sensibility Edward evinces in his reading of Cowper, see 1:17–18.

48. Seneca, "Of Favours," in *Moral and Political Essays*, ed. and trans. John M. Cooper and J. F. Procopé (Cambridge: Cambridge University Press, 1995), 296–97.

49. Visser, *Gift of Thanks*, 382.

50. See Margaret Russett, *Fiction and Fakes: Forging Romantic Authenticity, 1760–1845* (Cambridge: Cambridge University Press, 2006); and Susan Stewart, *Crimes of Writing: Problems in the Containment of Representation* (New York: Oxford University Press, 1991).

51. *Johnsonian Miscellanies*, ed. George Birkbeck Hill, 2 vols. (New York: Harper and Brothers, 1897), 2:344. Tyers echoes the same passage of Roscommon's "Essay on Translated Verse" that Hume had echoed in "Of the Standard of Taste." I draw here on Robert DeMaria Jr., *Samuel Johnson and the Life of Reading* (Baltimore: Johns Hopkins University Press, 1997).

52. See Bonnell, "Most Disreputable Trade" and Piper, *Dreaming in Books*, 59.

53. In his 1762 life of James Thomson, for instance, Patrick Murdoch had defended literary biography on the grounds that the public's desire to be more acquainted with authors' histories proceeded not from "mere curiosity, but chiefly from affection and gratitude to those by whom they have been entertained and instructed" ("An Account of the Life and Writings of Mr. James Thomson," in *The Works of James Thomson, with His Last Corrections and Improvements* [London: A. Millar, 1762], 1:i). Johnson's ambivalence about such accounts is more than a function of his worry that the public will be the losers should the life of the author claim attention that should by rights be accorded to that author's works. Certainly, Johnson did believe that the best of an author is "in general to be found in his book" (*Johnsoniana: A Collection of Miscellaneous Anecdotes and Sayings of Dr. Samuel Johnson* [London: Henry G. Bohn, 1845], 113). Here, however, in seeking to nuance how we assess his views on literary biography, I am primarily interested in tracking Johnson's resistance to the personalizing of the aesthetic transaction—the very personalizing that will, among literary biography's later practitioners, seem one motive for the form.

54. Gail Kern Paster, Katherine Rowe, and Mary Floyd-Wilson, introduction to *Reading the Early Modern Passions: Essays in the Cultural History of Emotion* (Philadelphia: University of Pennsylvania Press, 2004), 19.

55. Samuel Johnson, *The Lives of the Most Eminent English Poets*, ed. Roger Lonsdale, 4 vols. (Oxford: Clarendon Press, 2006): 2:149. Subsequent references to *Lives* are to this edition and will henceforth be included parenthetically in the text.

56. On this passage, see Lawrence Lipking, *Samuel Johnson: The Life of an Author* (Cambridge, MA: Harvard University Press, 1998), 283; and Laura Quinney, *Literary Power and the Criteria of Truth* (Gainesville: University Press of Florida, 1995), 61–62.

57. Roger Lonsdale, introduction to *Lives*, 1:110–12; Christine Rees, *Johnson's Milton* (Cambridge: Cambridge University Press, 2010), 126.

58. See Rees, *Johnson's Milton*, 126–27.

59. "We have had too many honey-suckle lives of Milton," Johnson reportedly told Edmond Malone, promising that his "should be in another strain" (quoted in *Johnsonian Miscellanies*, ed. Hill, 1:483).

60. David Schalkwyk, *Shakespeare, Love, and Service* (Cambridge: Cambridge University Press, 2008), 57, 7. In Johnson's day as in Shakespeare's, when domestic service or apprenticeship remained part of the life cycle for the majority of the population, books on household management continued, clinging to a rhetoric that increasingly lagged behind reality, to portray servants primarily as the children of the household and only secondarily as workers exchanging labor for wages. As children, servants owed (so they were reminded) a grateful affection to their masters and mistresses.

61. John Milton, *Paradise Lost*, in *Poetical Works*, ed. Douglas Bush (Oxford: Oxford University Press, 1966), 276, book 4, lines 53-54.

62. John A. Dussinger, "Dr. Johnson's Solemn Response to Beneficence," in *Domestick Privacies: Samuel Johnson and the Art of Biography*, ed. David Wheeler (Lexington: University of Kentucky Press, 1987), 69.

63. Helen Deutsch notes how even in portrayals meant to honor him Johnson "remains proximate to the realm of erotic desire, but never part of it" (*Loving Dr. Johnson* [Chicago: University of Chicago Press, 2005], 4).

64. Samuel Egerton Brydges, *The Autobiography, Times, Opinions and Contemporaries of Sir Egerton Brydges*, 2 vols. (London: Cochrane and M'Crone, 1834), 2:418, 1:171, 1:170.

65. Sonnet by H. F. Cary, printed as a prefatory address to Seward's *Original Sonnets on Various Subjects* (1799), cited in Harriet Guest, *Small Change: Women, Learning, Patriotism, 1750-1810* (Chicago: University of Chicago Press, 2000), 253.

66. In preface to *Poetical Works of Anna Seward*, ed. Walter Scott, 3 vols. (Edinburgh: Ballantyne, 1810), 1:xiii.

67. Letter to Edward Jerningham, February 23, 1801, in *Letters of Anna Seward: Written between the Years 1785 and 1807*, 6 vols. (Edinburgh: A. Constable, 1811), 5:362. Because the letter books that Seward had prepared for posthumous publication were ruthlessly abridged by her literary executor, Sir Walter Scott, and her publisher, Archibald Constable, these published letters provide only a partial representation of her concerns. Tessa Barnard in her recent biography, *Anna Seward: A Constructed Life* (Farnham, UK: Ashgate, 2009), relies therefore on the manuscripts in the National Library of Scotland and elsewhere so as to correct the image of the "book-obsessed figure" (9) that these men produced through their emendations (they tended to leave her belletristic letters intact). As this image conditioned Seward's reputation through the early nineteenth century I have decided to base my discussion on the published edition of 1811.

68. In preface to *Poetical Works of Anna Seward* (Edinburgh: Ballantyne, 1810), 1:xiii.

69. James Boswell, letter in *Gentleman's Magazine* 64, part 1 (January 1794): 33.

70. Such criticism of the *Lives* overlooked the role that the booksellers in charge of the volumes Johnson prefaced had played in determining the volumes' table of contents and their reluctance to shell out for new copyrights.

71. Letter to William Seward, May 17, 1795, *Letters of Anna Seward*, 4:57.

72. James Boswell, letter in *Gentleman's Magazine* 63, part 2 (November 1793): 1011. In *Anna Seward and the End of the Eighteenth Century* (Baltimore: Johns Hopkins University Press, 2012), which appeared just as I was completing this book, Claudia Thomas Kairoff analyzes the controversy between Boswell and Seward in detail: see 243-63.

73. On the morbid deficiency of readers who do not commit to rereading "Lycidas," see To George Hardinge, October 4, 1786, in *Letters of Anna Seward*, 1:191. Seward wrote that among her acquaintance in general she made "Lycidas" a "test-composition" with which to measure a capacity for poetry love or, alternately, detect frigidity (1:191). On Johnson's ingratitude, see To Miss Weston, July 7, 1791, *Letters of Anna Seward*, 3:86 and To William Seward, May 17, 1795, *Letters of Anna Seward*, 4:57. On Johnson's "gloomy spirit," see To Hester Piozzi, March 7, 1788, *Letters of Anna Seward*, 2:43.

74. Anthologized in *Anna Seward*, in *Bluestocking Feminism: Writings of the Bluestocking Circle, 1733-1785*, ed. Gary Kelly, vol. 4, ed. Jennifer Kelly (London: Pickering and Chatto, 1999), 196.

75. Anthologized in ibid. As Kairoff notes, the example of Milton's sonnets, themselves more often devoted to "critical assault" than to "amour," would have licensed Seward when she chose this literary form for her battle against Johnson: *Anna Seward and the End of the Eighteenth Century*, 190.

76. Another motive for the care Seward took to preserve these letters was her conviction that "genius" declared itself not only in print but also on "the page which [was] designed for the eye

288 NOTES TO PAGES 55-60

of friendship" exclusively (Letter to Reverend Berwick, October 6, 1788, *Letters of Anna Seward,* 2:165-66). Seward's resistance to the understanding of the author and critic spawned by an emergent world of professional letters is described in Gillen D'Arcy Wood, "The Female Penseroso: Anna Seward, Sociable Poetry, and the Handelian Consensus," *Modern Language Quarterly* 67, no. 4 (December 2006): 451-77; and John Brewer, *The Pleasures of the Imagination: English Culture in the Eighteenth Century* (New York: Farrar, Straus and Giroux, 1997), 573-612.

77. In many respects the psychodynamics of envy from which Seward (perhaps deludedly) so firmly dissociates her own reading practices had been on the agenda of observers of literary culture since Pope's *Essay on Criticism* (1711). There Pope first posits a moment in the past when praise was issued liberally and then notes that, by contrast, "*Now,* they who reach *Parnassus'* lofty Crown, / Employ their Pains to spurn others down" (*Poetry and Prose of Alexander Pope,* ed. Aubrey Williams [Boston: Houghton Mifflin, 1969], 51, lines 514-15). What was novel in Seward's account of this dynamic was her insistence that the reading public too should be concerned by such rivalries, which would put a damper on their admiration and affection.

78. To Thomas Swift, June 5, 1788, *Letters of Anna Seward,* 2:130; Letter to Court Dewes, January 30, 1786, *Letters of Anna Seward,* 1:115.

79. *Life with the Ladies of Llangollen,* ed. Elizabeth Mavor (Harmondsworth, UK: Viking Penguin, 1984), 40. For more on the Ladies' literary studies, recently recognized as a rich archive for scholars intent on establishing the links connecting literariness and emerging concepts of the sexual person, see also *The Hamwood Papers of the Ladies of Llangollen and Caroline Hamilton,* ed. G. H. Bell (London: Macmillan, 1930).

80. Letter to Rev. Henry White, Sept. 7, 1795, *Letters of Anna Seward,* 4:99-100. See also Seward, *Llangollen Vale, with Other Poems* (London: G. Sael, 1796), 11.

81. Hume, "Of the Delicacy of Taste and Passion," 13.

82. Margaret Ashmun, *The Singing Swan: An Account of Anna Seward and Her Acquaintance with Dr. Johnson, Boswell, and Others of Their Time* (New Haven, CT: Yale University Press, 1931), 279-80.

83. When Southey called on her in Lichfield, as he recollected in a letter, Seward informed him "that she had that minute finished transcribing some verses upon one of my poems": listening "to my own praise and glory set forth, in sonorous rhymes, and declared by one who read them with theatrical effect," Southey found it an effort to "keep down the risible muscles." Quoted in Clarke, *The Rise and Fall of the Woman of Letters* (London: Pimlico, 2004), 16-17. Southey's story is often repeated: see Brewer, *Pleasures,* 575-76, and Wood, "The Female Penseroso," 477. Seward's role in it also seems to be to embody the absurdity that the cultural order assigns to the female fan, the woman of overheated feeling who loves literature too much.

84. *Oxford English Dictionary,* 2nd ed., s.v. "appreciation," www.oed.com, accessed March 27, 2014.

85. In fact, Johnson concludes the point-by-point parallel between Dryden and Pope that he incorporates into the life of the latter by outing himself as someone with predilections and declaring that he foresees that his readership will suspect him, "as I suspect myself, of some partial fondness for the memory of Dryden" (*Lives,* 4:66).

86. To the Reverend Dr. Warner, October 13, 1786, *Letters of Anna Seward,* 1:183. There is perhaps a faint allusion to Thomas Creech's translation of the sixth epistle of the First Book of Horace in Seward's phrase "NOT admiring": The version of "nihil admirari" Creech gives—translating what was an influential statement of Stoicism in the classical world—reads (lines 1-3) "Not to admire, as most are wont to do, / It is the only method that I know, / To make Men happy and to keep 'em so": *The Odes, Satyrs, and Epistles of Horace,* trans. Thomas Creech (London: J. Tonson, 1684), 487. Stoicism was not Seward's cup of tea.

87. William Cowper, *The Task: A Poem in Six Books* (London: J. Johnson, 1785), 266 (British Museum shelf mark C71.c22). Cowper's comments on the Shakespeare Jubilee are in *The Task,*

book 6, lines 664–93, where they are preceded by more overtly hostile comments about the religious trappings of the Handel centenary celebration of 1784.

88. Seneca, "Of Favours," 209.

89. Walter Scott, *The Fortunes of Nigel*, ed. Frank Jordan (Edinburgh: Edinburgh University Press, 2004), 9.

CHAPTER TWO

1. Preface to Samuel Johnson, *A Dictionary of the English Language*, in *The Oxford Authors: Samuel Johnson*, ed. Donald Greene (New York: Oxford University Press, 1984), 328.

2. "I shall be ambitious to have it said of me," states Mr. Spectator on March 12, 1711, "that I have brought Philosophy out of Closets and Libraries, Schools and Colleges, to dwell in Clubs and Assemblies, at Tea-tables and in Coffee-houses": Joseph Addison, *Spectator* 10, in *The Spectator*, ed. Donald Bond, 5 vols. (Oxford: Clarendon, 1965), 1:44.

3. Letter to Joseph Warton, April 19, 1755, *The Correspondence of Thomas Warton*, ed. David Fairer (Athens: University of Georgia Press, 1995), 43.

4. *The Yale Edition of the Works of Samuel Johnson*, vol. 2, *The Idler* and *The Adventurer*, ed. W. J. Bate, John M. Bullitt, and L. F. Powell (New Haven, CT: Yale University Press, 1963), 102. The senior fellow's diary scrupulously records his repeated examinations of his weather-glass (there being, in the eighteenth century, no Internet for an academic to surf); his meals are another recurrent topic. "The inexpressible charms of the elbow-chair" had been touted in the ninth number of *The Idler* (June 10, 1758) by an unknown correspondent who lamented that Johnson had not successfully lived down to his title (29).

5. A. D. Nuttall, *Dead from the Waist Down: Scholars and Scholarship in Literature and the Popular Imagination* (New Haven, CT: Yale University Press, 2003). Nuttall borrows his title from Robert Browning's 1855 poem "A Grammarian's Funeral, Shortly after the Revival of Learning in Europe," line 132. The poem is the song the grammarian's students sing as they carry the corpse of their teacher, who "decided not to Live but to Know" (line 139), to its place of burial.

6. Jonathan Brody Kramnick, "Literary Criticism among the Disciplines," *Eighteenth-Century Studies* 35, no. 3 (Spring 2002): 346.

7. Johnson, preface to *A Dictionary of the English Language*, 318–19.

8. Marjorie Garber, *Academic Instincts* (Princeton, NJ: Princeton University Press, 2001), 48.

9. Richard Hurd, *Letters on Chivalry and Romance*, ed. Edith J. Morley (London: Henry Frowde, 1911), 148. Subsequent quotations from this work appear parenthetically in the text. Cf. Alok Yadav, who outlines how beginning in the later eighteenth century it will be a mark of the modern critic to insist on "the essential uniqueness and incompatibility of the classical world, the Biblical world, the medieval European world, the world of the Renaissance, and that of modern Europe, and of the literary art produced in each of those 'worlds'" (*Before the Empire of English: Literature, Provinciality, and Nationalism in Eighteenth-Century Britain* [Basingstoke, UK: Palgrave Macmillan, 2004], 171).

10. Edmund Spenser, *The Faerie Queene*, in *Poetical Works*, ed. J. C. Smith and E. De Selincourt (Oxford: Oxford University Press, 1970), 139, book 2, canto 12, stanza 80.

11. To Thomas Warton, July 17, 1754, in *Letters of Samuel Johnson*, ed. Bruce Redford, 5 vols. (Princeton, NJ: Princeton University Press, 1992), 1:81.

12. This is the honor that René Wellek's *The Rise of English Literary History* (Chapel Hill: University of North Carolina Press, 1941) bestowed on Warton—"the first historian of English Literature in the full sense of the term" (201).

13. Richard Mant, "Memoirs of the Life and Writings of Thomas Warton," in *The Poetical Works of the Late Thomas Warton*, ed. Richard Mant (Oxford: The University Press for W. Hanweel and J. Parker, and F. and C. Rivington, London, 1802), xxviii.

14. Thomas Warton, *Observations on the Fairy Queen of Spenser*, 2 vols., 2nd ed. (London: R. and J. Dodsley, 1762), 2:84n, the edition that is hereafter cited in the text, as *Observations*, and by volume and page number; Thomas Tyrwhitt, preface, *Canterbury Tales*, 3 vols. (Oxford: J. Cooke, and G. G. and J. Robinson, 1795), 1:117.

15. Alexander Pope, "A Gothic Library!": *The Dunciad in Four Books*, in *Poetry and Prose of Alexander Pope*, ed. Aubrey Williams (Boston: Houghton Mifflin, 1969), 313, book 1, line 145; "all such reading as was never read" in ibid., 365, book 4, line 250.

16. In D. Nichol Smith, ed., *Eighteenth-Century Essays on Shakespeare*, 2nd. ed. (Oxford: Clarendon, 1963), 151-202; quotation on 201.

17. "On the Revival of a Taste for Ancient Literature," *Blackwood's Magazine* 4 (1818), quoted in David Fairer's introduction to *Thomas Warton's History of English Poetry*, 4 vols. (1774-81; rept. London: Routledge/Thoemmes, 1998), 1:12. Subsequent references to the *History* are to this facsimile edition.

18. Jonathan Brody Kramnick, *Making the English Canon: Print-Capitalism and the Cultural Past, 1700-1770* (Cambridge: Cambridge University Press, 1998), 4.

19. Walter Scott, "On Ellis's Specimens of the Early English Poets," *Edinburgh Review*, 1804; rept. in *The Miscellaneous Prose Works of Sir Walter Scott*, vol. 17, *Periodical Criticism, Volume 1, Poetry* (Edinburgh: Robert Cadell, 1843), 4-5.

20. Joseph M. Levine, *The Battle of the Books: History and Literature in the Augustan Age* (Ithaca, NY: Cornell University Press, 1991), 83.

21. Thomas Percy, *Reliques of Ancient English Poetry*, 2 vols. (London: J. M. Dent, 1906), 1:2. Nick Groom's *The Making of Percy's* Reliques (Oxford: Clarendon, 1999) is a good guide to the split personality of the *Reliques*. See also David Matthews, *The Making of Middle English, 1765-1910* (Minneapolis: University of Minnesota Press, 1999), 3-24.

22. Quoted in James Boswell, *Life of Johnson*, introd. Pat Rogers, ed. R. W. Chapman (Oxford: Oxford University Press, 1980), 937. See Simon Jarvis, *Scholars and Gentlemen: Shakespearean Textual Criticism and Representations of Scholarly Labour, 1725-1765* (Oxford: Clarendon, 1995). The *Critical Review* of November 1782 ascribed to Thomas Ritson, the son of a corn merchant's clerk and of that merchant's servant, a "mind anxious about little things, intent only on the examination of extrinsic and unimportant parts, and unable to comprehend the whole" and dismissed Ritson's research into medieval romance as "minute investigations" (cited in Bertrand H. Bronson, *Joseph Ritson: Scholar-at-Arms*, 2 vols. [Berkeley: University of California Press, 1938], 1:336). As we'll see later in this chapter, Ritson came to public attention in the 1780s as the most severe of Warton's critics.

23. John Pinkerton, *An Essay on Medals* (1784), cited in Rosemary Sweet, *Antiquaries: The Discovery of the Past in Eighteenth-Century Britain* (London: Hambledon, 2004), 356n72.

24. Scott identifies Warton and Ellis as the cold-tempered, sterile-minded antiquaries that Godwin has in mind in his review of the *Life of Chaucer*: *Periodical Criticism*, 17:72. In lamenting the coldness of antiquaries, "who, by their phlegmatic and desultory industry, have brought discredit upon" the "science," Godwin was also announcing that his was meant to be a "work of a new species": *Life of Geoffrey Chaucer, the Early English Poet*, 2 vols. (London: Richard Phillips, 1803), 1:x.

25. Isaac D'Israeli, *A Dissertation upon Anecdotes* (London: C. and G. Kearsley, 1793), 5; Johnson, preface to *The Plays of William Shakespeare*, in *Oxford Authors: Samuel Johnson*, 455.

26. Letter to George Hardinge, October 4, 1786, in *Letters of Anna Seward: Written between the Years 1785 and 1807*, 6 vols. (Edinburgh: A. Constable, 1811), 1:191.

27. David Simpson, *The Academic Postmodern and the Rule of Literature: A Report on Half-Knowledge* (Chicago: University of Chicago Press, 1995), 81.

28. Kramnick, *Making the English Canon*, 144.

29. Louise Fradenburg and Carla Freccero, preface to *Premodern Sexualities*, ed. Fradenburg and Freccero (New York: Routledge, 1996), xix.

30. Aranye O. Fradenburg, "'So That We May Speak of Them': Enjoying the Middle Ages," *New*

Literary History 28, no. 2 (Spring 1997): 214. Fradenburg's essay is republished in revised form as the epilogue to her *Sacrifice Your Love: Psychoanalysis, Historicism, Chaucer* (Minneapolis: University of Minnesota Press, 2002): the bibliographical record for this more recent volume gives her name as L. O. Aranye Fradenburg.

31. As Slavoj Žižek, on whom Fradenburg draws, explains, "What we conceal by imputing to the Other the theft of enjoyment is the traumatic fact that we never possessed what was allegedly stolen from us." Put otherwise, lovable works of literature elude the monopoly possession that they also appear to solicit—the scandal that the thief of enjoyment publicizes is that *nobody* owns them ("Eastern Europe's Republics of Gilead," *New Left Review* 183 [1990]: 54).

32. David Mallet, "Of Verbal Criticism. An Epistle to Mr. Pope, Occasioned by Theobald's Shakespeare and Bentley's Milton," quoted in Jarvis, *Scholars and Gentlemen*, 80n68. See also Marcus Walsh, *Shakespeare, Milton, and Eighteenth-Century Literary Editing* (Cambridge: Cambridge University Press, 1997).

33. On this ethic of sacrifice see Fradenburg, "Enjoying the Middle Ages," and Nuttall, *Dead from the Waist Down*.

34. Georg Simmel, *The Sociology of Georg Simmel*, trans. and introd. Kurt H. Wolff (New York: Free Press, 1950), 330.

35. Johnson, preface to Shakespeare, 453.

36. Jürgen Habermas, *The Structural Transformation of the Public Sphere*, trans. Thomas Burger (Cambridge, MA: MIT Press, 1989), especially 44–51; for Kramnick's citations, see *Making the English Canon*, 4–6; 21–22; 28–29. See also Michael McKeon, *The Secret History of Domesticity: Public, Private, and the Division of Knowledge* (Baltimore: Johns Hopkins University Press, 2005), 110–12 and 219–68.

37. On Warton's sanctuary at the Bodleian see I. G. Philip, "Libraries and the University Press," in *The History of the University of Oxford*, ed. L. S. Sutherland and L. G. Mitchell, vol. 5, *The Eighteenth Century* (Oxford: Clarendon, 1986), 732. In fact, the carrels in modern academic libraries—though that particular term for our cubicle homes-away-from-home doesn't, the *Oxford English Dictionary* explains, enter usage until the twentieth century—hearken back to the enclosures, known as "carols," that medieval builders sometimes built into monastic cloisters. Each time we visit our carrels to escape students and return to our "own work," we have reason to recall Enlightenment complaints about the dark ages of cloistered virtues, when learning suffered because priestly institutions set it apart from the world. *Oxford English Dictionary*, 2nd ed., s. v. "carrel," www.oed.com, accessed March 27, 2014.

38. I cite the English translation: *The odes, epodes, and carmen seculare of Horace, in Latin and English: with a translation of Dr. Bentley's notes*, 2 vols. (London: Bernard Lintott, 1713); 1:11–13. The passage is discussed by Levine, *Battle of the Books*, 248.

39. James Boswell, *The Journal of a Tour to the Hebrides*, ed. Peter Levi (Harmondsworth, UK: Penguin, 1984), 180.

40. These titles, of works that Hearne published alongside his 1724 edition of a thirteenth-century manuscript chronicle by Robert of Gloucester, are supplied by William Huddesford, ed., *The Lives of Those Eminent Antiquaries: John Leland, Thomas Hearne, and Anthony à Wood*, 2 vols. (Oxford: J. and J. Fletcher, 1772), 1:79–85. (The first volume is not paginated continuously, but recommences its page numbering with the opening of the life of Hearne.) Hearne should, more fairly, be remembered, as well, as an insightful commentator on the problems of authorial attribution inherent in the scribal culture of the Middle Ages.

41. Susan Manning, "Antiquarianism, the Scottish Science of Man, and the Emergence of Modern Disciplinarity," in *Scotland and the Borders of Romanticism*, ed. Leith Davis, Ian Duncan, and Janet Sorensen (Cambridge: Cambridge University Press, 2004), 72.

42. Scott, "On Ellis's Specimens of the Early English Poets," *Periodical Criticism*, 17:4.

43. Scott, "On Ellis's Specimens of Early English Metrical Romances . . . and Ancient English Metrical Romances Selected by Joseph Ritson" (1806), rept. in *Periodical Criticism*, 17:19.

292 NOTES TO PAGES 81–89

44. Shenstone's reputation for exquisite taste had made him a useful addition to the ad hoc editorial committee that advised Percy as he attempted to write the popular oral canon of balladeering into the high-culture story of the British literary tradition.

45. Thomas Percy, *The Percy Letters*, 7 vols. (New Haven, CT: Yale University Press, 1977), 7:136.

46. Georg Simmel, *The Philosophy of Money*, trans. Tom Bottomore and David Frisby (London: Routledge Kegan Paul, 1978), 150. I am also inspired here by Manning's suggestion that antiquaries are readable as "the misers of historiography" ("Antiquarianism," 67).

47. Percy, *Reliques*, 1:1; Groom, *Making of Percy's* Reliques, 8; 38.

48. Scott, Review of Godwin's *Life of Chaucer*, in *Periodical Criticism*, 17:79.

49. *Remarks Critical and Illustrative, on the Text and Notes of the Last Edition of Shakespeare*, cited in Bronson, *Joseph Ritson*, 2:389. After traveling to Revolutionary France in 1791 Ritson declared his admiration for the nationalization of aristocratic libraries occurring there (ibid., 1:145).

50. The differences between Ritson and Percy involved, for a start, questions of editorial method, Percy subjecting his material to "improvements" prior to publication and Ritson in his own collections of song and romance promising authenticity.

51. *Observations on the Three First Volumes of the History of English Poetry in a Familiar Letter to the Author* (London: J. Stockdale, 1782), Advertisement.

52. The remarks are found in a Ritson manuscript and paraphrased in Bronson, *Joseph Ritson*, 1:331. On the memorial bookcase, see ibid., 1:130.

53. The dissertations are unpaginated.

54. William R. McKelvy, *The English Cult of Literature: Devoted Readers, 1774–1880* (Charlottesville: University of Virginia Press, 2007), 64. For additional commentaries on how Warton's *History* is complicated by this impulse to oppose learning and the poetical imagination, see Trevor Ross, *The Making of the English Literary Canon, from the Middle Ages to the Late Eighteenth Century* (Montreal: McGill-Queen's University Press, 1998), 261–67; Lawrence Lipking, *The Ordering of the Arts in Eighteenth-Century England* (Princeton, NJ: Princeton University Press, 1970), 375; James Simpson, "The Rule of Medieval Imagination," in *Images, Idolatry and Iconoclasm in Late Medieval England*, ed. Jeremy Dimmick et al. (Oxford: Oxford University Press, 2002), 4–24.

55. In 1745 the young Thomas Warton began drafting a never-completed "Essay on Romantic Poetry." That this title seems to us better suited to an essay that somebody—say, a young Matthew Arnold—might draft in 1845 confirms how thoroughly we have forgotten the eighteenth century's success in constructing the very critical paradigm that would ultimately dismiss it as an age lacking in romance, capable only of producing "classics of our prose" rather than of our poetry.

56. The description of historiography as a discourse of separation comes from Michel de Certeau, *The Writing of History*, trans. Tom Conley (New York: Columbia University Press, 1988), 4.

57. John Milton, *Poems upon Several Occasions, English, Italian, and Latin with Translations*, ed. Thomas Warton (London: Dodsley, 1785), 95n.

58. "Milton . . . may be reckoned an old English poet," Warton declared in his 1785 edition (xxi). On the historical revisionism that reinvented Milton as an Elizabethan author and enabled Milton's eighteenth-century readers to forget that he was actually the contemporary of John Dryden, see Jack Lynch, *The Age of Elizabeth in the Age of Johnson* (Cambridge: Cambridge University Press, 2003), 145–58; and Douglas Lane Patey, "The Eighteenth Century Invents the Canon," *Modern Language Studies* 18, no. 1 (1998): 17–37, especially 27–28.

59. Godwin, *Life of Chaucer*, 2:561.

60. Published in *The Museum: or the Literary and Historical Register*, no. 19 (December 6, 1746): 176–79.

61. *The Poetical Works of the Late Thomas Warton*, ed. Richard Mant (Oxford: Oxford University Press, 1802), 87n; Johnson's letter of June 10, 1755, addressed to Joseph Warton, *Correspondence of Thomas Warton*, 53.

62. Edmond Malone, preface to *Plays and Poems of William Shakspeare*, 10 vols. (London: Rivington, Davis, White, Longman, Law et al., 1790), 1:lvi; William Henry Ireland, *Miscellaneous Pa-*

pers and Legal Instruments under the Hand and Seal of William Shakspeare (London: Egerton, White, Leigh, Sotheby, Robson, Faulder, and Sael, 1796), xviii.

63. Warton in the *History* knowingly invites this diagnosis, as Fairer has noted (introduction, 9), by describing his narrative process as a journey and then avowing his susceptibility to being "seduced" from the straight line of his narrative path. Hence, for example, the passage in volume 3, in which Warton announces himself to have been seduced into "an irresistible digression" by "the magic of Shakespeare's name" (3:295).

64. The fascination with "Sir Thopas" as a premonitory *Don Quixote* was widespread: see Warton, *History* 1:433; Hurd, *Letters*, 147; Percy, *Reliques*, 1:294. I quote the recollection of "The Squire's Tale" in Milton's "Il Penseroso" (*Milton: Poetical Works*, ed. Douglas Bush [Oxford: Oxford University Press, 1966], 94–95, lines 110 and 114). Rita Copeland mentions "Sir Thopas" while tracing how romance from its medieval beginning always self-consciously archaized its thematic content: see "Between Romans and Romantics," *Texas Studies in Language and Literature* 33, no. 2 (Summer 1991): 215–24.

65. Ian Duncan, "Authenticity Effects: The Work of Fiction in Romantic Scotland," *South Atlantic Quarterly* 102, no. 1 (Winter 2003): 107.

66. "We are upon enchanted ground, my friend, and you are to think yourself well used that I detain you no longer in this fearful circle": Hurd, *Letters*, 113.

67. Leigh Hunt, *Literary Criticism*, ed. Lawrence Huston Houtchens and Carolyn Washburn Houtchens (New York: Columbia University Press, 1956), 456.

68. Harriet Guest, "The Wanton Muse: Politics and Gender in Gothic Theory after 1760," in *Beyond Romanticism: New Approaches to Texts and Contexts, 1780–1832*, ed. Stephen Copley and John Whale (London: Routledge, 1993), 125; Johnson, "Life of Dryden," in *The Lives of the Most Eminent English Poets*, ed. Roger Lonsdale, 4 vols. (Oxford: Clarendon, 2006), 2:120.

69. Kramnick, *Making*, 214; Guest, "Wanton Muse," 125.

70. Samuel Johnson to Thomas Warton, April 14, 1758, in Fairer, ed., *Correspondence*, 70.

71. The poem's occasion was Reynolds's design of a new window for New College's fourteenth-century chapel. I cite the second, corrected edition of 1783, from *Eighteenth-Century Poetry: An Annotated Edition*, ed. David Fairer and Christine Gerrard (Oxford, UK: Blackwell, 1999), 378.

72. Guest, "Wanton Muse," 119.

73. Ted Underwood, "Romantic Historicism and the Afterlife," *PMLA* 117, no. 2 (March 2002): 245. On Celtic, druidical, and fairy matters, I cite here a letter written in 1762 by Elizabeth Montagu, so-called Queen of the Bluestockings, following her reading of Hurd and Warton: *Bluestocking Feminism: Writings of the Bluestocking Circle*, ed. Gary Kelly, vol. 1, *Elizabeth Montagu*, ed. Elizabeth Eger (London: Pickering and Chatto, 1999), 164.

74. Walpole is cited in Groom, *Making of Percy's Reliques*, 241.

75. I quote William Shenstone, *The School-Mistress, A Poem, In Imitation of Spenser* (London: R. Dodsley, 1742), n.p., stanza 13. The poem's complicated history of revision and reprinting is traced in Adela Pinch, "Learning What Hurts: Romanticism, Pedagogy, Violence," in *Lessons of Romanticism*, ed. Thomas Pfau and Robert F. Gleckner (Durham, NC: Duke University Press, 1999), 413–28.

76. Godwin, *Life of Chaucer*, 1:39.

77. Boswell, *Life of Johnson*, 35–36.

78. In J. G. Lockhart, *Memoirs of the Life of Sir Walter Scott*, 8 vols. (Philadelphia: Carey, Lea, and Blanchard, 1838), 1:29; Groom, *Making of Percy's* Reliques, 237–38. I am guided here by the account of Scott and Percy's *Reliques* given in Stephen Newman, *Ballad Collection, Lyric, and the Canon: The Call of the Popular from the Restoration to the New Criticism* (Philadelphia: University of Pennsylvania Press, 2007), 185–87.

79. See Michèle Cohen, " 'To Think, to Compare, to Combine, to Methodise': Girls' Education in Enlightenment Britain," in *Women, Gender, and Enlightenment*, ed. Sarah Knott and Barbara Taylor (Basingstoke, UK: Palgrave Macmillan, 2005), 224–42.

80. Monsieur de St. Palaye, *Memoirs of Ancient Chivalry, to Which Are Added the Anecdotes of*

the Times, from the Romance Writers and Historians of those Ages, trans. Susannah Dobson (London: Dodsley, 1784), xviii.

81. Clara Reeve, *The Progress of Romance*, 2 vols. (Colchester, UK: W. Keymer, 1785), 1:8.

82. David Fairer writes superbly about these traditions in "Oxford and the Literary World," in *History of the University of Oxford*, vol. 5, *The Eighteenth Century*, 779–806, demonstrating how eighteenth-century Oxford's uneasy, even guilty, relationship with the outside world may be read as "a fascinating exemplar of the wider eighteenth-century debate about the function of literature" (779). The contention that "good cheer, especially good liquor [was] the very life and support of Jacobitism in this kingdom," originating in E. Bentham's 1749 *Letter to a Fellow* and repeated in the Tory don William King's reply to the pamphlet, is cited in W. R. Ward, *Georgian Oxford: University Politics in the Eighteenth Century* (Oxford: Oxford University Press, 1958), 164.

83. This information comes from the manuscript autobiography of Francis Newbery, excerpted in Charles Welsh, *A Bookseller of the Last Century, Being Some Account of the Life of John Newbery* (New York: E. P. Dutton, 1885), 67–68, and from John Nichol, *Literary Anecdotes of the Eighteenth Century*, 6 vols. (London: For the author, 1812), 3:702.

84. Nicholas Amhurst, *Terrae-Filius: Or, the Secret History of the University of Oxford, in Several Essays* (London: R. Francklin, 1726), 132, 135, 139.

85. Richard Graves, "Life of Shenstone," in *Poems, by William Shenstone* (Manchester, UK: G. Nicholson, 1798), iv.

86. Thomas Frognall Dibdin, *Reminiscences of a Literary Life*, 2 vols. (London: J. Major, 1836), 1:105, 1: 95, 1:103.

87. "The passion of secrecy . . . gives the group-form depending on it, a significance that is far superior to the significance of content": Simmel, *Sociology of Georg Simmel*, 363.

88. Amhurst, *Terrae-Filius*, 211. Warton appears to have been highly aware of secrecy's capacity, explored later by Simmel in his sociology, to engender "the possibility of a second world alongside the manifest world" (*Sociology of Georg Simmel*, 360).

89. *Life and Letters of Gilbert White of Selborne*, ed. Rashleigh Holt-White, 2 vols. (London: John Murray, 1901), 1:110.

90. Arthur Johnston, *Enchanted Ground: The Study of Medieval Romance in the Eighteenth Century* (London: Athlone Press, 1964), 25.

91. Ritson, *Observations*, 48.

92. Ibid., viii.

CHAPTER THREE

1. I owe the knowledge of Malone's memorandum to *Correspondence of Thomas Warton*, ed. David Fairer (Athens: University of Georgia Press, 1995), 512n.

2. Walter Benjamin, "Unpacking My Library," in *Illuminations*, ed. Hannah Arendt, trans. Harry Zohn (New York: Schocken, 1969), 64; see also Bill Brown, "The Collecting Mania," *University of Chicago Magazine* 94, no. 1 (October 2001), http://magazine/uchicago/edu/0110/features.mania .html.

3. Kristian Jensen, *Revolution and the Antiquarian Book: Reshaping the Past, 1780–1815* (Cambridge: Cambridge University Press, 2011), 87. See also H. J. Jackson, *Romantic Readers: The Evidence of Marginalia* (New Haven, CT: Yale University Press, 2005), especially 198–248.

4. Consequently, as Jon Klancher has outlined, the debut of what promised to be a new book history was almost immediately succeeded by its demise, and when a "historiography of print, books, and reading" was assembled in the 1950s its practitioners basically started again from scratch: "Wild Bibliography: The Rise and Fall of Book History in Nineteenth-Century Britain," in *Bookish Histories: Books, Literature, and Commercial Modernity, 1700–1900*, ed. Ina Ferris and Paul Keen (Basingstoke, UK: Palgrave Macmillan, 2009), 20.

5. Ibid., 27.

6. *The Bibliographical and Retrospective Miscellany* (London: John Wilson, 1830), 96; Philip Dormer Stanhope, fourth Earl of Chesterfield, Letters to his son, March 19, 1750, and January 10, 1749, in *Lord Chesterfield's Letters*, ed. David Roberts (Oxford: Oxford University Press, 1992), 201, 131.

7. Barbara Benedict, *Curiosity: A Cultural History of Early Modern Inquiry* (Chicago: University of Chicago Press, 2001), 3.

8. John Ferriar, "The Bibliomania," in *Illustrations of Sterne: With Other Essays and Verses*, 2nd ed. (London: Cadell and Davies, 1812), 212. An earlier version of this poem was published in 1809.

9. Andrew Piper, *Dreaming in Books: The Making of the Bibliographic Imagination in the Romantic Age* (Chicago: University of Chicago Press, 2009), 12.

10. Bernhard Metz, "Bibliomania and the Folly of Reading," *Comparative Critical Studies* 5, no. 2 (2008): 250.

11. Ibid.; Paul Keen, *Literature, Commerce, and the Spectacle of Modernity, 1750–1800* (Cambridge: Cambridge University Press, 2012), 83.

12. Samuel Egerton Brydges, *The Autobiography, Times, Opinions and Contemporaries of Sir Egerton Brydges*, 2 vols. (London: Cochrane and M' Crane, 1834), 2:196, 2:194.

13. The quoted phrase is also Brydges's: ibid., 1:25.

14. "The entire and constant possession of the object" of one's passion is in one dictionary of the late eighteenth century the trait that distinguishes "love" from "gallantry": see John Trusler, *The Difference between Words Esteemed Synonymous in the English Language, and the Proper Choice of Them Determined*, 2 vols. (Dublin: R. Moncrieffe, 1776), 2:54.

15. Thomas Frognall Dibdin, *Bibliomania; or Book-Madness: A Bibliographical Romance in Six Parts* (London: for the author, 1811), 745. Subsequent references to this text will be to *Bibliomania* (1811), since I will also be referring later in this chapter to Dibdin's first (and briefer) 1809 edition of *Bibliomania; or Book-Madness*.

16. L. Annaeus Seneca, *Minor Dialogues Together with the Dialogue on Clemency*, trans. Aubrey Stewart (London: George Bell, 1889), 270.

17. Ibid., 269.

18. I owe the distinction between obsessed and diseased human psyches to Lennard Davis's brief discussion of the bibliomania in *Obsession: A History* (Chicago: University of Chicago Press, 2008), 124.

19. Michel Foucault, *The History of Sexuality, Volume 1: An Introduction*, trans. Robert Hurley (New York: Vintage, 1980), 43; Ferriar, *Illustrations of Sterne*, 201; Louis Bollioud de Mermet, *De la Bibliomanie* (The Hague, 1761), 58. The article on "Bibliotaphe" in volume 17 of Diderot and D'Alembert's *Encyclopédie* calls the sufferers of the "bibliotaphie" the "peste" of letters, ascribing their accumulation of books to their selfish desire to prevent others from making use of them: see Metz, "Bibliomania," 259. Michael Robinson analyzes the erotic, campy, and queer dimensions of the bibliomania in his "Ornamental Gentlemen: Thomas F. Dibdin, Romantic Bibliomania, and Romantic Sexuality," *European Romantic Review* 22, no. 5 (October 2011): 685–706.

20. Isaac D'Israeli, "The Man of One Book," in *Literary Curiosities*, 2nd ser. (London: John Murray, 1824), 3:121.

21. See Walter Scott, *The Fortunes of Nigel*, ed. Frank Jordan (Edinburgh: Edinburgh University Press, 2004), 267; Scott, *The Antiquary*, ed. David Hewitt (Edinburgh: Edinburgh University Press, 1995), 23–24; Scott, *Woodstock, or, The Cavalier: A Tale of the Year 1651*, ed. Tony Inglis (Edinburgh: Edinburgh University Press, 1995), 23–25.

22. Dibdin, *Bibliomania* (1811), vi.

23. Thomas Frognall Dibdin, *The Bibliographical Decameron, or Ten Days Pleasant Discourse upon Illuminated Manuscripts and Subjects Connected with Early Engraving, Typography, and Bibliography*, 3 vols. (London: W. Bulmer, 1817), 3:50. My list of the newspapers reporting on the auction is borrowed from Jensen, *Revolution and the Antiquarian Book*, 129.

24. Didbin, *Bibliographical Decameron*, 3:52.

25. Thomas Frognall Dibdin, *Reminiscences of a Literary Life*, 2 vols. (London: J. Major, 1836), 1:357.

26. Ibid., 1:356. I draw here on the assessments of the Roxburghe sale's significance offered in David Matthews, *The Making of Middle English, 1765–1810* (Minneapolis: University of Minnesota Press, 1999), 85–87; and Jensen, *Revolution and the Antiquarian Book*, 127–31.

27. The quoted passage, lifted from the *Morning Chronicle*'s report on the sale, is found in Dibdin's *Bibliographical Decameron*, as are the prices: see 3:52, 3:65n, 3:57n. On Caxton pages being sold as wastepaper, see Jensen, *Revolution and the Antiquarian Book*, 80.

28. *A Catalogue of the Library of the Late John Duke of Roxburghe, Arranged by G. and W. Nichol, Booksellers to His Majesty, Pall-Mall* (London: G. and W. Nichol, 1812), 6.

29. Ferriar, *Illustrations of Sterne*, 203.

30. Jensen, *Revolution and the Antiquarian Book*, 75.

31. Thomas Frognall Dibdin, *Bibliomania; or, Book-Madness*, (London: Longman, Hurst, Rees, and Orme, 1809), 14. Subsequent references to this edition will appear parenthetically in the text of this chapter.

32. *Oxford English Dictionary*, s.v. "hobby," www.oed.com, accessed March 27, 2014.

33. The more direct connection between the bibliomania and modern English studies came about as a consequence of the founding of the exclusive book club and printing society, the Roxburghe Club, which came into being in June 1812 when Dibdin and his patron, Earl Spencer, invited a group of "choice bibliomaniacal spirits" to a tavern dinner organized in anticipation of the bidding war that was about to erupt over the Roxburghe Boccaccio. At that dinner the group agreed to an arrangement, which continues to this day, that saw each club member underwriting on an annual basis the reprinting, later in facsimile form, of a rare text from his library and its gratis distribution among the membership. This scheme contributed indirectly to the later nineteenth-century emergence of a professionalized medieval studies. Frederick J. Furnivall, later of the Early English Text Society, got his start in the 1860s editing for the club.

34. William St. Clair, *The Reading Nation in the Romantic Period* (Cambridge: Cambridge University Press, 2004), 115; Mike Goode, *Sentimental Masculinity and the Rise of History, 1790–1890* (Cambridge: Cambridge University Press, 2009), 207n43.

35. *Bibliosophia; or, Book-Wisdom. Containing Some Account of the Pride, Pleasures, and Privileges of That Glorious Vocation, Book-Collecting* (London: William Miller, 1810), 30; ellipses in the original. The *Oxford Dictionary of National Biography* ascribes "Bibliosophia" (published pseudonymously, "By an Aspirant") to the clergyman James Beresford.

36. Neil Kenny, "Books in Space and Time: Bibliomania and Early Modern Histories of Learning and 'Literature' in France," *Modern Language Quarterly* 61, no. 2 (June 2000): 256.

37. John Plotz, "Out of Circulation: For and Against Book Collecting," *Southwest Review* 84, no. 4 (Fall 1999): 468.

38. Philip Connell, "Bibliomania: Book Collecting, Cultural Politics, and the Rise of Literary Heritage in Romantic Britain," *Representations* 71 (Summer 2000): 24–47; see especially 24–30.

39. Jane Austen, *Pride and Prejudice*, vol. 2, *The Novels of Jane Austen*, ed. R. W. Chapman, 3rd ed. (Oxford: Oxford University Press, 1933), 38.

40. *The Peerage of England*, rev. ed, 9 vols. (London: Rivington, 1812), 1:x (I owe this reference to Connell, "Bibliomania," 27); Dibdin, *Bibliographical Decameron*, 3:65n.

41. Jon Klancher, "Wild Bibliography," 21. The deluge had been prefigured when the books from the libraries of the Jesuit order, suppressed in 1767 by multiple European kingdoms and principalities, entered the market.

42. Connell, "Bibliomania," 28.

43. I adapt here Jonah Siegel's helpful remarks on late twentieth-century cultural theory in his *Desire and Excess: The Nineteenth-Century Culture of Art* (Princeton, NJ: Princeton University Press, 2000), 283–84n1.

44. The author of *Bibliosophia* even claims to view Ovid as a prototype for Dibdin, on the grounds that the former similarly advocates for the very pursuit that he has pretended to identify as a disease. Ovid, this author notes, had both presented a *Remedium Amoris* that might work a cure upon his reader and "in the same scroll" supplied "the most copious instructions on '*De Arte Amandi*'": *Bibliosophia*, 3.

45. John Ferriar, See *The Bibliomania: An Epistle, to Richard Heber, Esq.* (London: T. Cadell and W. Davies, 1809), 11. These lines do not appear in the revised version of the poem included in Ferriar's 1812 *Illustrations of Sterne.*

46. Leigh Hunt, "Pocket-Books and Keepsakes," in *The Keepsake for 1828*, ed. Frederick Mansel Reynolds (London: Hurst, Chance, 1827), 12; "My Books," in *Essays and Miscellanies Selected from the Indicator and Companion*, 3 vols. in 1 (New York: Derby and Jackson, 1857), 2:136. Under ordinary circumstances in early nineteenth-century English culture "kissing the book" was an act involving a New Testament and a person called to testify in front of a court of law; Hunt rewrites here to wayward ends a ceremony of subjection intended to confirm how the state and the state church define and incorporate the individual.

47. Leigh Hunt, "Men Wedded to Books," *Indicator* 32 (May 17, 1820), in *The Indicator*, 2 vols. (London: Joseph Appleyard, 1820), 1:250.

48. Ibid., 1:251.

49. Charles Lamb, "Readers against the Grain," in *The Works of Charles and Mary Lamb*, 5 vols., ed. E. V. Lucas (New York: G. P. Putman's; London: Methuen, 1903), 1:272–73.

50. Compare Plotz, "Out of Circulation" and Leah Price's discussion of "the repellent book," in *How to Do Things with Books in Victorian Britain* (Princeton, NJ: Princeton University Press, 2012), 45–71.

51. Hunt, "My Books," in *Essays and Miscellanies* 2:138. Subsequent references to this essay will appear parenthetically in the text, keyed to page number.

52. Lamb, "Detached Thoughts on Books and Reading," in *Works of Charles and Mary Lamb*, 2:172. Subsequent references to this essay appear parenthetically in the text of this chapter. On the essay as a reader's genre see Scott Black, *Of Essays and Reading in Early Modern Britain* (Basingstoke, UK: Palgrave Macmillan, 2006).

53. I take this phrase from Ina Ferris's "Antiquarian Authorship: D'Israeli's Miscellany of Literary Curiosity and the Question of Secondary Genres," *Studies in Romanticism* 45, no. 4 (Winter 2006): 534.

54. Thomas De Quincey, "Recollections of Charles Lamb, II," in *The Works of Thomas De Quincey*, ed. Grevel Lindop, vol. 10, *Articles from* Tait's Edinburgh Magazine, *1834–38*, ed. Alina Clej (London: Pickering and Chatto, 2003), 274.

55. William Hazlitt, "Introduction," *Retrospective Review* 1 (1820): xiii. Cf. William Hazlitt, "On Reading Old Books" (first published in the *London Magazine*, February 1821), in *The Complete Works of William Hazlitt*, 21 vols., ed. P. P. Howe (London: J. M. Dent, 1931), 12:220.

56. Margaret Russett, *De Quincey's Romanticism: Canonical Minority and the Forms of Transmission* (Cambridge: Cambridge University Press, 1997), 9; see also John Guillory, *Cultural Capital: The Problem of Literary Canon Formation* (Chicago: University of Chicago Press, 1993), 55.

57. I receive guidance here from Jacqueline George, "'All These Lovers of Books Have Themselves Become Books!': Leigh Hunt in His Library," *Eighteenth Century* 50, nos. 2–3 (Summer/Fall 2010): 245–61.

58. Lamb, "New Year's Eve," in *Works of Charles and Mary Lamb*, 2:30.

59. As Russett argues in *De Quincey's Romanticism*, 122.

60. Lamb, "The Two Races of Men," in *Works of Charles and Mary Lamb*, 2:25. Compare the passage in De Quincey's *Confessions of an English Opium Eater* (published in the *London Magazine* in 1821) in which he paints the picture of "the interior of a scholar's library, in a cottage among the mountains," that library being his own: *Confessions of an English Opium-Eater and Other Writings*, ed. Grevel Lindop (Oxford : Oxford University Press, 1985), 60–61.

61. Hazlitt, "On Reading Old Books," in *Complete Works*, 12:224; Hunt, *Autobiography of Leigh Hunt*, new ed. (London: Smith, Elder, 1885), 69.

62. Price, *How to Do Things with Books*, 2.

63. Peter Manning, "Detaching Lamb's Thoughts," *Prose Studies* 25, no. 1 (April 2002): 140.

64. Russett, *De Quincey's Romanticism*, 213.

65. De Quincey, "The Street Companion," in *The Works of Thomas De Quincey*, ed. Grevel Lindop, vol. 4, *Articles and Translations from the London Magazine; Walladmor*, ed. Frederick Burwick (London: Pickering and Chatto, 2000), 450. Subsequent references appear parenthetically in the text. I owe this reference to Connell, "Bibliomania."

66. Thomas Frognall Dibdin, *The Library Companion; or, the Young Man's Guide, and the Old Man's Comfort, in the Choice of a Library* (London: Hardy, Triphook, and Lepard, 1824), ii, i.

67. Ibid., *Library Companion*, vii, 811n.

68. Hazlitt, "On the Pleasures of Painting," in *Complete Works*, 8:14; "On a Landscape of Nicolas Poussin," in *Complete Works*, 8:173; both essays appeared originally in Hazlitt's *Table Talk* (1821).

69. Hazlitt, "On the Pleasures of Painting," 8:14; Mary A. Favret, "A Home for Art: Painting, Poetry, and Domestic Interiors," in *At the Limits of Romanticism: Essays in Cultural, Feminist, and Materialist Criticism*, ed. Mary A. Favret and Nicola J. Watson (Bloomington: Indiana University Press, 1994), 64. See also the discussion of Hazlitt's essays on painting in Siegel, *Desire and Excess*, 168-72.

70. Lamb, "The Two Races," 2:25; cf. Price, *How to Do Things with Books*, 1-3.

71. Leigh Hunt, *Autobiography of Leigh Hunt*, 124.

72. De Quincey, "The Street Companion," in *Works of De Quincey*, 4:451n. On Spencer's libraries, see Clive Wainwright, "The Library as Living Room," in *Property of a Gentleman: The Formation, Organisation and Dispersal of the Private Library*, ed. Robin Myers and Michael Harris (New Castle, DE: Oak Knoll Press; Winchester, St. Paul's Bibliographies, 1996), 15; for Heber, I draw on Arthur Sherbo's entry in the *Oxford Dictionary of National Biography*.

73. A later passage in the essay, however, in which Hunt declares his "love of bookstall urbanity" does present the street as an alternate, open-air form of library. See also Lamb's "Detached Thoughts on Books and Reading," which concludes by engaging the "street-readers" who "filch" their learning from book stalls (*Works of Charles and Mary Lamb*, 2:176).

74. Ina Ferris, "Bibliographic Romance: Bibliophilia and the Book Object," in *Romantic Libraries*, ed. Ina Ferris, Romantic Circles Praxis Series (February 2004), http://www.rc.umd.edu /praxis/libraries/ferris/ferris.html, para. 1.

75. See Thomas F. Bonnell, *The Most Disreputable Trade: Publishing the Classics of English Poetry, 1765-1810* (Oxford: Oxford University Press, 2008), 262.

76. Hunt, *Autobiography*, 69.

77. Ferris, "Antiquarian Authorship," 534.

78. Plotz, "For and Against Book Collecting," 476.

79. See James Raven, "From Promotion to Proscription: Arrangements for Reading and Eighteenth-Century Libraries," in *The Practice and Representation of Reading in England*, ed. James Raven, Helen Small, and Naomi Tadmor (Cambridge: Cambridge University Press, 1996), 175-201. Raven states that an unprecedented number of domestic libraries were built in the second half of the eighteenth century in Britain.

80. Hazlitt, "Of Persons One Would Wish to Have Seen," in *Complete Works*, 17:123.

81. Didbin, *Library Companion*, vii.

82. The discussions of painting carried on in late eighteenth-century Britain provide an illuminating analogy here, since in parallel ways they too differentiated, as Sir Joshua Reynolds did in his *Discourses to the Royal Academy*, the history paintings that contributed to the project of national definition from the "cabinet pictures" or "portfolio pictures"—portraits, comic paintings, genre paintings, caricatures, works in watercolor rather than in oil—that did not.

83. Among Lamb's essays see "The Two Races of Men" particularly. This array of sources also provide glimpses of how Mary Lamb contributed to the script that the Lambs' Bloomsbury household devised to guide its cohabitation with literature. The brother and sister enacted their book love as if performing a duet. "Both great readers," but in "different directions," according to the account of Elia and Bridget given in Lamb's essay "Mackery End, in Hertfordshire," they appear to have arranged matters so that Charles would be the book collector, and Mary the book borrower, a client of the circulating libraries that kept their "common reading-table" supplied with daily doses of "some modern tale or adventure" (*Works of Charles and Mary Lamb*, 2:75).

84. E. V. Lucas, *The Life of Charles Lamb*, 6th ed. (London: Methuen, 1914), 369, 589.

85. As Lucy Newlyn notes (*Reading, Writing, and Romanticism: The Anxiety of Reception* [Oxford: Oxford University Press, 2000], 209), the works that Elia won't consider as books—Hume, Gibbon, Adam Smith, and other writers of history and moral philosophy all write "*books which are no books*"—are just the works that we, subsequent to the discursive reorganization of Lamb's day, now find it difficult to consider as literature.

86. The "tickling sense of property" I mentioned earlier is aroused by the trophies Elia carries away from these bookstalls, which are generally, he explains, works without hope of ever being reprinted, or works that though they have been reprinted have not "endenizened themselves in . . . the national heart" (2:174). By contrast, the possession of works by Shakespeare or Milton "confers no distinction" (2:173)—a claim that takes the role of collector to outrageous levels of fastidiousness.

87. On Hunt's rooms in prison, see his *Autobiography*, 216–20. Hunt and his brother John, co-proprietor and printer of the *Examiner*, were convicted of political libel for the article "The Prince on St. Patrick's Day," which the *Examiner* published on March 22, 1812.

88. Hunt, "Men Wedded to Books," *Indicator* 32 (May 17, 1820), 251.

89. "A Member of the University of Cambridge," Letter to the Editor, *Times*, Friday, October 10, 1823, 2, column D, in *The Times Digital Archive, 1785–1985*, find.galegroup.com.myaccess.library .utoronto.ca.

90. Jensen, *Revolution and the Antiquarian Book*, 66.

91. Review of L. C. F. Petit Rodel, *Recherches sur les bibliothèques anciennes et modernes . . . et sur les causes qui ont favorisé l'accroisement succesif du nombre des livres*, *Edinburgh Review* 34, no. 68 (1820): 418.

92. Lamb, "Readers against the Grain," in *Works*, 1:273.

93. H. J. Jackson suggests that the "reading boom" was over by 1826. Fashion had moved on, and a general economic depression had set in (*Romantic Readers*, 51).

94. Thomas Frognall Dibdin, *Bibliophobia: Remarks on the Present Languid and Depressed State of Literature and the Book Trade* (London: Henry Bohn, 1832), 14, 27, 29; Leigh Hunt, "Men and Books," in *Leigh Hunt's Literary Criticism*, ed. Lawrence Huston Houtchens and Carolyn Washburn Houtchens (New York: Columbia University Press, 1956), 402, 405, Benjamin, "Unpacking My Library," 66–67.

95. Hazlitt, "The Sick Chamber," in *Complete Works*, 17:376.

96. Lamb, "Oxford in the Vacation," in *Works of Charles and Mary Lamb*, 2:10; Jackson, *Anatomy of Bibliomania*, quoted in Ferris, "Bibliographical Romance," para 8.

97. See Lamb's letter to Samuel Taylor Coleridge, tentatively dated autumn 1820, in *The Selected Letters of Charles Lamb*, ed. T. S. Matthews (New York: Farrar, Straus and Cudahy, 1956), 153.

98. I reference here Susan Stewart's discussion of how the collection in detaching objects from their contexts enables the forgetting of the labor that created the objects originally: see *On Longing: Narratives of the Gigantic, the Miniature, the Souvenir, the Collection* (Baltimore: Johns Hopkins University Press, 1984), 151.

99. Holbrook Jackson, *The Fear of Books* (New York: Charles Scribner's, 1932), 157.

100. See Sonia Hofkosh, "A Woman's Profession: Sexual Difference and the Romance of Authorship," *Studies in Romanticism* 32, no. 2 (Summer 1993): 245–72.

101. Dibdin, *Reminiscences*, 2:949.

102. My generalizations about these books are based on an examination of about sixty such volumes from the period 1790–1850. Helpful discussions of this primarily female pastime can be found in Patrizia Di Bello, *Women's Albums and Photography in Victorian England* (Aldershot, UK: Ashgate, 2007); David Allan, *Commonplace Books and Reading in Georgian England* (Cambridge: Cambridge University Press, 2010); Stephen Colclough, *Consuming Texts: Readers and Reading Communities, 1695–1870* (Basingstoke, UK: Palgrave Macmillan, 2007), 118–44; Corin Throsby, "Byron, Commonplacing, and Early Fan Culture," in *Romanticism and Celebrity Culture, 1750–1850*, ed. Tom Mole (Cambridge: Cambridge University Press, 2009), 227–44.

103. Anna Maria McNeill was later famous as the mother of the painter James Whistler; her album is in the Special Collections Department of the University of Glasgow Library. Anne Wagner's "Memorials of Friendship" has been digitized by the Pforzheimer Collection of the New York Public Library and may be viewed at http://exhibitions.nypl.org/biblion/node/2738.

104. David Hume, "Of the Delicacy of Taste and Passion," in *Selected Essays*, ed. Stephen Copley and Andrew Edgar (Oxford: Oxford University Press, 1993), 12. These books come in many varieties, of course, spanning a spectrum that runs from the private commonplace book for study to the parlor table book for show. Sometimes the affections they document are those of fellow readers for one another; these readers connect through the shared texts clipped and transcribed in the books' pages. Most critical commentary on these books stresses their instrumentality for such sociability, ruling out the possibility that sometimes the copied-out texts are themselves the objects of affection. This is the possibility I mean to explore, keeping in mind how readily the identities of devoted reader and devoted friend were fused by participants in album culture.

105. Judith Pascoe, "Poetry as Souvenir: Mary Shelley in the Annuals," in *Mary Shelley in Her Times*, ed. Betty T. Bennett and Stuart Curran (Baltimore: Johns Hopkins University Press, 1997), 174.

106. Lamb, "The Latin Poems of Vincent Bourne" (1831), quoted in Samantha Matthews, "'O All Pervading Album!': Place and Displacement in Romantic Albums and Album Poetry," in *Romantic Localities: Europe Writes Place*, ed. Christoph Bode and Jacqueline Labbe (London: Pickering and Chatto, 2010), 113.

107. Di Bello, *Women's Albums*, 3.

108. The Dyce-Hoe Shakespeare as it is now known, after editor, extra-illustrator, and author (in that order), is in the Folger Shakespeare Library: see Erin C. Blake and Stuart Sillars, *Extending the Book: The Art of Extra-Illustration* (Washington, DC: Folger Library, 2010).

109. Dibdin, *Bibliomania*, 62–63; Southey, *Letters from England*, quoted in Lucy Peltz, "Facing the Text: The Amateur and Commercial Histories of Extra-Illustration, ca. 1770–1840," in *Owners, Annotators, and the Signs of Reading*, ed. Robin Myers et al. (New Castle, DE: Oak Knoll Press; London, British Library, 2005), 94.

110. Ellen Gruber Garvey, "Imitation is the Sincerest Form of Appropriation," *Common-Place* 7, no. 3 (April 2007), http://www.commonplace.org.

111. Colclough discusses an example of such a change: *Consuming Texts*, 133.

112. Eliza Graeme commonplace book, circa 1820–70, National Library of Scotland, Ms. 16404.

113. Eliza Reynolds, "Medley, or Scrap Book," Sir Harry Page Collection of Victorian Scrapbooks, Albums and Commonplace Books held at Manchester Metropolitan University Special Collections, no. 178.

114. Anonymous scrapbook, circa 1830–40, Sir Harry Page Collection, no. 33.

115. Margaret Visser describes the votive as operating in the context of popular piety as a gift of a particular kind. It operates not just as documentation of the proper gratitude for blessings received from on high, but also an instrument that the blessed deploy to create a rapprochement with supernatural power; it is a means of achieving a temporary closeness "between the two hugely

distant sides": *The Gift of Thanks: The Roots, Persistence, and Paradoxical Meanings of a Social Ritual* (Toronto: HarperCollins, 2008), 155.

116. Sir Harry Page Collection, no. 88.

117. Leah Price, *The Anthology and the Rise of the Novel* (Cambridge: Cambridge University Press, 2003), 102.

118. Di Bello, *Women's Albums*, 2.

119. Hazlitt, "On Reading Old Books," in *Complete Works*, 12:221.

120. Jean Baudrillard, *The System of Objects*, trans. James Benedict (London: Verso, 1996), 86.

CHAPTER FOUR

1. Samuel Johnson, Letter to Thomas Warton, July 16, 1754, in *The Correspondence of Thomas Warton*, ed. David Fairer (Athens: University of Georgia Press, 1995), 27.

2. For the "Life of Cowley," in *Lives of the Most Eminent English Poets*, ed. Roger Lonsdale, 4 vols. (Oxford: Clarendon Press, 2006), 1:191; for the "Life of Shenstone," in ibid., 4:126. The lines that Johnson recalls in his "Life of Cowley" are found in Cowley's essay "Of My Self," in *Works of Mr. Abraham Cowley*, 11th ed. (London: J. Tonson, 1710), 2:782.

3. Leah Price, *The Anthology and the Rise of the Novel* (Cambridge: Cambridge University Press, 2000), 71, 70. Also relevant here is Barbara M. Benedict's proposal that the eighteenth-century literary miscellany marks a new acknowledgment of readers as participants in and makers of literary culture: *Making the Modern Reader: Cultural Mediation in Early Modern Literary Anthologies* (Princeton, NJ: Princeton University Press, 1996), 5.

4. Leigh Hunt, *A Book for a Corner, or Selections in Prose and Verse from Authors the Best Suited to That Mode of Enjoyment* (London: Chapman and Hall, 1849), 8, v; Hunt quotes Johnson's "Life of Shenstone" on 2.

5. Steve Connor, "Dickens, The Haunting Man (On L-iterature)," paper given at the conference "A Man for All Media: The Popularity of Dickens, 1902-2002," Institute for English Studies, 2002; online at http://www.stevenconnor.com/haunting/.

6. Harold Bloom, *The Western Canon* (New York: Harcourt Brace, 1994), 30. I receive assistance here from William Paulson, "The Literary Canon in the Age of Its Technical Obsolescence," in *Reading Matters: Narrative in the New Media Ecology*, ed. Joseph Tabbi and Michael Wutz (Ithaca, NY: Cornell University Press, 1997), 240-41.

7. See, for example, François Roustang, "On Reading Again," in *The Limits of Theory*, ed. Thomas M. Kavanagh (Stanford, CA: Stanford University Press, 1989), 121-38; Matei Calinescu, *Rereading* (New Haven, CT: Yale University Press, 1993); Roland Barthes, *S/Z*, trans. Richard Miller (New York: Farrar, Straus and Giroux, 1974), 15-16.

8. Michael Warner, "Uncritical Reading," in *Polemic: Critical or Uncritical*, ed. Jane Gallop (New York and London: Routledge, 2004), 13-38. "Critical reading" itself is of course more than simply a transparent medium for knowledge acquisition. It carries more ideological baggage than that. As Warner observes, it is often assigned a formative role within an ethical program specific to modern political culture, with the result that the legitimacy of the profession of English currently owes a lot to an "imputed relationship" between this mode of textual engagement and "critical reason" and "liberal openness" (15). Warner's essay is a polemic designed to remind us that there are "other cultures of textualism" out there and other ways of harnessing reading to the ethical problematic of subject formation: I would underline, however, that this also holds *within* the culture of English departments.

9. Henry Reed, cited in Adam Potkay, "Wordsworth, Henry Reed, and Bishop Doane: High Church Romanticism on the Delaware," in *Wordsworth in American Literary Culture*, ed. Joel Pace and Matthew Scott (Basingstoke, UK: Palgrave Macmillan, 2005), 110.

10. John Gillis, "Making Time for Family: The Invention of Family Time(s) and the Reinvention of Family History," *Journal of Family History* 21, no. 1 (1996): 4-21.

11. "I am not satisfied if a year passes without my having read [*Rasselas*] through": James Boswell, *Life of Johnson*, introd. Pat Rogers, ed. R. W. Chapman (Oxford: Oxford University Press, 1980), 242.

12. See, for example, Erasmus Darwin, *Zoonomia, or, the Laws of Organic Life* (1796) and George Henry Lewes, *The Physical Basis of Mind* (1877).

13. William Hazlitt, "On Reading Old Books" (first published *London Magazine*, February 1821), in *The Complete Works of William Hazlitt*, ed. P. P. Howe, 21 vols. (London: J. M. Dent, 1931), 12:221. Subsequent references to this essay are to volume and page numbers in this edition and appear parenthetically in the text.

14. Gillis, "Making Time for Family," 11.

15. See Kirstie Blair, "John Keble and the Rhythm of Faith," *Essays in Criticism* 53, no. 2 (April 2003): 129-50; John Ruskin, "Fiction Fair and Foul," in *The Complete Works of John Ruskin*, ed. E. T. Cook and Alexander Wedderburn, 39 vols. (London: G. Allen, 1902), 34:349; *John Clare by Himself*, ed. Eric Robinson and David Powell (Ashington, UK: MidNorthumberland Arts Group and Carcanet Press, 1996), 56; E. F. G. [i.e., Edward FitzGerald], "Memoir of Bernard Barton," in *The Poems and Letters of Bernard Barton, Edited by his Daughter* (London: Hall, Virtue, and Co., 1849), xxxiv. Barton likewise knew by heart "all of the good things" in Boswell's *Life of Johnson* and would "sit at table, his snuff-box in his hand, . . . repeating some favourite passage, and glancing his fine brown eyes about him as he recited" (xxxiv).

16. I owe this quotation and many additional insights to Mary A. Favret's "Jane Austen at 25: A Life in Numbers," *English Language Notes* 46, no. 1 (Spring/Summer 2008): 9-20.

17. Adolphus Jack, *Essays on the Novel: As Illustrated by Scott and Miss Austen* (London: Macmillan, 1897), 257.

18. Devastating satire of this late nineteenth-century sanctification of literary domesticity is to be found in Evelyn Waugh's novel *A Handful of Dust* (1934; rept. Harmondsworth, UK: Penguin, 1972): Waugh's protagonist Tony Last ends his days in a little bit of England that has been re-created in the deepest jungle of British Guiana, reading Dickens aloud to his captor, Mr. Todd, "tomorrow and the day after that and the day after that.""Let us read *Little Dorrit* again," said Mr. Todd: "There are passages in that book I can never hear without the temptation to weep" (209).

19. For examples of this reassessment, see Saba Mahmood, *The Politics of Piety: The Islamic Revival and the Feminist Subject* (Princeton, NJ: Princeton University Press, 2005), especially 119-27; and James N. Baker, "The Presence of the Name: Reading Scripture in an Indonesian Village," in *The Ethnography of Reading*, ed. Jonathan Boyarin (Berkeley: University of California Press, 1993), 98-138.

20. See, for instance, John Brewer, "Readers and the Reading Public," chapter 4 of *The Pleasures of the Imagination: English Culture in the Eighteenth Century* (New York: Farrar, Straus and Giroux, 1997), which draws on the periodizing framework introduced by Rolf Engelsing's 1969 "Die Perioden der Lesergeschichte in der Neuzeit." For the shift from the Bible to a generalized *biblios* see Garrett Stewart, *The Look of Reading : Book, Painting, Text* (Chicago: University of Chicago Press, 2006), 39.

21. Danièle Hervieu-Léger, *Religion as a Chain of Memory*, trans. Simon Lee (New Brunswick, NJ: Rutgers University Press, 2000), 45; William McKelvy, *The English Cult of Literature: Devoted Readers, 1774-1880* (Charlottesville: University of Virginia Press, 2006).

22. Stuart Sherman, *Telling Time: Clocks, Diaries, and English Diurnal Form, 1660-1785* (Chicago: University of Chicago Press, 1996), 225.

23. Ibid., 35-36. See also Anne-Martin Fugier's description of the rhythms idealized by promoters of bourgeois domesticity in nineteenth-century France: "Bourgeois Rituals," in *A History of Private Life*, vol. 4, *From the Fires of Revolution to the Great War*, ed. Michelle Perrot, trans. Arthur Goldhammer (Cambridge, MA: Harvard University Press, 1990), 261-338.

24. Samuel Johnson, *Letters of Samuel Johnson*, ed. Bruce Redford, 5 vols. (Princeton, NJ: Princeton University Press, 1992), 1:48.

25. Sir George Otto Trevelyan, *The Life and Letters of Lord Macaulay* (1876; rept. Oxford: Oxford University Press, 1961), 1:348-49. See also *Letters of Macaulay*, ed. Thomas Pinney, 6 vols. (Cambridge: Cambridge University Press, 1976): 3:9, 3:22.

26. "Richardson sème dans les coeurs des germes de vertus qui y rêstent d'abord oisifs et tranquilles: ils y sont secrètement jusqu'à ce qu'il se présente une occasion qui les remue and les fasse éclore. Alors ils se développent; on se sent porter au bien avec une impétuosité qu'on ne se conaissait pas": Denis Diderot, *Éloge de Richardson*, ed. Henri Lafon, in Denis Diderot, *Contes et romans* (Paris: Gallimard, 2004), 898-99.

27. "O Richardson, Richardson, . . . tu seras ma lecture dans tous les temps" (900). Compare *Éloge*, 902: "lisez-le sans cesse." Such statements—"thou wilt at all times be the subject of my reading": "read him ceaselessly"—call for readers to repeat themselves.

28. Roger Chartier, "Richardson, Diderot et la lectrice impatiente," *MLN* 114, no. 4 (September 1999): 647-65; incorporated and translated in Chartier's *Inscription and Erasure: Literature and Written Culture*, trans. Arthur Goldhammer (Philadelphia: University of Pennsylvania Press, 2007): I quote 121-22.

29. Samuel Richardson, *Clarissa*, ed. Angus Ross (Harmondsworth, UK: Penguin, 1985), 1470-72; Richardson, *Correspondence of Samuel Richardson*, ed. Anna Letitia Barbauld, 6 vols. (rept. New York: AMS Press, 1966), 4:264; Richardson, *Pamela*, 2 vols. (London: Dent, 1914), 2:250.

30. Gillis, "Making Time for Family," 13.

31. Elizabeth Hamilton, Letter to Dr. H—, December 12, 1811, in Elizabeth Benger, *Memoirs of the Late Mrs. Elizabeth Hamilton, with a Selection from Her Correspondence and Other Unpublished Writing*, 2 vols. (London: Longman, Hurst, Rees, Orme, and Brown, 1818), 2:142.

32. John Aikin, *Letters to a Young Lady on a Course of English Poetry* (1804; 2nd ed., London: J. Johnson, 1807), 180 (on Edward Young's *Night Thoughts*, which Aikin would *not* like to see as his young lady's "favourite or closet companion") and 138 (on *Paradise Lost*).

33. Leigh Hunt, *The Literary Pocket-Book* (London: C. Ollier, 1819), 2, hereafter cited parenthetically in the text by page number. Hunt's introduction to this first volume compares his "Calendar of Nature" with Gilbert White's *Natural History and Antiquities of Selborne* (1789) and John Aikin and Arthur Aikin's *Natural History of the Year* (1799).

34. Benedict Anderson, *Imagined Communities: Reflections on the Origin and Spread of Nationalism*, rev. ed. (London: Verso, 1991), 24.

35. Thomas Hood, *The Letters of Thomas Hood*, ed. Peter F. Morgan (Edinburgh: Oliver and Boyd, 1973), 686.

36. For Franco Moretti's discussion of kitsch, see *The Way of the World: The Bildungsroman in European Culture* (London: Verso, 1987), 36-37.

37. This point is made by Sara Lodge, "Romantic Reliquaries: Memory and Irony in the Literary Annuals," *Romanticism* 10, no. 1 (April 2004): 25-26.

38. I quote from the unpaginated explanatory address found at the start of the 1830 edition (London: Thomas Tegg), which combines *The Every-Day Book* with Hone's later, 1827 *The Table Book*.

39. Gregory Dart, "Cockneyism," *London Review of Books*, December 18, 2003, 20 (review of *The Selected Writings of Leigh Hunt*, ed. Robert Morrison and Michael Eberle-Sinatra).

40. In the late Enlightenment it was *philosophes* who criticized fashionable consumption in the name of comfort, aiming to make the public sensible of the discomfort of domestic arrangements—smoky chimneys, for example—it had deemed acceptable: see John Crowley, "The Sensibility of Comfort," *American Historical Review* 104, no. 3 (June 1999): 750, 771. Suggestively, in 1794 Mary Wollstonecraft condemns ancien régime France—and establishes France's unreadiness for revolution—by noting that the French "have no word in their vocabulary to express *comfort*—that state of existence in which reason renders serene and useful the days" (*An Historical and Moral View of the Origin and Progress of the French Revolution* [London: J. Johnson, 1794], 511).

41. For an account of how middle-class Victorians learned to look in new locations for their "temporal convoys," and how they made relations with family members serve needs that were formerly fulfilled through their religious affiliations, see John R. Gillis, *A World of Their Own Making: Myth, Ritual, and the Quest for Family Values* (New York: Basic Books, 1996), 43; Gillis borrows the term "temporal convoy" from the sociologist David Cheal.

42. Alexander Gerard, *Essay on Genius* (1777), quoted in Gordon McKenzie, *Critical Responsiveness: A Study of the Psychological Current in Later Eighteenth-Century Criticism* (Berkeley: University of California Press, 1949), 133.

43. Henry Home, Lord Kames, *Elements of Criticism*, 3 vols. (London: A. Millar; Edinburgh: A. Kincaid and J. Bell, 1762), 1:91.

44. See David Perkins, "Romantic Reading as Revery," *European Romantic Review* 4, no. 2 (January 1994): 183-99.

45. Joseph Priestley, *A Course of Lectures on Oratory and Criticism* (London: J. Johnson, 1777), i, 83.

46. Francis Jeffrey, "Thomas Campbell" (1809), in *Essays on English Poets and Poetry from the Edinburgh Review* (London: George Routledge and Sons, n.d.), 186.

47. I am indebted here to Perkins's "Romantic Reading as Revery."

48. For a redescription of romantic poetic theory that makes this interest in unconscious mental operations crucial, see Alan Richardson, *British Romanticism and the Science of the Mind* (Cambridge: Cambridge University Press, 2001).

49. Lord Kames, *Elements of Criticism*, 1:82.

50. Linda M. Austin, *Nostalgia in Transition, 1780-1817* (Charlottesville: University of Virginia Press, 2007), 36.

51. Joseph Warton, "Reflections on Didactic Poetry," in *The Works of Virgil, in Latin and English*, trans. Christopher Pitt, ed. Joseph Warton, 4 vols. (London: R. Dodsley, 1753), 1:400.

52. Erasmus Darwin, *Zoonomia, or, the Laws of Organic Life* (New York: T. and J. Swords, 1796), 28.

53. Priestley, *Course of Lectures on Oratory and Criticism*, 80-81.

54. John Locke, *An Essay concerning Human Understanding*, ed. Peter H. Nidditch (Oxford: Clarendon, 1975), 397, 395; Alison, cited in Perkins, "Romantic Reading as Revery," 184.

55. The phrase occurs in Martin Priestman, *Cowper's "Task": Structure and Influence* (Cambridge: Cambridge University Press, 1983), 22.

56. Cited in Nicholas Dames, *Amnesiac Selves: Nostalgia, Forgetting, and British Fiction, 1810-1870* (New York: Oxford University Press, 2001), 140.

57. Edward Mangin, *A View of the Pleasure Arising from a Love of Books: In Letters to a Lady* (London: Longman, Hurst, Rees, Orme, and Brown, 1814), 199; Jeffrey, "Thomas Campbell," 186.

58. David Hartley, *Observations on Man*, 2 vols. (London: James Leake and William Frederick, 1749), 1:397; David Hume, *A Treatise of Human Nature*, ed. Ernest C. Mossner (Harmondsworth, UK: Penguin, 1965), 367. Cf. Adela Pinch's discussion of Hume in *Strange Fits of Passion: Epistemologies of Emotion, from Hume to Austen* (Stanford, CA: Stanford University Press, 1996), 32-37; and Jonathan Lamb's discussion of Hume together with Hartley in *Sterne and the Double Principle* (Cambridge: Cambridge University Press, 1989), 67-83.

59. Pinch, *Strange Fits*, 24.

60. Jerome Christensen, *Practicing Enlightenment: Hume and the Formation of a Literary Career* (Madison: University of Wisconsin Press, 1987), 12.

61. Maurice Blanchot, "Everyday Speech," trans. Susan Hanson, *Yale French Studies* 73 (1987): 14.

62. Warner, "Uncritical Reading," 14. Pressed to explain this understanding of aesthetic experience's medicinal effects, most of us, would, I suspect, mention a concept of defamiliarization that we would trace to the romantic poets' antipathy toward self-defeating patterns of being and thinking. One wonders, though, how this orthodoxy would fare if practitioners of English studies

thought harder about how the reading that we do for our classes takes us in circles: those recurrent reunions with the texts we teach to shake our students up—semester in and semester out—themselves represent a tacit admission that some patterns are worth repeating.

63. Austin, *Nostalgia in Transition*, 3.

64. Catherine Gallagher, "Formalism and Time," *Modern Language Quarterly* 61, no. 1 (March 2000): 229–51; Longinus, "On the Sublime," in *Classical Literary Criticism*, trans. T. S. Dorsch (London: Penguin, 1965), 100.

65. Samuel Taylor Coleridge, *Biographia Literaria*, ed. James Engell and W. Jackson Bate, 2 vols. in 1 (Princeton, NJ: Princeton University Press, 1983), 1:80, hereafter cited parenthetically in the text by volume and page number.

66. William Wordsworth, preface to *Lyrical Ballads* (1802), in *The Oxford Authors: William Wordsworth*, ed. Stephen Gill (Oxford: Oxford University Press, 1984), 611, hereafter cited parenthetically in the body of this chapter.

67. Michel de Montaigne, "Upon the Verses of Virgil," in *Montaigne's Essays*, trans. Charles Cotton, 6th ed. (London: Barker, Strahan, Ballard, *et al.*, 1743), 3:71. Here is, at length, William Hone's preface to *The Table Book*: "Perhaps, if the good old window-seats had not gone out of fashion, it might be called a parlour-window book—a good name for a volume of agreeable reading selected from the book-case and left lying about, for the constant recreation of the family, and the casual amusement of visitors" ([London: Hunt and Clarke, 1827], n.p.). Introducing her edition of *Selections from the Spectator, Tatler, Guardian and Freeholder* (London: J. Johnson, 1804), Anna Letitia Barbauld muses on how with time, even a book that is "respected as a classic" will be "withdrawn from the parlour-window, and laid upon the shelf in an honourable repose" (iv). On Sterne's *Tristram Shandy* and the parlour window-book, see my "The Shandean Lifetime Reading Plan," in *The Work of Genre: Selected Essays from the English Institute*, ed. Robyn Warhol (Cambridge, MA: The English Institute in collaboration with the American Council of Learned Societies, 2011), http://quod.lib.umich.edu/cgi/t/text/text-idx?c=acls;idno=heb90055.0001.001.

68. Hazlitt, "My First Acquaintance with Poets," in *Complete Works*, 17:120. If this was true, it was almost too good to be so: remember that in Johnson's *Lives*, Cowley is said to have made another version of this discovery, finding that spellbinding copy of *The Faerie Queene* lying in the window of his mother's parlor.

69. See, for example, James Robert Allard, *Romanticism, Medicine, and the Poet's Body* (Aldershot, UK: Ashgate, 2007).

70. Clifford Siskin discusses the resemblance linking poets' and doctors' professional authority in "Wordsworth's Prescriptions: Romanticism and Professional Power," in *The Romantics and Us: Essays on Literature and Culture*, ed. Gene W. Ruoff (New Brunswick, NJ: Rutgers University Press, 1990), 303–21.

71. The 1805 *Prelude*, in *Oxford Authors: William Wordsworth*, 453, book 6, lines 117–18.

72. Angela Willey, "'Christian Nations,' 'Polygamic Races,' and Women's Rights: Toward a Genealogy of Non/Monogamy and Whiteness," *Sexualities* 9, no. 5 (December 2006): 530–46, referring to George Combe, *Elements of Phrenology* (1834).

73. Thank you to Leah Price for this formulation.

74. Benjamin Rush, *Medical Inquiries and Observations upon the Diseases of the Mind* (Philadelphia, 1812; rept. New York: Hafner, 1962), 37.

75. Sianne Ngai, *Ugly Feelings* (Cambridge, MA: Harvard University Press, 2005), 7, 10.

76. Susan J. Wolfson, "Romanticism and the Measures of Meter," *Eighteenth-Century Life* 16, no. 3 (November 1992): 232. Cf. Pinch, *Strange Fits*, 86–88.

77. It is intriguing to see a poet whose characteristic lyrics record and reenact the sudden and freakish returns of past sensations—the uncanny hauntings of the mind by itself that in *The Prelude* Wordsworth called "spots of time" (*Oxford Authors: William Wordsworth*, 565, book 11, line 258)—taking pains to put readers' experience of this untimeliness on a schedule. The effort reveals

a Wordsworth inclined to assimilate the passions of poetry and passions for poetry to an ethic of moral health.

78. Gallagher, "Formalism and Time," 229.

79. Mary Russell Mitford, *Recollections of a Literary Life, or, Books, Places and People* (1851; rept. New York: Harper and Brothers, 1862), 343.

80. Dino Franco Felluga, *The Perversity of Poetry: Romantic Ideology and the Popular Male Poet of Genius* (Albany: State University of New York Press, 2005), 42. Felluga describes how Scott's fiction was presented in early nineteenth-century critical and medical writing as a panacea for modern nervous disorders while Byron's poetry was pathologized. See also the discussion of the novel's increasing respectability, likewise pegged to Scott's example, in Kathleen Tillotson, *Novels of the Eighteen-Forties* (Oxford: Clarendon, 1954), 13–20.

81. Benjamin Rush mentions Cowper in his *Medical Inquiries and Observations upon the Diseases of the Mind* while describing the methods by which maniacs may be restored to regularity. Rush's source is likely to have been William Hayley's *The Life and Posthumous Writings of William Cowper*, 2 vols. (Boston: W. Pelham, Manning, and Loring, and E. Lincoln, 1803); see especially, 2:113. Rush is named the father of bibliotherapy on the website of the National Association for Poetry Therapy: http://www.poetrytherapy.org/history.html. I quote John Johnson's account of these years in Cowper's life, included in Johnson's edition of *The Poems of William Cowper, Containing His Posthumous Poetry, and a Sketch of His Life*, 3 vols. (London, T. C. and J. Rivington, 1815), 3:lx, 3:lix.

82. Richardson, *Clarissa*, 1336.

83. Samuel Richardson, *The History of Sir Charles Grandison*, ed. Jocelyn Harris, 3 parts in 1 (Oxford: Oxford University Press, 1986), part 3, vol. 7, Letter xv, 321; Laurence Sterne, *The Life and Opinions of Tristram Shandy, Gentleman*, ed. Melvyn New and Joan New, 3 vols. (Gainesville: University Presses of Florida, 1978), 1:82.

84. J. Paul Hunter, "Serious Reflections on Farther Adventures: Resistances to Closure in Eighteenth-Century English Novels," in *Augustan Subjects: Essays in Honor of Martin C. Battestin* (Newark: University of Delaware Press, 1997), 284.

85. Macaulay, Letter to Mrs. Edward Cropper, October 3, 1834, *Letters* 3:76.

86. Franco Moretti, "Serious Century," in *The Novel*, ed. Franco Moretti, 2 vols. (Princeton, NJ: Princeton University Press, 2006), 1:376, 1:368.

87. J. E. Austen-Leigh, *A Memoir of Jane Austen, and Other Family Recollections*, ed. Kathryn Sutherland (Oxford: Oxford University Press, 2002), 71.

88. Moretti, "Serious Century," 368.

89. Susan Ferrier's 1816 letter to a Miss Clavering is cited in B. W. Southam, comp., *Jane Austen: The Critical Heritage*, vol. 1 (London: Routledge Kegan Paul, 1968), 15. Walter Scott's 1816 review of *Emma* for the *Quarterly Review* declared the sacrifice of narrative excitement to be the essence of a new "style of novel" that had "arisen in the last fifteen or twenty years" and which presented to the reader a "correct and striking representation of that which is daily taking place around him": in *Jane Austen: Critical Assessments*, ed. Ian Littlewood (London: Helm Information, 1998), 291.

90. Jane Austen, *Emma*, in *The Oxford Illustrated Jane Austen*, ed. R. W. Chapman, 6 vols. (Oxford: Oxford University Press, 1933), 4:20. Subsequent references are to this edition: page numbers are given parenthetically in the text.

91. The phrase "stationary movement" is from Blanchot's "Everyday Speech," 15.

92. The canonical critical statements about *Emma*'s rereadability include W. J. Harvey, "The Plot of *Emma*," *Essays in Criticism* 17, no. 1 (January 1967): 48–63; and Adena Rosmarin, "Misreading *Emma*: The Powers and Perfidies of Interpretive History," *ELH* 51, no. 2 (Summer 1984): 315–42.

93. In a passage of free indirect discourse that precedes this scene, we find Emma reminding herself that for a long time "from family attachment and habit . . . [Knightley] had loved her" (326).

94. *Cyclopaedia of English Literature*, ed. Robert Chambers (Edinburgh: William and Robert Chambers, 1844), 2:572.

95. Austen-Leigh, *Memoir*, 112.

96. Edward FitzGerald, *The Letters of Edward FitzGerald*, vol. 3 (1867–1876), ed. Alfred McKinley Terhune and Annabelle Burdick Terhune (Princeton, NJ: Princeton University Press, 1980), 240.

97. Thomas De Quincey, "Walladmor: Sir Walter Scott's German Novel," in *The Works of Thomas De Quincey*, ed. Grevel Lindop, vol. 4, *Articles and Translations from the London Magazine; Walldamor*, ed. Frederick Burwick (London: Pickering and Chatto, 2000), 236.

98. *The Golden Treasury of the Best Songs and Lyrical Poems in the English Language, Selected and Arranged with Notes by Francis Turner Palgrave*, ed. Christopher Ricks (London: Penguin, 1991), 6. Subsequent references appear parenthetically in the text.

99. The *Oxford English Dictionary*'s first illustrative quotation is from a publication of 1841, Richard W. Hamilton's *Nugae literariae: Prose and Verse*: "He has not slept for the last three nights. No wonder he is ill: he is quite mistimed." The usage is marked as being largely restricted to Scotland and northern England.

100. Charles Kingsley, "On English Literature," in *The Nineteenth-Century History of English Studies*, comp. and ed. Alan Bacon (Aldershot, UK: Ashgate, 1998), 92.

101. Francis Turner Palgrave, "On Readers in 1760 and 1860," *Macmillan's Magazine* 1 (1859–60): 489. I am indebted here to Price's discussion of Palgrave in *Anthology and the Rise of the Novel*, 4.

102. B. W. Southam, introduction to *Jane Austen: The Critical Heritage*, vol. 2 (London: Routledge Kegan Paul, 1987), 13.

103. Thomas Noon Talfourd, *Memoirs of Charles Lamb* (1838), ed. Percy Fitzgerald (London: Gibbings and Co., 1894), 269; Lamb, "The Convalescent," in *The Works of Charles and Mary Lamb*, ed. E. V. Lucas, 5 vols. (New York: G. P. Putman's; London: Methuen, 1903), 2:186.

104. Maria H. Frawley, *Invalidism and Identity in Nineteenth-Century Britain* (Chicago: University of Chicago Press, 2004), 5.

105. I think of questions that Wayne Booth posed and left unanswered in his tellingly titled vindication of literary experience as moral education, *The Company We Keep: An Ethics of Fiction* (Berkeley: University of California Press, 1988): "Could we not say that even an addiction to a Shakespeare . . . would be potentially disastrous? . . . Is one ever justified in giving 'all for love' (of literature) as some educational programs have implicitly suggested?" (184n12). See also Tillotson, *Novels of the 1840s*, 18: "Where does the devotee shade off into the addict?"

CHAPTER FIVE

1. Samuel Taylor Coleridge, *Biographia Literaria*, ed. James Engell and W. Jackson Bate, 2 vols. in 1 (Princeton, NJ: Princeton University Press, 1983), 2:106. Subsequent references are to this edition and appear parenthetically in the text.

2. Erasmus Darwin, *Zoonomia; or, the Laws of Organic Life* (New York: T. and J. Swords, 1796), 187, 161.

3. Thomas Percival, "Miscellaneous Observations on the Influence of Habit and Association," in *Moral and Literary Dissertations*, 2nd ed. (Warrington, UK: W. Eyres for J. Johnson, 1789), 162; John Locke, *The Conduct of the Understanding* (Cambridge, UK: Nicholson, 1781), 230. Cf. Kevis Goodman, "Romantic Poetry and the Science of Nostalgia," in *The Cambridge Companion to British Romantic Poetry*, ed. James Chandler and Maureen N. McLane (Cambridge University Press, 2008), 195–216; and Ashley Miller, "Involuntary Metrics and the Physiology of Memory," *Literature Compass* 6, no. 2 (February 2009): 549–56.

4. John Keats, Letter to John Taylor, February 27, 1818, in *Keats's Poetry and Prose: A Norton Critical Edition*, ed. Jeffrey N. Cox (New York: W. W. Norton, 2009), 128.

5. The figure comes from Robert Miles, "The 1790s: The Effulgence of Gothic," in *The Cambridge Companion to Gothic Fiction*, ed. Jerrold E. Hogle (Cambridge: Cambridge University Press, 2002), 42. Franz J. Potter notes that "the era of the great circulating libraries—Bell's, Lackington's, and Lane's—coincided with the rise and development of Gothic fiction" (*The History of Gothic Publishing, 1800–1835: Exhuming the Trade* [Basingstoke, UK: Palgrave Macmillan, 2005], 15).

6. Ann Radcliffe, *The Mysteries of Udolpho*, ed. Bonamy Dobrée, introd. Terry Castle (Oxford: Oxford University Press, 1998), 103; Anon, *The Monks of St. Andrews, or, Castle of Haldenstein* (London: Bailey, n.d. [circa 1808–27]), 17. Subsequent references to *The Mysteries of Udolpho* are to this edition and appear parenthetically in the text.

7. For these inscription poems see, among many examples, Radcliffe, *Mysteries of Udolpho*, 7–9, and 558–59; Ann Radcliffe, *The Romance of the Forest*, ed. Chloe Chard (Oxford: Oxford University Press, 1986), 67; Mary Robinson, *Vancenza; or, the Dangers of Credulity*, 4th ed. (1793), in *The Works of Mary Robinson*, ed. William D. Brewer, vol. 2, ed. Dawn M. Vernooy-Epp (London: Pickering and Chatto, 2009): 275–76. The final section of this chapter will return to this presentation of poetry.

8. On the quoted poetry in this fiction see Ingrid Horrocks, "'Her Ideas Arranged Themselves': Re-membering Poetry in Radcliffe," *Studies in Romanticism* 47, no. 1 (Winter 2008): 507–27; Marshall Brown, "Poetry and the Novel," in *The Cambridge Companion to Fiction in the Romantic Period*, ed. Richard Maxwell and Katie Trumpener (Cambridge: Cambridge University Press, 2007), 107–28; Leah Price, *The Anthology and the Rise of the Novel* (Cambridge: Cambridge University Press, 2000), 95–97; Mary A. Favret, "Telling Tales about Genre," *Studies in the Novel* 26, no. 2 (Fall 1994): 153–72; Gillian Beer, "'Our Unnatural No-Voice': the Heroic Epistle, Pope, and Women's Gothic," *Yearbook of English Studies* 12 (1982): 53–81.

9. On Scott's intimate yet vexed relationship to the gothic mode, see Fiona Robertson, *Legitimate Histories: Scott, Gothic, and the Authorities of Fiction* (Oxford: Clarendon, 1994) and my own article (remote ancestor of this chapter), "Gothic Libraries and National Subjects," *Studies in Romanticism* 40, no. 1 (Spring 2001): 29–48.

10. Michael Gamer, *Romanticism and the Gothic: Genre, Reception, and Canon Formation* (Cambridge: Cambridge University Press, 2000).

11. Robinson, *Vancenza*, 2:276. Subsequent references appear parenthetically in the text.

12. If Radcliffe in her final pages tends to naturalize the supernatural and subject it to rational explanation, she also, by a kind of recoil, supernaturalizes consciousness, as Terry Castle has shown in a classic essay. Accordingly Radcliffe's portrayal of ordinary life in the opening and concluding sections of her fiction is when scrutinized closely anything but ordinary. In Radcliffe's characteristic arrangement, which also structures the fiction of many of her imitators, the mental images that possess the thoughts of her heroine of sensibility—mental images of an absent lover or a much-mourned parent—take on, in her moments of reverie, some of the apparitional attributes of the very ghosts that the novelist will ultimately banish from her fictional world. Castle's discussion of how Radcliffe stages late eighteenth-century psychology's "new obsession with the internalized images of other people" does not consider the literary enthusiasms distinguishing Radcliffe's protagonists, though her discussion provides one framework in which their import can be understood. Reading forms part of this story of the secularization of the invisible, and the beings of the mind whom the reader of imaginative literature comes to know during her reading contribute to the mind's hauntedness. See Castle, *The Female Thermometer: Eighteenth-Century Culture and the Invention of the Uncanny* (Oxford: Oxford University Press, 1995), 121–35: I quote 125.

13. Eliza Parsons, *The Mysterious Warning: A German Tale*, 4 vols. (London: William Lane, 1796), 1:3.

14. Eliza Parsons, *The Castle of Wolfenbach*, 2 vols. (1793; rept. London: Folio, 1968), 1:3, 1:15, 1:74.

15. Castle, *Female Thermometer*, 123.

16. See Garrett Stewart, *Dear Reader: The Conscripted Audience in Nineteenth-Century British Fiction* (Baltimore: Johns Hopkins University Press, 1996), 93–94.

17. Matthew Lewis, *The Monk*, ed. Howard Anderson (Oxford: Oxford University Press, 1973), 313–18.

18. See Karen Swann, "The Strange Time of Reading," *European Romantic Review* 9, no. 2 (1998): 275–82.

19. Parsons, *Mysterious Warning*, 2:261, 2:215.

20. Radcliffe, *Romance of the Forest*, 116. Subsequent references, likewise to the edition cited in note 7 above, are henceforth included parenthetically in the text.

21. Here as elsewhere Radcliffe's description of her character's reading converges with the discussion of "Emotions caused by Fiction" that Lord Kames undertakes in his *Elements of Criticism* (3 vols. [London: A. Millar; Edinburgh: A. Kincaid and J. Bell, 1762], 1:104–27): there Kames celebrates the reading of fiction as a process of auto-hallucination in which representations come alive before the reader's eyes.

22. "Genealogy . . . is the hidden structuring principle of the plot that must finally be brought to light. Fortuitous contact with strangers or strange places gives rise to a multitude of blood connections": E. J. Clery, *The Rise of Supernatural Fiction, 1762–1800* (Cambridge: Cambridge University Press, 1995), 112.

23. Anthologized in *Literary Mushrooms: Tales of Terror from the Gothic Chapbooks*, ed. Franz J. Potter (Camarillo: Zittaw Press, 2009), 114–38; see especially 121–25.

24. Such volumes may be found, as well, in the hands of the novels' necromancers, props to the magic spells with which they bedazzle the credulous (the key characteristic of those books is that they are presented not as texts, but as fundamentally unknowable objects, in which none may read). For examples of these talismanic books, see from the Minerva Press in 1794 Laurence Flammenberg, *The Necromancer, or, The Tale of the Black Forest*, trans. Peter Teuthold (London: Folio, 1968), 27; and, also from the Minerva Press, Eleanor Sleath's 1810 *The Nocturnal Minstrel, or, The Spirit of the Woods: A Romance*, 2 vols. (rept. New York: Arno Press, 1962), 2:88.

25. Jane Austen, *Northanger Abbey*, in *The Oxford Illustrated Jane Austen*, ed. R. W. Chapman, 5 vols. (Oxford: Oxford University Press, 1933), 5:38.

26. In the chapbook's opening, so as to enliven an evening at home Lady Emily sings an air, titled "Mutual Love," to which the narrator obligingly provides the words: Potter, ed., *Literary Mushrooms*, 116.

27. Parsons, *Castle of Wolfenbach*, 1:3.

28. As this heroine, like others, will discover many pages later, it is her own family history, balefully estranged, that she has brushed up against, since the portrait will be found to depict an aunt or a father whom she never knew. This is the uncanniness that invites descriptions of gothic narrative as a proto-psychoanalytic account of individuals' confrontations with repressed memories and desires they cannot know they have.

29. On the gothic's exploration of interrupted mourning, see Dale Townshend, "Gothic and the Ghost of *Hamlet*," in *Gothic Shakespeares*, ed. John Drakakis and Dale Townshend (London: Routledge, 2008), 60–97.

30. Walter Scott, "Horace Walpole," in *Sir Walter Scott on Novelists and Fiction*, ed. Ioan Williams (London: Routledge and Kegan Paul, 1968), 88.

31. The episodes in gothic novels in which characters are unnerved by echoes' uncanny repetitions of their words also supply these prose fictions with the means of displaying their own canonical affiliations. These episodes may themselves be echoes, deliberately reminiscent of the final sequence of *Hamlet*, act 1, scene 5, in which the ghost installed beneath the stage—a part legendarily associated with Shakespeare himself—repeats Hamlet's demand that his companions swear to keep secret the sights they have seen on Elsinore's battlements. See, for example, the episode in *The Mysteries of Udolpho* in which Montoni's menaces to Emily are repeated by a mysterious voice "which seemed to rise from underneath the chamber they were in" (394–95). For the Marchese de Montferrat, who fills the Montoni role in Eleanor Sleath's Minerva Press novel of 1798, *The Orphan of the Rhine*, the evidence that he lives with a phantom comes as he wakes up from a

nightmare, repeats the last word uttered by the Inquisitor he encountered in his dream, and then hears it echoed once more. "He pronounced the word 'Confess.' 'Confess,' repeated a voice apparently proceeding from a distant part of the room, in a tone at once deep and impressive": *The Orphan of the Rhine: A Romance* (New York: Folio, 1968), 4:268.

32. The effects of love are also portrayed in terms belonging to this associational network. After he first sees the beautiful orphan Ellena Rosalba, in the incident that opens Radcliffe's *The Italian*, the hero, Vivaldi, feels "the touching accents of her voice still vibrating on his heart" (*The Italian*, ed. Frederick Garber [Oxford: Oxford University Press, 1968], 7). Poetry love, we are made to understand, works in a comparable fashion.

33. Scott, "Horace Walpole," 88.

34. Brown, "Poetry and the Novel," 116.

35. Included in Thomas Frognall Dibdin, *Reminiscences of a Literary Life*, 2 vols. (London: J. Major, 1836), 1:305.

36. Thomas Sheridan, *British Education: or, the Source of the Disorders of Great Britain* (London: R. and J. Dodsley, 1756), 257. With the book appearing in 1756, just as war broke out between Britain and France, this roll call of canonical names was probably read in part as a call to arms. Admittedly, Sheridan's canon is not precisely the one manifested in scattershot form in the chapter epigraphs of 1790s gothic fictions. It is instead geared to the programs of politeness that were during the eighteenth century enrolling increasing numbers of Irish and Scots eager to prove their acquaintance with metropolitan norms of linguistic correctness.

37. Compare John Pinkerton in *A Dissertation on the Origin and Progress of the Scythians or Goths* (London: George Nicol, 1787), who aligns "the contempt we bear to the Goths" with "that of a spendthrift heir to a great and prudent father" (xiv). This is the same John Pinkerton who appeared in chapter 2, seen trying to teach his fellow antiquaries manners.

38. Ian Duncan, *Modern Romance and Transformations of the Novel: The Gothic, Scott, Dickens* (Cambridge: Cambridge University Press, 1992), 4.

39. Dryden, Preface to *Fables Ancient and Modern*, in *The Works of John Dryden*, ed. Niles Hooker and H. T. Swedenberg Jr., vol. 7, *Poems 1697–1700*, ed. Vinton A. Dearing (Berkeley: University of California Press, 2000), 25; I also quote Lucy Newlyn, *Reading, Writing, and Romanticism: The Anxiety of Reception* (Oxford: Oxford University Press, 2000), 67.

40. Michel Foucault, *History of Sexuality, Volume 1: An Introduction*, trans. Robert Hurley (New York: Pantheon, 1978), 108.

41. Charlotte Smith, *Emmeline, the Orphan of the Castle*, in *The Works of Charlotte Smith*, ed. Stuart Curran, vol. 2, ed. Judith Stanton (London: Pickering and Chatto, 2005), 414. On *Emmeline* as the urtext for the female Gothic tradition, see Diane Long Hoeveler, *Gothic Feminism: The Professionalization of Gender from Charlotte Smith to Charlotte Bronte* (College Park: Pennsylvania State University Press, 1998), 37.

42. Smith, *Emmeline*, 2:5.

43. Ibid., 2:322, 2:323.

44. Elvira's attainment of knowledge of the truth of her birth also brings about the close of the novel, not because this knowledge has made her an heiress, as in *Emmeline*, but because it kills her. In learning her parentage Elvira learns that the man she is about to marry is the son of her mother's seducer and so her own half brother—a shock that ends her life.

45. Paul Westover, "William Godwin, Literary Tourism, and the Work of Necromanticism," *Studies in Romanticism* 48, no. 2 (Summer 2009): 300.

46. Martin Thom, *Republics, Nations and Tribes* (London: Verso, 1995), 60.

47. Raymond Williams, *Keywords: A Vocabulary of Culture and Society* (New York: Oxford University Press, 1976), 87–93. See also David Hill Radcliffe, "Ossian and the Genres of Culture," *Studies in Romanticism* 31, no. 2 (Summer 1992): 213–32.

48. Edmund Burke, *Reflections on the Revolution in France*, ed. Conor Cruise O'Brien (Har-

mondsworth, UK: Penguin, 1968), 194–95; I follow here Esther M. Schor's reading of Burke in *Bearing the Dead: The British Culture of Mourning, from the Enlightenment to Victoria* (Princeton, NJ: Princeton University Press, 1994), 82.

49. Burke, *Reflections on the Revolution in France*, 136, 119.

50. William Godwin, *Essay on Sepulchres*, in *Political and Philosophical Writings of William Godwin*, ed. Mark Philp, 7 vols. (London: William Pickering, 1993), 6:28 (on dead authors' superiority to other kinds of dead people); 6:24 (on calling the dead from their tombs).

51. Nicola J. Watson, *The Literary Tourist* (Basingstoke, UK: Palgrave Macmillan, 2006), 31.

52. Godwin, *Essay on Sepulchres*, 6:18, 6:22, 6:20.

53. Quoted in Watson, *Literary Tourist*, 44.

54. Julie A. Carlson, *England's First Family of Writers: Mary Wollstonecraft, William Godwin, Mary Shelley* (Baltimore: Johns Hopkins University Press, 2007), 150.

55. Godwin, *Essay on Sepulchres*, 6:22. I have underscored the *Essay*'s resonances with novels' happy endings—the family reunions that in the Radcliffean universe reunite the living to the "pleasing shades" of the dead—in part because such dimensions of the *Essay* make it something more than a recapitulation of an earlier Renaissance-humanist account of reading as a speaking with the dead. The late eighteenth-century and early nineteenth-century readers and writers I've been discussing share the humanists' presupposition that people from the vanished past retain their voices in the texts they have left behind. However, Machiavelli's famous 1513 letter to Francesco Vettori does not depict dead authors as figures who define readers' sense of home: instead, these authors hold court. Preparatory to entering his study, Machiavelli writes, "I put on my regal and courtly garments," and only then "decently reclothed," garbed in symbols of respect and reserve, "I enter the ancient courts of ancient men, where, received by them lovingly, I feed on that food that alone is mine and that I was born for." (I follow the translation of Machiavelli's letter given in Jurgen Pieters, *Speaking with the Dead: Explorations in Literature and History* [Edinburgh: Edinburgh University Press, 2005], 21.)

56. Benedict Anderson, "Narrating the Nation," *Times Literary Supplement*, June 13, 1986, quoted in Gyan Prakash, "The Modern Nation's Return in the Archaic," *Critical Inquiry* 23, no. 3 (Spring 1997): 536.

57. Marlon Ross, "Romancing the Nation-State: The Poetics of Romantic Nationalism," in *Macropolitics of Nineteenth-Century Literature*, ed. Jonathan Arac and Harriet Ritvo (rept. Durham, NC: Duke University Press, 1995), 58.

58. W. J. Alexander, "Inaugural Address," quoted in A. B. McKillop, *Matters of Mind: The University in Ontario, 1791–1951* (Toronto: University of Toronto Press, 1994), 110; William Spalding, *A History of English Literature . . . For the Use of Schools and of Private Students*, new rev. ed. (Toronto: Adam Miller, 1878), 21 (first published 1853).

59. Samuel Johnson, preface to *The Plays of William Shakespeare*, in *The Oxford Authors: Samuel Johnson*, ed. Donald Greene (Oxford: Oxford University Press, 1984), 419; Jonathan Brody Kramnick, *Making the English Canon: Print-Capitalism and the Cultural Past, 1700–1770* (Cambridge: Cambridge University Press, 1998), 207.

60. See Brown, "Poetry and the Novel," 116.

61. Philippe Ariès, *The Hour of our Death*, trans. Helen Weaver (London: Allen Lane, 1981), 449, 471.

62. Watson, *Literary Tourist*, 29.

63. Ariès, *Hour of our Death*, 471.

64. Sleath, *Nocturnal Minstrel*, 1:1.

65. Ibid., 1:72.

66. Godwin, *Essay on Sepulchres*, 6:29. This passage first appeared in an essay included in Godwin's earlier *The Enquirer* (1797).

67. Godwin, *Essay on Sepulchres*, 6:29.

68. Sigmund Freud, *Totem and Taboo*, trans. James Strachey (London: Routledge Kegan Paul, 1960), 65.

69. Joseph Roach, *Cities of the Dead: Circum-Atlantic Performance* (New York: Columbia University Press, 1996), 77.

70. The causes of that ephemerality include the fact that almost half of the print run of a novel would be claimed by circulating libraries; in addition, few of the new titles produced by firms like Lane's Minerva Press ever saw a reprinting.

71. Susan Stewart, *On Longing: Narratives of the Miniature, the Gigantic, the Souvenir, the Collection* (rept. Durham, NC: Duke University Press, 1984), 19.

72. Paul Magnuson, *Reading Public Romanticism* (Princeton, NJ: Princeton University Press, 1998), 38.

73. See Christina Lupton, "Gray and Mackenzie Printing on the Wall," chapter 5 of her *Knowing Books: The Consciousness of Mediation in Eighteenth-Century Britain* (Philadelphia: University of Pennsylvania Press, 2011), 122–50.

74. Juliet Fleming, *Graffiti and the Writing Arts of Early Modern England* (Philadelphia: University of Pennsylvania Press, 2001), 20.

75. Lewis, *Monk*, 51–53.

76. Parsons, *Castle of Wolfenbach*, 1:26, 1:24.

77. When Emily encounters it for the second time, she finds that her own name now forms part of the verse and "she start[s] as if she had seen a stranger" (*Mysteries of Udolpho*, 9). In the aftermath of this poem's discovery, the novel is abruptly shifted out of the time frame of pastoral idyll in which it commences, as if registering the disruptive potential of the female sexuality that, as a love lyric, the sonnet heralds, or creates. First Madame St. Aubert dies, and then Emily's father follows her to the grave, leaving their daughter adrift in a dangerous world.

78. Diana Fuss, "Corpse Poem," *Critical Inquiry* 30, no. 1 (Autumn 2003): 27.

CHAPTER SIX

1. See, for example, Eve Kosofsky Sedgwick, "Paranoid Reading and Reparative Reading, or, You're So Paranoid, You Probably Think This Essay Is about You," in *Touching Feeling: Affect, Pedagogy, Performativity* (Durham, NC: Duke University Press, 2003), 123–52; Rita Felski, "After Suspicion," *Profession* 2009, ed. Rosemary G. Feal (New York: Modern Language Association, 2009): 28–35. Cottom mentions an "Erotic Rearmament Campaign" in *Why Education Is Useless* (Philadelphia: University of Pennsylvania Press, 2003), 51.

2. Virginia Jackson, "Who Reads Poetry?" *PMLA* 123, no.1 (January 2008): 181.

3. I owe this characterization of literary biography to Julian North's *The Domestication of Genius: Biography and the Romantic Poet* (Oxford: Oxford University Press, 2009).

4. James Boswell, *Life of Johnson*, introd. Pat Rogers, ed. R. W. Chapman (Oxford: Oxford University Press, 1980), 19. All references to the *Life* are to this edition and from here on occur parenthetically in the body of my text. See also the April 30, 1785, letter to Anna Seward in which Boswell describes his book as "an Egyptian Pyramid in which there will be a compleat mummy of Johnson" (quoted in William H. Epstein, *Recognizing Biography* [Philadelphia: University of Pennsylvania Press, 1987], 125).

5. John Durham Peters, *Speaking into the Air: A History of the Idea of Communication* (Chicago: University of Chicago Press, 1999), 6, 16.

6. Quotations are from the 1805 *Prelude* in *The Oxford Authors: William Wordsworth*, ed. Stephen Gill (Oxford: Oxford University Press, 1984). My source for Shakespeare's sonnet is *The Norton Shakespeare*, ed. Stephen Greenblatt et al. (New York: W. W. Norton, 1997), 1944.

7. Commenting on this passage, Adela Pinch notes how "the mere presence of a quotation here satisfies mixed emotions," in so far as a quotation hovers "between being something that one has

and something that belongs elsewhere" (*Strange Fits of Passion: Epistemologies of Emotion, Hume to Austen* [Stanford, CA: Stanford University Press, 1996], 169).

8. Ian Reid, *Wordsworth and the Formation of English Studies* (Aldershot, UK: Ashgate, 2004); Clifford Siskin, "Wordsworth's Prescriptions: Romanticism and Professional Power," in *The Romantics and Us: Essays on Literature and Culture*, ed. Gene W. Ruoff (New Brunswick, NJ: Rutgers University Press, 1990), 303–21; Jonathan Arac, *Critical Genealogies: Historical Situations for Postmodern Literary Studies* (New York: Columbia University Press, 1987).

9. Wordsworth's lines center Helen Vendler's 1980 "Presidential Address to the Modern Language Association," anthologized as "What We Have Loved," in *Teaching Literature: What Is Needed Now*, ed. James Engell and David Perkins (Cambridge, MA: Harvard University Press, 1988), 13–25; see also Roger Lundin, "What We Have Loved," *Pedagogy* 4, no. 1 (Winter 2004): 133–40.

10. David Simpson, *Wordsworth, Commodification, and Social Concern: The Poetics of Modernity* (Cambridge: Cambridge University Press, 2009), 208.

11. "Ode ('There was a time')," *Oxford Authors: William Wordsworth*, 298, line 56—henceforth I'll be referring to this by its familiar, shorthand title, the "Intimations Ode." Tellingly, echoes of this ode become audible at the very moment in William Hazlitt's "On Reading Old Books" when Hazlitt's constancy to literature falters, and he admits that love dies and habit numbs. "Books have in a great measure lost their power over me, . . . The sharp luscious flavour . . . *is fled*, and nothing but the stalk, the bran, the husk of literature is left. . . . But it was not always so. *There was a time* when to my thinking, every word was a flower": William Hazlitt, *The Complete Works*, ed. P. P. Howe (London: J. M. Dent, 1931), 12:225; my emphasis. For fuller discussion of Wordsworth's and Hazlitt's accounts of their reading practices, see Kevis Goodman, "'Uncertain Disease': Nostalgia, Pathologies of Motion, Practices of Reading," *Studies in Romanticism* 49, no. 2 (Summer 2010): 197–227.

12. I cite Ann Wierda Rowland's description of how definitions of literature came in the nineteenth century to intersect with new theories about infancy and mental development: see *Romanticism and Childhood: The Infantilization of British Literary Culture* (Cambridge: Cambridge University Press, 2012), 250.

13. Wordsworth, *Oxford Authors: William Wordsworth*, 599.

14. Andrew Piper, *Dreaming in Books: The Making of the Bibliographic Imagination in the Romantic Age* (Chicago: University of Chicago Press, 2009), 3.

15. Joseph Warton, *An Essay on the Genius and Writings of Pope* (London: J. Dodsley, 1782), 2:477 (notoriously, Warton excluded Pope himself from that category of poetic poetry); Samuel Johnson, preface to *A Dictionary of the English Language, The Oxford Authors: Samuel Johnson*, ed. Donald Greene (Oxford: Oxford University Press, 1984), 319.

16. Book historians' accounts of the late eighteenth century remind us that during the copyright window created by the 1774 decision in *Becket v. Donaldson*, it was an "old canon" of out-of-copyright works that became affordable. New works—which is to say works authored by their contemporaries—were out of reach for vast sectors of the reading nation. See William St. Clair, *The Reading Nation in the Romantic Period* (Cambridge: Cambridge University Press, 2004).

17. Jacques Derrida, *Specters of Marx: The State of the Debt, the Work of Mourning, and the New International*, trans. Peggy Kamuf (New York: Routledge, 1994), 38.

18. Ted Underwood, "Romantic Historicism and the Afterlife," *PMLA* 117, no. 2 (March 2002): 240.

19. In a complementary discussion, Andrew Bennett describes how, in the face of their uncertainty about their contemporary reception, the romantic poets reinvented response, deferred it to an indefinite time after the poet's death, and so made posterity the major trope of reading. As Bennett puts it, since "posterity validates the artist, but does so in the future perfect tense," "the artist is one who will have been": "On Posterity," *Yale Journal of Criticism* 12, no. 1 (Spring 1999): 132.

20. Underwood, "Romantic Historicism and the Afterlife," 245. The readiness of people in the past to believe that ghosts could act within this world instanced how truth was specific to discrete

historical circumstances. Mentions of ghost belief could accordingly anchor a division between the pre-modern and modern and prove useful to the project of periodizing the past.

21. Underwood, "Romantic Historicism and the Afterlife," 244. Cf. Trevor Ross, *The Making of the English Literary Canon, from the Middle Ages to the Late Eighteenth Century* (Montreal: McGill-Queen's University Press, 1998); and Jonathan Brody Kramnick, *Making the English Canon: Print-Capitalism and the Cultural Past, 1700–1770* (Cambridge: Cambridge University Press, 1998).

22. Isaac D'Israeli, *A Dissertation on Anecdotes* (London: C. and G. Kearsley and J. Murray, 1793), 4–5. On the anecdote and the culture of subjectification, see David Simpson, *The Academic Postmodern and the Rule of Literature* (Chicago: University of Chicago Press, 1995), 55.

23. Ina Ferris, "Melancholy, Memory, and the 'Narrative Situation' of History in Post-Enlightenment Scotland," in *Scotland and the Borders of Romanticism*, ed. Leith Davis, Ian Duncan, and Janet Sorensen (Cambridge: Cambridge University Press, 2004), 78.

24. Geoffrey Hartman, *The Unremarkable Wordsworth* (Minneapolis: University of Minnesota Press, 1987), 34, 42.

25. "We learn how to grieve from the poets" is for Schor a central assertion of Thomas Gray's elegiac sonnet to Richard West (1742): *Bearing the Dead: The British Culture of Mourning from the Enlightenment to Victoria* (Princeton, NJ: Princeton University Press, 1994), 59. I also quote Samantha Matthews, *Poetical Remains: Poets' Graves, Bodies, and Books in the Nineteenth Century* (Oxford: Oxford University Press, 2004), 12.

26. Susan Stewart, *Crimes of Writing: Problems in the Containment of Representation* (New York: Oxford University Press, 1991), 102–31.

27. William Hazlitt, *Lectures on the English Poets; The Spirit of the Age* (London: J. M. Dent, 1910), 9; Thomas Love Peacock, *Peacock's Four Ages of Poetry*, ed. H. F. B. Brett-Smith (Oxford: Basil Blackwell, 1921), 15; Walter Scott, *The Lady of the Lake*, canto 1, line 6 (New York: Wiley and Putnam, 1837), 25.

28. Virginia Jackson, *Dickinson's Misery: A Theory of Lyric Reading* (Princeton, NJ: Princeton University Press, 2005), 51

29. Jackson, "Who Reads Poetry?" 183.

30. Jackson, *Dickinson's Misery*, 100.

31. Jackson, "Who Reads Poetry?" 183, 181; John Stuart Mill, "Thoughts on Poetry and Its Varieties," in *Collected Works of John Stuart Mill*, ed. John M. Robson, vol. 1, *Autobiography and Literary Essays*, ed. John M. Robson and Jack Stillinger (Toronto: University of Toronto Press, 1981), 348.

32. Proposing that writers of the romantic period were the first in literary history to confront a fully standardized English, Andrew Elfenbein's *Romanticism and the Rise of English* (Stanford, CA: Stanford University Press, 2009) recovers one strand in the institutional history behind this perception that the best authors are dead authors. That standardization enshrined a canon of dead writers—exemplars of good usage—and the standardizers made it seem, Elfenbein suggests, as though there were no "pressing need for new literature at all" (40).

33. *Reminiscences of the Lakes and the Lake Poets* is only one of the titles by which the essays as an ensemble have come to be known; I use here the title they bore when, revised, they were republished by De Quincey in book form in 1862. For purposes of quotation I draw on *The Works of Thomas De Quincey*, ed. Grevel Lindop, vol. 11, *Articles from* Tait's Magazine *and* Blackwood's Magazine, *1838–41*, ed. Julian North (London: Pickering and Chatto, 2003).

34. See Annette Wheeler Cafarelli, *Prose in the Age of Poets: Romanticism and Biographical Narrative from Johnson to De Quincey* (Philadelphia: University of Pennsylvania Press, 1990), 165–68, and North, *Domestication of Genius*, 1–3, 23–30.

35. Adam Sisman, *Boswell's Presumptuous Task* (New York: Farrar, Straus and Giroux, 2001), 292.

36. "Letter to Mr. Tait Concerning the Poetry of Wordsworth" (dated May 16, 1838), in De Quincey, *Works*, 11:588. This unpublished article proposes a cheap popular edition of Wordsworth's poetry and proposes that De Quincey should edit it.

37. I follow Margaret Russett's suggestive analysis in *De Quincey's Romanticism: Canonical Minority and the Forms of Transmission* (Cambridge: Cambridge University Press, 1997). As Russett observes, "De Quincey's residence in the Lakes may be read as a lesson in the perils of mistaking rhetoric for psychology—of an imaginary subjection to poetry as friendship with the poet" (213).

38. Cafarelli, *Prose in the Age of Poets*, 165; De Quincey, "Wordsworth," in *Works*, 11:46.

39. John E. Jordan, *De Quincey to Wordsworth: A Biography of a Relationship* (Berkeley: University of California Press, 1962), 33; Russett, *De Quincey's Romanticism*, 197.

40. Thomas Babington Macaulay, Review of Henry Hallam, *The Constitutional History of England*, quoted in Phillips, *Society and Sentiment: Genres of Historical Writing in Britain, 1740-1820* (Princeton, NJ: Princeton University Press, 2000), 347.

41. Stephen Bann, "The Historian as Taxidermist: Ranke, Barante, Waterton," in *Comparative Criticism: A Yearbook*, ed. E. S. Shaffer (Cambridge: Cambridge University Press, 1981), 3:21-49; on the "photo-prophetic desires" that preceded the invention of photography, see Geoffrey Batchen, *Burning with Desire: The Conception of Photography* (Cambridge, MA: MIT Press, 1997), 52.

42. I receive assistance here from Meredith L. McGill, "Introduction: Someone Said," in *Taking Liberties with the Author: Selected Essays from the English Institute*, ed. McGill (Cambridge, MA: English Institute in collaboration with the American Council of Learned Societies, 2013), uod.lib.umich.edu/cgi/t/text/text-idx?c=acls;idno=heb90058.0001.001.

43. Kevin Hart, *Samuel Johnson and the Culture of Property* (Cambridge: Cambridge University Press, 1999), 18.

44. John Guillory, *Cultural Capital: The Problem of Literary Canon Formation* (Chicago: University of Chicago Press, 1993), 30. In opening *Poetical Remains*, Samantha Matthews also plays off the idea of the king's two bodies (1).

45. James Boswell, *Boswell's London Journal, 1762-1763*, ed. Frederick A. Pottle (New York: McGraw-Hill, 1950), 176.

46. Michael Holroyd, Lecture for the Hay Literary Festival, published in *Guardian*, June 1, 2002, http://www.theguardian.com/books/2002/jun/01/featuresreviews.guardianreview36.

47. James Boswell, *Boswell on the Grand Tour: Germany and Switzerland, 1764*, ed. Frederick A. Pottle (New York: McGraw Hill, 1953), 321.

48. In a forthcoming book on writing for fame H J. Jackson describes the concept of literary immortality—and the related assumption that over the long term artistic merit will out—as involving for Johnson's generation and ours a version of a belief in Providence. She notes how this faith-based structure continues to claim adherents even among determinedly secular authors and readers.

49. De Quincey, "Lake Reminiscences, No. 1," in *Works*, 11:61; emphasis added.

50. Ibid., 11:59.

51. North, *Domestication of Genius*, 164.

52. De Quincey, "Lake Reminiscences, No. 1," in *Works*, 11:49. On this passage, see Russett, *De Quincey's Romanticism*, 182; Charles J. Rzepka, *Sacramental Commodities: Gift, Text, and the Sublime in De Quincey* (Amherst: University of Massachusetts Press, 1995), 189-93; and Eric Eisner, *Nineteenth-Century Poetry and Literary Celebrity* (Basingstoke, UK: Palgrave Macmillan, 2009), 6-10.

53. Paul Westover, *Necromanticism: Travelling to Meet the Dead, 1750-1860* (Basingstoke, UK: Palgrave Macmillan, 2010), 95.

54. I owe the phrase "canonical coffin" to Matthews's *Poetical Remains* (9).

55. Thomas De Quincey, *Shakspeare* [*sic*] (Edinburgh: Adam and Charles Black, 1864), 74; Nathan Drake, *Literary Hours, or, Sketches Critical and Narrative* (London: T. Cadell and W. Davies, 1798), 93, 90; William Pearce, *The Haunts of Shakespeare* (London: D. Browne, 1778), 26, 16. In the process of becoming a poet James Beattie's Minstrel goes through a phase in which he "dreams of graves, and corses pale; / And ghosts, that to the charnel-dungeon throng" (*The Minstrel; or, the Progress of Genius: A Poem, Book the First* [London: E. C. Dilly, 1771], 18).

56. Richard Terry, *Poetry and the Making of the English Literary Past, 1660-1781* (Oxford: Oxford University Press, 2001), 86-90.

57. Jacques Derrida, *Mémoires: For Paul De Man*, trans. Cecile Lindsay, Jonathan Culler, and Eduoardo Cadava (New York: Columbia University Press, 1986), 58-59.

58. Stephen Greenblatt, *Hamlet in Purgatory* (Princeton, NJ: Princeton University Press, 2003), 41.

59. Ibid., 18-19.

60. On how the idea of ghosts was "reformulated and internalized as an imaginative tool" in the eighteenth century, see Sasha Handley, *Visions of an Unseen World: Ghost Beliefs and Ghost Stories in Eighteenth-Century England* (London: Pickering and Chatto, 2007): I quote 18. Discerning in nineteenth-century Protestant theology a longing to undo the Reformation and restore the doctrine of purgatory, Michael Wheeler traces the emergence of a new doctrine of the "intermediate state" in his *Death and the Future Life in Victorian Literature and Theology* (Cambridge: Cambridge University Press, 1990), 73-79.

61. James Boswell, *London Journal*, 54 (November 28, 1762): "I have a warm heart and a vivacious fancy: I am therefore given to love, and also to piety or gratitude to GOD, and to the most brilliant and showy method of public worship."

62. I quote Shane McCorristine's development of Castle's argument in *Spectres of the Self: Thinking about Ghosts and Ghost-Seeing in England, 1750-1920* (Cambridge: Cambridge University Press, 2010), 31; Terry Castle, *The Female Thermometer: Eighteenth-Century Culture and the Invention of the Uncanny* (New York: Oxford University Press, 1995), 168-89.

63. Boswell, *London Journal*, 79.

64. I draw on Adela Pinch's work on Victorian Shelley lovers: "A Shape All Light," in *Taking Liberties with the Author*, ed. McGill.

65. Matthews, *Poetical Remains*, 5, 30.

66. Nicola Watson, *The Literary Tourist* (Basingstoke, UK: Palgrave Macmillan, 2006), 34.

67. William Howitt, *The Rural Life of England*, 3rd ed. (London, 1844; rept. Shannon: Irish University Press, 1971), 386; see also Westover, *Necromanticism*, 95-96. William Howitt, who published *The Homes and Haunts of the British Poets* in 1847, was by the start of the 1860s involved with haunts in a different sense of the term as a leading spiritualist journalist and contributor to the *Spiritual Magazine*.

68. William Wordsworth, "Illustrated Books and Newspapers," in *Last Poems, 1821-1850*, ed. Jared Curtis (Ithaca, NY: Cornell University Press, 1999), 405-6.

69. William and Mary Howitt, *Ruined Abbeys and Castles of Great Britain* (London: A. W. Bennett, 1862), preface (n.p.).

70. Ibid.

71. See Paul Duguid's discussion of these futurological tropes in "Material Matters: The Past and Futurology of the Book," in *The Future of the Book*, ed. Geoffrey Nunberg (Berkeley: University of California Press, 1996), 63-65.

72. Stephen Gill, *Wordsworth and the Victorians* (Oxford: Clarendon, 1998), 14.

73. Garrett Stewart, "Painted Readers, Narrative Regress," *Narrative* 11, no. 2 (May 2003): 141.

74. William Wordsworth, preface to *Our English Lakes, Mountains and Waterfalls, As Seen by William Wordsworth, Photographically Illustrated* (London: A. W. Bennett, 1864), v.

75. William Wordsworth, *The Excursion*, ed. Sally Bushell, James A. Butler, and Michael C. Jaye, with the assistance of David García (Ithaca, NY: Cornell University Press, 2007), 289-90, book 9, lines 513-18.

76. Helen Groth, *Victorian Photography and Literary Nostalgia* (Oxford: Oxford University Press, 2003), 7.

77. Gillen D'Arcy Wood, *The Shock of the Real: Romanticism and Visual Culture, 1760-1860* (New York: Palgrave Macmillan, 2001), 187.

78. William Samuel Wright, *The Loved Haunts of Cowper; or The Photographic Remembrancer of Olney and Weston* (Olney: For William Samuel Wright, 1876), vii-viii.

79. On photography's weak intentionality, see Carol Armstrong, *Scenes in a Library: Reading the Photograph in the Book, 1843-1875* (Cambridge, MA: MIT Press, 1998), 2; on how poetic references could help market the photograph, see Groth, *Victorian Photography*, 4.

80. The quoted phrase is from William Howitt's *Homes and Haunts of the British Poets* (rept. London: Routledge, 1894), 24.

81. Celeste Langan, "Understanding Media in 1805: Audiovisual Hallucination in *The Lay of the Last Minstrel*," *Studies in Romanticism* 40, no. 1 (Spring 2001): 49-70; Laura Mandell, "Imaging Interiority: Photography, Psychology, and Lyric Poetry," *Victorian Studies* 49, no. 2 (Winter 2007): 218-27.

82. J. L. Williams, *The Home and Haunts of Shakespeare*, quoted in John Taylor, *A Dream of England: Landscape, Photography, and the Tourist's Imagination* (Manchester, UK: Manchester University Press, 1994), 83-84.

83. Susan Sontag, *On Photography* (New York: Dell, 1977), 57; Roland Barthes, *Camera Lucida*, trans. Richard Howard (New York: Hill and Wang, 1981), 88.

84. Michel de Certeau, *The Writing of History*, trans. Tom Conley (New York: Columbia University Press, 1988), 5. "The home of the photographed is the cemetery": Eduardo Cadava, *Words of Light: Theses on the Photography of History* (Princeton NJ: Princeton University Press, 1997), 8.

85. Wordsworth, *Our English Lakes, Mountains and Waterfalls*, 54.

86. Projection in a literal sense as well as a psychological one: by the 1850s, and a decade before the advent of spirit photography, psychologists and spiritualists alike had learned to use analogies with the camera to describe the process by which individuals would move from an experience of ideation, of the inner world of their memories and imaginations, to an experience of an apparition. The possibility that the sensitive individual might "daguerreotype" the subject of her thoughts upon the external world became for the psychologists a way of describing hallucinations, while spiritualists, suggesting that human beings were hardwired to see the dead, described how the brains of gifted individuals operated as "photographic plates" that could both bring the spirit world into visibility and project it into our world. See McCorristine, *Spectres*, 56, 94-97.

87. Arac, *Critical Genealogies*, 3.

88. Wordsworth, ["Intimations Ode"], lines 124-25.

89. Henry Newbolt, Chair, *The Teaching of English in England: Report of the Departmental Committee Appointed . . . to Inquire into the Position of English in the Educational System of England* (London: H. M. Stationery Office, 1921), 16-17, 24; Stanley Fish, *Doing What Comes Naturally: Change, Rhetoric, and the Practice of Theory in Literary and Legal Studies* (Durham, NC: Duke University Press, 1989), 205.

90. See Catherine Robson, *Heart Beats: Everyday Life and the Memorized Poem* (Princeton, NJ: Princeton University Press, 2012).

91. Wordsworth, ["Intimations Ode"], lines 124-25.

92. Martha Banta, "Editor's Column: Mental Work, Metal Work," *PMLA* 113, no. 2 (March 1998): 206. Cf. Rei Terada's shrewd response in a subsequent *PMLA* Forum, which questions how Banta casts passion as an *obligation,* and notes that this move undermines the intellectual freedom Banta's column means to promote (Rei Terada, "Passion and Mental Work," *PMLA* 114, no. 1 [January 1999]: 99).

93. Hazlitt, "On Reading Old Books," in *Works*, 12:225.

Index